SPARKNOTES™

SAT II Biology

2003–2004 Edition

Series Editor Ben Florman

Editor Paul Fyfe

Contributors Rachel Friedman, Rob Superty

Cover Design Dan O. Williams

Illustrations Matt Daniels

Technology Tammy Hepps

This edition published by Spark Publishing

Spark Publishing
A Division of SparkNotes LLC
120 Fifth Avenue, 8th Floor
New York, NY 10011

02 03 04 05 SN 9 8 7 6 5 4 3 2 1

Please send all comments and questions or report errors to feedback@sparknotes.com.

Library of Congress information available upon request

Printed and bound in Canada

ISBN 1-58663-430-5

Welcome to SparkNotes Test Preparation™

S O YOU'RE PLANNING to take the SAT II Biology test. Not only that, you're planning to get a great score on the SAT II Biology test. You've come to the right book. In order to help you reach your goal of extreme SAT II Biology success, the Spark–Notes guide to SAT II Biology provides:

The precise topics of biology you'll need to know to do well on the test. This book is not designed to teach you all of biology. It's designed to teach you the biology you need to know to do well on the SAT II Biology test. SparkNotes recognizes the value of your time and won't waste it by telling you to study the wrong topics. Yet while the biology we teach is tailored to the test, we don't simply feed you facts and formulas and tell you to memorize them, as other books do. The SAT II Biology test demands flexibility and understanding, not rigid memorization. We teach the biology you need to know so that you truly know it and are able to deal with whatever the SAT II Biology throws at you.

Critical-thinking skills and specific SAT II Biology test-taking strategies. Understanding biology is the most important ingredient in achieving success on the SAT II Biology. But only the proper test-taking strategies can make your biology knowledge really shine. SparkNotes explains all the strategies, from general approaches to taking the test to specific vulnerabilities of the different types of questions found on the SAT II Biology.

Three full-length practice tests, and a study method that will maximize their usefulness and teach you to learn from your mistakes. Taking practice tests can and should be an extremely important part of your preparation for any standardized test. Practice tests help you to hone your test-taking skills, familiarize you with the format and time limits of the test, and show you your progress. In addition, if you follow our methods for studying the practice tests you take, the tests can be a powerful diagnostic study tool that will help you to identify and eliminate your weaknesses.

General information about SAT II Subject Tests. Beyond teaching you what you need to know to do well on a particular SAT II test, we think it's also important to discuss the SAT IIs in general. This first chapter of the book is dedicated to helping you figure out how the SAT II tests are used by colleges, which SAT II tests are right for you, when to take the tests, and how to register for them.

Contents

SAT II BIOLOGY REVIEW

The Cell 37

Organic and Biochemistry 51

Cell Processes 71

Mendelian and Molecular Genetics 93

Evolution and Diversity

Organismal Biology

Ecology

Glossary

PRACTICE TESTS
Practice Tests Are Your Best Friends   **251**

ORIENTATION

Introduction to the SAT II

The SAT II Subject Tests are created and administered by the College Board and the Educational Testing Service (ETS), the two organizations responsible for the dreaded SAT I, which most people just call the SAT. The SAT II Subject Tests were created to act as complements to the SAT I. Whereas the SAT I is a three-hour test that assesses your critical-thinking skills by asking math and verbal questions, the SAT II Subject Tests are hour-long affairs that test specific subjects covered in standard American high school classes. There are SAT II Subject Tests on writing, literature, history, math, science, and a host of languages from Korean to Hebrew.

In our opinion, the SAT II Subject Tests are better tests than the SAT I because they cover clearly defined topics rather than an ambiguous set of critical thinking skills. However, just because the SAT II Subject Tests do a better job of testing your actual knowledge doesn't mean the tests are necessarily easier or demand less study. A "better" test isn't necessarily "better for you" in terms of how easy it will be. But a "better" test will probably reflect your knowledge of that subject better than your SAT I verbal result will reflect your reading abilities.

In comparison to taking the SAT I, there are good things and bad things about taking an SAT II Subject Test.

The Good

- Because SAT II Subject Tests cover actual topics like Biology, Chemistry, and American History, you can very effectively study for them. If you don't know a topic in biology, such as the process of protein synthesis, you can look it up and learn it. The SAT II tests are straightforward tests: if you know your stuff, you will do well on them.

- Often, the classes you've taken in school have already prepared you for the test. If you took a biology course in high school, you probably covered most of the topics that are tested on the SAT II Biology test. All you need is some refreshing and focusing, which this book provides.

- In studying for the SAT II Biology, Chemistry, or American History, you really are learning biology, chemistry, and American history. In other words, you are accumulating valuable, interesting knowledge. If learning is something you enjoy, you might actually find the process of studying for an SAT II test to be worthwhile and gratifying. You can't say that about studying for the SAT I.

The Bad

- Because SAT II subject tests quiz you on specific knowledge, it is much harder to "beat" or "outsmart" an SAT II test than it is to outsmart the SAT I. For the SAT I, you can use all sorts of tricks or strategies to figure out an answer. There are far fewer strategies to help you on the SAT II. Don't get us wrong: having test-taking skills will help you on an SAT II, but knowing the subject will help you much, much more. In other words, to do well on the SAT II, you can't just rely on your quick thinking and intelligence. You need to study.

Colleges and the SAT II Subject Tests

Why would you take an SAT II Subject Test? Is it to prove to yourself how much you've learned in the year? That seems unlikely. Is it to prove to your teacher how much you've learned? No, you've got finals for that. Is it to win a new car? You wish. No, there's only one reason to take an SAT II Subject Test: colleges want you to, and sometimes they require you to.

Colleges care about SAT II Subject Tests for two related reasons:

1. Your performance on SAT II tests demonstrates your interest, knowledge, and skill in a broad range of topics.

2. Because SAT II tests are standardized, they show your abilities in these topics *in relation to the entire country.* The grades you get in high school don't offer such a measurement to colleges: some high schools are more difficult than others, meaning that students of equal ability might receive different grades, even in biology classes that have basically the same curriculum. By contrast, SAT II tests provide colleges with a definite yardstick against which they can measure your, and every other applicant's, knowledge and skills.

When it comes down to it, colleges like the SAT II tests because the tests make the college's job easier. The tests are tools that allow the colleges to compare students easily.

But because you know how colleges use the SAT II, you can make the tests your tool as well. Since SAT II tests provide an objective standard by which colleges can judge all their applicants, the tests provide you with an ideal opportunity to shine. If you got a 93 in biology and some other kid got a 91, colleges won't necessarily know what to make of that difference. But if you get a 720 on the SAT II Biology and that other kid gets a 670, colleges will be far more convinced.

The Importance of SAT II Tests in College Applications

Time for some perspective: SAT II tests are *not* the primary tools that colleges use to decide whether to admit an applicant. High school grades, extracurricular activities, and SAT or ACT scores are all more important to colleges than your scores on SAT II tests. If you take AP tests, those scores will also be more important to colleges than your SAT II scores. But because SAT II tests provide colleges with such a nice and easy measurement tool, they are an important *part* of your application to college. Good SAT II scores can give your application the extra shove that pushes you from the maybe pile into the accepted pile.

College Placement

Occasionally, colleges use SAT II tests to determine placement. For example, if you do very well on the SAT II Biology, you might be exempted from a basic science class. Though colleges do not often use SAT II tests for placement purposes, it's worth finding out whether the colleges to which you are applying do.

Scoring the SAT II Subject Tests

There are three different names for your SAT II score. The "raw score" is a simple score of how you did on the test, like the grade you might receive on a normal test in school. The "percentile score" takes your raw score and compares it to the rest of the raw scores in the country for the same test. Percentile scores let you know how you did on the test in comparison to your peers. The "scaled score," which ranges from 200–800, compares your score to the scores received by all students who have ever taken that subject SAT II.

The Raw Score

Your will never see your SAT II raw score because the raw score is not included in the SAT II score report. But you should understand how it is calculated, as this knowledge can affect your strategy on the test.

Your raw score on SAT II tests is based on a few simple rules:

- You earn 1 point for every correct answer

- You lose $\frac{1}{4}$ of a point for each incorrect answer.

- You receive 0 points for each question left blank

Calculating the raw score is easy. Simply add up the number of questions answered correctly and the number of questions answered incorrectly. Then multiply the number of wrong answers by ¼, and subtract this value from the number of right answers.

$$\text{raw score} = \text{right answers} - \left(\frac{1}{4} \times \text{wrong answers}\right)$$

In the chapter called General SAT II Strategies, we'll discuss how the rules for calculating a raw score should influence your strategies for guessing and leaving questions blank.

The Percentile Score

Your percentile score describes your score in relation to everyone else who took the same test as you. Another way to think of the score is as a marker of what percentage of test-takers received a lower raw score than you did. For example, if Gregor Mendel took the SAT II Biology Test and got a score that placed him in the ninety-third percentile, that means he scored better on that particular test than did 92 percent of the other students who took the same test. It also means that 7 percent of the students taking that test got the same score or scored better than he did.

The Scaled Score

ETS takes the raw score and uses a formula to turn that raw score into the the scaled score, which ranges between 200 and 800. The scaled score is the one your parents will brag about and your curious classmates will want to know.

The curve to convert raw scores to scaled scores varies from test to test. For example, a raw score of 33 on the Math IC might scale to a 600, while the same 33 on the Math IIC might scale to a 700. In fact, the scaled score can even vary on different editions of the *same* test. A raw score of 33 on the February 2002 Math IIC might scale to a 710, while a 33 in June of 2002 might scale to a 690. These differences in scaled scores reflect the differences in difficultly level of the test from edition to edition. The difference in the curve for various versions of the same test will not vary by more than 20 points or so.

Which SAT II Subject Tests to Take

There are three types of SAT II test: those you must take, those you should take, and those you shouldn't take. The SAT II tests you *must* take are those that are required by the colleges you are interested in. The SAT II tests you *should* take are tests that aren't required, but which you'll do well on, thereby impressing the colleges looking at your application. The SAT II tests you *shouldn't* take are those that aren't required and that cover a subject in which you don't feel confident.

Determining Which SAT II Tests are Required

To find out if the colleges to which you are applying require that you take a particular SAT II test, you'll need to do a bit of research. Call the schools you're interested in, look at their web pages online, or talk to your guidance counselor. Often, colleges request that you take the following SAT II tests:

- The Writing SAT II test

- One of the two Math SAT II tests (either Math IC or Math IIC)

- Another SAT II in some other subject of your choice

The SAT II Biology is not usually required by colleges. But taking it and doing well can show a liberal arts college that you are well rounded, or a science-oriented college that you are serious about science. In general, it is a good idea to take one science-based SAT II, such as Biology, Chemistry, or Physics.

Determining Whether You Should Take an SAT II
Even if it isn't Required

There are two rules of thumb for deciding which additional test to take beyond the Writing and Math tests:

1. **Go with what you know.** If history is your field, a strong score on the American History test will impress admissions officers far more than a bold but mediocre effort on the Physics test.

2. **Try to show breadth.** Scoring well on similar subject tests such as Math, Biology, and Chemistry will not be as impressive as good scores in more diverse subjects, such as Math, Writing, World History, and Biology.

Of course, the bottom line is that you need to get a good score on the tests you do take. Before you decide to take a specific SAT II test, you should know two things:

1. What a good score on that SAT II test is

2. Whether you can get that score

Below, we have included a list of the most commonly taken SAT II tests and the average scaled score on each.

Test	Average Score
Writing	590–600
Literature	590–600
American History	580–590
World History	570–580
Math IC	580–590
Math IIC	655–665
Biology E&M	590–600
Chemistry	605–615
Physics	635–645

For most schools, a score that is 50 points above this average will provide a significant boost to your college application. If you are applying to an elite school, you may need to aim closer to 100 points above the average. A little research in this area can get you a long way: call the schools you're interested in or talk to a guidance counselor.

AP vs. SAT II

As we've said, it's a good idea to take three SAT II tests that cover a range of topics, such as one math SAT II, one humanities SAT II (history or writing), and one science SAT II. However, there's no real reason to take *more* than three SAT II tests. Once you've taken the SAT II tests you need to take, the best way to set yourself apart from other students is to take AP courses and tests.

AP tests are harder than the SAT II tests, and, as a result, they carry quite a bit more distinction. SAT II test give you the opportunity to show colleges that you can learn and do well when you need to. Taking AP tests shows colleges that you are a disciplined, sophisticated student who *wants* to learn as much as possible.

When to Take an SAT II Subject Test

The best time to take an SAT II subject test is right after you've finished a yearlong course in that subject. If, for example, you take biology in tenth grade, then you should take the SAT II Biology near the end of that year, when you've learned all the material and it's still fresh in your mind. This rule does not apply for the Writing, Literature, and Foreign Language SAT II tests; it's best to take those after you've had as much study in the area as possible.

Make sure to finish taking all your SAT II Subject Tests by the end of November of your senior year of high school. Unless the colleges to which you are applying use the SAT II for placement purposes, there is no point in taking SAT II tests after November of your senior year, since you won't get your scores back from ETS until after the college application deadline has passed.

ETS usually sets testing dates for SAT II subject tests in October, November, December, January, May, and June. However, not every subject test is administered in each of these months. To check when the test you want to take is being offered, visit the College Board website at www.collegeboard.com, or do some research in your school's guidance office.

Registering for SAT II Tests

To register for the SAT II tests of your choice, you have to fill out some forms and pay a registration fee. We know—it's ridiculous that *you* have to pay for a test that colleges require you to take in order to make *their* jobs easier, but, sadly, there isn't anything we, or you, can do about it. It is acceptable for you to grumble here about the unfairness of the world.

After grumbling, of course, you still have to register. There are two ways to register: online or by mail. To register online, go to www.collegeboard.com. To register by mail, fill out and send in the forms enclosed in the *Registration Bulletin*, which should be available in your high school's guidance office. You can also request a copy of the *Bulletin* by calling the College Board at (609) 771-7600, or writing to:

> College Board SAT Program
> P.O. Box 6200
> Princeton, NJ 08541–6200

You can register to take up to three SAT II tests for any given testing day. Unfortunately, even if you decide to take three tests in one day, you'll still have to pay a separate registration fee for each.

Introduction to the SAT II Biology

T HE BEST WAY TO DO WELL ON THE SAT II Biology is to be really good at biology. For that, there is no substitute. But the biology whiz who spends the week before taking the SAT II cramming on the nuances of mitochondrial DNA and the physiological role of the amygdala probably won't fare any better on the test than the average student who reviews this book carefully. Why? Because the SAT II Biology doesn't cover mitochondrial DNA or the amygdala.

Happy? Good. This chapter will tell you precisely what the SAT II Biology *will* test you on, how the test breaks down, and what format the questions will take. Take this information to heart and base your study plan around it. There's no use spending hours studying topics you won't be tested on, or spending countless hours studying bacterial diversity while ignoring meiosis, which is covered far more extensively by the test.

The Strange Dual Nature of the SAT II Biology

The official name of the SAT II Biology test is not SAT II Biology. The test is actually called the SAT II Biology E/M. The test has this strange name because it's actually two tests built into one. One test, the Biology E test, emphasizes ecology and evolution. The other test, the Biology M test, emphasizes molecular biology and evolution. On test day, you will take either the Biology E or Biology M test. You can't take both.

The Biology E and Biology M tests aren't completely dissimilar. In fact, the two tests share a core of 60 questions. No matter which test you sign up to take, you will

13

have to answer the 60 core questions. In addition to the core questions, the Biology E/ M test contains 40 more questions, split equally between two specialty sections. If you decide to take the Biology E test, then you will only have to answer the ecology and evolution specialty section. If you decide to take Biology M, you need only answer the molecular biology and evolution section. In total, both the SAT II Biology E and Biology M contain 80 questions.

Content of the SAT II Biology

The SAT II Biology is written to test your understanding of the topics of biology taught in a standard American high school biology course, with particular emphasis on either ecology or molecular biology. ETS provides the following breakdown of the test covering five basic categories:

Topic	Number of Questions
Cellular and Molecular Biology	8–11
Ecology	8–11
Classical Genetics	7–9
Organismal Biology	22–26
Evolution and Diversity	7–10

As we said, depending on which specialty section you elect to take, you will also face 20 questions (25 percent of the total questions you will see) on either ecology/evolution or molecular biology/evolution.

The breakdown from ETS is a pretty accurate assessment of what appears on the test. But, frankly, some of its categories are so broad that it isn't all that helpful as a tool to help you focus your study. It may be that you have cell structure down pat, but biochemistry throws you for a loop, and you would like to get a sense of how much of the test is devoted to these two topics. To help you out, we've broken the core of the test down even further, so that you'll know exactly where to expect to feel the squeeze.

Topic	Number of Questions
Cellular and Molecular Biology	**8–12**
The Cell and Cell Structure	4–6
Biochemistry and Organic Chemistry	3–5
Cell Processes	1–3

Topic	Number of Questions
Mendelian and Molecular Genetics	**8–10**
Evolution and Diversity	**8–10**
Evolution	2–4
Diversity	4–6
Organismal Biology	**20–26**
Animal Structure, Function, and Behavior	9–13
Plant Structure and Function	9–13
Ecology	**7–9**

This book is organized according to these categories, giving you the ability to focus on each topic to whatever degree you feel necessary. Also, each question in the practice tests at the back of this book has been categorized according to these categories, so that when you study your practice tests you can very precisely identify your weaknesses and then use this book to address them.

Format of the SAT II Biology

Whether you take the SAT II Biology E or Biology M, the test will last an hour and consist of 80 questions. These questions will be organized in two main groups. The 60 core questions will come first, followed by a 20 question specialty section. All this information you already know. Now for what you don't know.

The core section of the test (and occasionally the specialty sections) contains two different types of questions. Classification questions make up the first 10–12 questions of the core, while the last 48–50 questions of the core are five-choice multiple-choice questions. What are classification and five-choice multiple-choice questions? Funny you should ask—we were just about to tell you.

Classification Questions

Classification questions are the opposite of your normal multiple-choice question: they give you the answers first and the questions second. A classification question presents you with five possible answer choices, and then a string of three to five questions to which those answer choices apply. The answer choices are usually either graphs or the names of five related laws or concepts. Because they allow for several questions on the same topic, classification questions will ask you to exhibit a fuller understanding of the topic at hand.

The level of difficulty within any set of questions is generally pretty random: you can't expect the first question in a set to be easier than the last. However, each set of classification questions is generally a bit harder than the one that came before. In the core questions, for example, you should expect questions 10–12 to be harder than questions 1–3.

Classification Question Example

Directions: Each set of lettered choices below refers to the numbered questions or statements immediately following it. Select the one lettered choice that best answers each question or best fits each statement, and then fill in the corresponding oval on the answer sheet. A choice may be used once, more than once, or not at all in each set.

Questions 1–3 refer to the following organelles.

    (A)   Chloroplast
    (B)   Mitochondria
    (C)   Nucleus
    (D)   Cytoplasm
    (E)   Cell Membrane

1.   Location of cellular respiration in prokaryotes

2.   Maintains proper concentrations of substances within the cell

3.   Found in plant cells, but not in animal cells

You can usually answer classification questions a bit more quickly than the standard five-choice completion questions, since you only need to review one set of answer choices to answer a series of questions. Don't worry if you didn't know the answers to these questions. The material in this question and more will be covered in the chapter on Cell Structure. This example is meant mainly to show you how a classification question is formatted. If you're burning with curiosity, though, the answers to the questions are (C), (E), and (A), respectively.

Five-Choice Completion Questions

These are the multiple-choice questions we all know and love, and the lifeblood of any multiple-choice exam. You know the drill: they ask a question, and give you five possible answer choices, and you pick the best one.

Directions: Each of the questions or incomplete statements below is followed by five suggested answers or completions. Some questions pertain to a set that refers to a laboratory or experimental situation. For each question, select the one choice that is the best answer to the question and then fill in the corresponding oval on the answer sheet.

As the directions imply, some five-choice completion questions are individual questions in which the five answer choices refer to only one question. But more than half of the five-choice completion questions are group questions, in which a set of questions all refer to the same biological scenario, figure, or experiment.

4. Giraffes with longer necks can reach more food and are more likely to survive and have offspring. This is an example of

(A) Lamarck's principle
(B) natural selection
(C) adaptive radiation
(D) convergent evolution
(E) speciation

A series of about 20 individual multiple-choice questions are found in the core section just after the classification questions. About five individual multiple-choice questions will begin each specialty section. In both the core and the specialty sections, there is a general tendency for the questions to become progressively more difficult. The answer to the example question is (B); we cover this material in the chapter on evolution.

There are actually two types of group questions. Group questions that refer to figures often test your knowledge in a very straightforward manner. For example, the test might contain a figure of a flower, with each part labeled with a number. The questions will ask you to match a function with the correct part of the flower. Group questions that deal with an experiment or scenario are usually more complicated. Some of the questions in the group may test your ability to read the data in the experiment; others may test your understanding of the experiment itself by asking you how the experiment might have been improved, or how the results of the experiment might have changed along with a particular variable.

In both the core and specialty sections, group questions appear after the individual multiple-choice questions. The difficulty of the questions within a group follows no pattern, but each group will generally be more difficult than the last. We provide examples of both kinds of group question below.

Figure-Based Group Questions

Figure-based group questions present you with an image or graphic and ask you to identify the structures or functions being represented. The questions are all five-choice multiple-choice questions. Most of the questions dealing with figures demand only simple recognition and recall. The first two questions in the following sample fit this type: you either know the name for a structure or you don't. Some figure-based questions go further, though, and ask about the major processes associated with the images you're identifying.

Questions 5–7 refer to the diagram below.

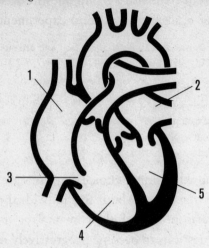

5.   Oxygen-rich blood is pumped out to the body by structure

(A)   1
(B)   2
(C)   3
(D)   4
(E)   5

6.   Structure 1 is termed the

(A)   aorta
(B)   right atrium
(C)   left atrium
(D)   pulmonary artery
(E)   right ventricle

7.   Which of the following muscle types are involved in circulating the blood?

I.   skeletal
II.   smooth
III.   cardiac

(A)   I only
(B)   II only
(C)   III only
(D)   II and III only
(E)   I, II, and III

The third question is of this second kind: it requires you to make a leap from recognizing the heart to knowing the general characteristics of the circulatory system. Don't worry about the answers now: you'll learn about the major structures of the heart and circulation in the chapter on Animal Structure and Function. (If you're interested, the answers to questions 5, 6, and 7 are (E), (B), and (E).)

Before you start answering questions within a figure-based group, try to figure out what is being depicted and remember what biological phenomena are associated with it. For instance, if you recognize a drawing of mitochondria, chances are you'll be asked about cellular respiration. If the drawing specifies a molecule or organism, keep in mind the general characteristics of the class of molecules or organisms it represents. If you're not sure what the image or graphic in the figure-group represents, you can probably pick up hints from the answer choices. Scanning the questions above and seeing the words "atrium," "ventricle," and "circulating the blood" provides pretty strong clues that the image shows a heart. Be careful, though: test writers love to seed misleading answers among the correct ones.

Experiment-Based Group Questions

The SAT II Biology uses group questions based on experiments, biological situations, and data to measure your scientific reasoning and laboratory skills. There is no standard appearance for the experiments; the data can be presented in paragraphs, tables, and/or graphs.

These groups can be the most intimidating part of the SAT II Biology test: they often describe scenarios that are more complex or advanced than what you've been exposed to in biology class or labs. But stay confident: the two main purposes of these group questions are to test how you understand scientific data and how you apply knowledge of biological principles to this data. Any unfamiliar terms or experimental techniques mentioned in the groups usually just mask simple concepts addressed by the individual questions. In fact, some questions might simply ask you to interpret the data. For these questions you won't have to think much about the concept at all.

Questions 8–10 refer to the following experiment and results obtained.

Dialysis bags are semipermeable membranes, allowing the transport of small molecules while prohibiting larger ones. In an experiment, students filled dialysis bags with different concentrations of sucrose solution and placed them in a beaker of distilled water. The bags were each weighed before being placed in the beaker. After two minutes, they were removed from the beaker, dried, and weighed again.

Contents in Dialysis Bag	Initial Mass	Final Mass
Distilled Water	25.1 g	25.3 g
0.2 M sucrose	25.9 g	28.4 g
0.4 M sucrose	26.1 g	30.0 g
0.6 M sucrose	26.3 g	30.1 g
0.8 M sucrose	25.9 g	35.6 g
1.0 M sucrose	30.7 g	37.6 g

8. Which dialysis bag experiences the largest percent change in mass?

    (A) 0.2 M sucrose
    (B) 0.4 M sucrose
    (C) 0.6 M sucrose
    (D) 0.8 M sucrose
    (E) 1.0 M sucrose

9. If the 0.6 M sucrose solution bag was left in the beaker for four minutes, all of the following occur EXCEPT

    (A) mass of the dialysis bag increases to more than 30.1 g
    (B) water travels down its concentration gradient
    (C) decrease in the bag's molarity of sucrose
    (D) sucrose leaks into the beaker
    (E) volume of water in the beaker decreases

10. A glucose molecule is small enough to pass through the bag. If glucose was substituted for sucrose in the dialysis experiment above, by what process does it cross the membrane?

    (A) osmosis
    (B) active transport
    (C) simple diffusion
    (D) facilitated diffusion
    (E) transpiration

For each experiment, identify the following: What is being tested and why? What are the variables, and what factors stay the same? In this example, the mass of the dialysis bags changes with the variable of sucrose concentration. Changes in mass can only come from water entering or leaving the bags, so the question deals with osmosis. (You'll learn all about osmosis, diffusion, and transport over membranes in the chapter covering the cell.)

The three sample questions are good examples of the various types of questions the SAT II Biology asks in experiment groups. You don't have to know anything about concentrations, osmosis, or membrane transport to answer the first question in this group; determining percent change in mass demands only simple data interpretation. The second question requires you to extrapolate and make predictions from the data. The third question asks you to make predictions on what would occur if the experiment were slightly modified. This last type of question goes beyond the numbers and requires knowledge of the topic. If you can identify the general biological properties of the experiment in advance, you should have no trouble answering questions of this sort. (Answers to the sample questions: 8 (D), 9 (D), and 10 (C).)

The SAT II Biology may also present data in graph form. For graphs, make sure you know what the axes represent. Think about what relationship exists between these concepts and identify in advance any general trends you can think of. If it helps, sketch out your own tables or notes to sort the data and identify trends or exceptions. For all experiment-based questions, elimination is a helpful tool. You can eliminate answer choices that do not relate to the experiment's variables or what is being tested, or those choices that contradict your knowledge of the biological principles working in the experiment or scenario.

How Your Knowledge of Biology Will Be Tested

The SAT II Biology tests your knowledge of biology in three different ways. Knowing how your knowledge may be tested should help you better prepare yourself for the exam.

Recall Questions. These questions test your basic knowledge of the fundamental facts and terminology of biology. A typical recall question might ask you to pick out the function of ribosomes, or to name the nitrogenous base that DNA and RNA do not have in common. These questions are straightforward—they're simply a matter of knowing your stuff. Some recall questions might be organized in sets around a figure, as in the example of the questions about the structure of a flower we described earlier.

Interpretation and Application Questions. These questions test your ability to digest data or biological scenarios and to extrapolate answers from that understanding. These questions often necessitate that you are able to use, in tandem, your knowledge of different topics in biology. An interpretation and application question might present a scenario in which the temperature drops and then ask you to predict how this change will affect the metabolism of a lizard and a dog. To answer this question you have to realize, first, that a question about the change in metabolism due to temperature is asking about warm-blooded and cold-blooded animals. To get the question right, you must first recall that a dog is warm-blooded and a lizard cold-blooded. Then you have to understand how a lowered temperature will affect each type of animal (as temperatures decrease, the metabolism of a cold-blooded animal will slow down, while the metabolism of the warm-blooded animal will remain constant).

Laboratory Questions. Laboratory questions describe a situation in a laboratory and often provide you with data. To answer these questions you must be able to read and understand the data, to form hypotheses and conclusions based on the data, and to be able to identify the goals and assumptions underlying the experiment.

You'll find all three types of question all over the test, and at all different levels of difficulty. Ultimately, they all test the very same thing: whether you've grasped the basic principles of biology.

Basic Math and the SAT II Biology

The writers of the SAT II Biology assume that you are able to deal with basic mathematical concepts, such as ratios and proportions. They also assume that you know the metric system. You will not be allowed to use a calculator on the test; this isn't a big deal because you won't have to do any calculations more difficult than multiplication.

Scoring the SAT II Biology

Scoring on the SAT II Biology is very similar to the scoring for all other SAT II tests. For every right answer, you earn 1 point. For every wrong answer, you lose ¼ of a point. For each question you leave blank, you earn 0 points. Add all these points up, and you get your raw score. ETS then converts your raw score to a scaled score according to a special curve. On page 23 we've included a raw-score-to-scaled-score conversion chart, so you can translate your raw score on a practice test into scaled scores. But to give you a sense of what sorts of performances convert into what sorts of scores, here's a synopsis. You could score:

- 800 if you answered 79 right and left 1 blank

- 750 if you answered 73 right, 4 wrong, and left 3 blank

- 700 if you answered 67 right, 8 wrong, and left 5 blank

- 650 if you answered 60 right, 12 wrong, and left 8 blank

- 600 if you answered 54 right, 16 wrong, and left 10 blank

This chart should show you that your score doesn't plummet with every question you can't answer confidently. You can do very well on this test without knowing or answering everything. The key to doing well on the SAT II Biology is to follow a strategy that ensures you will see and answer all the questions you can answer, while intelligently guessing on those slightly fuzzier questions. We will talk about these strategies in the next chapter.

Raw Score	Scaled Score	Raw Score	Scaled Score	Raw Score	Scaled Score
80	800	49	600	18	420
79	800	48	590	17	410
78	790	47	590	16	410
77	780	46	580	15	400
76	770	45	580	14	390
75	770	44	570	13	390
74	760	43	560	12	380
73	760	42	560	11	370
72	750	41	550	10	360
71	740	40	550	9	360
70	740	39	540	8	350
69	730	38	540	7	350
68	730	37	530	6	340
67	720	36	520	5	340
66	710	35	520	4	330
65	700	34	510	3	330
64	700	33	500	2	320
63	690	32	500	1	320
62	680	31	490	0	310
61	680	30	490	-1	310
60	670	29	480	-2	300
59	660	28	480	-3	300
58	660	27	470	-4	290
57	650	26	470	-5	280
56	640	25	460	-6	280
55	640	24	450	-7	270
54	630	23	450	-8	270
53	620	22	440	-9	260
52	620	21	440	-10	260
51	610	20	430		
50	600	19	420		

The SAT II Biology

Strategies for Taking the SAT II Biology

A MACHINE, NOT A PERSON, WILL SCORE your SAT II test. The tabulating machine sees only the filled-in ovals on your answer sheet and doesn't care how you came to these answers; it cares only whether your answers are correct. A lucky guess counts in your favor just as much as an answer you give confidently. By the same token, if you accidentally fill in (B) where you meant (C), you won't get any credit for having known what the answer was. Think of the multiple-choice test as a message to you from ETS: "We score your answers—not any of the work behind them."

That may be a dumb way to run a test, but that's the hand that ETS deals you. You might as well take advantage of it. Give them right answers, as many as possible, using whatever means possible. It's obvious that the SAT II Biology test allows you to exhibit your knowledge of biology; but the test gives you the same opportunity to show off your fox-like cunning by figuring out what strategies will allow you to best display that knowledge.

Chapter Contents

The Strategies

Most of these "strategies" are common sense, and many of them you already know. The funny thing, though, is that in high-pressure situations, common sense often goes out the window. If you review anything in the minutes before taking the test, review these strategies. Of course, that doesn't mean you should skip this section now. It's full of juicy hints, some of which might be new to you.

Be Calm

The best way to do poorly on a test is to psych yourself out. If your mind starts thrashing about wildly, it will have a hard time settling on the right answers. There are a number of preventative measures you can take, beginning weeks, or even months, before you take the test. Buying this book was a good start: it's reassuring to see all the information you'll need to ace the test in a compact, manageable form. But you ought to keep a number of other things in mind:

Study in advance. If you've studied at regular intervals leading up to the test, rather than cramming the night before, the information will sit more easily in your mind.

Be well rested. Get a good night's sleep on the two nights leading up to the test. If you're frazzled or wired you're going to have a harder time buckling down and concentrating when it really counts.

Come up for air. Don't assume that the best way to take an hour-long test is to spend the full hour nose to nose with the test questions. If you lift your head occasionally, look about you, and take a deep breath, you'll return to the test with a clearer mind. You'll lose maybe ten seconds of your total test-taking time and will be all the more focused for the other fifty-nine minutes and fifty seconds.

Grid Your Answers Carefully

No kidding. People make mistakes while entering their answers into the grid and it can cost them big-time. This slip up occurs most frequently after you skip a question. If you left question 43 blank, and then unthinkingly put the answer to question 44 into row 43, you could be starting a long, painful chain of wrong answers. Don't do this.

Some test prep books advise that you fill in your answer sheet five questions at a time rather than one at a time. Some suggest that you should fill out each oval as you answer the question. We think you should fill out the answer sheet whatever way feels most natural to you, but make sure you're careful while doing it. In our opinion, the best way to ensure that you're being careful is to talk to yourself. As you figure out an answer in the test booklet and transfer it over to the answer sheet ovals, say to yourself: "Number 23, B. Number 24, E, Number 25, A."

Pace Yourself

At the very least, aim to at least look at every question on the test. You can't afford to lose points because you didn't find the time to look at a question you could have easily answered. You can spend an average of forty-eight seconds on each question, though you'll probably breeze through some in ten seconds and dwell on others for two minutes. Knowing how to pace yourself is a critical skill—these three guidelines should help:

Don't dwell on any one question for too long: If you've spent a couple minutes laboring over the question, you might just want to make a note of it and move on. If you feel the answer is on the tip of your tongue, it might come more easily if you just let it rest and come back to it later. Not only is it demoralizing to spend five minutes on a single question, but it also eats up precious time in which you might have answered a number of easier questions.

Nail the easy questions: As we said in the previous chapter, the test questions get progressively harder as you go along. Nonetheless, there will be some tough ones thrown in right at the start, and you'll be finding gimmes right up until the end. One of the reasons you don't want to dwell too long on tough questions is to ensure that you get a look at all the questions and snatch up the easy ones. Remember: you get as many points for correctly answering an easy question as a difficult one. You get a lot more points for five quickly answered easy questions than one hard-earned victory.

Skip the unfamiliar: If you encounter a question you can't make heads or tails of, just skip it. Don't sweat too hard trying to sort out what's going on. If you have time at the end, you can come back to it and see if you can make an educated guess. Your first priority should be to get all the easy questions, and your second priority should be to work through the questions you can solve with difficulty. Unfamiliar material should be at the bottom of your list of priorities.

Strategies

Set a Target Score

You can make the job of pacing yourself much easier if you go into the test knowing how many questions you have to answer correctly in order to earn the score you want. What score do you want to get? Obviously, you should strive for the best score possible, but be realistic: consider how much you know about biology and how well you do, generally, on these sorts of tests. You should also do a little research and find out what counts as a good score to the colleges to which you're applying: is it a 600? 680? Talk to the admissions offices of the colleges you might want to attend, do a little research in college guidebooks, or talk to your guidance counselor. Find out the average score of a student admitted to the schools of your choice, and set your target score above it (you want to be above average, right?). Then take a look at the chart we showed you before. You can score:

- 800 if you answered 79 right and left 1 blank

- 750 if you answered 73 right, 4 wrong, and left 3 blank

- 700 if you answered 67 right, 8 wrong, and left 5 blank

- 650 if you answered 60 right, 12 wrong, and left 8 blank

- 600 if you answered 54 right, 16 wrong, and left 10 blank

Suppose the average score on the SAT II Biology for the school you're interested in is 650. Set your target at about 700. To get that score, you need to get 67 questions right, while leaving yourself room to get 8 wrong and leave 5 blank. In other words, you can leave a number of tough questions blank, get a bunch more wrong, and still earn the score you want. As long as you have some idea of how many questions you need to answer, bearing in mind that you'll likely get some questions wrong, you can pace yourself accordingly. Taking practice tests is the best way to work on your pacing. See how many questions you can leave blank and still get the score you want, and you'll have a better sense of what to aim at on the big day.

If you find yourself effortlessly hitting your target score when you take the practice tests, don't just pat yourself on the back. Set a higher target score and start gunning for that one. The purpose of buying this book and studying for the test is to improve your score as much as possible, so be sure to push your limits.

Know What You're Being Asked

You can't know the answer until you know the question. This might sound obvious, but many a point has been lost by the careless student who scans the answer choices hastily before properly understanding the question. Take the following example:

Mammalian cell membranes work to maintain a concentration gradient in which there is a high water concentration inside the cell and a high sodium concentration outside the cell. If the cell membrane contains transport channels, these channels would allow sodium to

(A) flow out of the cell by simple diffusion
(B) flow into the cell by simple diffusion
(C) flow out of the cell by facilitated diffusion
(D) flow into the cell through facilitated diffusion
(E) flow into of the cell by phagocytosis

This is not a difficult question. The sodium will move by simple diffusion from a high concentration gradient to a low concentration gradient. But the question is long and contains a great deal of information, so that by the end, a hasty student might have mixed up whether there was a higher concentration of sodium inside or outside the cell. This sort of mix-up might happen to the hasty student on only a few questions, but a few questions are the difference between a 730 and a 680 on the SAT II Biology.

To avoid getting confused on any questions, take a moment to *understand* the question before answering it. Read the question, and then vocalize to yourself what the question is asking and what the pertinent information is. This process should not take more than a second or two. But those brief moments can make all the difference. For this question, once you've recognized what you're dealing with, you will have little trouble in correctly answering (B).

Think of the Answer Before Looking at the Answer Choices

This hint goes hand in hand with the last one. In fact, this hint provides a method to stop yourself from speeding through the test carelessly. Imagine the hasty student who read the last example question too quickly and thought that the sodium concentration was higher inside the cell than outside. The hasty student, of course, doesn't realize this error, and looks through the answers. And there sits choice (A), which is the right answer based on the information lodged in the hasty test-taker's head. So the hasty test-taker answers (A) and continues on her way, having lost points she should have gotten.

But if the hasty test taker had instead tried to answer the question without looking at the answers, she wouldn't have been so hasty. Instead, she would have had to stop for a second, and look at the information in the question a second time; then she would have sorted everything out and gotten the question right. If you force yourself to answer the question before looking at the answer choices, you force yourself to come to grips with the question and therefore will cut down on the careless errors you might normally make.

Know How To Guess

ETS doesn't take off ¼ of a point for each wrong answer in order to punish you for guessing. They do it so as not to reward you for blind guessing. Suppose, without even glancing at any of the questions, you just randomly entered responses in the first 20 spaces on your answer sheet. Because there's a one-in-five chance of guessing correctly on any given question, odds are you would guess right for 4 questions and wrong for 16 questions. Your raw score for those 20 questions would then be:

$$4 \times 1 - 16 \times \frac{1}{4} = 0$$

Because of the ¼ point penalty for wrong answers, you would be no better off and no worse off than if you'd left those twenty spaces blank.

Now suppose in each of the first 20 questions you are able to eliminate just 1 possible answer choice so that you guess with a ¼ chance of being right. Odds are, you'd get 5 questions right and 15 questions wrong, giving you a raw score of:

$$5 \times 1 - 15 \times \frac{1}{4} = 1.25$$

All of a sudden, you're more than a point up. It's not much, but every little bit helps.

The lesson to be learned here is that blind guessing doesn't help, but educated guessing does. If you can eliminate even one of the five possible answer choices, *you must guess.* We'll discuss how to eliminate answer choices on certain special kinds of questions later in this chapter.

Guessing as Partial Credit

Some students feel that guessing is similar to cheating—that guessing correctly means getting credit where none is due. But instead of looking at guessing as an attempt to gain undeserved points, you should see it as a form of partial credit. For example, suppose you're stumped on the question above—which asks about sodium ions and transport channels in an animal's cell membrane—because you can't remember if the sodium should flow into the cell or out of the cell. But let's say you *do* know that phagocytosis occurs when a cell engulfs a particle that is much larger than an ion. And suppose you are pretty sure that the answer isn't simple diffusion, because sodium ions do not cross cell membranes without help. Don't you deserve something for that extra knowledge? Well, you do get something: when you look at this question, you can throw out (A), (B), and (E) as answer choices, leaving you with a one-in-two chance of getting the question right if you guess. Your extra knowledge gives you better odds of getting this question right, exactly as extra knowledge should.

Eliminate Wrong Answers

We've already said that if you can eliminate one answer in a question, the scoring odds are in your favor, and you should guess. This means that you shouldn't skip a question juts because you realize you don't know the right answer. Before skipping any question, check to see if you can at least eliminate an answer. For every question, you should go through a checklist of priorities:

- **First priority:** Answer the question correctly.

- **Second priority:** If you don't know the answer, try to eliminate answer choices and then guess.

- **Third priority:** If you can't eliminate any answer choices, move on to the next question.

On most questions, there will be at least one or two answer choices you can eliminate. There are also certain styles of question that lend themselves to particular processes of elimination.

Classification Questions

The weakness of classification questions is that the same five answer choices apply to several questions. Invariably, some of these answer choices will be tempting for some questions, but not for others.

Questions 1–3 relate to the following molecules:

(A)   phospholipid
(B)   carbohydrate
(C)   protein
(D)   DNA
(E)   RNA

1.   Contains the nitrogenous base uracil

2.   Acts as storage for long strings of sugars

3.   One side is hydrophilic, while the other is hydrophobic

For instance, you can be pretty sure that uracil doesn't appear in protein, carbohydrates, or phospholipids, since nitrogenous bases are only found in RNA and DNA.

Another point that may help you guess in a pinch: you'll rarely find the same answer choice being correct for two different questions. True, the directions for classification questions explicitly state that an answer choice "may be used once, more than once, or not at all," but on the whole, the ETS people shy away from the "more than once" possibility. This is by no means a sure bet, but if you're trying to eliminate answers, you might want to eliminate those choices that you've already used on other questions in the same set.

Strategies

If you're wondering, the answers to the above questions are 1 (E), 2 (B), and 3 (A). Don't worry if you didn't know these answers. After reading this book, you will. The same goes for the following example questions.

"EXCEPT" Questions

"EXCEPT" questions are five-choice multiple-choice questions that contain a bunch of right answers and one wrong answer. The questions always contain an all-caps EXCEPT, LEAST, or some other, similar word. Even if you aren't sure of the answer (which is actually the wrong answer), you should be able to identify one or two of the answer choices as true statements and eliminate them.

Most birds are characterized by all of the following EXCEPT

    (A)   four-chambered heart
    (B)   strong, heavy bones
    (C)   powerful lungs
    (D)   eggs protected by hard shells
    (E)   evolved from reptiles

Perhaps you're not sure which of the five answer choices is wrong. But you should be able to identify that birds *do* lay eggs protected by shells and that they evolved from dinosaurs. Already, you've eliminated two possible answers and can make a pretty good guess from there.

If you're interested, the answer is (B): the bones of birds are extremely light. Heavy bones would make flight much more difficult for birds.

"I, II, and III" Questions

"I, II, and III" questions are multiple-choice questions that provide you with three possible answers, and the five answer choices list different combinations of those three.

A population of animals is split in two by the formation of a river through their territory. The two populations gain different characteristics due to the different natures of their new habitats. When the river disappears, the two populations can no longer interbreed. What has occurred?

I. Natural selection
II. Convergent evolution
III. Speciation

(A) I only
(B) II only
(C) I and III only
(D) II and III only
(E) I, II, and III

There's an upside and a downside to questions like this. Suppose you know that the scenario described by this question does involve speciation, but you aren't sure about natural selection or convergent evolution. The downside is that you can't get the right answer for sure. The upside is that you can eliminate (A) and (B) and significantly increase your chance of guessing the right answer. As long as you're not afraid to guess—and you should never be afraid to guess if you've eliminated an answer—these questions shouldn't be daunting. By the way, the answer is (C): changes in organisms' characteristics due to changes in habitat are a result of natural selection, and the inability of the members of a former population to interbreed after being separated for a long time is speciation.

SAT II
BIOLOGY
REVIEW

The Cell

THE EARTH IS HOME TO MILLIONS OF different kinds of organisms, from slime molds to kelp, and blue whales to naked mole rats. Yet the vast diversity of size and structure evident in all of these organisms emerges from one fundamental building block: the cell. A cell is a small, membrane-bound compartment capable of performing all the basic functions of life. Since all living organisms, from the simplest to the most complex, are composed of cells, developing a thorough grounding in how cells work is integral to understanding larger life processes—not to mention the fact that the cell and its structure are common topics tested by the SAT II Biology.

The Discovery of Cells

Most cells are too small to be observed with the naked eye. For this reason, even the existence of cells escaped notice until scientists first learned to harness the magnifying power of lenses in the second half of the seventeenth century. At that time a Dutch clothing dealer named **Antonie van Leeuwenhoek** (1632–1723) fashioned extraordinarily accurate single-lens microscopes. Gazing into the lens of these microscopes, he discovered single-celled organisms, which he called "animalcules" and which, today, we call bacteria and protists.

Englishman Robert Hooke (1635–1703) expanded on Leeuwenhoek's observations with the newly developed compound microscope, which uses two or more aligned lenses to increase magnification while reducing blurring. When Hooke turned the microscope on a piece of cork, he noticed that the tiny, boxlike compartments of the wood resembled the cells of a monastery. The term "cell" was born.

Cell Theory Emerges

As microscope technology improved, scientists were able to study cells in ever-greater detail. Hooke had no way to tell if cells were living things, but researchers who could see the nucleus and the swirling motion of the cytoplasm were convinced that cells were indeed alive. By 1839, enough evidence had accumulated for German biologists Matthias Schleiden and Theodore Schwann to proclaim that cells are "the elementary particles of organisms." But many researchers still did not believe that cells arose from other cells until 1855, when famous German pathologist Rudolph Virchow pronounced, "all cells come from cells." Nearly 200 years after the discovery of cells, the observations of Virchow, Schleiden, and Schwann established the cell theory:

- All living things are made of cells.

- All cells arise from preexisting cells.

These two tenets made clear that the cell is the fundamental unit of life.

Cell Size

Cells could not be studied until the development of microscopes because they are very small. This fact raises two related questions: why are cells so small, and why are living things made up of millions of tiny cells?

Cells are small because their surface area and volume must be balanced. In order to stay alive, cells with a larger volume need to carry out more chemical activity than smaller cells do. However, for metabolic activity to take place, the cell must also have enough surface area to allow an adequate supply of nutrients and waste products to move in and out of the cell. Because surface area increases at a slower rate than volume as objects get bigger, the surface area–to–volume ratio in a cell decreases dramatically as the cell gets larger. It turns out that a size of 10 μ provides the surface area to volume ratio necessary for the survival of most cells. (μ, the micrometer, is one thousandth of a millimeter.)

Microscopes

Two major types of microscopes allow scientists to study the miniature world of the cell.

The Light Microscope

Light microscopes use light and lenses to magnify their subjects. The most common of these used in the laboratory is the compound microscope, which creates high magnification by combining two relatively low-power lenses. The total power of a compound microscope is the power of the ocular lens, located in the eyepiece, multiplied by the power of the objective lens, located near the slide. For example, an ocular lens of 10x and an objective lens of 11x yield a total magnification of 110x. Typical high school microscopes offer magnifications of up to about 430x.

From time to time the SAT II Biology tests your knowledge of the various parts of the compound microscope, usually by showing you an image and asking you to identify the parts.

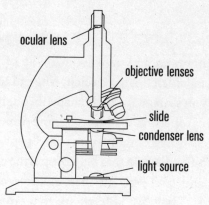

Many parts of the cell are hard to see under microscopes because they are colorless. In order to view them, scientists sometimes employ stains that mark various cell parts differently. One alternative to staining is a technique called phase contrast microscopy, which uses filters to emphasize the contrast between different parts of the cell.

The Electron Microscope

At high magnifications, light microscopes produce blurry images. In the 1950s, scientists invented a new type of microscope called the electron microscope, which offers increased image clarity, or resolving power. Electron microscopes are powerful enough to resolve individual fats and proteins. Light microscopes are still widely used, however, because electron microscopes are expensive and can only be used to view matter that is not living.

Types of Cells

There are two major types of cells: prokaryotes and eukaryotes. Eukaryotic cells, whose name derives from the Greek "eu", meaning "good," and karyon, "kernel" or "nucleus," have a nucleus and membrane-bound organelles. Prokaryotic cells, whose name derives from the Greek "pro," meaning "before," contain neither nucleus nor organelles. As the names imply, prokaryotic cells are less evolutionarily advanced than eukaryotic cells.

The Cell

Prokaryotes

Prokaryotes include some of the most primitive forms of life: bacteria and blue-green algae (also known as cyanobacteria). Prokaryotic organisms are generally single-celled.

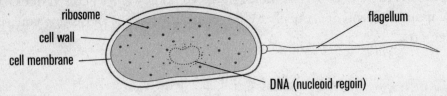

Prokaryotes have a cell membrane, and they are made up of generally undifferentiated fluid, called the **cytoplasm**, in which floats a circular ring of DNA that controls the functioning of the cell. Prokaryotes maintain their shape through a cytoskeleton, and have ribosomes that float in the cytoplasm. In addition, some prokaryotes have a special type of cell wall made of a protein-sugar combination called peptidoglycan. A few prokaryotes possess whiplike tails called **flagella** that help propel the cells through water.

Though less complex and less efficient than eukaryotes, prokaryotes are hardy because of their simplicity. They are able to survive environmental extremes that would kill higher life forms.

Eukaryotes

All living things besides bacteria and cyanobacteria consist of eukaryotic cells, which are larger and structurally more complex than prokaryotic cells. Like prokaryotes, eukaryotes are surrounded by a lipid bilayer cell membrane and have cytoplasm and ribosomes. However, unlike prokaryotes, eukaryotes also contain **organelles** and a defined **nucleus** containing DNA.

Eukaryotes benefit enormously from the presence of membrane-bound organelles. Each organelle creates an additional compartment in the cell that can specialize in particular activities or processes, increasing productivity as a result. The structure of eukaryotic cells and the specific functions of the various organelles are often tested by the SAT II Biology.

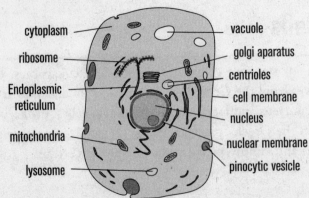

Cytoplasm

The cytoplasm refers to the entire area of the cell outside of the nucleus. The cytoplasm has two parts, the organelles and the **cytosol**, a grayish gel-like liquid that fills the interior of the cell. The cytosol provides a home for the nucleus and organelles as well as a location for protein synthesis and other fundamental chemical reactions.

Cytoskeleton

The cytoskeleton is a protein structure that maintains cell shape and helps move organelles around the cell. There are two types of cytoskeleton proteins: **microtubules** and **microfilaments**. Microtubules are thick, hollow rods that provide a strong scaffold for the cell. The smaller microfilaments are thin rods made of a protein called actin; they are strung around the perimeter of the cell to help it withstand strain. In some organisms, the microtubules power limbs called cilia and flagella, creating movement. Contraction of the microfilaments powers muscle movement in animals and facilitates the creeping motion of creatures like amoebas. The microtubules also form protein tracks on which organelles can slide around the cell.

The Organelles

Floating in the cytoplasm are the many membrane-bound organelles, each with a distinct structure and an important function in the processes of the cell.

Nucleus: stores the cell's genetic material in strands of **DNA**, and choreographs life functions by sending detailed messages to the rest of the cell. The interior of the nucleus is separated from the cytosol by a membrane called the **nuclear envelope**, which lets only select molecules in and out. The DNA itself is wrapped around proteins known as **histones** in an entangled fibrous network called **chromatin**. When the nucleus is about to split in two, this amorphous mass coils more tightly, forming distinct structures called **chromosomes**. The nucleus also houses a small, dark structure called the **nucleolus**, which helps manufacture ribosomes.

Ribosomes: synthesize proteins for the cell. Some ribosomes are mounted on the surface of the endoplasmic reticulum (see below), and others float freely in the cytoplasm. All ribosomes have two unequally sized subunits made of proteins and a substance called RNA. All living cells, prokaryotic and eukaryotic alike, have ribosomes. Ribosomes are explained in more detail in the chapter on Cell Processes as part of the larger discussion about the way the cell manufactures proteins.

Mitochondria: produces energy for the cell through a process called cellular respiration (see the chapter on Cell Processes). The mitochondria has two membranes: the

The Cell

inside membrane has many folds, called cristae. Many of the key cell-respiration enzymes are embedded in this second membrane. The chemical reactions of respiration take place in the compartment formed by the second membrane, a region called the **mitochondrial matrix.**

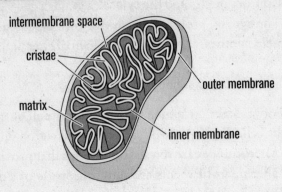

Endoplasmic Reticulum: an extensive network of flattened membrane sacs that manufactures proteins. These proteins are transferred to the Golgi apparatus, from which they will be exported from the cell. There are two types of endoplasmic reticulum: rough and smooth. Rough endoplasmic reticulum is studded by ribosomes covering its exterior. These ribosomes make rough endoplasmic reticulum a prime location for protein synthesis. The smooth endoplasmic reticulum moves the proteins around the cell and then packages them into small containers called vesicles that travel to the Golgi apparatus. The smooth endoplasmic reticulum also functions in the synthesis of fats and lipids.

Golgi apparatus: a complex of membrane-bound sacs that package proteins for export from the cell. Proteins enter the Golgi complex from the endoplasmic reticulum and proceed through the stacks where they are modified and stored before secretion. When proteins are ready for export, pieces of the Golgi membrane bud off, forming vesicles that send them to the cell membrane.

Lysosomes: small membrane-bound packages of acidic enzymes that digest compounds and worn-out cellular components that the cell no longer needs.

Cell Organelles

Organelle	Function	Found in which Type of Cell
Cytoplasm	Home for the organelles	Prokaryotes and Eukaryotes
Cytoskeleton	Maintains cell shape, moves organelles, moves cell	Eukaryotes
Nucleus	Contains the genetic material	Eukaryotes
Mitochondria	Produces energy for the cell	Eukaryotes
Ribosomes	Synthesize proteins	Prokaryotes and Eukaryotes
Endoplasmic Reticulum	Manufactures and transports proteins, manufacture fats	Eukaryotes
Golgi Complex	Packages proteins for secretion	Eukaryotes
Lysosomes	Digest wastes	Eukaryotes
Chloroplasts	Make food	Plant Eukaryotes
Vacuoles	Storage	Plant Eukaryotes (contractile vacuoles are found in some animal cells)
Cell Wall	Stability and protection	Plant Eukaryotes; some prokaryotes have a cell wall made of peptidoglycan

Plant Cell Organelles

The organelles described above are found in both animal and plant eukaryotic cells. But plants have additional organelles—chloroplasts, vacuoles, and cell walls—that support their unique life cycles.

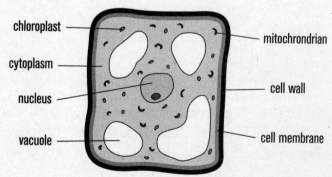

The Cell

Chloroplasts: Animal cells break down the food that they ingest to produce energy. Plants do not need to ingest food; they manufacture their own from sunlight, using the process of photosynthesis (covered in the chapter on Plant Structure and Function). Chloroplasts are the organelles in which **photosynthesis** takes place. They are large oval-shaped structures containing a green pigment called **chlorophyll** that absorbs sunlight. Chloroplasts, like mitochondria, are built from two membranes: an external membrane forming the boundary of the organelle, and a stacked inner membrane within the organelle.

Vacuoles: large liquid-filled storage containers found in plant cells. Plant cells can put virtually anything in their vacuoles, from nutrients to wastes to water to pigments. Vacuoles can be quite large, allowing plant cells to grow to substantial volumes without making new cytoplasm. Some animal cells in freshwater microorganisms have specialized contractile vacuoles that pump water out of the cell to prevent bursting.

Cell Wall: Plant cells have a rigid cell wall surrounding their cell membrane. This wall is made of a compound called cellulose. The tough wall gives the plant cell added stability and protection from harm.

The Cell Membrane

The cells of all organisms, prokaryotic and eukaryotic alike, are surrounded by a thin sheet called the cell membrane. This barrier keeps cellular materials in and foreign objects out. The membrane is key to the life of the cell. By regulating what gets into and out of the cell, the membrane maintains the proper chemical composition, which is crucial to the life processes the cell carries out.

Structure of the Cell Membrane

The cell membrane is made up of two sheets of special fat molecules called **phospholipids**, placed on top of each other.

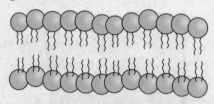

This arrangement is known as a **phospholipid bilayer**. Phospholipid molecules naturally arrange in bilayers because they have a unique structure. The long chains of carbon and hydrogen that form the tail of this molecule do not dissolve in water; they are said to be hydrophobic or "water fearing." The hydrophilic phosphorous heads are attracted to water. Forming a bilayer satisfies the water preferences of both the "heads" and "tails" of phospholipids: the hydrophilic heads face the watery regions inside and outside the cell and the hydrophobic tails face each other in a water-free junction. The bilayer forms spontaneously because this situation is so favorable.

The Fluid Mosaic Model

Phospholipids form the fundamental structure of the cell membrane, but they are not the only substance found there. According to the fluid-mosaic model of the cell membrane, special proteins called membrane proteins float in the phospholipid bilayer like icebergs in a sea.

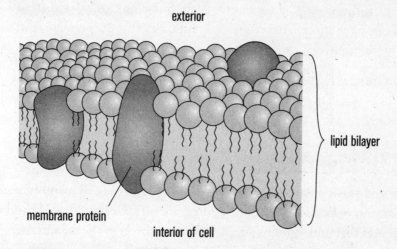

The sea of phospholipid molecules and gatekeeper membrane proteins is in constant motion. The membrane's fluidity keeps the cell from fracturing when placed under strain.

Transport Through the Cell Membrane

The most important property of the cell membrane is its selective permeability: some substances can pass through it freely, but others cannot. Small and nonpolar (hydrophobic) molecules can freely pass through the membrane, but charged ions and large molecules such as proteins and sugars are barred passage. The selective permeability of the cell membrane allows a cell to maintain its internal composition at necessary levels.

Molecules that can pass freely through the membrane follow concentration gradients, moving from the higher concentration area to the region of lower concentration. These processes take no energy and are called passive transport. The molecules that cannot pass freely across the phospholipid bilayer can be carried across the membrane in various processes that require energy, and are therefore called active transport.

Passive Transport

There are three main types of passive transport: diffusion, facilitated diffusion, and osmosis. In fact, osmosis is simply the term given to the diffusion of water.

Diffusion

In the absence of other forces, substances dissolved in water move naturally from areas where they are abundant to areas where they are scarce—a process known as diffusion. If there is a higher concentration of carbon dioxide gas dissolved in the water inside the cell than in the water outside the cell, carbon dioxide will naturally flow out from the cell until its distribution is balanced, without any energy required from the cell.

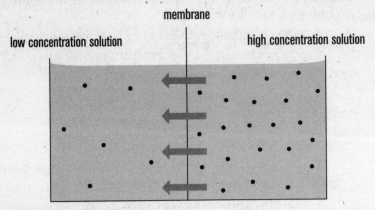

Nonpolar and small polar molecules can pass through the cell membrane, so they diffuse across it in response to concentration gradients. Carbon dioxide and oxygen are two molecules that undergo this simple diffusion through the membrane.

The simple diffusion of water is known as **osmosis**. Because water is a small polar molecule, it undergoes simple diffusion. SAT II Biology problems on osmosis can be tricky: water moves from areas where it is in high concentration to areas where it is in low concentration. Remember, however, that water is found in low concentrations in places where there are many dissolved substances, called solutes. Therefore, water moves from places where there are few dissolved substances (known as **hypotonic** solutions) to places where there are many dissolved substances (**hypertonic** solutions). An **isotonic** solution is one in which the concentration is the same as that found inside a cell, meaning osmotic pressure in both sides is equal.

Immersing cells in unusually hypotonic or hypertonic solutions can be disastrous: water can rush into cells in hypotonic conditions, causing them to fill up so fast that they burst! To combat this possibility, many cells that need to survive in freshwater environments possess contractile vacuoles to pump out excess water.

Facilitated Diffusion

Certain compounds important to the functioning of the cell, such as ions, cannot enter the cell through simple diffusion because they cannot pass through the cell membrane.

As with water, these substances "want" to enter the cell if the concentration gradient demands it. For that reason, cells have developed a way for such compounds to bypass the cell membrane and flow into the cell on the basis of concentration. The cell has protein channels through the phospholipid membrane. The channels can open and close based on protein membranes. When closed, nothing can get through. When open, the protein channels allow compounds to pass through along the concentration gradient, which is diffusion.

Active Transport

Quite often, cells have to transport a substance across the cell membrane *against* the normal concentration gradient. In these cases, cells use another class of membrane proteins. Instead of relying on diffusion, these proteins actively pump compounds in the direction the cell wants them to go, a process that requires energy. Cells can turn active transport on and off as needed.

Endocytosis and Exocytosis

Cells use yet another type of transport to move large particles through the cell membrane. In exocytosis, waste products that need to be removed from the cell are placed in vesicles that then fuse with the cell membrane, releasing their contents into the space outside the cell. Endocytosis is the opposite of exocytosis: the cell membrane engulfs a substance the cell needs to import, and then pinches off into a vesicle that is inside the cell.

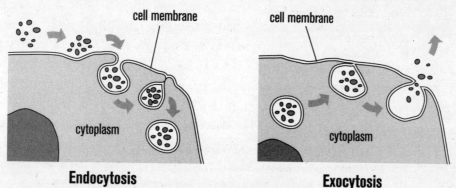

Endocytosis   **Exocytosis**

There are two kinds of endocytosis: in **phagocytosis** the cell takes in large solid food particles that it then digests. In **pinocytosis**, the cell takes in drops of cellular fluid containing dissolved nutrients.

Review Questions

1. A microscope has an ocular lens with a magnification of 10x and objective lenses with magnifications of 10x, 20x, 30x, and 43x. Which of the following are not possible magnifications that can be achieved with this microscope?

    A. 10x
    B. 100x
    C. 200x
    D. 300x
    E. 430x

2. Which of the following are features of the prokaryotic cell?

    A. nucleus
    B. ribosomes
    C. mitochondria
    D. vacuoles
    E. Golgi bodies

3. What is the function of the Golgi apparatus?

    A. It controls the cell's activities and stores its DNA.
    B. It is the site of protein synthesis.
    C. It synthesizes lipids and transports synthesized proteins.
    D. It sorts and packages proteins made in the endoplasmic reticulum.
    E. It provides structure to the prokaryotic cell.

4. Proteins manufactured in the endoplasmic reticulum are secreted from the cell by which of the following processes:

    A. diffusion
    B. osmosis
    C. pinocytosis
    D. exocytosis
    E. passive transport

5. Why is the "rough" endoplasmic reticulum rough?

    A. It is studded with ribosomes that form a bumpy coat.
    B. It functions in lipid synthesis.
    C. It contains cellulose which gives the membrane rigidity and structure.
    D. It lacks the ribosomes characteristic of the cytosol.
    E. It engages in lipid synthesis, which gives it a rough texture.

6. Which of the following functions is performed by the lysosome?

    A. digestion of intracellular debris
    B. production of energy through photosynthesis
    C. regulation of transport
    D. storage of nutrients
    E. lipid synthesis

7. What two classes of molecules make up the phospholipid bilayer?

   A. sugars and phosphoproteins
   B. proteins and phospholipids
   C. phosphoproteins and lipids
   D. DNA and carbohydrates
   E. phosphoDNA and lipids

8. What is the name of the natural process by which molecules flow from an area of higher concentration to an area of lower concentration?

   A. diffusion
   B. pinocytosis
   C. endocytosis
   D. respiration
   E. exocytosis

9. Which of the following is not a property of the cell membrane?

   A. fluidity
   B. permeability to nonpolar compounds
   C. permeability to water and gases
   D. rigidity
   E. impermeability to large polar compounds

10. A cell is placed in a bath of water that has a much higher salt concentration than the concentration inside the cell. What happens?

   A. The cell will fill with water.
   B. Water will rush out of the cell.
   C. The distribution of water will not change.
   D. Salt will move from the cell to the exterior.
   E. The cell will clearly burst.

Explanations

1. (A)

Total magnification is calculated by multiplying the power of the ocular and objective lenses. Since, in this case, the ocular lens has a magnification power of 10x, and none of the possible objective lenses has a magnification power of 1x, it's impossible for the microscope to have a total magnification power of 10x.

2. (B)

Prokaryotes lack membrane-bound organelles, but must have ribosomes for protein synthesis. Prokaryotes do not have a nucleus; DNA is stored in a coil in the cytoplasm.

3. (D)
The Golgi apparatus packages proteins for secretion by the cell. As for the other answer choices: the nucleus controls the cell's activities, proteins are made in the cytoplasm and endoplasmic reticulum by ribosomes, and lipids are synthesized by the smooth endoplasmic reticulum.

4. (D)
All of the answers are forms of transport, but only exocytosis is used to remove synthesized proteins from the cell. These proteins cannot undergo diffusion because they are too large to fit through the cell membrane. Osmosis refers only to the transport of water. Pinocytosis is a form of transport that involves taking liquids into the cell rather than secreting them. Passive transport includes diffusion and osmosis.

5. (A)
The ribosomes attached to the ER membrane give it its roughness. The smooth ER, not the rough ER, functions in lipid synthesis. Cellulose is part of the cell wall in plants.

6. (A)
Lysosomes digest cellular debris. The other choices refer to functions that are performed by organelles, but not by lysosomes. Chloroplasts produce energy through photosynthesis, vacuoles store nutrients, the cell membrane regulates the movement of substances in and out of the cell, and lipid synthesis takes place in the smooth endoplasmic reticulum.

7. (B)
Clearly phospholipids must be a type of molecule in the phospholipid bilayer. The bilayer also contains proteins, which float in the bilayer like icebergs in a sea.

8. (A)
All of the processes listed are means of transport, except for respiration. However, only diffusion is a process by which molecules move from high to low concentration. Pinocytosis, endocytosis, and exocytosis are means of active transport, while diffusion is a type of passive transport.

9. (D)
The cell membrane consists of a floating sea of phospholipids. If the membrane were rigid, organisms would fracture when they move.

10. (B)
Water is in lower concentration outside the cell because there is more salt there. Since substances diffuse from areas of high concentration to low concentration, water will move out of the cell.

Organic and Biochemistry

ON A PHYSICAL LEVEL, ORGANISMS ARE NO more than enormous complexes of interacting chemicals. Even complicated large-scale processes, like the behavior of animals, have a basis in chemistry. This chapter will begin by explaining the rudiments of chemistry and then using that foundation to describe the chemistry of life.

The Building Blocks of Matter

All matter, from a rock to an animal to the magma at the center of the Earth, is made from different combinations of 92 naturally occurring substances known as **elements**. The smallest quantity of an element that still exhibits the characteristics of that element is known as an **atom**. One atom of carbon, for example, is the smallest piece of matter that still retains the chemical and physical characteristics of carbon.

Atoms are made up of even smaller particles called **electrons**, **protons**, and **neutrons**. Each of these particles has a different electrical charge. Protons are positively charged, neutrons have no charge, and electrons are negatively charged. The protons and neutrons of an atom reside in a central body called a nucleus. Electrons appear around the nucleus within orbitals of varying energy. Overall, the atom is neutrally charged with equal numbers of positively charged protons and negatively charged electrons.

Elements are distinguished by the number of protons in their nuclei. All atoms containing six protons are called carbon. Any element with one proton is called hydrogen. Only the number of protons—and not the number of neutrons or electrons—distinguishes elements from each other.

Isotopes and Ions

Though the number of neutrons and electrons in an atom won't change the atom's status as a particular element, it can affect the properties of an element in subtle ways. An atom that contains a larger or smaller number of neutrons than usual is called an isotope. Carbon usually has six protons and six neutrons, and can be called carbon-12 because the number of its protons and neutrons add up to 12. But some carbon atoms have seven or even eight neutrons. These two isotopes are called carbon-13 and carbon-14. Isotopes do not have charge, because the numbers of positive and negative particles remain balanced. Even though they have different masses, isotopes of the same element all have similar chemical properties, because the number of electrons (not the number of neutrons or protons) determines the way an atom will interact with other atoms.

Ions are atoms that either lack or have extra electrons. Because these atoms have unequal numbers of electrons and protons, they are charged particles, and are often quite chemically interactive with other atoms. Though the SAT II Biology test rarely asks direct questions about ions, ions do play an important role in many biological processes and phenomena, so understanding the basics of ions can help you understand the processes that the test covers.

Molecules and Compounds

Atoms combine with each other in chemical reactions to create molecules, unique substances with physical and chemical properties distinct from those of their constituent elements. Combining two hydrogen atoms with one oxygen atom creates water, which has very different characteristics than hydrogen or oxygen do alone. Molecules such as water containing more than one type of element can also be called compounds. A water molecule made up of oxygen and hydrogen can be called a compound; a hydrogen molecule, which contains only two hydrogen atoms, cannot be called a compound.

You may have heard water referred to as H_2O. This notation is the standard way of representing molecules and compounds by shorthand. The "H" and "O" stand for the elements hydrogen and oxygen, and the subscript indicates that water contains two parts hydrogen for every one part oxygen. You can create the formula for any compound by writing down the letter symbol of each of its constituent elements and using subscripted numbers to indicate how many atoms of each element are present.

Chemical Bonds

The connections between the atoms in a compound are called chemical bonds. Atoms form bonds by sharing their electrons with each other, relying on the power of electric charge to keep themselves attached. Molecules and compounds can also bond with each other. Important bonds between atoms are covalent and ionic bonds. Bonds between molecules or compounds are called dipole-dipole bonds.

Covalent bonds

Bonds formed through the more or less equal sharing of electrons between atoms are known as covalent bonds.

If the electrons in a covalent bond are shared equally, the resulting bond is called a **nonpolar covalent bond**. When one atom pulls the shared electrons towards itself a little more tightly than the other, the resulting covalent bond is said to be a **polar bond**. In a polar bond, the atom that pulls electrons towards itself gains a slight negative charge (because electrons have a negative charge). Since the other atom partially loses an electron, it gains a slight positive charge. For example, the atoms in water form polar bonds because oxygen, which has eight protons in its nucleus, has a greater pull on electrons than hydrogen, which has only one proton.

Ionic Bonds

Polar covalent bonds involve the unequal sharing of electrons. This inequality is brought to an extreme in a bonding arrangement called an ionic bond. In an ionic bond, one atom pulls the shared electrons away from the other atom entirely. Ionic bonds are stronger than polar bonds.

One example of ionic bonding is the reaction between sodium (Na) and chlorine (Cl) to form table salt (NaCl). The chlorine atom steals an electron from the sodium atom. Because it loses an electron, the sodium atom develops a charge of +1. The chlorine atom has a charge of –1, since it gained an electron.

Dipole-Dipole Bonds

As seen in polar covalent compounds, due to the unequal sharing of electrons, some molecules have a slightly positive and a slightly negative end to them, or a dipole (dipole = two magnetic poles). These compounds can form weak bonds with one another without combining together completely to create new compounds. This type of bonding, known as dipole-dipole interaction, takes places when the positively charged end of one polar covalent compound ($\delta+$) comes in contact with the negatively charged end of another polar covalent compound ($\delta-$):

$$
\begin{array}{ccc}
\overset{\delta+}{H} & & \overset{\delta+}{H} \\
\diagdown & & \diagdown \\
\overset{\delta-}{O} - \overset{\delta+}{H} - - - - - \overset{\delta-}{O} \\
& & \diagdown \\
& & \underset{H}{\overset{\delta+}{}}
\end{array}
$$

Dipole-dipole interactions are much weaker than the bonds within molecules, but they play a very important role in the chemistry of life. Perhaps the most important dipole-dipole bond in biochemistry (and on the SAT II Biology) is the dipole-dipole interaction between positively charged hydrogen molecules and negatively charged oxygen molecules. This reaction is so important it gets its own special name: **hydrogen bond**. These bonds account for many of the exceptional properties of water and have important effects on the structure of proteins and DNA.

Acids and Bases

Sometimes atoms give their electrons up altogether instead of sharing them in a chemical bond. This process is known as disassociation. Water, for instance, dissociates by the following formula:

$$H_2O \rightarrow H^+ + OH^-$$

The hydrogen atom gives up a negatively charged electron, gaining a positive charge, and the OH compound gains a negatively charged electron, taking on a negative charge. The H^+ is known as a **hydrogen ion** and OH^- ion is known as a **hydroxide ion**.

The disassociation of water produces equal amounts of hydrogen and hydroxide ions. However, the disassociation of some compounds produces solutions with high proportions of either hydrogen or hydroxide ions. Solutions high in hydrogen ions are known as **acids**, while solutions in high hydroxide ions are known as **bases**. Both types of solution are extremely reactive—likely to form bonds—because they contain so many charged particles.

The technical definition of an acid is that it is a hydrogen ion donor, or a proton donor, as hydrogen ions are comprised of only a single proton. Acids put H^+ ions into solution. The definition of a base is a little more complicated: they are H^+ ion or proton acceptors, which means that they remove H^+ ions from solution. Some bases can directly produce OH^- ions that will take H^+ out of solution. NaOH is an example of this type of base:

$$NaOH \rightarrow Na^+ + OH^-$$

A second type of base can directly take H⁺ out an H_2O solution. Ammonia (NH_3) is a common example of this sort of base:

$$NH_3 + H_2O \rightarrow NH_4^+ + OH^-$$

From time to time, the SAT II Biology has been known to ask whether ammonia is a base.

The pH Scale

The pH scale, measured on a scale of 0–14, is used to measure the degree to which a solution is acidic or basic. If the proportion of hydrogen ions in a solution is the same as the proportion of hydroxide ions or equivalent, the solution has a pH of 7, which is neutral. The most acidic solutions (those with a high proportion of H⁺) have pHs approaching 0, while the most basic solutions (those with a high proportion of OH⁻ or equivalent) have pHs closer to 14.

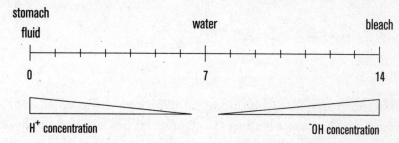

Water has a pH of 7 because it has equal proportions of H⁺ and OH⁻ ions. In contrast, when a compound called hydrogen fluoride (HF) disassociates, it only forms hydroxide ions. HF is therefore quite acidic and has a pH well below 7. Some acids are more acidic than others because they put more H⁺ ions into solution. Stomach fluid, for example, is more acidic than saliva.

When sodium hydroxide (NaOH) disassociates, it forms only hydroxide ions, making it a base and giving it a pH above 7. Like acids, bases can be strong or weak depending on how many hydroxide ions they put in solution, or how many hydrogen ions they take out of solution.

Buffers

Some substances resist changes in pH even when acids or bases are added to them. These substances are known as buffers. The cell contains many buffers because wide swings in pH can negatively impact the chemical reactions of cell processes.

Organic and Biochemistry

The Chemistry of Life

Of the 92 naturally existing elements on the Earth, only 25 play a role in the chemical processes of life. Of these 25, there are four elements that comprise more than 98 percent of all biological matter: carbon (C), oxygen (O), hydrogen (H) and nitrogen (N). Virtually every important organic compound is made up of these four elements. The Big 4 of organic elements can be cut down even further to a Supreme 1: carbon is the most important biological molecule, both for life as we know it and on the SAT II.

Carbon

Carbon is the central element of life. Its important role stems from its ability to form four chemical bonds with other elements at the same time:

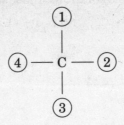

Carbons often attach to other carbon atoms, forming long chains called hydrocarbons. These molecules get their name because the central carbons also bond to hydrogen:

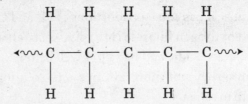

In addition to making a connection to four other atoms, carbon also has the ability to make two or three separate connections with the same single partner (and make its remaining one or two bonds with other substances). These bonds, which are stronger than single bonds, are known as double or triple bonds, respectively.

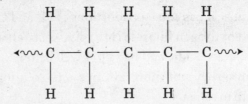

Monomers and Polymers

Many biological molecules consist of basic units that are strung together to form long chains, much like beads are placed on a string to make a necklace. There can be some variation in these basic units, which are known as monomers. Two monomers connected to each other are known as a dimer; a chain of monomers is called a polymer.

Polymers can be formed by many different types of chemical reactions. One special reaction, however, is particularly important in producing the polymers found in the chemistry of life. This reaction involves a carbon that has a hydrogen atom attached and a carbon that has an OH^- group attached. When the carbons bond to each other, they release a water molecule formed from the oxygen atom and the two hydrogen atoms.

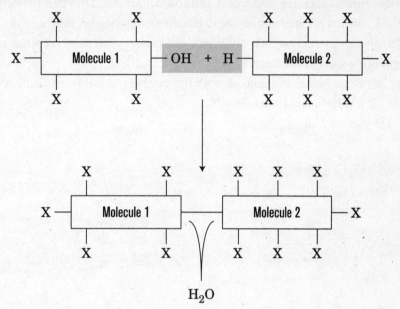

Because a water molecule is created in order to join the two monomers, this reaction is known as **dehydration synthesis**. The reverse of dehydration synthesis, when a water molecule is inserted into a polymer to break off a monomer, is called **hydrolysis**.

The Molecules of Life

The elements involved in life processes can, and do, form millions of different compounds. Thankfully, these millions of compounds fall into four major groups: carbohydrates, proteins, lipids, and nucleic acids. Though all of these groups are organized around carbon, each group has its own special structure and function.

Organic and Biochemistry

Carbohydrates

Carbohydrates are compounds that have carbon, hydrogen, and oxygen atoms in a ratio of about 1:2:1. If you're stuck on an SAT II Biology question about whether a compound is a carbohydrate, just count up the atoms and see if they fit this ratio. Carbohydrates are often sugars, which provide energy for cellular processes.

Like all of the biologically important classes of compounds, carbohydrates can be monomers, dimers, or polymers. The names of most carbohydrates end in -ose: **glucose**, fructose, sucrose, and maltose are some common examples.

Monosaccharides

Carbohydrate monomers are known as monosaccharides. This group includes glucose, $C_6H_{12}O_6$, which is a key substance in biochemistry. Sugars that an animal eats are converted to glucose, which is then converted into energy to fuel the animal's activities by respiration (see Cell Processes).

Glucose has a cousin called fructose with the same chemical formula. But these two compounds have different structures:

Glucose and fructose differ in one important way: glucose has a double-bonded oxygen on the top carbon, while fructose has its double-bonded carbon on the second carbon. This difference is most apparent when the two monosaccharides are in their ring forms. Glucose generally forms a hexagonal ring (six-sided), while fructose forms a pentagonal ring (five-sided). Whereas fructose is the sugar most often found in fruits, glucose is most often used as the major source of energy for cellular activities.

Disaccharides

Disaccharides are carbohydrate dimers. These dimers are formed from two monomers by dehydration synthesis. Any two monosaccharides can form a disaccharide. For example, maltose is formed by the dehydration synthesis of two glucose molecules. Sucrose, common table sugar, comes from the linkage of one molecule of glucose and one of another monosaccharide called fructose.

Polysaccharides

Polysaccharides can consist of as few as three and as many as several thousand monosaccharides. Depending on their structure and the monosaccharides they contain, polysaccharides can function as a means of storing excess energy or provide structural support.

When cells ingest more carbohydrates than they need for fuel, they link the sugars together to form polysaccharides. The structure of these polysaccharides is different in plants and animals: in plants, polysaccharides take the form of **starch**, whereas in animals, they are linked in a structure called **glycogen**.

Polysaccharides can also have structural roles in plants and animals. Cellulose, which forms the cell walls of plant cells, is a structural polysaccharide. In animals, the polysaccharide chitin forms the hard outer armor of insects, crabs, spiders, and other arthropods. Many fungi also use chitin as a structural carbohydrate.

Proteins

More than half of the organic compounds in cells are proteins, which play an important function in almost every cellular process. Proteins, for example, provide structural support to the cell in the cytoskeleton and that make up many of the hormones that send messages around the body. **Enzymes**, which regulate chemical reactions in the cell, are also proteins.

Amino Acids

Proteins are made up of monomers called amino acids. The names of many, but not all amino acids, end in –ine: methionine, lysine, serine, etc. Each amino acid consists of a central carbon atom attached to a set of three designated groups: an atom of hydrogen (–H), an amino group ($-NH_2$), and a carboxyl group (–COOH). The final group, designated (–R) in the diagram below, varies between different amino acids.

Organic and Biochemistry

It is possible to make an infinite number of amino acids by attaching different compounds to the R position of the central carbon. However, only 20 types of R groups exist in nature, so there are only 20 naturally occurring amino acids.

Polypeptides

All proteins are made of chains of some or all of these 20 amino acids. The bond formed between two amino acids by dehydration synthesis is known as a **peptide bond**.

A particular protein has a specific sequence of amino acids, which is known as its **primary structure**. Every protein also winds, coils and folds in three-dimensional space in specific and predetermined ways, taking on a unique secondary (initial winding and coiling) and tertiary structure (overall folding). In harsh conditions, such as high temperature or extreme pH, proteins can lose their normal tertiary shape and cease to function properly. When a protein unfolds in harsh conditions, it has been "denatured."

Lipids

Lipids are carbon compounds that do not dissolve in water. They are distinguished from other macromolecules by characteristic **hydrocarbon** chains—long strings of carbon molecules with hydrogens attached. Such chains do not dissolve well in water because they are nonpolar.

Triglycerides

Triglycerides consist of three long hydrocarbon chains known as **fatty acids** attached to each other by a molecule called glycerol.

glycerol   fatty acids

Because they include three fatty acids, fats and oils are also known as triglycerides. As you might expect by this point, glycerol and each fatty acid chain are joined to each other by dehydration synthesis.

Some fats are saturated, while others are unsaturated. These terms refer to the presence or absence of double bonds in the fatty acids of fats. Saturated fats have no double bonds, whereas unsaturated fats contain one or more such bonds. In general, plant fats are unsaturated and animal fats are saturated. Saturated fats are generally solid at room temperature, while unsaturated fats are typically liquid.

Organic and Biochemistry

Phospholipids

Phospholipids, which are important components of cell membranes, consist of a glycerol molecule attached to two fatty acid chains and one phosphate group (PO_4^{-2}):

glycerol   fatty acids

Like all fats, the hydrocarbon tails of phospholipids do not dissolve in water. However, phosphate groups do dissolve in water because they are polar. The different solubilities of the two ends of phospholipid molecules allow them to form the bilayers that make up the cell membrane.

Steroids

Steroids are the primary structure in hormones, substances that play important signaling roles in the body. Structurally, steroids are made up of four fused carbon rings attached to a hydrocarbon chain.

HCCH$_3$(CH$_2$)$_3$CH(CH$_3$)$_2$

CH$_3$

CH$_3$

HO

The linked rings indicate that each carbon atom is attached to other carbon atoms that form multiple loops. Cholesterol, the steroid in the image above, is the central steroid from which other steroids, such as the sex hormones, are synthesized. Cholesterol is only found in animal cells.

Nucleic Acids

Cells use a class of compounds called nucleic acids to store and use hereditary information. Individual nucleic acid monomers, known as **nucleotides**, consist of three main units: a **nitrogenous base** (a compound made with nitrogen), a phosphate group, and a sugar:

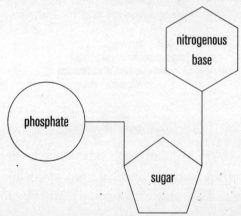

There are two main types of nucleotides, differentiated by their sugars: **deoxyribonucleic acid (DNA)** and **ribonucleic acid (RNA)**. DNA nucleotides have one less oxygen than RNA nucleotides. The "deoxy" in deoxyribonucleic acid refers to the missing oxygen molecule. In terms of function, DNA molecules store genetic information for the cell, while RNA molecules carry genetic messages from the DNA in the nucleus to the cytoplasm for use in protein synthesis and other processes.

Organic and Biochemistry

Within both DNA and RNA, there are further subdivisions of nucleotides by nitrogenous bases. For DNA, there are four different kinds of nitrogenous bases:

1. adenine (A)

2. guanine (G)

3. cytosine (C)

4. thymine (T)

The nitrogenous base of a nucleotide provides it with its chemical identity, so the nucleotides are called by the name of their nitrogenous base. RNA also has four nitrogenous bases. Three—adenine, guanine and cytosine—are identical to those found in DNA. The fourth, uracil, replaces thymine.

DNA and RNA

In 1953, James Watson and Francis Crick published the discovery of the three-dimensional structure of DNA. Watson and Crick hypothesized that DNA nucleotides are organized into a polymer that looks like a ladder twisted into a coil. They called this structure the **double helix**.

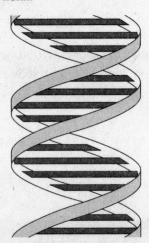

Two separate DNA polymers make up each side of the ladder. The sugar and phosphate molecules of the DNA form the vertical supports, while the nitrogenous bases stick out to form the rungs. The rungs attach to each other by hydrogen bonding.

Cytosine	Guanine	DNA and RNA
Adenine	Thymine	DNA only
Adenine	Uracil	RNA only

The nitrogen bases attach to each other according to two simple rules: Adenine (A) pairs with thymine (T), and guanine (G) pairs with cytosine (C). The exclusivity of the attachments between nitrogen bases is known as **base pairing**.

The rules of base pairing are frequently tested on the SAT II Biology. A test question might ask, "What is the **complementary** DNA strand to 'CAT'." Following the rules of DNA base pairing, you can deduce that the answer is 'GTA'. ('DOG' is the wrong answer, smart guy.)

RNA Structure

Unlike the double stranded DNA, RNA is single stranded. It looks like a ladder cut down the middle. As you will see when we discuss protein synthesis in the chapter on Cell Processes, this structure of RNA is very important to its functions as a messenger from the DNA in the nucleus to the cytoplasm.

	DNA	**RNA**
Bases	Adenine, guanine, cytosine, thymine	Adenine, guanine, cytosine, uracil
Structure	Double helix	Single helix
Function	Store genetic material and pass it from generation to generation	Carry messages from the nucleus to the cytoplasm

Summary of the Molecules of Life

	Proteins	**Lipids**	**Nucleic Acids**	**Carbohydrates**
Function	Structure, signaling, catalysis	Energy storage, signaling, membrane constituents	Store genetic material	Energy source, energy storage, structural
Monomer	Amino acid		Nucleotide	Monosaccharide
Polymer	Polypeptide, Protein		RNA, DNA	Polysaccharide
Example	Insulin, transcriptase (an enzyme)	Corn oil	A chromosome	Glucose

Organic and Biochemistry

Enzymes

Some chemical reactions simply happen when the two reactants come into contact. For example, you may be familiar with the bubbly "volcano" that forms when baking soda and vinegar are placed together in a glass. This reaction is spontaneous because it does not require outside energy to force it to occur.

Most reactions, however, require energy. For example, the chemical reactions that produce a cake do not take place when baking soda, flour, and the other ingredients of a cake are simply left in a pan on the kitchen counter. Heat is required to break the existing chemical bonds in the ingredients so that they can undergo chemical reactions and combine with each other in new ways.

In the laboratory, chemists use heat to create the activation energy needed to get nonspontaneous reactions started. Animals, however, can't rely on internal Bunsen burners to get their chemical reactions cooking. In order to perform chemical reactions at low temperatures, the body uses special proteins called enzymes, which lower the activation energy necessary for chemical reactions to achievable levels. Enzymes lower the activation energy by interacting with the **substrates**, the primary molecules or compounds involved in the reaction. If you think of the activation energy needed for a chemical reaction as a mountain that the reactants have to climb, think of an enzyme as opening up a tunnel though the mountain. Less energy is required to go through the tunnel than to climb all the way up the mountain.

Enzymes are not themselves altered when they help reactions along. Consequently, a single enzyme can be used repeatedly in many reactions. Because enzymes can be used over and over again, and because they can act very quickly, a relatively small amount of enzyme is needed to facilitate reactions involving relatively large amounts of material.

Each enzyme is designed to fit only the substrates in the reaction that the enzyme is meant to control. The one-to-one correspondence between enzyme and substrate is referred to as **specificity**. An analogy to a **lock and key** is useful for understanding the specificity of enzymes. Each enzyme can be thought of as a lock and that can interact only with the appropriate key, or substrate. The region of the enzyme that interacts with the substrate is known as the **active site**.

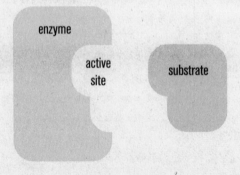

Enzymes help form bonds by holding two substrates near each other in the active site. Compounds can form bonds with each other more easily when they are adjacent than when they are floating around the cell randomly.

Often, enzymes are named for their substrate. The name of the enzyme is the name of the starting material followed by the "-ase". For example, maltase is an enzyme that breaks down maltose, a common sugar. (Be careful not to confuse sugars, which end in "-ose,", with enzymes that end in "-ase.")

Factors Affecting Enzymes

Like all proteins, enzymes have a unique three-dimensional structure that changes under unusual environmental conditions. Enzymes do not function well when their structure is altered.

Temperature and pH

Depending on where it is normally located in the body, an enzyme will have different temperature and pH values at which its structure is most stable. As conditions deviate from this point, the enzymes' ability to help along reactions decreases.

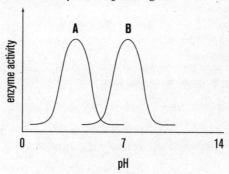

A - optimum pH for stomach enzyme

B - optimum pH for cytoplasm enzyme

Most enzymes work best near a pH of 7, but some enzymes operate most effectively in particularly acidic environment, such as the stomach; a neutral environment impairs their function. Likewise, the enzymes of creatures that live at high temperatures, such as bacteria that live in hot springs, do not function properly at human body temperature.

Cofactors and Inhibitors

In order to control enzyme activity more precisely, the body has developed a number of compounds that turn enzymes on or off and make them work faster or slower. Sometimes these compounds attach to the active site along with the substrate and sometimes they bind to another site on the enzyme. Activators of enzymes are known as cofactors or **coenzymes**. Many vitamins are coenzymes. Molecules that prevent enzymes from functioning properly are known as inhibitors.

Organic and Biochemistry

Review Questions

1. All of the following statements are true EXCEPT

   A. Hydrogen ions have different chemical properties from elemental hydrogen.
   B. Carbon isotopes have different chemical properties from elemental carbon.
   C. Carbon-14 has six protons and eight neutrons.
   D. Hydrogen ions are missing an electron.
   E. Ions have equal numbers of protons and neutrons.

2. How many atoms are there in $C_6H_{12}O_6$?

   A. 3
   B. 6
   C. 12
   D. 24
   E. 144

3. Electrons are shared equally in which of the following chemical bonds?

   A. nonpolar covalent bond
   B. polar covalent bond
   C. ionic bond
   D. dipole-dipole bond
   E. hydrogen bond

4. How many single bonds can carbon form with other atoms at the same time?

   A. 1
   B. 2
   C. 3
   D. 4
   E. 5

5. What chemical reaction takes place when two glucose monomers, or monosaccharides, form a dimer?

   A. disassociation
   B. dehydration synthesis
   C. hydrolysis
   D. ionization
   E. isomerization

6. Which of the following polysaccharide stores carbohydrates in animals?

   A. cellulose
   B. glycogen
   C. starch
   D. glucose
   E. fructose

7. What are the primary lipids found in cell membranes?

   A. glycerol
   B. cholestrol
   C. fatty acids
   D. phospholipids
   E. oils

8. What are the components of nucleotides?

   A. glycerols, fatty acids, and phosphates
   B. sugars, phosphates, and nitrogenous bases
   C. amino groups, hydrogens, and carboxyl groups
   D. protons, neutrons, and electrons
   E. protons and neutrons only

9. Which of the following represent a correct pairing of nitrogenous bases?

   A. glycerol and uracil
   B. guanine and uracil
   C. nucleic acids and bases
   D. cytosine and adenine
   E. adenine and thymine

10. Which of the following statements is incorrect?

   A. Enzymes are made from proteins.
   B. One enzyme can facilitate the reaction of many different substrates.
   C. Enzymes sometimes use induced fits to break apart their substrates.
   D. Enzymes are not required for spontaneous reactions.
   E. Not all catalysts are enzymes.

Explanations

1. (B)
Isotopes of elements share the same chemical properties as standard elements. They differ only in their number of neutrons, which has no effect on chemistry.

2. (D)
To compute the number of atoms in a compound, add the subscripts in the formula. In this case, 6 + 12 + 6 = 24.

3. (A)
Electrons are shared equally only in nonpolar covalent bonds. In polar covalent bonds, electrons are shared, but their distribution between the partners is unequal. In ionic bonds, one partner hogs all the electrons. Dipole-dipole and hydrogen bonds are weak intermolecular interactions.

4. (D)

Carbon is the element common to all organic compounds. Its unique properties arise from the fact that it can form up to four bonds with other atoms.

5. (B)

Bonds between monosaccharides are formed by dehydration synthesis, a common biochemical reaction in which a new compound is formed by the joining of two monomers with the by-product of water. Hydrolysis is the reverse of dehydration synthesis; "lysis" means breaking, and "hydro" means water, so hydrolysis is the splitting of a polymer with the uptake of a water molecule.

6. (B)

Glycogen is the molecule animals use to store carbohydrates. Plants use starch to store the glucose produced in photosynthesis. Cellulose is also a polysaccharide, but it is a structural component of cell walls. Glucose and fructose are monosaccharides.

7. (D)

The fluid mosaic model states that the cell membrane is made up primarily of phospholipids and proteins. Though cholesterol is found in the membrane, it is not a major constituent.

8. (B)

Nucleotides are made of sugars, phosphates, and nitrogenous bases. Glycerols and fatty acids are part of fats; when these combine with a phosphate, you get phospholipids. Amino groups (NH_2) and carboxyl groups (COOH) are found in proteins. Protons, neutrons, and electrons are the basic components of the atom.

9. (E)

Adenine binds only to thymine and uracil. Cytosine binds exclusively to guanine. None of the other answer choices contain correct pairings of nitrogenous bases.

10. (B)

Enzymes cannot work on many different substrates. In fact, the reason enzymes are able to function as they do is because of their specificity in the substrates they can catalyze.

Cell Processes

Cell Processes

Staying alive is no easy business. To keep from dying, cells must constantly juggle a wide range of tasks. They need to turn food into energy and produce the proteins and enzymes that choreograph crucial life processes. But no matter how efficient a cell is, in the end, it will die. To make sure its work does not die with it, every cell must be able to reproduce. This chapter reviews cellular respiration, protein synthesis, and cellular reproduction, the three crucial cellular life processes.

Cell Respiration

Respiration is the process by which organisms burn food to produce energy. The starting material of cellular respiration is the sugar **glucose**, which has energy stored in its chemical bonds. You can think of glucose as a kind of cellular piece of coal: chock full of energy, but useless when you want to power a stereo. Just as burning coal produces heat and energy in the form of electricity, the chemical processes of respiration converts the energy in glucose into usable form.

Adenosine triphosphate (ATP) is the usable form of energy produced by respiration. ATP is like electricity: it contains the same energy as coal, but it's easier to transport and is just what's needed when the cell needs some power to carry out a task.

ATP

ATP is a nucleic acid similar to those found in RNA. It has a ribose sugar attached to the nitrogenous base adenine. However, instead of the single phosphate group typical of RNA nucleotides, ATP has three phosphate groups. Each of the ATP phosphate groups carries a negative charge. In order to hold the three negative charges in such proximity, the bonds holding the phosphate groups have to be quite powerful. If one or two of the bonds are broken and the additional phosphates are freed, the energy stored in the bonds is released and can be used to fuel other chemical reactions. When the cell needs energy, it removes phosphates from ATP by hydrolysis, creating energy and either adenosine diphosphate (ADP), which has two phosphates, or adenosine monophosphate (AMP), which has one phosphate.

Respiration is the process of making ATP rather than breaking it down. To make ATP, the cell burns glucose and adds new phosphate groups to AMP or ADP, creating new power molecules.

There are actually two general types of respiration, aerobic and anaerobic. Aerobic respiration occurs in the presence of oxygen, while anaerobic respiration does not use oxygen. Both types of cell respiration begin with the process of glycolysis, after which the two diverge. We'll first discuss aerobic respiration, and then move to anaerobic.

Aerobic Cell Respiration

Aerobic respiration is more efficient and more complicated than anaerobic respiration. Aerobic respiration uses oxygen and glucose to produce carbon dioxide, water, and ATP. More precisely, this process involves six oxygen molecules for every sugar molecule:

$$6O_2 + C_6H_{12}O_6 \rightarrow 6CO_2 + 6H_2O + ATP \text{ energy}$$

This general equation for aerobic respiration (which you should know for the test) is actually the product of three separate stages: glycolysis, the Krebs cycle, and the electron transport chain. Typically, the SAT II Biology only asks questions about the starting and ending products of each stage and the location where each takes place. Understanding the internal details of stages will help you remember these key facts and prepare you in case the testers throw in a more difficult question, but the details of all the complex reactions will probably not be tested by the SAT II.

Glycolysis

Glycolysis is the first stage of aerobic (and anaerobic) respiration. It takes place in the cytoplasm of the cell. In glycolysis ("glucose breaking"), ATP is used to split glucose molecules into a three-carbon compound called **pyruvate**. This splitting produces energy that is stored in ATP and a molecule called **NADH**. The chemical formula for glycolysis is:

$$C_6H_{12}O_6 + 2ATP + 2NAD^+ \rightarrow 2Pyruvate + 4ATP + 2NADH$$

As the formula indicates, the cell must invest 2 ATP molecules in order to get glycolysis going. But by the time glycolysis is complete, the cell has produced 4 new ATP, creating a net gain of 2 ATP. The 2 NADH molecules travel to the mitochondria where, in the next two stages of aerobic respiration, the energy stored in them is converted to ATP.

The most important things to remember about glycolysis are:

- Glycolysis is part of both aerobic and anaerobic respiration.

- Glycolysis splits glucose, a six-carbon compound, into two pyruvate molecules, each of which has three carbons.

- In glycolysis, a 2 ATP investment results in a 4 ATP payoff.

- Unlike the rest of aerobic respiration, which takes place in the mitochondria, glycolysis takes place in the cytoplasm of the cell.

- Unlike the rest of aerobic respiration, glycolysis does not require oxygen.

The Krebs Cycle

After glycolysis, the pyruvate sugars are transported to the mitochondria. During this transport, the three-carbon pyruvate is converted into the two-carbon molecule called acetate. The extra carbon from the pyruvate is released as carbon dioxide, producing another NADH molecule that heads off to the electron transport chain to help create more ATP. The acetate attaches to a coenzyme called Coenzyme A to form the compound **acetyl-CoA**. The acetyl-CoA then enters the Krebs cycle. The Krebs cycle is called a cycle because one of the molecules it starts with, the four-carbon oxaloacetate, is regenerated by the end of the cycle to start the cycle over again.

The Krebs cycle begins when acetyl-CoA and oxaloacetate interact to form the six-carbon compound citric acid. (The Krebs cycle is also sometimes called the **citric acid cycle**.) This citric acid molecule then undergoes a series of eight chemical reactions that strip carbons to produce a new oxaloacetate molecule. The extra carbon atoms are expelled as CO_2 (the Krebs cycle is the source of the carbon dioxide you exhale). In the process of breaking up citric acid, energy is produced. It is stored in ATP, NADH, and $FADH_2$. The NADH and $FADH_2$ proceed on to the electron transport chain.

Cell Processes

The entire Krebs cycle is shown in the figure below. For the SAT II Biology, you don't have to know the intricacies of this figure, but you should be able to recognize that it shows the Krebs cycle.

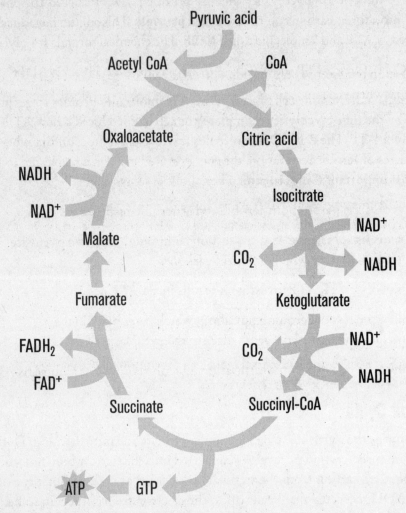

It is also important to remember that each glucose molecule that enters glycolysis is split into two pyruvate molecules, which are then converted into the acetyl-CoA that moves through the Krebs cycle. This means that for every glucose molecule that enters glycolysis, the Krebs cycle runs twice. Therefore, for one glucose molecule running through aerobic cell respiration, the equation for the Krebs cycle is:

$$2\text{Acetyl-CoA} + 2\text{Oxaloacetate} \rightarrow 4CO_2 + 6\text{NADH} + 2\text{FADH}_2 + 2\text{ATP} + 2\text{Oxaloacetate}$$

For the SAT II Biology, the most important things to remember about the Krebs cycle are:

- The Krebs cycle results in 2 ATP molecules for each glucose molecule run through glycolysis.

- The Krebs cycle sends energy-laden NADH and FADH$_2$ molecules on to the next step in respiration, the electron transport chain. It does not export carbon molecules for further processing.

- The Krebs cycle takes place in the mitochondrial matrix, the innermost compartment of the mitochondria.

- Though the Krebs cycle does not directly require oxygen, it can only take place when oxygen is present because it relies on byproducts from the electron transport chain, which requires oxygen. The Krebs cycle is therefore an aerobic process.

The Electron Transport Chain

A great deal of energy is stored in NADH and FADH$_2$ molecules formed in glycolysis and the Krebs cycle. This energy is converted to ATP in the final phase of respiration, the electron transport chain:

$$10 \text{ NADH} + 2 \text{ FADH}_2 \rightarrow 34 \text{ ATP}$$

The electron transport chain consists of a set of three protein pumps embedded in the inner membrane of the mitochondria. FADH$_2$ and NADH are used to power these pumps. Using the energy in NADH and FADH$_2$, these pumps move positive hydrogen ions (H$^+$) from the mitochondrial matrix to the intermembrane space. This creates a concentration gradient over the membrane.

In a process called **oxidative phosphorylation**, H$^+$ ions flow back into the matrix through a membrane protein called an ATP synthase. This channel is the opposite of the standard membrane pumps that burns ATP to transport molecules against their concentration gradient: ATP synthase uses the natural movement of ions along their concentration gradient to make ATP. All told, the flow of ions through this channel

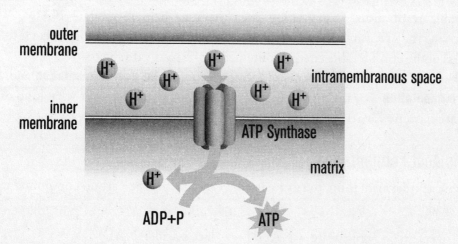

produces 34 ATP molecules. The waste products from the powering of the electron transport chain protein pumps combine with oxygen to produce water molecules. By accepting these waste products, oxygen frees NAD^+ and FAD to play their roles in the Krebs cycle and the electron transport chain. Without oxygen, these vital energy carrier molecules would not perform their roles and the processes of aerobic respiration could not occur.

For the SAT II Biology, the most important things to remember about the electron transport chain and oxidative phosphorylation are:

- Four ATP molecules are produced by glycolysis and the Krebs cycle combined. The electron transport chain produces 34 ATP.

- The electron transport chain occurs across the inner membrane of the mitochondria.

- The electron transport chain requires oxygen.

Anaerobic Respiration

Aerobic respiration requires oxygen. However, some organisms live in places where oxygen is not always present. Similarly, under extreme exertion, muscle cells may run out of oxygen. Anaerobic respiration is a form of respiration that can function without oxygen.

In the absence of oxygen, organisms continue to carry out glycolysis, since glycolysis does not use oxygen in its chemical process. But glycolysis does require NAD^+. In aerobic respiration, the electron transport chain turns NADH back to NAD^+ with the aid of oxygen, thereby averting any NAD^+ shortage and allowing glycolysis to take place. In anaerobic respiration, cells must find another way to turn NADH back to NAD^+.

This "other way" is called **fermentation**. Fermentation's goal is not to produce additional energy, but merely to replenish NAD^+ supplies so that glycolysis can continue churning out its slow but steady stream of ATP. Because pyruvates are not needed in anaerobic respiration, fermentation uses them to help regenerate NAD^+. While employing the pyruvates in this way does allow glycolysis to continue, it also results in the loss of the considerable energy contained in the pyruvate sugars.

There are two principle forms of fermentation, **lactic acid fermentation** and **alcoholic fermentation**. For the SAT II Biology, remember that no matter what kind of fermentation occurs, anaerobic respiration only produces 2 net ATP in glycolysis.

Lactic Acid Fermentation

In lactic acid fermentation, pyruvate is converted to a three-carbon compound called lactic acid:

$$\text{pyruvate} + \text{NADH} \rightarrow \text{lactic acid} + NAD^+$$

In this reaction, the hydrogen from the NADH molecule is transferred to the pyruvate molecule.

Lactic acid fermentation is common in fungi and bacteria. Lactic acid fermentation also takes place in human muscle cells when strenuous exercise causes temporary oxygen shortages. Since lactic acid is a toxic substance, its buildup in the muscles produces fatigue and soreness.

Alcoholic Fermentation

Another route to NAD^+ produces alcohol (ethanol) as a by-product:

$$pyruvate + NADH \rightarrow ethyl\ alcohol + NAD^+ + CO_2$$

Alcoholic fermentation is the source of ethyl alcohol present in wines and liquors. It also accounts for the bubbles in bread. When yeast in bread dough runs out of oxygen, it goes through alcoholic fermentation, producing carbon dioxide. These carbon dioxide bubbles create spaces in the dough and cause it to rise.

Like lactic acid, the ethanol produced by alcoholic fermentation is toxic. When ethanol levels rise to about 12 percent, the yeast dies.

From DNA to Protein

DNA directs the cell's activities by telling it what proteins to make and when. These proteins form structural elements in the cell and regulate the production of other cell products. By controlling protein synthesis, DNA is hugely important in directing life.

Protein synthesis is a two-step process. DNA resides in the nucleus, but proteins are made in the cytoplasm. The cell copies the information held in DNA onto RNA molecules in a process called transcription. Proteins are synthesized at the ribosomes from the codes in RNA in a process called translation.

Before getting into the way that the information on DNA can be transcribed and then translated into protein, we have to spend some time studying the major players in the process: DNA and RNA.

DNA and the Genetic Code

The sequence of nucleotides in DNA makes up a code that controls the functions of the cell by telling it what proteins to produce. Cells need to be able to produce 20 different amino acids in order to produce all the proteins necessary to function. DNA, however, has only four nitrogen bases. How can these four bases code for the 20 amino acids? If adenine, thymine, guanine, and cytosine each coded for one particular amino acid, DNA would only be able to code for four amino acids. If two bases were used to specify an amino acid there would only be room to code for 16 (4×4) different amino acids.

In order to be able to code for 20 amino acids, it is necessary to use three bases (which offer a total of 64 coding combinations) to code for each amino acid. These triplets of nucleotides that make up a single coding group are called **codons** or **genes**. Two examples of codons are CAG, which codes for the amino acid glutamine, and CGA, which codes for argenine.

Codons are always read in a non-overlapping sequence. This means that any one nucleotide can only be a part of one codon. Given the code AUGCA, AUG could be a codon for the amino acid methionine, with CA starting a new codon. Alternatively, GCA could be a codon specifying alanine, while the initial AU was the last two letters of a previous codon. But AUG and GCA cannot both be codons at the same time.

Degeneracy of the Genetic Code

There are 64 codons but only 20 amino acids. What happens to the other 44 coding possibilities? It happens that some of the different codons call for the same amino acid. The genetic code is said to be **degenerate** because of its redundancy.

Experiments have shown that there are also three **stop codons** that signal when a protein is fully formed and one start codon which signals the beginning of an amino acid sequence.

Mutations of the Genetic Code

Since the sequence of nucleotides in DNA determines the order of amino acids in proteins, a change or error in the DNA sequence can affect a protein's function. These errors or changes in the DNA sequence are called mutations.

There are two basic types of mutations: substitution mutations, and frameshift mutations.

Substitution Mutation

A substitution mutation occurs when a single nucleotide is replaced by a different nucleotide. The effects of substitution mutations can vary. Certain mutations might have no effect at all; these are called silent mutations. For instance, because the genetic code is degenerate, if the particular codon GAA becomes GAG, it will *still* code for the amino acid glutamate and the function of the cell will not change. Other substitution mutations can drastically affect cellular and organismal function. Sickle-cell anemia, which cripples human red blood cells, is caused by a substitution mutation. A person will suffer from sickle-cell anemia if he has the amino acid valine in his hemoglobin rather than glutamic acid. The codon for valine is GUA or GUG, while the codon for glutamic acid is GAA or GAG. A simple substitution of A for U results in the disease.

Frameshift Mutation

A frameshift mutation occurs when a nucleotide is wrongly inserted or deleted from a codon. Both types of frameshifts usually have debilitating or lethal effects. An insertion or deletion will affect *every* codon in a particular genetic sequence by throwing the entire three by three codon structure out of whack. For example, if the A in the GAU were to be deleted, the code:

GAU GAC UCC GCU AGG

would become:

GUG ACU CCG CUA GG

and code for an entirely different set of amino acids in translation. The results of such mutations on an organism are usually catastrophic.

The only sort of frameshift mutation that might not have dire effects is one in which an entire codon is inserted or deleted. This will result in the gain or loss of one amino acid, but will not affect surrounding codons.

Chromosomes

Even the tiniest cells contain meters upon meters of DNA. With the aid of special proteins called histones, this DNA is coiled into an entangled fibrous mass called chromatin. When it comes time for the cell to replicate (a process covered later in this chapter), these masses gather into a number of discrete compact structures called chromosomes.

In eukaryotes, the chromosomes are located in the nucleus of the cell. Prokaryotes don't have a nucleus; their DNA is located in a single chromosome that is joined together in a ring. This ring chromosome is found in the cytoplasm. In this chapter, when we talk about chromosomes, we will be referring to eukaryotic chromosomes.

Different eukaryotes have varying numbers of chromosomes. Humans, for example, have 46 chromosomes arranged in 23 pairs. (Dogs have 78 chromosomes in 39 pairs. A larger number of chromosomes is not a sign of greater biological sophistication.) The total number of distinct chromosomes in a cell is the cell's **diploid number**.

The cells in a human body that are not passed down to offspring, called **somatic** cells, contain chromosomes in two closely related sets—one set of 23 each from a person's mother and father—making up a total of 46 chromosomes. These sets pair up, and the pairs are known as **homologous chromosomes**. Each homologous pair consists of one maternal and one paternal chromosome. The **haploid number** of a cell refers to half of the total number of chromosomes in a cell (half the diploid number), or the number of homologous pairs in somatic cells.

In humans and other higher animals, only the sex cells that are passed on to offspring have the haploid number of chromosomes. These sex cells are also called **gametes**.

RNA

Ribonucleic acid (RNA) helps DNA turn stored genetic messages into proteins. As discussed in the biochemistry chapter, RNA monomers (nucleotides) are similar to those of DNA, but with three crucial differences:

- DNA's five-carbon sugar is deoxyribose. RNA nucleotides contain a slightly different sugar, called ribose.

- RNA uses the nitrogenous base uracil in place of DNA's thymine.

- The RNA molecule takes the form of a single helix—half a spiral ladder—as compared with the double helix structure of DNA.

Two different types of RNA play important roles in protein synthesis. During transcription, DNA is copied to make **messenger RNA (mRNA)**, which then leaves the nucleus to bring its still encoded information to the ribosomes in the cytoplasm. In order to use the information contained in the transcribed mRNA to make a protein, a second type of RNA is used. **Transfer RNA (tRNA)** moves amino acids to the site of protein synthesis at the ribosome according to the code specified by the mRNA strand. There are many different tRNAs, each of which bond to a different amino acid and the mRNA sequence corresponding to that amino acid.

Protein Synthesis

Now that we've described DNA and RNA, it's time to take a look at the process of protein synthesis. The synthesis of proteins takes two steps: transcription and translation. Transcription takes the information encoded in DNA and encodes it into mRNA, which heads out of the cell's nucleus and into the cytoplasm. During translation, the mRNA works with a ribosome and tRNA to synthesize proteins.

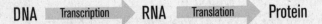

DNA → Transcription → RNA → Translation → Protein

Transcription

The first step in transcription is the partial unwinding of the DNA molecule so that the portion of DNA that codes for the needed protein can be transcribed. Once the DNA molecule is unwound at the correct location, an enzyme called RNA polymerase helps line up nucleotides to create a **complementary strand** of mRNA. Since mRNA is a single-stranded molecule, only one of the two strands of DNA is used as a template for the new RNA strand.

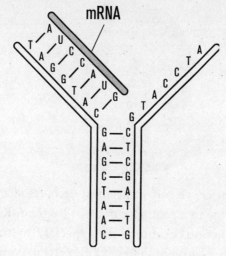

The new strand of RNA is made according to the rules of base pairing:

- DNA cytosine pairs with RNA guanine

- DNA guanine pairs with RNA cytosine

- DNA thymine pairs with RNA adenine

- DNA adenine pairs with RNA uracil

For example, the mRNA complement to the DNA sequence TTGCAC is AACGUG. The SAT II Biology frequently asks about the sequence of mRNA that will be produced from a given sequence of DNA. For these questions, don't forget that RNA uses uracil in place of thymine.

After transcription, the new RNA strand is released and the two unzipped DNA strands bind together again to form the double helix. Because the DNA template remains unchanged after transcription, it is possible to transcribe another identical molecule of RNA immediately after the first one is complete. A single gene on a DNA strand can produce enough RNA to make thousands of copies of the same protein in a very short time.

Translation

In translation, mRNA is sent to the cytoplasm where it bonds with ribosomes, the sites of protein synthesis. Ribosomes have three important binding sites: one for mRNA and two for tRNA. The two tRNA sites are labeled the A-site and P-site.

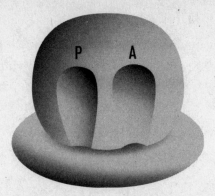

Once the mRNA is in place, tRNA molecules, each associated with specific amino acids, bind to the ribosome in a sequence defined by the mRNA code. tRNA molecules can perform this function because of their special structure. tRNA is made up of many nucleotides that bend into the shape of a cloverleaf. At its tail end, tRNA has an acceptor stem that attaches to a specific amino acid. At its head, tRNA has three nucleotides that make up an **anticodon**.

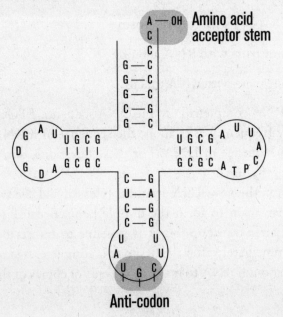

Amino acid acceptor stem

Anti-codon

An anticodon pairs complimentary nitrogenous bases with mRNA. For example if mRNA has a codon AUC, it will pair with tRNA's anticodon sequence UAG. tRNA molecules with the same anticodon sequence will always carry the same amino acids, ensuring the consistency of the proteins coded for in DNA.

The Process of Translation

Translation begins with the binding of the mRNA chain to the ribosome. The first codon, which is always the start codon methionine, fills the P-site and the second codon fills the A-site. The tRNA molecule whose anticodon is complementary to the mRNA forms a temporary base-pair with the mRNA in the A-site. A peptide bond is formed between the amino acid attached to the tRNA in the A-site and the methionine in the P-site.

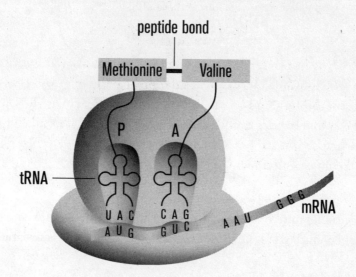

The ribosome now slides down the mRNA, so that the tRNA in the A-site moves over to the P-site, and a new codon fills the A-site. (One way to remember this is that the A-site brings new amino acids to the growing polypeptide at the P-site.) The appropriate tRNA carrying the appropriate amino acid pairs bases with this new codon in the A-site. A peptide bond is formed between the two adjacent amino acids held by tRNA molecules, forming the first two links of a chain.

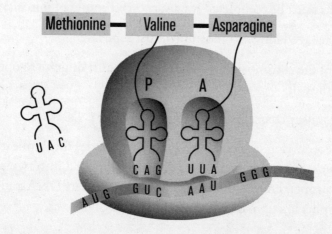

The ribosome slides again. The tRNA that was in the P-site is let go into the cytoplasm where it will eventually bind with another amino acid. Another tRNA comes to bind with the new codon in the A-site, and a peptide bond is formed between the new amino acid to the growing peptide chain.

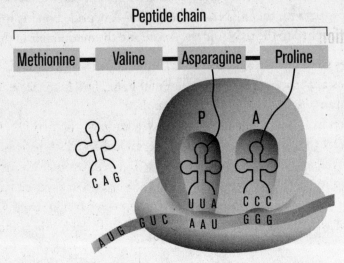

The process continues until one of the three stop codons enters the A-site. At that point, the protein chain connected to the tRNA in the P-site is released. Translation is complete.

Cell Replication

Eukaryotic cell replication is a process by which cells duplicate their genetic material and then divide to yield two daughter cells. In this section, we will discuss one type of cell reproduction called **mitosis** that produces an exact copy of the original cell, including an exact replication of DNA. In the next chapter, we will move on to discuss meiosis, a different form of cell replication that leads to the creation of sex cells. Millions of rounds of mitosis take place during the development of large multicellular organisms. Three separate tasks must be completed for a successful round of mitosis:

1. DNA packaged into chromosomes must replicate.

2. Copies of the chromosomes and organelles must migrate to opposite ends of the cell.

3. The cell must physically split into two separate cells.

The **cell cycle** is the recurring sequence of events that includes the duplication of a cell's contents and its subsequent division. The cell cycle is divided into two phases: interphase and mitosis proper. During interphase, the cell copies its DNA and prepares for division. The cell splits into two daughters in the stages of mitosis.

Interphase

During interphase, the cell prepares for the division it will undergo during mitosis. Such preparation involves maintaining its normal activities, growing to a size that can support cell division, and replicating its DNA.

DNA Replication

DNA replicates so that from one helix of DNA emerge two "daughter" helices. These daughter helices are exact copies of the parental helix. DNA creates daughter helices by using the parental strands of DNA as a template.

The first step in DNA replication is the separation of the two DNA strands that make up the helix that is to be copied. An enzyme called DNA helicase untwists the helix to form a Y shape called a replication fork. The replication fork moves down the DNA strand, splitting it into two single strands. Next, an enzyme called DNA polymerase helps new nucleotides line up next to the two separated strands, according to the rules of base pairing: adenine and thymine pair with each other, and guanine and cytosine pair with each other.

As new nucleotides line up at the appropriate spots along the original strand, they form the "rungs" on the new DNA molecule. Ultimately replication produces two new DNA molecules that are identical to the original molecule. Replication is complete when both of the new strands have formed and rewound into their characteristic double helix shape.

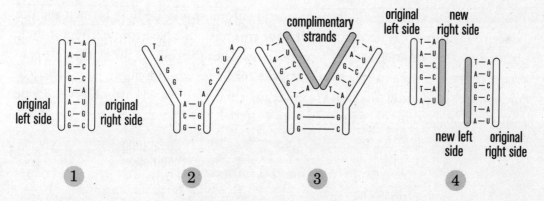

The Products of Replication

During interphase, every chromosome is replicated. In a human cell, for example, all 46 chromosomes are replicated. You might logically think that after replication, the 46 chromosomes would become 92 chromosomes. But you'd be wrong.

After a chromosome replicates, each of the two new chromosomes are joined together at their middle by a region called a centromere. The result is an X-shaped structure.

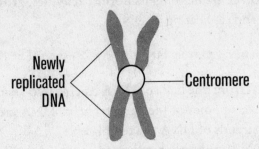

Newly replicated DNA — Centromere

The two halves of the structure are called **chromatids**. The entire structure, even though it has doubled in size, is still called a chromosome. Since we call each double-chromatid structure a chromosome, a cell that has replicated all of its DNA to prepare for division is still said to contain the diploid number of chromosomes, which is 46 in humans.

Mitosis

During mitosis, the cell divides into two daughter cells. Mitosis can be divided into four subphases: prophase, metaphase, anaphase, and telophase.

Prophase

Prophase begins when the double-chromatid chromosomes are fully formed and can be seen clearly under a microscope. After the chromosomes have formed, microtubule structures called **centrioles** move to opposite ends of the cell. As the centrioles separate, a fanlike array called the **mitotic spindle** forms between them. In later phases of mitosis, the spindle will function as a guide to help the replicated chromosomes divide neatly into two groups of complete genetic material.

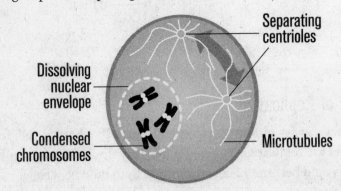

Dissolving nuclear envelope

Condensed chromosomes

Separating centrioles

Microtubules

In prophase, the nuclear membrane dissolves and the chromosomes attach to the spindle at their centromere. With chromosomes secured on the spindle, the cell is ready to enter the next phase of mitosis, metaphase.

Metaphase

Metaphase begins when the spindle is completely formed. The phase is marked by the alignment of chromosomes at the middle of the cell, halfway between each of the mitotic spindle poles along a plane called the metaphase plate.

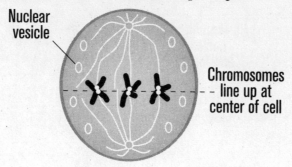

Nuclear vesicle

Chromosomes line up at center of cell

Once the chromosomes are aligned correctly, the cell enters anaphase, the third stage of mitosis.

Anaphase

During anaphase, the pairs of chromosomes at the center of the cell separate into individual chromosomes, which move to opposite sides of the cell. The microtubule and spindle fibers facilitate this motion. The cell also begins to elongate in preparation for splitting.

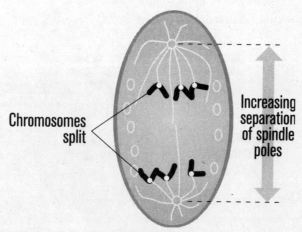

Chromosomes split

Increasing separation of spindle poles

When the chromosomes reach their destination at the opposite poles of the cell, anaphase gives way to telophase, the fourth and final stage of mitosis.

Telophase

Telophase begins when the chromosomes reach opposite poles. Small pieces of nuclear membrane in the cell begin to reform around the group of chromosomes at each end, creating two nuclei in one cell. When the chromosomes are once again surrounded by a protective envelope, they relax and resume their interphase appearance as a stringy tangle. No longer needed, the spindles fall apart during this stage, and a nucleolus reforms inside each nucleus.

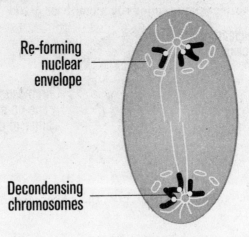

Re-forming nuclear envelope

Decondensing chromosomes

Cytokinesis

Although mitosis officially ends with telophase, at this point, the cell is not yet actually split into two new cells. The final cleavage is not exactly its own stage, but it does have its own name: cytokinesis, literally "cell division."

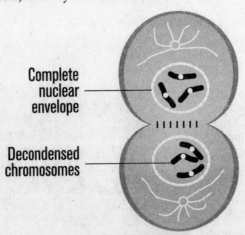

Complete nuclear envelope

Decondensed chromosomes

When the two nuclei reach opposite poles of the cell, the cell pinches in the middle, ultimately leading to cleavage.

Review Questions

1. Cellular respiration is the process by which cells convert the energy available in food to which energy-rich compound?

   A. ADP
   B. Glucose
   C. Water
   D. ATP
   E. Oxygen

2. Which of the following processes does not occur in the mitochondria?

   A. glycolysis
   B. the citric acid cycle
   C. electron transport chain
   D. photosynthesis
   E. oxidative phosphorylation

3. How many nucleotides specify an amino acid?

   A. 1
   B. 3
   C. 6
   D. 9
   E. 12

4. What tRNA anticodons correspond to the mRNA nucleotide sequence AUGCUG?

   A. TAC and GAC
   B. UAC and GAC
   C. UA, CG and AC
   D. GAC and TAC
   E. SAT and ACE

5. What DNA sequence codes for the tRNA anticodon CAU?

   A. GUA
   B. CAT
   C. GTA
   D. CAU
   E. UAC

6. During which of the following cell cycle phases does DNA replication take place?

   A. mitosis
   B. prophase
   C. interphase
   D. metaphase
   E. cytokinesis

7. Chromosomes are made up of which of the following substances?

   A. carbohydrates
   B. adenosine triphosphate
   C. adenosine diphosphate
   D. deoxyribonucleic acid
   E. phospholipid bilayer

8. Which of the following is the human haploid number?

   A. 10
   B. 23
   C. 30
   D. 46
   E. 92

9. What is the name for the process by which the cytoplasm of a cell divides to form two daughter cells?

   A. Cytokinesis
   B. Prophase
   C. Metaphase
   D. Anaphase
   E. Telophase

10. Which compound is both an initial reactant and final product of the Krebs cycle?

   A. Pyruvate
   B. Glucose
   C. Citric Acid
   D. NADH
   E. Oxaloacetic Acid

Explanations

1.   (D)

Adenosine triphosphate, ATP, is the molecule that provides most of the energy used by cells. When the bond between the second and third phosphate molecules in ATP is hydrolyzed, or broken, energy is released. The by-product of this process is a molecule of ADP, adenosine diphosphate, which can be recycled into another ATP molecule through the process of cellular respiration. Respiration uses oxygen to break down glucose and releases water as a by-product.

2.   (A)

Glycolysis, the first step in aerobic cellular respiration, takes place in the cytoplasm. The citric acid cycle, electron transport chain, and oxidative phosphorylation constitute the remaining steps in aerobic respiration and take place in the mitochondria. Photosynthesis occurs in the chloroplasts of plant cells.

3.   (B)

A codon, the nucleotide sequence on mRNA used to specify an amino acid, is composed of three nucleotides. Although there are some amino acids that can be indicated by more than one codon, every three-nucleotide codon specifies only one amino acid.

4.   (B)

In RNA, cytosine pairs with guanine, and adenine pairs with uracil. Therefore, the tRNA anticodons corresponding to the mRNA AUGCUG are UAC and GAC.

5.   (B)

To solve this question, trace the sequence back through mRNA, and from there, to DNA. GUA is the mRNA sequence that corresponds to CAU. (Remember: C pairs with G and A pairs with T in DNA; in RNA A pairs with U.) The DNA sequence that would code for this mRNA codon is CAT. If you memorize the rule that tRNA sequence is the same as DNA sequence only with U substituted for T, you can answer this type of question without doing any scratch work.

6.   (C)

DNA replication occurs during interphase. During this phase, chromosomes are replicated to provide a full set of genetic material for both daughter cells. Mitosis is the phase during which the cell splits into two daughter cells, but the DNA is replicated before the cell enters this process. Prophase is the first stage of mitosis, while metaphase is the second stage of mitosis.

7. **(D)**

Chromosomes are composed of deoxyribonucleic acid (DNA), a polymer made up of nucleotides strung together through covalent bonding. Adenosine triphosphate (ATP) is the primary energy source of cellular processes, and adenosine diphosphate (ADP) is the by-product formed when the third phosphate bond is broken to release ATP's energy. The phospholipid bilayer is the major component of all biological membranes.

8. **(B)**

The haploid number is the number of unique chromosomes, or homologous pairs, in a cell. The human haploid number is 23. A normal human somatic (not sperm or ova) cell has 46 total chromosomes in its nucleus. However, these chromosomes are found in pairs, so there are actually 23 pairs of what are called homologous chromosomes.

9. **(A)**

The part of the cell cycle in which cell division occurs is called cytokinesis. During prophase, homologous chromosomes begin to separate with the help of the spindle. Metaphase is marked by the formation of the metaphase plate and the lining up of the chromosomes along the midline of the cell. During anaphase, each chromosome splits into its two chromatids, which are separated to opposite poles of the cell. Telophase is the last phase of mitosis before the cell splits in two.

10. **(E)**

In the Krebs cycle, also called the citric acid cycle, acetyl Co-A produced from pyruvate in the pyruvate deoxygenase complex combines with oxaloacetic acid to form citric acid. At the end of the cycle, oxaloacetic acid is formed again, making it both a reactant and a product. NADH is only a product of the Krebs cycle and is broken down after glycolysis.

Mendelian and Molecular Genetics

Genetics

THE WORD "INHERITANCE" USUALLY BRINGS to mind money or property left by a relative who has passed away. But there's another type of inheritance that is right under our noses—actually, your nose is part of the inheritance. Every living organism has characteristics or features that it passes on to its offspring. These tendencies of **heredity** are obvious: even a child knows cows give birth only to other cows, and that children often look like their parents. But, in fact, the specific biological mechanisms that allow parents to transmit their features to their offspring were an enormous mystery until about 140 years ago. Scientists back then knew that parents somehow made a tiny copy of themselves inside an egg or a sperm, but they had no idea what these copies were or how they worked.

Then, in the 1860s, an Austrian monk named **Gregor Mendel** started breeding peas in his garden. Where others saw only plants, Mendel looked deeper and found the basic units of heredity we now call **genes**. If you remember from last chapter, genes are the portions of a chromosome that are transcribed to mRNA, and are ultimately translated to the proteins essential to cellular processes. Mendel had no knowledge of protein synthesis and had never seen a chromosome, but his simple experiments with peas and the laws he developed to describe the behavior of hereditary—now termed classical genetics—have provided the foundation for the modern field of molecular genetics, the study of heredity on the molecular level.

For the SAT II Biology, you should have a good grasp of the basic laws and patterns of both classical genetics and molecular genetics. Questions on genetics can comprise anywhere from 14 to 20 percent of the core of the SAT II Biology. In addition, the "M" section of the Biology E/M test focuses on evolution in terms of molecular biology, including genetics.

Basis of Inheritance: Meiosis

Mitosis takes a diploid cell and creates a nearly exact copy. Mitosis has two main functions: 1) it leads to the creation of all of the somatic (body) cells in humans and other living organisms; 2) in organisms that undergo **asexual reproduction**, diploid parent cells undergo mitosis to create identical daughter copies of themselves. Mitosis creates a daughter cell with chromosomes that are identical to the chromosomes in its parent cell.

But humans and most other complex plants and animals each have a unique set of chromosomes. This diversity of chromosomes is the result of **sexual reproduction**, which involves the contribution of the genetic material from not one, but two parents. During sexual reproduction the father's haploid sperm cell and the mother's haploid ovum (egg) cell fuse to form a single-celled diploid **zygote** that then divides billions of times to form a whole individual.

In order for sexual reproduction to take place, however, the parents first need to *have* haploid sperm or ova, also called **sex cells**, **germ cells**, or **gametes**. Meiosis is the name for the special type of cell division that produces gametes.

Process of Meiosis

Unlike the single-cell division of mitosis, meiosis involves two cellular divisions: meiosis I and meiosis II. Each stage of meiosis runs through the same five stages as discussed in mitosis. During the first round of division, two intermediate daughter cells are produced. By the end of the second round of meiotic division (meiosis II), the original diploid (2n) cell has become four haploid (n) daughter cells.

Meiosis I

Meiosis I is quite similar to mitosis. However, there are a number of crucial differences between meiosis I and mitosis, all of which will be outlined in the discussion of each individual stage below.

Interphase I: Just as in mitosis, the cell undergoes DNA replication during this intermediate phase. After replication, the cell has a total of 46 chromosomes, each made up of two sister chromatids joined by a centromere.

Prophase I: The major distinction between mitosis and meiosis occurs during this phase. In mitotic prophase, the double-stranded chromosomes line up individually along the spindle. But in meiotic prophase I, chromosomes line up along the spindle in homologous pairs. Then, in a process called **synapsis**, the homologous pairs actually join together and intertwine, forming a **tetrad** (two chromosomes of two chromatids each, or four total chromatids). Often this intertwining leads the chromatids of homologous chromosomes to actually exchange corresponding pieces of DNA, a process called **crossing-over** or genetic reassortment. Throughout prophase I, sister chromatids behave as a unit, and are identical except for the region where crossover occurred.

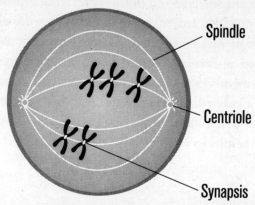

Metaphase I: After prophase I, the meiotic cell enters metaphase I. During this phase, the nuclear membrane breaks down, allowing microtubules access to the chromosomes. Still joined at their crossover regions in tetrads, the homologous pairs of chromosomes, with one maternal and one paternal chromosome in each pair, align at the center of the cell via microtubules, as in mitotic metaphase. The pairs align in random order.

Anaphase I: Anaphase I differs slightly from its mitotic counterpart. In mitotic anaphase, sister chromatids split at their centromeres and are pulled apart towards opposite poles. In contrast, during anaphase I, the centromeres do not split: the entire maternal chromosome of a homologous pair is pulled to one end, and the paternal chromosome is pulled to the other end.

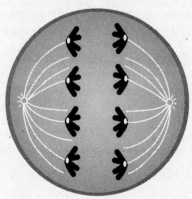

Genetics

Telophase I: During telophase I, the chromosomes arrive at separate poles and decondense. Nuclear membranes re-form around them. The cell physically divides, as in mitotic cytokinesis.

The Product of Meiosis I

Meiosis I results in two independent cells. One cell contains the maternal homologous pair, with a small segment of the paternal chromosome from crossover. The other cell contains the paternal homologous pair, likewise with a small segment of the maternal chromosome. Despite the small region of crossover in the chromosomes of each cell, the maternal sister **chromatids** are still quite similar, as are the paternal sister chromatids. Both cells formed by meiosis I contain a haploid amount of DNA.

The cells produced in meiosis I are different from those produced in mitosis because both haploid members of the meiotic pair derive from random assortments of either the maternal or paternal chromosomes from each homologous pair (with the exception of the small crossover sections). In mitosis, the cellular division separates sister chromatids and results in diploid cells containing one maternal and one paternal copy in each diploid pair.

Meiosis II

The cells produced by meiosis I quickly enter meiosis II. These cells *do not* undergo DNA replication before entering meiosis II. The two cells that move from meiosis I into meiosis II are haploid—each have 23 replicated chromosomes, rather than the 46 that exist in cells entering both mitosis and meiosis I.

Meiotic division II occurs through the familiar phases from meiosis I and mitosis. To distinguish the phases, they are called prophase II, metaphase II, anaphase II, and telophase II. One important difference between the events of meiosis I and II is that no further genetic reassortment takes place during prophase II. As a result, prophase II is much shorter than prophase I. In fact, all of the phases of meiosis II proceed rapidly.

During meiosis II, chromosomes align at the center of the cell in metaphase II exactly the way they do in mitotic metaphase. In anaphase II, the sister chromatids separate, once again in the same fashion as occurs in mitotic anaphase. The only difference is that since there was no second round of DNA replication; only one set of chromosomes exists. When the two cells split at the end of meioisis II, the result is four haploid cells.

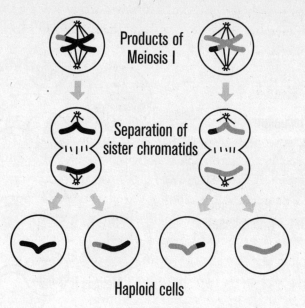

Of the four haploid cells, one cell is composed completely of a maternal homologue, another of a maternal homologue with a small segment of paternal DNA from cross-over in meiosis I, another complete paternal homologue, and a final paternal homologue with a small segment of maternal DNA from crossover in meiosis I. These four haploid cells are the gametes, the sperm or egg cells, that fuse together in sexual reproduction to create new individuals.

Spermatogenesis and Oogenesis

Meiosis, the process by which gametes are formed, can also be called **gametogenesis**, literally "creation of gametes." The specific type of meiosis that forms sperm is called spermatogenesis, while the formation of egg cells, or ova, is called oogenesis. The most important thing you need to remember about both processes is that they occur through meiosis, but there are a few specific distinctions between them.

Spermatogenesis

The male testes have tiny tubules containing diploid cells called spermatogonium that mature to become sperm. The basic function of spermatogenesis is to turn each one of the diploid spermatogonium into four haploid sperm cells. This quadrupling is accomplished through the meiotic cell division detailed in the last section. During interphase before meiosis I, the spermatogonium's 46 single chromosomes are replicated to form 46 pairs of sister chromatids, which then exchange genetic material through synapsis before the first meiotic division. In meiosis II, the two daughter cells go through a sec-

Genetics

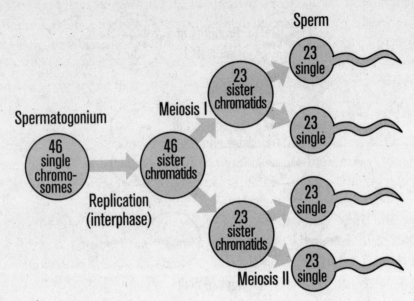

ond division to yield four cells containing a unique set of 23 single chromosomes that ultimately mature into four sperm cells. Starting at puberty, a male will produce literally millions of sperm every single day for the rest of his life.

Oogenesis

Just like spermatogenesis, oogenesis involves the formation of haploid cells from an original diploid cell, called a primary oocyte, through meiosis. The female ovaries contain the primary oocytes. There are two major differences between the male and female production of gametes. First of all, oogenesis only leads to the production of one final ovum, or egg cell, from each primary oocyte (in contrast to the four sperm

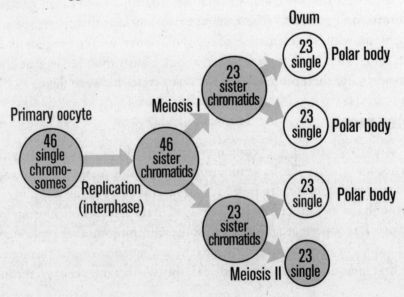

that are generated from every spermatogonium). Of the four daughter cells that are produced when the primary oocyte divides meiotically, three come out much smaller than the fourth. These smaller cells, called polar bodies, eventually disintegrate, leaving only the larger ovum as the final product of oogenesis. The production of one egg cell via oogenesis normally occurs only once a month, from puberty to menopause.

Mendel's Experiments

Gregor Mendel lived in an Austrian monastery and tended the monastery garden. In 1865, through his observations of the garden pea plants that grew there, Mendel developed three basic principles that—although ignored at the time by his scientific colleagues—would later become the foundation for the new science of genetics.

Every pea plant contains both male and female reproductive parts and will normally reproduce through self-pollination. Mendel noticed that the self-pollinating pea plants in his garden were true-breeding: they all produced offspring with characteristics identical to their own. Mendel looked at seven different characteristics, or **traits**, that showed up in all of the plants. Each of these traits had two contrasting natures, only one of which would show up in a given true-breeding plant. For example, plant height could be either short or tall: short, true-breeding plants would only produce short offspring, and tall plants would only produce tall offspring. At some point, Mendel wondered what would happen if he manually mated these true-breeding plants with each other—would a tall plant mated with a short plant produce a tall, medium, or short offspring? Focusing on only one trait at a time, Mendel cross-pollinated plants with each of the seven contrasting traits and examined their offspring. He called the original true-breeding parents the P (for parental) generation, and called their first set of offspring the F_1 (for "first filial", from the Latin word "filius" meaning son). The F_1 offspring that result from two parents with different characteristics are also called **hybrids**.

Law of Dominance

When Mendel crossed a purebred tall plant with a purebred short plant, all of the offspring in the first generation (the F_1 generation) were tall. The same thing happened with the other pairs of contrasting traits he studied: hybrid offspring in the first generation always showed just one of the two forms.

Mendel used the word **dominant** to describe the form that dominated the phenotype, or physical appearance, in the F_1 generation. The other form he called **recessive**, because the characteristic receded into the background in the F_1 generation. Mendel was the first to realize that hereditary information for two different forms of a trait can coexist in a single individual, with one form masking the expression of the other form. This principle, referred to as the Law of Dominance, provided the basis for Mendel's subsequent work.

Law of Segregation

Mendel discovered that mating a tall pea and a short pea would produce an F_1 generation of only tall pea plants. But, he wondered, were these offspring tall pea plants really identical to their tall parents, or might they still contain some element of their short parents? To answer this question, Mendel let all seven types of hybrid F_1 generation plant self-pollinate, producing what he called the F_2 (second filial) generation.

Lo and behold, in each F_2 generation some of the recessive forms of the traits— which had visibly disappeared in the F_1 generation—reappeared! Approximately one fourth of the F_2 plants exhibited the recessive characteristic, and three fourths continued to exhibit the dominant form of the trait, like their F_1 parents. This 3:1 ratio of dominant to recessive remained consistent in all of the F_2 offspring.

P — 1 tall / 1 short

F_1 — 4 tall

F_2 — 6 tall / 2 short

Mendel came up with a simple but revolutionary explanation for the results he saw in the F_2 generation. He concluded that within an individual, hereditary information came in paired units, with one unit derived from each parent. Each simple physical trait, such as stem height, was determined by the combined action of a single pair of units. Each unit could come in either a dominant form, which he denoted with a capital letter "A," or a recessive form, which he denoted with a lowercase "a." Two units with two possible forms gave four possible combinations: AA, Aa, aA, and aa; since Aa and aA were equivalent, there were really only three functional combinations. Because "A" is dominant over "a," both AA and Aa produced plants with the same physical characteristics. Only "aa" produced a plant that showed the recessive characteristic.

Mendel realized that the results he saw in the F_2 generation could only be explained if, during the formation of reproductive cells, paired units are separated at random so that each gamete contains only one of the two units. This postulate is now known as the Law of Segregation.

Genetics

Modern Explanation of Mendel's Results

With our modern understanding of genes, chromosomes, and cellular reproduction, we can explain the biological basis of Mendel's observations and make pretty accurate predictions about the offspring that any given cross (short for cross-breeding) will produce.

Alleles

Each of the traits that Mendel observed in his pea plants came in one of two varieties; modern science calls any gene that gives rise to more than one version of the same trait an allele. So, for example, the tall gene and the short gene are different alleles (variations) of the height gene.

Every somatic cell contains two complete sets of chromosomes, one from each parent. Now you can understand why homologous chromosomes are similar, but not identical: although they contain the same genes, they may not contain the same alleles for these genes.

Homozygous and Heterozygous

Going back to Mendel's plants, we can now say that all of his true-breeding plants contained two of the same alleles for each of the observed genes. Tall plants in this P generation had two alleles for tallness (TT), and short P generation plants had two alleles for shortness (tt). Anytime an organism's two alleles for a specific trait are identical, that the individual is said to be *homozygous* ("homo" means same) for that trait.

On the other hand, crossing the tall and short plants to produce F_1 hybrids created a generation of plants with one tall allele and one short allele (Tt). An organism with two opposing alleles for a single gene is said to be *heterozygous* for that trait.

Genotype and Phenotype

Although the P generation of pure-breeding tall plants *looked* the same as their hybrid F_1 offspring, the P and F_1 generations did not have identical genetic makeups. The genetic makeup of a certain trait (e.g., TT, Tt, or tt) is called its genotype, while the physical expression of these traits (e.g., short or tall) is called a phenotype.

For any given trait, an organism's genotype will indicate alleles from both parents, while the phenotype only indicates the allelic form that is physically expressed in that individual. This distinction between genetic makeup and physical appearance explains the apparent "disappearance" of the recessive alleles in the F_1 generation. Mendel's results for the F_2 generation can also be reinterpreted in light of these new distinctions. Mendel's results showed that 75 percent of the F_2 offspring exhibited the dominant phenotype, a ratio of 3:1 dominant to recessive. But from a genetic perspective, the breakdown would actually be around 25 percent homozygous dominant (TT), 50 percent heterozygous with a dominant phenotype (Tt), and 25 percent homozygous recessive (tt)—a ratio of 1:2:1.

Punnett Squares

The Punnett square is a convenient graphical method for representing the genotypes of the parental gametes and all the possible offspring they produce. The Punnett square below shows the mating of two F_1 hybrids (Aa genotype). We call this mating a **monohybrid cross**, because it involves only one gene. According to the Law of Segregation, two possible gametes are formed: A and a. The paternal gametes are listed as columns across the top of the square, and maternal gametes are listed as rows down the left side of the square. Combining the gametes in the intersecting boxes provides the genotypes of all possible offspring.

Paternal Gametes

	A	a
A	AA	Aa
a	aA	aa

Maternal Gametes

In this case, 25 percent of the F_2 offspring will be AA, 50 percent will be Aa, and 25 percent will be aa. Both AA and Aa will have the dominant phenotype, giving the 3:1 ratio (75 percent to 25 percent) of dominant to recessive phenotypes that Mendel observed.

For the SAT II Biology, if you are given the genotypes of two parents, you should be able to predict the genotypes and phenotypes of their offspring by using a Punnett Square.

The Law of Independent Assortment

After finishing his monohybrid crosses, Mendel moved onto **dihybrid crosses**, in which he bred pure, parental varieties that had two traits distinguishing them from each other. He wanted to determine whether the inheritance of one trait was connected in any way to the inheritance of the other.

The color and shape of the pea seeds provided two convenient traits to study. The seeds were either yellow or green, with yellow dominant; in shape, they were either round or wrinkled, with round dominant. Mendel crossed double dominant (phenotype yellow and round, genotype RRYY) plants with double recessive (phenotype green and wrinkled, genotype rryy) plants. As expected, the F_1 generation consisted of hybrid offspring all with the double dominant (round yellow) phenotype, and a heterozygous genotype (RrYy). The key test came in the proportions of different phenotypes in the F_2 generation. If the inheritance of one trait did not influence the inheritance of the other, then each parent should make equal numbers of the four possible gametes, and sixteen different genotypes would be equally represented in the offspring. As seen in the Punnett Square below, there should be four different phenotypes (yellow and round, green and round, yellow and wrinkled, green and wrinkled) occurring in the proportions 9:3:3:1.

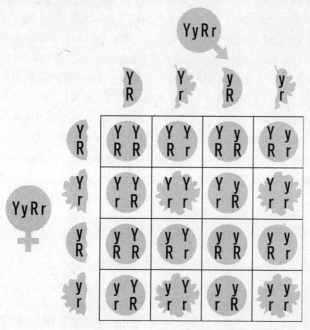

Mendel's phenotype counts of F_2 seeds did indeed show the 9:3:3:1 proportions anticipated in the Punnett square for the dihybrid cross. From these results, he concluded that the inheritance of one trait was unrelated to the inheritance of a second trait. The units from any one hereditary pair segregate into the gametes independently of the segregation of the units from any other pair. This principle is known as the Law of Independent Assortment.

Calculating Probabilities

Drawing Punnett Squares is a helpful way to visualize simple genetics problems, but with problems involving several different genes, it is often easier to use the rules of probability. (A Punnett Square for a three-gene hybrid cross would have 64 squares!) There are two rules of probability that you will need to solve genetics problems. First, the probability of an outcome that depends on the occurrence of two or more independent events is obtained by multiplying together the probability of each necessary independent event. This is the *and* rule of probability:

Genetics

> If A *and* B must occur in order to bring about outcome C,
> then the probability of outcome $C = P(a) \times P(b)$.

In contrast, if an outcome depends on the occurrence of any one of several mutually exclusive alternatives, then the probability of the outcome is obtained by adding together the probabilities of the alternatives. This is the *or* rule of probability:

> If A *or* B must occur to get outcome C, then the probability of $C = P(a) + P(b)$

As an example, we can calculate the probability of getting an 11 when rolling two dice, die A and die B. In order to roll an 11, we need a 5 *and* a 6. The probability of rolling a 5 on die A and a 6 on die B is $1/6 \times 1/6 = 1/36$. But we can also roll an 11 with a 6 on die A and a 5 on die B. This is a mutually exclusive alternative to the first roll we considered; its probability is also 1/36. Since either A5, B6 *or* A6, B5 gives us a total of 11, the final probability of rolling an 11 using two dice is $1/36 + 1/36 = 2/36 = 1/18$.

Moving from gambling to genetics, we can calculate the probability that a cross between genotypes AABBCc and aaBbCc will produce an offspring with genotype AaBbcc. Taking one gene at a time, the probability of the Aa combination is a perfect 1, since an AA and aa cross can only produce Aa offspring.

	a	a
A	Aa	Aa
A	Aa	Aa

The probability of the Bb combination is 1/2, because the BB and Bb cross will produce Bb offspring 50 percent of the time.

	B	b
B	BB	Bb
B	BB	Bb

The probability of the cc combination is 1/4, because the Cc and Cc cross gives cc offspring 25 percent of the time.

	C	c
C	CC	Cc
c	cC	cc

Since Aa *and* Bb *and* cc must occur to produce our desired outcome, the probability is $1 \times 1/2 \times 1/4 = 1/8$.

Test Crossing (Back Crossing)

A test cross is the means by which a scientist can determine whether an individual with a dominant phenotype has a homozygous (AA) or heterozygous (Aa) dominant genotype. The test cross involves mating the individual with the dominant phenotype to an individual with a recessive (aa) phenotype, and observing the offspring produced. If the individual being tested is homozygous dominant, then all offspring will have a dominant phenotype, since all the offspring will have at least one A allele and the A is dominant.

	a	a
A	Aa	Aa
A	Aa	Aa

If the tested individual is heterozygous dominant, then half of the offspring will show the dominant phenotype, while the other half show the recessive phenotype.

	a	a
A	Aa	Aa
a	aa	aa

Incomplete Dominance and Codominance

Mendel's Law of Dominance is generally true, but there are many exceptions to the law. In some instances, instead of a heterozygote expressing only one of two alleles, both alleles could be partially expressed. For example, the flower color of the four o'clock plant is determined by a single gene with two alleles: plants homozygous for the R1 allele have red flowers, while plants homozygous for the R2 allele have white

Genetics

flowers. If interbred, the heterozygous R1R2 plants have pink flowers. Incomplete dominance is the term used to describe the situation in which the heterozygote phenotype is intermediate between the two homozygous phenotypes.

If the heterozygote form simultaneously expresses both alleles fully, then the relationship between the two alleles is called codominance. An example of codominance appears in human blood type. Blood type is determined by two alleles, *A* and *B*, that code for the presence of antigen *A* and antigen *B* on the surface of red blood cells. Allele *A* and *B* are codominant. If only the allele *A* is present, then only antigen *A* exists on the blood cell. If only allele *B* is present, then only antigen *B* exists on the blood cell. If both alleles *A* and *B* are present, neither dominates the other and both antigens appear on the red blood cell. A third allele, *i*, is recessive: if only it appears, then the blood is of type O. The following is a summary of the genotypes that result in the four different blood types:

$$AA \text{ and } Ai \rightarrow \text{ Type A blood}$$
$$BB \text{ and } Bi \rightarrow \text{ Type B blood}$$
$$AB \text{ and } BA \rightarrow \text{ Type AB blood}$$
$$ii \rightarrow \text{ Type O blood}$$

Linkage and Crossing-Over

Fortunately for Mendel, the genes encoding his selected traits did not reside close together on the same chromosome. If they had, his dihybrid cross results would have been much more confusing, and he might not have discovered the Law of Independent Assortment. The Law of Independent Assortment holds true as long as two different genes are on separate chromosomes. When the genes are on separate chromosomes, the two alleles of one gene (A and a) will segregate into gametes independently of the two alleles of the other gene (B and b). Equal numbers of four different gametes will result: AB, aB, Ab, ab. But if the two genes are on the same chromosome, then they will be linked and will segregate together during meoisis, producing only two kinds of gametes.

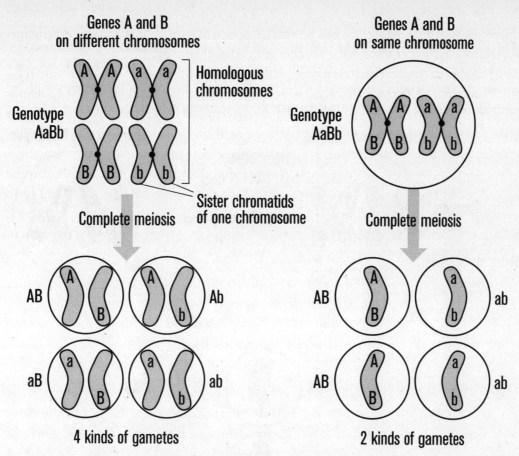

Genes A and B
on different chromosomes

Genes A and B
on same chromosome

Genotype
AaBb

Homologous
chromosomes

Genotype
AaBb

Sister chromatids
of one chromosome

Complete meiosis

Complete meiosis

AB

Ab

AB

ab

aB

ab

AB

ab

4 kinds of gametes

2 kinds of gametes

For instance, if the genes for seed shape and seed color were on the same chromosome, and a homozygous double dominant (yellow and round, RRYY) plant was crossed with a homozygous double recessive (green and wrinkled, rryy), the F_1 hybrid offspring, as usual, would be double heterozygous dominant (yellow and round, RrYy). However, since in this example the R and Y are linked together on the chromosome inherited from the dominant parent, with r and y linked together on the other chromosome, only two different gametes can be formed: RY and ry. Therefore, instead of 16 different genotypes in the F_2 offspring, only three are possible: RRYY, RrYy, rryy. And instead of four different phenotypes, only the original two will exist. Notice that the inheritance pattern now resembles that seen in a monohybrid cross, with a 3:1 phenotypic ratio, rather than the 9:3:3:1 ratio expected from the dihybrid cross. If physically linked on a single chromosome, the round and yellow alleles would segregate together, and the wrinkled and green alleles would segregate together: no round green seeds or wrinkled yellow seeds would ever appear.

The above explanation, however, neglects the influence of the crossing over of genetic material that occurs during meiosis. The further away two genes are from one another, the more likely an exchange point for crossing over will form between them.

At these exchange points, the alleles of one gene switch to the opposite homologous chromosome, while the other gene alleles remain with their original chromosomes. When alleles switch places like this, the resulting gametes are called recombinant. In the example above, the original parental gametes would be RY and ry, while the recombinant gametes would be Ry and rY. Thus four different kinds of gametes will be formed, instead of only two formed when the genes were linked.

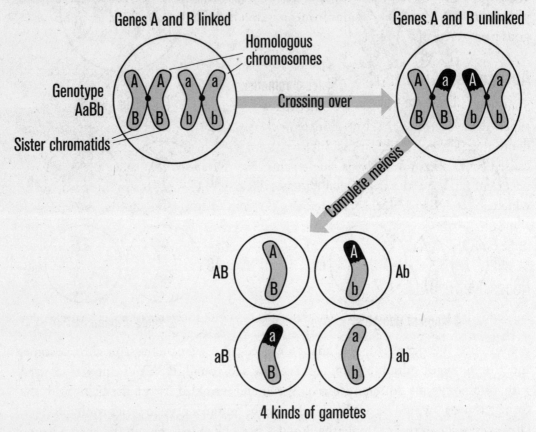

4 kinds of gametes

If two genes are extremely close together, crossing over will almost never occur between them, and recombinant gametes will almost never form. If they are very far apart on the chromosome, crossing over will almost certainly occur between them, and recombinant gametes will form just as often as if the genes were on different chromosomes (50 percent of the time). If the genes are at an intermediate distance from one another, crossing over may sometimes occur between them, and sometimes not. Therefore, the percentage of recombinant gametes (reflected in the percentage of recombinant offspring), correlates with the distance between two genes on a chromosome. By comparing the recombination rates of multiple different pairs of genes on the same chromosome, the relative position of each gene along the chromosome can be determined. This method of ordering genes on a chromosome is called a linkage map.

Mutations

Mutations are errors in the genotype that create new alleles and can result in a variety of genetic disorders. In order for a mutation to be inherited from one generation to another, they must occur in sex cells, such as eggs and sperm, rather than in somatic cells. The best way to detect whether a genetic disorder exists is to use a **karyotype**, a photograph of the chromosomes from an individual cell, usually lined up in homologous pairs, according to size.

Autosomal Mutations

Some human genetic illnesses are inherited in a Mendelian fashion. The disease phenotype will have either a clearly dominant or clearly recessive pattern of inheritance, similar to the traits in Mendel's peas. Such a pattern will usually only occur if the disease is caused by an abnormality in a single gene. The mutations that cause these diseases occur in genes on the **autosomal chromosomes**, as opposed to sex-linked diseases, which we cover later in this chapter. (Be careful not to confuse autosomal chromosomes with somatic cells; autosomal chromosomes are the chromosomes that determine bodily characteristics and exist in *all* cells, both sex and somatic.)

Recessive Disorders

A Mendelian genetic illness initially arises as a new mutation that changes a single gene so that it no longer produces a protein that functions normally. Some mutations, however, result in an allele that produces a non-functional protein. A disease resulting from this sort of mutation will be inherited in a recessive fashion: the disease phenotype will only appear when both copies of the gene carry the mutation, resulting in a total absence of the necessary protein. If only one copy of the mutated allele is present, the individual is a heterozygous carrier, showing no signs of the disease but able to transmit the disease gene to the next generation. Albinism is an example of a recessive illness, resulting from a mutation in a gene that normally encodes a protein needed for pigment production in the skin and eyes. The **pedigree** shown below diagrams three generations of a hypothetical family affected by albinism.

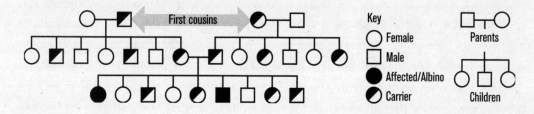

The pedigree demonstrates the characteristic features of autosomal recessive inheritance. The parents of an affected individual usually show no signs of disease, but both must at least be heterozygous carriers of the disease gene. Among the offspring of two carriers, 25 percent will have the disease, 50 percent will be carriers, and 25 percent will be non-carriers. No offspring produced by a carrier and a non-carrier will have the disease, but 50 percent will be carriers. Although not shown in this pedigree, offspring produced by two individuals who have the disease in their phenotype, which means both parents are recessive homozygous, will all develop the disease.

Many recessive illnesses occur with much greater frequency in particular racial or ethnic groups that have a history of intermarrying within their own community. For example, Tay-Sachs disease is especially common among people of Eastern European Jewish descent. Other well-known autosomal recessive disorders include sickle-cell anemia and cystic fibrosis.

Dominant Disorders

Usually, a dominant phenotype results from the presence of at least one normal allele producing a protein that functions abnormally. In the case of a dominant genetic illness, there is a mutation that results in the production of a protein with an abnormal and harmful action. Only one copy of such an allele is needed to produce disease, because the presence of the normal allele and protein cannot prevent the harmful action of the mutant protein. If a recessive mutation is like a car with an engine that cannot start, a dominant mutation is like a car with an engine that explodes. A spare car will solve the problem in the first case, but will do nothing to protect the garage in the second case.

Huntington's Disease, which killed folksinger Woody Guthrie, is a dominant genetic illness. A single mutant allele produces an abnormal version of the Huntington protein; this abnormal protein accumulates in particular regions of the brain and gradually kills the brain cells. By middle age, this progressive brain damage produces severely disturbed physical movements, loss of intellectual functions, and personality changes. The pedigree shown below diagrams three generations of a hypothetical family with Huntington's Disease.

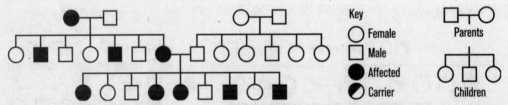

This pedigree demonstrates the characteristic features of autosomal dominant inheritance. Notice that all affected individuals have at least one parent with the disease. Unlike recessive inheritance, there is no such thing as a carrier: the disease will affect *all* heterozygous individuals. Among the offspring of an affected heterozygote and an unaffected person, 50 percent will be affected and 50 percent will be unaffected. None of the children born to two unaffected individuals will have the disease. (Although not shown in this pedigree, homozygous dominant mutations often produce very severe cases of the disease, because the amount of the abnormal protein is doubled and the normal protein is entirely absent.)

Chromosomal Disorders

Recessive and dominant characteristics result from the mutation of a single gene. Some genetic disorders result from the gain or loss of an entire chromosome. Normally, paired homologous chromosomes separate from one another during the first division of meiosis. If one pair fails to separate, an event called **nondisjunction**, then one daughter cell will receive both chromosomes and the other daughter cell will receive none. When one of these gametes joins with a normal gamete from the other parent, the resulting offspring will have either one or three copies of the affected chromosome, rather than the usual two.

Trisomy

A single chromosome contains hundreds to thousands of genes. A zygote with three copies of a chromosome (trisomy), instead of the usual two, generally cannot survive embryonic development. Chromosome 21 is a major exception to this rule; individuals with three copies of this small chromosome (trisomy 21) develop the genetic disorder called Down's syndrome. People with Down's syndrome show at least mild mental disabilities, and have unusual physical features including a flat face, large tongue, and distinctive creases on their palms. They are also at a much greater risk for various health problems such as heart defects and early Alzheimer's disease.

Monosomy

The absence of one copy of a chromosome (monosomy) causes even more problems than the presence of an extra copy. Only monosomy of the X chromosome (discussed below) is compatible with life.

Polyploidy

Polyploidy occurs when a failure occurs during the formation of the gametes during meiosis. The gametes produced in this instance are diploid rather than haploid. If fertilization occurs with these gametes, the offspring receive an entire extra set of chromosomes. In humans, polyploidy is always fatal, though in many plants and fish it is not.

Genetics

Sex Chromosomes and Sex-linked Traits

Dominant and recessive illnesses occur with equal frequency in males and females. This is because the genes involved are located on autosomes, which are the same in both genders. Many physical traits, however, obviously do differ between the two genders. In addition, gender dramatically affects the inheritance of certain traits and illnesses that have no obvious connection to sexual characteristics.

These sex-linked traits are controlled by genes located on the sex chromosomes. Humans have 46 chromosomes, including 44 autosomes (nonsex chromosomes) and the two sex chromosomes, which can be either X or Y. The autosomes come in 22 homologous pairs, present in both males and females. Females also possess a homologous pair of X chromosomes, while males have one X chromosome and one Y chromosome (the master gene for "maleness" is located on the Y chromosome). All eggs have an X chromosome, so the sex of a child is determined at the time of fertilization by the type of sperm. If the fertilizing sperm carries an X chromosome the child will be female; if it carries a Y chromosome the child will be male. The X chromosome is much larger than the tiny Y chromosome, and most of the genes on the X chromosome do not have a homologous counterpart on the Y.

Genes on autosomes will always be present in two copies: one inherited from the maternal parent, the other from the paternal parent. The traits controlled by such autosomal genes will be generally unaffected by gender, and will follow Mendelian patterns of inheritance (with the exceptions noted in previous sections). In contrast, genes on the X chromosome (X-linked genes) are present in two copies in females but only one copy in males. Female offspring will inherit one copy of an X-linked gene from each parent, but male offspring must inherit the Y chromosome from their father and therefore always inherit only the maternal allele of any X-linked gene. For example, color-blindness and hemophilia are sex-linked disorders. The mutated gene that causes these disorders is recessive and exists on the X-chromosome. In order for a female, who is XX, to have a phenotype that is color-blind or hemophiliac, both of her parents have to have the recessive gene. But since males have only one X-chromosome inherited from their mother, if their mother expresses the recessive mutation, that trait will *automatically* be expressed in the male child's phenotype, since the male has no other gene to assert dominance over the recessive mutation.

The pedigree shown below diagrams three generations of a hypothetical family affected by hemophilia A.

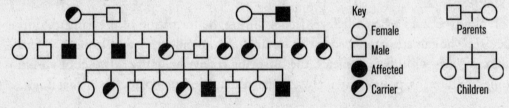

This pedigree demonstrates many of the characteristic features of X-linked recessive inheritance. Heterozygous females are carriers who do not express the disease. In contrast, all males with the mutated allele will express the disease; there are no male carriers. Affected males will transmit the mutated allele to none of their sons but to all of their daughters, who will then all be carriers. Heterozygous females will transmit the disease to one-half of their sons, and one-half of their daughters will be carriers. Affected males generally have an unaffected father and a mother who is a carrier; 50 percent of their maternal uncles will have the disease.

Review Questions

1.   During which meiotic phase are sister chromatids separated?

   A.   Prophase I
   B.   Metaphase I
   C.   Metaphase II
   D.   Anaphase I
   E.   Anaphase II

2.   One cell that undergoes meiosis will yield how many independent cells?

   A.   1
   B.   2
   C.   3
   D.   4
   E.   5

3.   In which generation of a monohybrid cross do all the individuals look the same?

   A.   Parental
   B. F_1
   C. F_2
   D. F_3

4.   In a monohybrid cross, the two parental genotypes are AA and aa. The genotype of all F_1 plants is Aa. If the F_1 plants are crossed to get an F_2 generation, what percentage of the F_2 generation will have the dominant phenotype?

   A.   0%
   B.   25%
   C.   50%
   D.   75%
   E.   100%

5.   You are performing a dihybrid cross with two traits encoded by two different genes. These genes are on two different chromosomes and follow the Law of Independent Assortment. The two parental genotypes are AABB and aabb. The genotype of all F_1 plants is AaBb. What phenotype ratio will you observe in the F_2 generation?

A.   8:4:2:1
B.   1:1:1:1
C.   4:2:2:1
D.   1:2:2:1
E.   9:3:3:1

6.   A scientist is studying the inheritance of two traits: stem height and stem color. Tall is dominant over short; brown is dominant over green. The scientist wants to do a test cross to determine the genotype of a tall, brown F_1 hybrid individual. What will be the height and color of the other plant he uses in this test cross?

A.   Tall and brown
B.   Tall and green
C.   Short and brown
D.   Short and green
E.   It doesn't matter; any of the above will work.

7.   You are studying the inheritance of stem height and stem color. For height, the tall phenotype is dominant over short; for color, the brown phenotype is dominant over green. You mate a purebred tall, brown plant to a purebred short, green plant and all of the F_1 offspring are tall and brown. You then mate two of these F_1 hybrid offspring together, and you count the following phenotypes in their F_2 offspring: 61 tall and brown, 1 tall and green, 2 short and brown, and 18 short and green. Which of the following is probably true?

A.   The two genes controlling these traits are sex-linked.
B.   The two genes controlling these traits might be on different chromosomes.
C.   The two genes controlling these traits are linked with no crossing over.
D.   The two genes controlling these traits are nearby on the same chromosome.
E.   The two genes controlling these traits are far apart on the same chromosome.

8.   Which of the following is usually NOT true of an autosomal recessive disease?

A.   Most people with the disease have parents who do not have the disease.
B.   An equal number of males and females get the disease.
C.   If both parents have the disease, 50% of their offspring will have the disease.
D.   If both parents are heterozygous, 75% of their children will not get the disease.
E.   The genes for the disease are not located on the sex chromosomes.

Genetics

9. A woman who is a heterozygous carrier of the hemophilia allele marries a man who has hemophilia. What percentage of their female children would you expect to have hemophilia?

   A. 0%
   B. 25%
   C. 50%
   D. 75%
   E. 100%

10. A boy with red-green color blindness (an X-linked recessive condition) has a color-blind father and a mother who is not color-blind. From which parent did the boy inherit his color blindness?

    A. No way to know—it could have been either one.
    B. His father
    C. His mother
    D. It had to come partly from both his mother and father.
    E. It had nothing to do with either his mother or father

Explanations

1. (E)

In meiosis, sister chromatids separate during anaphase II. During prophase I, sister chromatids are linked at their centromeres. At metaphase I, each pair of sister chromatids lines up in the middle of the cell together with its homologous pair of sister chromatids, and only homologous chromosomes separate during anaphase I. During metaphase II, each pair of sister chromatids again lines up along the metaphase plate, but they do not separate until anaphase II.

2. (D)

Meiosis divides a single diploid cell into four haploid cells. In the case of oogenesis, only one of those daughter cells goes on to become a fully developed egg cell, leaving three "polar bodies" to disintegrate; the original product, however, is still four cells.

3. (B)

The first (F_1) generation of offspring from a hybrid cross will all look the same. A hybrid cross involves the mating of a homozygous dominant (RR) individual with a homozygous recessive (rr) individual, so the parents do not look the same. In the F_1 generation, all offspring will have genotype Rr, and will all show the dominant trait. Other generations will contain some individuals with the dominant phenotype (RR or Rr) and some with the recessive phenotype (rr), and so will not all look the same.

4.   (D)
Approximately 75% of the F$_2$ generation will exhibit the dominant phenotype. Genotypically, there will be three types of offspring: 25% homozygous dominant, 50% heterozygous dominant, and 25% homozygous recessive. Only the homozygous recessive will show the recessive phenotype—therefore, a total of 75% will have the dominant phenotype.

5.   (E)
Because these genes are on separate chromosomes and therefore act independently, we can use a Punnett square to work out the results of this dihybrid cross.

	AB	Ab	aB	aB
AB	AABB	AABb	AaBB	AaBb
Ab	AABb	AAbb	AaBb	Aabb
aB	AaBB	AaBb	aaBB	aaBb
ab	AaBb	Aabb	aaBb	aabb

For every sixteen offspring in the F$_2$ generation, approximately nine will exhibit the dominant phenotype of both genes (genotype AABB, AABb, AaBB, or AaBb); three will be dominant on gene A only (AAbb or Aabb); three will be dominant on gene B only (aaBB or aaBb); and one will show a recessive phenotype on both genes (aabb). The result is a phenotype ratio of 9:3:3:1.

6.   (D)
In order to determine the genotype of a dominant-appearing individual, the scientist would have to perform a test cross (also known as a back cross) using a fully recessive individual. In this case, that would be a short and green plant.

7.   (D)
Given the fact that the expected 3:1 dominant to recessive phenotype showed up on the same F$_2$ offspring plants, it looks like these genes are linked and were not acting independently of one another. From this information, you can predict that the two genes controlling these traits are on the same chromosome. Since crossing over limits the affects of linkage—and crossing over occurs more often when two genes are far apart on the same chromosome— you can further determine that the two genes must be near each other on the chromosome.

8. (C)

The genotype of a person who has an autosomal recessive disease must be homozygous recessive. Therefore, if two parents have the disease, 100 percent (not 50 percent as stated in the wrong answer choice) of their children should get the disease, since neither parent has dominant alleles to contribute.

9. (C)

50 percent of the couple's daughters would be expected to have hemophilia, an X-linked recessive disease. Using a Punnett square to do the cross of the father (X hemophilia/Y) and the mother (X normal/X hemophilia), you should find that half of the female children will be homozygous for the X hemophilia gene and have the disease, while half will be heterozygous and only be carriers of the disease.

	X^H	Y
X^H	X^HX^H	X^HY
X	XX^H	XY

10. (C)

Although the father is color-blind, the gene for this condition is located on the X chromosome. The father could not have given his son the condition, because he only contributes a Y chromosome to his son; therefore, the gene that causes the disease must have been inherited from the mother.

Evolution and Diversity

THE BIOLOGIST THEODOSIUS DOBSZHANSKY once said, "Nothing in biology makes any sense except in the light of evolution." Now, old Theodosius never had to take the SAT II Biology test, but if he had, he probably would have been quite pleased about the many questions the SAT II asks about evolution and the diversity of species. About 15 percent of the ques-

tions in the core of the SAT II Biology E/M test evolution or diversity in some way, and the E and M sections cover ecology and molecular biology, respectively, in the context of evolution.

But there is good news: evolution is not such a difficult concept. In fact, its beauty is that it is such an elegant, simple theory. And getting a handle on the classification of the species is largely a matter of memorization.

Origin of Life: The Heterotroph Hypothesis

Life on Earth began about 3.5 billion years ago. At that point in the development of the Earth, the atmosphere was very different from what it is today. As opposed to the current atmosphere, which is mostly nitrogen and oxygen, the early Earth atmosphere contained mostly hydrogen, water, ammonia, and methane.

In experiments, scientists have showed that the electrical discharges of lightning, radioactivity, and ultraviolet light caused the elements in the early Earth atmosphere to form the basic molecules of biological chemistry, such as nucleotides, simple proteins, and ATP. It seems likely, then, that the Earth was covered in a hot, thin soup of water and organic materials. Over time, the molecules became more complex, and began to collaborate to run metabolic processes. Eventually, the first cells came into being. These cells were **heterotrophs**, which could not produce their own food and instead fed on the organic material from the primordial soup. (These heterotrophs give this theory its name.)

The anaerobic metabolic processes of the heterotrophs released carbon dioxide into the atmosphere, which allowed for the evolution of photosynthetic **autotrophs**, which could use light and CO_2 to produce their own food. The autotrophs released oxygen into the atmosphere. For most of the original anaerobic heterotrophs, oxygen proved poisonous. The few heterotrophs that survived the change in environment generally evolved the capacity to carry out aerobic respiration. Over the subsequent billions of years, the aerobic autotrophs and heterotrophs became the dominant life-forms on the planet, and evolved into all of the diversity of life now visible on Earth.

Evidence of Evolution

Humankind has always wondered about its origins and the origins of the life around it. Many cultures have ancient creation myths that explain the origin of the Earth and its life. In Western cultures, ideas about evolution were originally based on the Bible. The book of Genesis relates how God created all life on Earth about 6,000 years ago in a mass creation event. Proponents of creationism support the Genesis account and state that species were created exactly as they are currently found in nature. This oldest formal conception of the origin of life still has proponents today.

However, about 200 years ago, scientific evidence began to cast doubt on creationism. This evidence comes in a variety of forms.

Rock and Fossil Formation

Fossils provide the only direct evidence of the history of evolution. Fossil formation occurs when sediment covers some material or fills an impression. Very gradually, heat and pressure harden the sediment and surrounding minerals replace it, creating fossils. Fossils of prehistoric life can be bones, shells, or teeth that are buried in rock, and they can also be traces of leaves or footprints left behind by organisms.

Taken together, fossils can be used to construct a **fossil record** that offers a timeline of fossils reaching back through history. To puzzle together the fossil record, scientists have to be able to date the fossil to a certain time period. The strata of rock in which fossils are found give clues about their relative ages. If two fossils are found in the same geographic location, but one is found in a layer of sediment that is beneath the other layer, it is likely that the fossil in the lower layer is from an earlier era. After all, the first layer of sediment had to already be on the ground in order for the second layer to begin to build up on top of it. In addition to sediment layers, new techniques such as radioactive decay or carbon dating can also help determine a fossil's age.

There are, however, limitations to the information fossils can supply. First of all, fossilization is an improbable event. Most often, remains and other traces of organisms are crushed or consumed before they can be fossilized. Additionally, fossils can only form in areas with sedimentary rock, such as ocean floors. Organisms that live in these environments are therefore more likely to become fossils. Finally, erosion of exposed surfaces or geological movements such as Earthquakes can destroy fossils even after they form. All of these conditions lead to large and numerous gaps in the fossil record.

Comparative Anatomy

Scientists often try to determine the relatedness of two organisms by comparing external and internal structures. The study of comparative anatomy is an extension of the logical reasoning that organisms with similar structures must have acquired these traits from a common ancestor. For example, the flipper of a whale and a human arm seem to be quite different when looked at on the outside. But the bone structure of each is quite similar, suggesting that whales and humans have a common ancestor way back in prehistory. Anatomical features in different species that point to a common ancestor are called **homologous structures**.

However, comparative anatomists cannot just assume that every similar structure points to a common evolutionary origin. A hasty and reckless comparative anatomist might assume that bats and insects share a common ancestor, since both have wings. But a closer look at the structure of the wings shows that there is very little in common between them besides their function. In fact, the bat wing is much closer in structure to the arm of a man and the fin of a whale than it is to the wings of an insect. In other words, bats and insects evolved their ability to fly along two very separate evolutionary paths. These sorts of structures, which have superficial similarities because of similarity of function but do not result from a common ancestor are called **analogous structures**.

In addition to homologous and analogous structures, **vestigial structures**, which serve no apparent modern function, can help determine how an organism may have evolved over time. In humans the appendix is useless, but in cows and other mammalian herbivores a similar structure is used to digest cellulose. The existence of the appendix suggests that humans share a common evolutionary ancestry with other mammalian herbivores. The fact that the appendix now serves no purpose in humans demonstrates that humans and mammalian herbivores long ago diverged in their evolutionary paths.

Comparative Embryology

Homologous structures not present in adult organisms often *do* appear in some form during embryonic development. Species that bear little resemblance to each other in their adult forms may have strikingly similar embryonic stages. In some ways, it is almost as if the embryo passes through many evolutionary stages to produce the

Evolution and Diversity

mature organism. For example, for a large portion of its development, the human embryo possesses a tail, much like those of our close primate relatives. This tail is usually reabsorbed before birth, but occasionally children are born with the ancestral structure intact. Even though they are not generally present in the adult organism, tails could be considered homologous traits between humans and primates.

In general, the more closely related two species are, the more their embryological processes of development resemble one another.

Molecular Evolution

Just as comparative anatomy is used to determine the anatomical relatedness of species, molecular biology can be used to determine evolutionary relationships at the molecular level. Two species that are closely related will have fewer genetic or protein differences between them than two species that are distantly related and split in evolutionary development long in the past.

Certain genes or proteins in organisms change at a constant rate over time. These genes and proteins, called **molecular clocks** because they are so constant in their rate of change, are especially useful in comparing the molecular evolution of different species. Scientists can use the rate of change in the gene or protein to calculate the point at which two species last shared a common ancestor. For example, ribosomal RNA has a very slow rate of change, so it is commonly used as a molecular clock to determine relationships between extremely ancient species. Cytochrome C, a protein that plays an important role in aerobic respiration, is an example of a protein commonly used as a molecular clock.

Theories of Evolution

In the nineteenth century, as increasing evidence suggested that species changed over time, scientists began to develop theories to explain how these changes arise. During this time, there were two notable theories of evolution. The first, proposed by Lamarck, turned out to be incorrect. The second, developed by Darwin, is the basis of all evolutionary theory.

Lamarck–Use and Disuse

The first notable theory of evolution was proposed by Jean-Baptiste Lamarck (1744–1829). He described a two-part mechanism by which evolutionary change was gradually introduced into the species and passed down through generations. His theory is referred to as the theory of transformation or **Lamarckism**.

The classic example used to explain Lamarckism is the elongated neck of the giraffe. According to Lamarck's theory, a given giraffe could, over a lifetime of straining to reach high branches, develop an elongated neck. This vividly illustrates Lamarck's belief that *use* could amplify or enhance a trait. Similarly, he believed that *disuse* would cause a trait to become reduced. According to Lamarck's theory, the wings of penguins, for example, were understandably smaller than the wings of other birds because penguins did not use their wings to fly.

The second part of Lamarck's mechanism for evolution involved the **inheritance of acquired traits**. He believed that if an organism's traits changed over the course of its lifetime, the organism would pass these traits along to its offspring.

Lamarck's theory has been proven wrong in both of its basic premises. First, an organism cannot fundamentally change its structure through use or disuse. A giraffe's neck will not become longer or shorter by stretching for leaves. Second, modern genetics shows that it is impossible to pass on acquired traits; the traits that an organism can pass on are determined by the genotype of its sex cells, which does not change according to changes in phenotype.

Darwin—Natural Selection

While sailing aboard the *HMS Beagle*, the Englishman Charles Darwin had the opportunity to study the wildlife of the Galapagos Islands. On the islands, he was amazed by the great diversity of life. Most particularly, he took interest in the islands' various finches, whose beaks were all highly adapted to their particular lifestyles. He hypothesized that there must be some process that created such diversity and adaptation, and he spent much of his time trying to puzzle out just what the process might be. In 1859, he published his theory of natural selection and the evolution it produced. Darwin explained his theory through four basic points:

- Each species produces more offspring than can survive.

- The individual organisms that make up a larger population are born with certain variations.

- The overabundance of offspring creates a competition for survival among individual organisms. The individuals that have the most favorable variations will survive and reproduce, while those with less favorable variations are less likely to survive and reproduce.

- Variations are passed down from parent to offspring.

Natural selection creates change within a species through competition, or the struggle for life. Members of a species compete with each other and with other species for resources. In this competition, the individuals that are the most **fit**—the individuals that have certain variations that make them better adapted to their environments—are the most able to survive, reproduce, and pass their traits on to their offspring. The competition that Darwin's theory describes is sometimes called **the survival of the fittest**.

Evolution and Diversity

Natural Selection in Action

One of the best examples of natural selection is a true story that took place in England around the turn of the century. Near an agricultural town lived a species of moth. The moth spent much of its time perched on the lichen-covered bark of trees of the area. Most of the moths were of a peppered color, though few were black. When the pepper-color moths were attached to the lichen-covered bark of the trees in the region, it was quite difficult for predators to see them. The black moths were easy to spot against the black-and-white speckled trunks.

The nearby city, however, slowly became industrialized. Smokestacks and foundries in the town puffed out soot and smoke into the air. In a fairly short time, the soot settled on everything, including the trees, and killed much of the lichen. As a result, the appearance of the trees became nearly black in color. Suddenly, the pepper-color moths that used to be hard to spot against the trees became easy to spot, while the black moths that had been easy to spot now blended in against the trees. Over the course of years, residents of the town noticed that the population of the moths changed. Whereas about 90 percent of the moths used to be light, after the trees became black, the moth population became increasingly black.

When the trees were lighter in color, natural selection favored the pepper-color moths because those moths were more difficult for predators to spot. As a result, the pepper-color moths lived to reproduce and had pepper-color offspring, while far fewer of the black moths lived to produce black offspring. When the industry in the town suddenly made the trees black, however, the selection pressure switched. Suddenly the black moths were more likely to survive and have offspring. In each generation, more black moths survived and had offspring, while fewer lighter moths survived to have offspring. Over time, the population as a whole evolved from mostly white in color to mostly black in color.

Types of Natural Selection

In a normal population without selection pressure, individual traits, such as height, vary in the population. Most individuals are of an average height, while fewer are extremely short or extremely tall. The distribution of height falls into a bell curve.

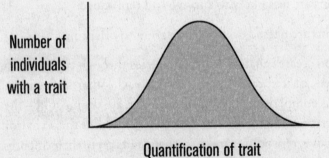

Number of individuals with a trait

Quantification of trait

Natural selection can operate on this population in three basic ways. **Stabilizing selection** eliminates extreme individuals. A plant that is too short may not be able to compete with other plants for sunlight. However, extremely tall plants may be more susceptible to wind damage. Combined, these two selection pressures act to favor plants of medium height.

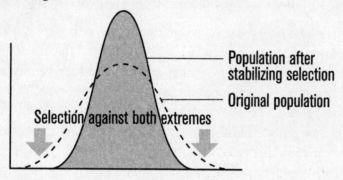

Directional selection selects against one extreme. In the familiar example of giraffe necks, there was a selection pressure against short necks, since individuals with short necks could not reach as many leaves on which to feed. As a result, the distribution of neck-length shifted to favor individuals with long necks.

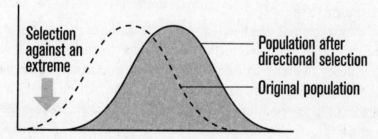

Disruptive selection eliminates intermediate individuals. For example, imagine a plant of extremely variable height that is pollinated by three different pollinator insects: one that was attracted to short plants, another that preferred plants of medium height, and a third that visited only the tallest plants. If the pollinator that preferred plants of medium height disappeared from an area, medium height plants would be selected against, and the population would tend toward both short and tall plants, but not plants of medium height.

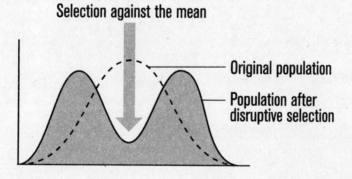

The Genetic Basis for Evolution

Darwin's theory of natural selection and evolution rests on two crucial ideas:

1. Variations exist in the individuals within a population.

2. Those variations are passed down from one generation to the next.

But Darwin had no idea how those variations came to be, or how they were passed down from one generation to the next. Mendel's experiments and the development of the science of genetics provided answers. Genetics explains that the phenotype—the physical attributes of an organism—is produced by an organism's genotype. Through the mechanism of mutations, genetics explains how variations arose among individuals in the form of different alleles of genes. Meiosis, sexual reproduction, and the inheritance of alleles explain how the variations between organisms are passed down from parent to offspring.

With the modern understanding of genes and inheritance, it is possible to redefine natural selection and evolution in genetic terms. The particular alleles that an organism inherits from its parents determine that organism's physical attributes, and therefore its fitness for survival. When the forces of natural selection result in the survival of the fittest, what those forces are really doing is selecting which alleles will be passed on from one generation to the next.

Once you see that natural selection is actually a selection of the passage of alleles from generation to generation, you can further see that the forces of natural selection can change the frequency of each particular allele within a population's **gene pool**, which is the sum total of all the alleles within a particular population. Using genetics, it is possible to create a new definition of evolution as the change in the **allele frequencies** in the gene pool of a population over time. For example, in the population of moths we discussed earlier, after the trees darkened, the frequency of the alleles for black coloration increased in the gene pool, while the frequency of alleles for light coloration decreased.

Hardy-Weinberg Equilibrium

The Hardy-Weinberg principle states that a sexually reproducing population will have stable allelic frequencies and therefore will not undergo evolution, given the following five conditions:

- large population size

- no immigration or emigration

- random mating

- random reproductive success

- no mutation

The Hardy-Weinberg principle proves that variability and inheritance alone are not enough to cause evolution; natural selection must drive evolution. A population that meets all of these conditions is said to be in **Hardy-Weinberg equilibrium**. Few natural populations ever experience Hardy-Weinberg equilibrium, though, since large populations are rarely found in isolation, all populations experience some level of mutation, and natural selection simply cannot be avoided.

Development of New Species

The scientific definition of a **species** is a discrete group of organisms that can only breed within its own confines. In other words, the members of one species cannot interbreed with the members of another species. Each species is said to experience **reproductive isolation**. If you think about evolution in terms of genetics, this definition of species makes a great deal of sense: if species could interbreed, they could share gene flow, and their evolution would not be separate. But since species cannot interbreed, each species exists on its own individual path.

As populations change, new species evolve. This process is known as **speciation**. Through speciation, the earliest simple organisms were able to branch out and populate the world with millions of different species. Speciation is also called **divergent evolution**, since when a new species develops it diverges from a previous form. All homologous traits are produced by divergent evolution. Whales and humans share a distant common ancestor. Through speciation, that ancestor underwent divergent evolution and gave rise to new species, which in turn gave rise to new species, which over the course of millions of years resulted in whales and humans. The original ancestor had a limb structure that, over millions of years and successive occurrences of divergent evolution, evolved into the fin of the whale and the arm of the human.

Speciation occurs when two populations become reproductively isolated. Once reproductive isolation occurs for a new species, it will begin to evolve independently. There are two main ways in which speciation might occur. **Allopatric speciation** occurs when populations of a species become geographically isolated so that they cannot interbreed. Over time, the populations may become genetically different in response to the unique selection pressures operating in their different environments. Eventually the genetic differences between the two populations will become so extreme that the two populations would be unable to interbreed even if the geographic barrier disappeared.

A second, more common form of speciation is **adaptive radiation**, which is the creation of several new species from a single parent species. Think of a population of given species, which we'll imaginatively name population 1. The population moves into a new habitat and establishes itself in a niche, or role, in the habitat (we discuss niches in more detail in the chapter on Ecology). In so doing, it adapts to its new environment and becomes different from the parent species. If a new population of the parent species, population 2, moves into the area, it too will try to occupy the same niche as population 1. Competition between population 1 and population 2 ensues, placing pressure on both groups to adapt to separate niches, further distinguishing them from each other and the parent species. As this happens many times in a given habitat, several new species may be formed from a single parent species in a relatively short period of time. The immense diversity of finches that Darwin observed on the Galapagos Islands is an excellent example of the products of adaptive radiation.

Convergent Evolution

When different species inhabit similar environments, they face similar selection pressures, or use parts of their bodies to perform similar functions. These similarities can cause the species to evolve similar traits, in a process called convergent evolution. From living in the cold, watery, arctic regions where most of the food exists underwater, penguins and killer whales have evolved some similar characteristics: both are streamlined to help them swim more quickly underwater, both have layers of fat to keep them warm, both have similar white and black coloration that helps them to avoid detection, and both have developed fins (or flippers) to propel them through the water. All of these similar traits are examples of analogous traits, which are the product of convergent evolution.

Convergent evolution sounds as if it is the opposite of divergent evolution, but that isn't actually true. Convergent evolution is only superficial. From the outside, the fin of a whale may look like the flipper of a penguin, but the bone structure of a whale fin is still more similar to the limbs of other mammals than it is to the structure of penguin flippers. More importantly, convergent evolution never results in two species gaining the ability to interbreed; convergent evolution can't take two species and turn them into one.

Classifying Life

The diversity of life on Earth is staggering. The science of identifying, describing, naming, and classifying all of these organisms is called **taxonomy**. Carolus Linnaeus, an eighteenth century Swedish botanist, is considered the father of modern taxonomy. He carefully observed and compared different species, grouping them according to the similarities and differences he found. Taxonomists today still use his system of organization, though they classify organisms based on their evolutionary relationships, or **phylogeny**, rather than on simple physical characteristics. The classification system used in taxonomy is hierarchical and contains seven levels. The seven levels of taxonomic classification, from broadest to most specific, are:

Kingdom → Phylum → Class → Order → Family → Genus → Species

A good way to remember the sequence of taxonomic categories is to use a mnemonic:

King Philip Came Over From German Shores

Each kingdom contains numerous phyla; each phyla contains numerous classes; each class contains numerous orders; etc. It is more accurate to draw the diagram of the taxonomic categories in a tree structure, with each level of the hierarchy branching into the next:

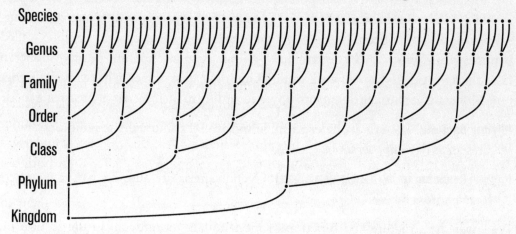

As one moves through the hierarchy from species to kingdom, the common ancestor of all the species at a certain level dates further back in evolutionary history than the common ancestor of organisms in more specific levels. For example, the common ancestor of humans and chimpanzees (which are both in the Order Primates) was alive more recently than the common ancestor of humans and dogs (which are both in the Class Mammalia). Members of the same Genus are more closely related than members of the same Family; members of the same Family are more closely related than members of the same Order; etc.

Each species is placed into the classification system with a two-part name. The first half of the name is the species' genus, while the second is the species' own specific name. The genus name is capitalized, and the species name is lower case. Humans belong to the genus *Homo* and the species *sapiens*, so the name for humans is *Homo sapiens*.

The Five Kingdoms

Taxonomy splits all living things into five kingdoms: Monera, Protista, Fungi, Plantae, and Animalia. For the SAT II Biology, you should know the basic characteristics of the organisms that belong in each of these kingdoms, and you should also be familiar with the names and features of the major phyla within each kingdom.

Evolution and Diversity

Kingdom Monera

Monerans are prokaryotic: they are single-celled organisms that lack a nucleus and membrane-bound organelles. Of the four kingdoms, monerans are the simplest, and they generally evolved the earliest. Of all the kingdoms, only monerans are prokaryotic.

Monerans are characterized by a single circular chromosome of DNA, a single cell membrane that controls the transport of substances into and out of the cell, and a process of asexual reproduction called binary fission that involves dividing into two identical clones. Some monerans have a cell wall made of a sugar-protein complex called peptidoglycan, which can be determined by Gram staining. A Gram-positive moneran has a thick peptidoglycan cell wall, while a Gram-negative moneran has a much thinner one. Monerans are broken down into phyla according to their means of procuring food.

Phylum Bacteria: Bacteria are heterotrophic and can act as mutualistic symbionts, parasites, or as decomposers.

Phylum Cyanobacteria (blue-green algae): Cyanobacteria are autotrophs that can perform photosynthesis.

We cover the structure and function of monerans in more detail in the section on microorganisms in the Organismal Biology chapter.

Kingdom Protista

Protists are eukaryotic. In general, protists are less complex than the other eukaryotes, and originated earlier in evolutionary history. Most are unicellular, though some are organized in colonies, and some others are multicellular. The kingdom Protista can be separated into three primary divisions: animal-like, plantlike, and funguslike.

The animal-like protists are heterotrophic and motile. The most important protozoa for the SAT II Biology are the amoeba, sporozoa, and ciliates:

Phylum Rhizopoda: The members of phylum Rhizopoda are **amoebas**, known for their constantly changing body structure. Amoebas use membrane extensions called pseudopods ("false feet") to move and to surround food particles, which they then engulf into their cytoplasm via phagocytosis. Amoebas generally live in fresh water, but some are found in soil or salt water. If an amoeba finds its way inside a human through contaminated drinking water, it can cause severe dysentery.

Phylum Apicomplexa: The phylum Apicomplexa consists of spore-forming parasitic organisms, also known as **sporozoa**. The adult form lives inside the cells of animals. The spores are transmitted to other host animals, usually by a carrier animal. For example, a mosquito bite transmits Plasmodium, an apicomplexan that lives in red blood cells and causes malaria.

Phylum Ciliophora: All members of the phylum Ciliophora propel themselves by waving many short, hair-like structures called cilia in a coordinated fashion; cilia also help draw food particles into the oral groove. Unlike other protozoa, ciliates have two nuclei: the smaller micronucleus is involved in reproduction, while the macronucleus controls the organism's metabolic processes. A **paramecium** is the classic example of a ciliate protozoan.

The plantlike protists include euglenoids and various kinds of algae. They are all photosynthetic autotrophs, transforming light energy into food. Some are unicellular, but many are multicellular, forming fibrous seaweed structures.

Phylum Euglenophyta: Euglenoids are classified with the plantlike Protists because many of them photosynthesize. But these unicellular organisms have flagella that allow them to move.

Phylum Phaeophyta: Brown algae of phylum Phaeophyta are all multicellular seaweeds, ranging in size from an inch to almost the length of a football field (the large varieties are called kelp). Brown algae provide both food and shelter to many animals in the coastal marine ecosystem.

Phylum Chlorophyta: Green algae of phylum Chlorophyta have the same photosynthetic pigments and the same cell wall structure as plants. In fact, they are believed to be the ancestors of modern plants. Some are unicellular, and some are multicellular; however, none have specialized tissues like plants, and therefore they remain classified with the simpler organisms in kingdom Protista.

The funguslike protists are called slime molds, which belong to the phyla Myxomycota and Acrasiomycota. All slime molds are heterotrophs.

Phylum Myxomycota: includes the plasmodial (acellular) slime molds. A plasmodium consists of a single cell with multiple nuclei. Plasmodial slime molds creep slowly along the decaying vegetation they digest; when food or water is scarce they produce small tough spores that germinate when environmental conditions improve.

Phylum Acrasiomycota: contains the cellular slime molds. The mold is really a large collection of individual amoebalike protists which congregate into a "pseudo-plasmodium" or "slug" only when food is scarce. In this cooperative form, they produce a single stalk that releases spores.

Kingdom Fungi

Fungi are typically non-motile and, like plants, have cell walls. Unlike plants, fungi are heterotrophic and have cell walls made of chitin rather than cellulose. Fungi secrete enzymes to digest their food externally and then absorb the nutrients. They usually live as decomposers, living off dead and decaying organisms, or as parasites, growing on or in other living organisms. With the exception of yeast, most fungi are multicellular. Structurally, multicellular fungi are composed of filaments called hyphae; some have hyphae that are segmented by divisions called septa, while others have a continuous cytoplasm with many nuclei in each hyphae. Many fungi exist as a tangle of hyphae, called a mycelium. Examples of fungi are yeast and mushrooms.

Most fungi can also exist in the form of a spore, a microscopic reproductive structure that is much more resistant to lack of food or water. Unlike most plants and animals that exist predominantly in a diploid state, fungi spend most of their time in a haploid state, with only a brief diploid phase during the reproductive cycle.

Some fungi grow in a mutually beneficial relationship with a photosynthetic algae or plant. Lichen is an example of such a partnership between a fungus and an algae. The benefits of the merger are apparent; lichen can grow in a wider range of temperatures than any individual plant or fungus, and lichen can often colonize rocks that will not support any other multicellular life forms.

Kingdom Plantae

Plants are complex multicellular photosynthetic autotrophs, with cellulose in their cell walls and a waxy cuticle covering their aboveground parts. They are easily distinguishable from members of all other kingdoms, with the possible exception of their simpler ancestors in the Protista kingdom, the green algae. Over evolutionary time, plants improved their ability to live on land by developing a variety of important features. Plants can be divided into four major groups, displaying a progressively greater degree of adaptation to the terrestrial environment.

Nonvascular Plants–Bryophytes

Bryophyta is the only phylum in the group of nonvascular seedless plants. These mosses and worts are the most primitive true plants. Because they lack a vascular system (vascular systems are discussed in much more detail in the chapter on Plant Structure and Function), bryophytes do not have a stem, leaves, or roots; they must distribute water and nutrients throughout their bodies by absorption and diffusion. As a result, they cannot grow beyond a small size and must keep their bodies close to moist Earth. Bryophytes reproduce by spores and need water in order to bring about fertilization. Because the male gamete is a flagellated sperm, reproduction requires water in which the sperm can swim. Unlike all other plants, which have a diploid adult stage, adult bryophytes are haploid, passing only briefly through a diploid phase during the reproductive cycle.

Seedless Vascular Plants

There are three phyla of seedless vascular plants: Lycophyta (club mosses), Sphenophyta (horsetails), and, most likely to appear on the SAT II Biology, Pterophyta (ferns). Vascular plants have a dual fluid transport system: xylem transports water and inorganic minerals from the roots upward, and phloem transports sugars and other organic nutrients up and down. This vascular system represents a major evolutionary step in the adaptation to life on land. The ability to transport water and nutrients across long distances allows plants to grow much larger, sending specialized photosynthetic structures (leaves) upwards toward sunlight, and specialized root structures downwards towards the water and minerals in the ground. Like bryophytes, seedless vascular phyla reproduce by spores and have flagellated sperm that require water in which to swim, limiting these plants to relatively moist environments.

Flowerless Seed Plants—Gymnosperms

The evolution of seeds provided plants with another advantage in their prolonged pilgrimage onto land. Unlike the spores of more primitive plants, seeds are multicellular, containing both a complete diploid embryo and a food supply. Having a food supply inside the seed provides the newborn plant with a period of growth that is independent of food resources in the environment. This independence allows seed plants to grow in a greater variety of environments. Further freeing seed plants, the male gametes of the seed plants take the form of pollen, making reproduction independent of water.

The seed plants that evolved first, called gymnosperms ("naked seeds"), do not produce flowers. Their seeds are exposed directly to the air, without any capsule or fruit enclosing them. The most important group of gymnosperms is phylum Coniferophyta; these plants, commonly called conifers, produce cones that carry seeds on their scales. Examples of gymnosperms are pines, firs, cedars, and sequoias.

Flowering Seed Plants—Angiosperms

Flowering plants, called angiosperms ("covered-seeds"), are vascular seed plants with specialized reproductive structures, which include both flowers and fruit. Instead of depending on currents of wind or water for the dispersal of their gametes and seeds, plants with flowers and fruit provide protection and attract animals that then serve as the means of fertilization.

Flowering plants are divided into two classes, monocots and dicots. Monocot seeds have a single cotyledon, while dicots have two cotyledons in each seed. Monocots and dicots are covered in more detail in the section on the structure and function of Plants, which is part of the organismal biology chapter.

Kingdom Animalia

Animals are eukaryotic, multicellular, and heterotrophic. Animals also have specialized tissues to perform various functions. Most animals are motile, at least during part of their lifecycle, reproduce sexually, and have nervous systems that allow them to respond rapidly to changes in their environment.

Taxonomists use several observable features to classify animals into groups according to their evolutionary relationships. One of the most important of these features is body symmetry. In **bilateral symmetry**, the left half of the organism is the mirror image of the right half, but the top does not resemble the bottom, and the front is dissimilar to the back. In **radial symmetry**, the organism has a circular body plan, with similar structures arranged like spokes on a wheel, such as a starfish. Most animals have three layers of cells: the ectoderm, mesoderm, and endoderm. Almost all animals have a hollow tube inside, which acts as a digestive tract; the opening where food enters is called the mouth, and the opening where digested material exists is called the anus.

Animals are the most diverse of the kingdoms. Any of their various phyla may come up on the SAT II Biology, though the vertebrates come up most often.

Phylum Porifera (Sponges): Sponges are sessile (non-moving), complex colonies of flagellated unicellular protozoa-like organisms. They do not exhibit any clear symmetry, and they are the only animal phylum that does not possess at least two distinct embryonic tissue layers. Their unique lack of tissue organization has prompted taxonomists to classify sponges as parazoa ("next-to-animals"). Nonetheless, some sponge cells are specialized for reproductive or nutritional purposes, and this slight organizational complexity gives them a toehold on the edge of the animal kingdom. Although sponges do have a hollow space inside, they do not have a digestive gut like other animals. Water flows into the central space through the many pores in the sponge's outer surface, and flows out through the large opening at the top of the sponge. The flow of water brings food and oxygen, and carries away waste and carbon dioxide. All sponges secrete a skeleton that maintains their shape (you might use these skeletal remains as "natural sponges" in bathing).

Phylum Cnidaria: Phylum Cnidaria includes all stinging marine organisms that exhibit radial symmetry, such as jellyfish, hydras, sea anemones, and coral. Cnidarians have a true digestive gut like other animals, but one opening serves as both the mouth and anus. Additionally, their body walls are made up of only two layers of cells: endoderm and ectoderm.

Phylum Platyhelminthes (Flatworms): Flatworms are bilaterally symmetric and are the most primitive animals to possess all three embryonic tissue layers. Like cnidarians, most flatworms have a digestive gut with only a single opening. Flatworms are also the most primitive animals to exhibit discernable organs, internal structures with at least two tissue layers and a specialized function. There are three main kinds of flatworms: free-living carnivorous planarians, parasitic flukes that feed off the blood of other animals, and parasitic tapeworms that live inside the digestive tracts of other animals.

Evolution and Diversity

Phylum Nematoda (Roundworms): Most nematodes, also called roundworms, are free-living; however, some live as parasites in the digestive tracts of humans and other animals. Soil-dwelling roundworms play an important ecological role by helping to decompose and recycle organic debris. Roundworms are bilaterally symmetric, have a complete gut tube with two openings, and possess all three embryonic tissue layers with a cavity in between the mesodermal and endodermal tissues. The roundworm species *C. elegans* was the first animal to have its entire genome sequence determined.

Phylum Mollusca: Phylum Mollusca includes many familiar animals such as snails, slugs, squid, octopuses, and shellfish like clams and oysters. Mollusks are bilaterally symmetric, and have a complete digestive tract and a circulatory system with a simple heart. They move by means of a muscular structure called a foot, and they have a rasping tongue called a radula and a mantle that secretes a hard shell. Mollusks generally live in aquatic regions.

Phylum Annelida (Segmented Worms): Annelida means "ringed" and refers to the repeated ringlike segments that make up the bodies of annelids like earthworms and leeches. Annelids exhibit bilateral symmetry, have a complete digestive tract with two excretory organs called **nephridia** in each segment, and a closed circulatory system. Their nervous system consists of a simple brain in front and a ventral (near the belly) nerve cord connecting smaller clusters of nerve cells, or **ganglia**, within each segment. Earthworms live freely within the soil, while most leeches, on the other hand, are blood-sucking parasites. All annelids must live in moist environments. Having not yet developed more sophisticated respiratory systems, they exchange gases directly with their surroundings.

Phylum Arthropoda: Arthropoda is the most diverse and numerous animal phylum. Insects, spiders, and crustaceans—which include lobsters, shrimp, and crabs—constitute the major arthropod groups. The name Arthropoda means "jointed-feet"; arthropods have jointed appendages and, like annelids, exhibit segmentation. Insects and crustaceans have three body segments consisting of the head, thorax, and abdomen, while arachnids only have two body segments. Arthropods are unique among animals in having a hard exoskeleton made of chitin. The arthropod nervous system resembles the annelid nervous system, with a simple brain, a ventral nerve cord, and smaller ganglia within the various body segments. However, many arthropods have very highly developed sensory perception, including hearing organs, antennae, and compound eyes. Arthropods have an open circulatory system, a full digestive tract, and structures called **Malphigian tubules** to eliminate waste.

Phylum Echinodermata: The name Echinodermata means "spiny-skin," and this phylum includes spiny marine animals such as starfish, sea urchins, and sand dollars, all of which exhibit radial symmetry. Echinoderms have several characteristic features, including an endoskeleton that secretes a spiny skin and an unusual vascular system of water-filled vessels that regulates the movement of their many **tube feet** and also permits the exchange of carbon dioxide for oxygen. Echinoderms have a very simple nervous system, with a ring of nerves around their mouth and no brain. Some echinoderms filter food out of the water, while others, like starfish, are carnivorous predators or scavengers. Despite their primitive appearance, patterns in early embryonic development strongly suggest that echinoderms are most closely related to the chordates, the animal phylum that developed most recently in evolutionary time.

Phylum Chordata

Human beings belong to Chordata, the phylum that evolved most recently in the animal kingdom. Chordates have three embryonic tissues, a complete digestive tract, and well-developed circulatory, respiratory, and nervous systems. Several features distinguish chordates from all other animal phyla. The primary feature, for which chordates are named, is the **notochord**, a tubular rod of tissue that runs longitudinally down the back. Just above the notochord runs a single, hollow nerve cord, the center of the nervous system. Other animals, such as earthworms, also have nerve cords; however, these run in ventral pairs along the belly, and are not hollow. Two other features, gill slits and tails, are present in all chordates during embryonic development, but disappear by adulthood in many members of the phylum.

There are two groups of chordates, subphylum Urochordata and subphylum Vertebrata. The former subphylum includes invertebrate marine animals such as tunicates and lancelets, and almost never appears on the SAT II Biology. Much more important for the test are the vertebrates.

Subphylum Vertebrata

Subphylum Vertebrata contains those chordates that have replaced the simple notochord with a segmented skeletal rod that wraps around and protects the brain and nerve cord. The skeletal segments, called vertebrae, are made of bone or cartilage, and the entire series of segments is called the vertebral column. The portion encasing the brain is called the skull. There are seven main classes of **vertebrates**:

Jawless fish: These fish are bottom-dwelling filter-feeders without jaws. They breathe through gills and lay eggs. Examples are lampreys and hagfish.

Cartilaginous fish: With a flexible endoskeleton made of cartilage, these fish have well-developed jaws and fins, and they breathe through gills. Their young hatch from eggs. Examples are sharks, eels, and rays.

Bony fish: Bony fish mark an advance since they have much stronger skeletons made of bone rather than cartilage. Bony fish are found in both saltwater and freshwater. They breathe through gills and lay soft eggs. Almost every fish you can think of is a bony fish, from goldfish to trout.

Amphibians: Amphibians like frogs and salamanders embody the transition from aquatic to terrestrial living. Born initially as fishlike tadpoles living in the water, they undergo a metamorphosis and develop legs and move onto land as adults. Most adult amphibians breathe through lungs that develop during their metamorphosis, though some can breathe through their skin. Their eggs lack shells, must be laid in water, and receive little parental care.

Reptiles: With the development of the fluid-filled **amniotic sac**, reptiles including dinosaurs were the first animals to be able to hatch their eggs on land and make the full transition to terrestrial life. Reptiles lay few eggs and provide some parental care. Reptiles also have thick, scaly skin that resists water loss, and efficient lungs.

All classes of vertebrates that evolved before birds are **cold-blooded** (ectothermic). The metabolism of these earlier classes is dependent on the environment. When the temperature drops their metabolism slows, and speeds up as the temperature rises. Birds and mammals, in contrast, are **warm-blooded** (endothermic). They have developed structures such as feathers, hair, and fur to help them maintain body temperature. The metabolism of birds and mammals stays constant through far larger extremes of temperature, making these two classes much more versatile.

Birds: Birds have specially evolved structures such as wings, feathers, and light bones that allow for flight. In addition, birds have four-chambered hearts and powerful lungs that can withstand the extreme metabolic demands of flight. Birds lay hard eggs, but provide a great deal of care for their eggs and developing young.

Mammals: Mammals have a number of unique features that have allowed them to adapt successfully to many different environments. They have the most highly developed nervous systems in the animal kingdom, providing them with complex and adaptable behaviors. With the exception of a few species such as the platypus, mammals do not lay eggs like other vertebrates; instead, mammalian embryos develop inside the mother and are not released until nearly or fully developed and equipped for survival. Mammals are also unique in having milk glands that provide nourishment for their infants. In this way, the protection and feeding of their young is built directly into mammalian bodies, dramatically increasing the ability of these animals to raise surviving offspring in diverse environments. Examples of mammals are whales, cows, mice, monkeys, and humans.

Evolution and Diversity

Life or Not Life? Viruses

Viruses are extremely small infectious agents that invade cells of all types. Once inside another cell, viruses become hijackers, using the cells' machinery to produce more viruses. Whether viruses constitute living organisms or not—because they can only reproduce by means of using another cell's machinery—has been a source of debate for many years. Because of their in-between status, viruses do not fit into the taxonomic system; neither do they commonly appear on the SAT II. All you need to know about viruses appears below.

Structure

All viruses have a protein capsid or head region that contains its genetic material. The genetic material can be either DNA, RNA, or even in some cases a limited number of enzymes. Some viruses also have an elaborate protein tail region. The tail aids in binding to the surface of the host cell and penetrating the surface of the host so that the virus' genetic material can be introduced.

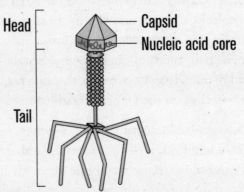

Virus "Life Cycle"

Though the details of virus infection and replication vary greatly with the type of host a particular virus attacks, all viruses share four basic steps in their replication cycles:

1. **Attachment:** Using specialized protein structures located on the exterior of the capsid or tail, the virus latches onto the cell it will attack and hijack. The protein structures are specific to specific cells. A virus that can attach to bacterium is unlikely to be able to attack animal cells.

2. **Penetration:** The virus breaks through the cell wall and cell membrane, releasing its genetic material into the host cell.

3. **Replication and assembly:** The viral genetic material hijacks the cell machinery. Host ribosomes begin to produce viral proteins and nucleic acids. The virus uses the host cell to assemble many new viruses.

4. **Release:** Viruses are bad guests. In addition to the production of new viruses, the viral genetic material usually forces the host cell to produce an enzyme that kills, or lyses, the host and breaks it open, freeing the many new viruses to go and hunt new host cells to attack. Almost always, the host cell is killed when it is invaded by a virus.

Review Questions

1. What feature clearly distinguishes kingdom Monera from other kingdoms?

    A.   All monerans are prokaryotes.
    B.   All monerans are eukaryotes.
    C.   Monerans have a cell wall, whereas other organisms only have cell membranes.
    D.   Monerans are angiosperms, whereas all other organisms are gymnosperms.
    E.   All monerans exhibit radial cleavage.

2. An autotrophic organism might

    A.   engage in photosynthesis
    B.   consume the organic nutrients in other living organisms
    C.   be a fungus
    D.   not be able produce its own organic nutrients
    E.   not require an external source of energy for metabolism

3. Which of the following has a chitinous cell wall?

    A.   spider
    B.   fungi
    C.   slime mold
    D.   euglena
    E.   cnidarian

4. All of the following are phylogenetic clues used by taxonomists to classify animals EXCEPT

    A.   motility
    B.   body symmetry
    C.   pattern of embryonic development
    D.   similarity of molecular clocks
    E.   complexity of tissue organization

Evolution and Diversity

5. As plants adapted to terrestrial living, they developed all of the following EXCEPT

    A. seeds
    B. phloem
    C. flowers
    D. xylem
    E. spores

6. According to the heterotroph hypothesis,

    A. anaerobic and aerobic organisms evolved simultaneously.
    B. photosynthetic autotrophs evolved first, since they required only energy from the sun and simple molecules from the environment.
    C. autotrophs evolved before a carbon source was made available.
    D. anaerobic heterotrophs evolved first.
    E. chemosynthesis was critical to the evolution of heterotrophic organisms.

7. Which of the following best characterizes Lamarckian evolution?

    A. Evolutionary change happens instantaneously.
    B. An animal that draws on a particular trait very often passes that trait on in reduced form to offspring because of overuse.
    C. The function of a body part plays no part in evolution.
    D. Acquired traits can be passed down from parent to offspring.
    E. Selection pressures push evolutionary change.

8. A river switches course and splits a population into two populations that cannot interbreed. What is likely to occur?

    A. Speciation
    B. Adaptive radiation
    C. Convergent evolution
    D. Natural selection
    E. Lamarckian evolution

9. Weather patterns on the Earth suddenly change, and the temperature in Alaska becomes much colder. Among the penguins, a few individuals have an extra layer of fat that allows them to function more efficiently in the cold. This is an example of

    A. speciation
    B. evolution
    C. natural Selection
    D. divergent Evolution
    E. convergent Evolution

10. An organism that lays hard eggs and gives little parental care to its offspring is a(n)

    A. prokaryote
    B. vertebrate
    C. amphibian
    D. reptile
    E. bird

Explanations

1.   (A)

All monerans are prokaryotes. Bacteria commonly have cell walls, but so do other organisms, such as in kingdoms Fungi and Plantae. Radial cleavage is a characteristic found in kingdom Animalia, and angiosperms and gymnosperms are distinctions within the Plant kingdom.

2.   (B)

Autotrophic ("self-feeding") organisms produce their own organic nutrients, using energy from sunlight (photosynthesis) or chemical energy (chemosynthesis). Heterotrophic ("other-feeding") organisms must consume the organic nutrients in other living organisms. Fungi are heterotrophic organisms.

3.   (B)

Fungi have chitinous cell walls. Spiders are arthropods, which have chitin incorporated into the exoskeleton. Like all animals, however, the cells of spiders do not have cell walls. The euglena and cnidarian do not possess cell walls. Protist molds and bryophytes both have cell walls made of cellulose.

4.   (A)

Taxonomists use body symmetry (e.g. bilateral vs. radial), patterns of embryonic development (e.g. spiral vs. radial cleavage), similarity of molecular clocks (e.g. cytochrome c), and complexity of tissue organization (particularly development of sensory organs and nervous tissue). Motility is characteristic of organisms in various kingdoms and is not used to determine evolutionary relationships among animals.

5.   (E)

Bryophytes reproduce using single-celled spores rather than seeds. Spores require a flagellated male gamete to travel through water for fertilization. Seeds contain both a complete embryo and a food supply, allowing the embryo to grow independently of outside food sources when it is smallest and most vulnerable. Also, the male gamete of seed plants is pollen, which can travel through the air. The vascular system has allowed plants to grow larger and develop different parts with specialized functions. Flowers and fruits increase the efficiency of reproduction by recruiting animals into pollen and seed distribution. Animals spread pollen and seeds in a more targeted fashion, and to a wider area, than wind or water usually do.

Evolution and Diversity

6. (D)

The heterotroph hypothesis suggests that anaerobic heterotropic organisms may have evolved first, releasing carbon compounds into the atmosphere and allowing the process of photosynthesis to evolve. Autotrophs then consumed the carbon dioxide. The oxygen released as waste facilitated the evolution of aerobic organisms. It would not make sense that anaerobic and aerobic organisms would evolve together. The latter would thrive in an oxygen-rich atmosphere, and the former would rely on other molecules. Autotrophs require carbon dioxide, which was not available in great quantity in the ancient atmosphere of the Earth. Chemosynthesis is an autotrophic process and did not contribute to the evolution of heterotrophs.

7. (D)

Lamarck argued that gradual changes acquired by individuals over a lifetime were passed on to offspring. Use enhanced or amplified a trait while disuse reduced it. Lamarck did not discuss the idea of recessive inheritance, and natural selection was an element of Darwinian evolution.

8. (A)

When a population is unable to interbreed, speciation occurs. Adaptive radiation is a specific type of speciation, but it refers to speciation that occurs by means of competition for a niche, not through geographical isolation. Convergent evolution occurs when two different species that have some similar functions develop similar-looking body parts. Natural selection is always happening; the diversion of the river does not begin natural selection. Lamarckian evolution never occurs, since it is an incorrect theory.

9. (C)

The situation described in the question only covers one generation of penguins. Evolution and speciation take a lot more time than one generation to begin to function, but natural selection occurs within a generation by picking out the most fit individuals.

10. (D)

Of the organisms in the answer choices, only birds and reptiles lay hard eggs. Reptiles do not provide parental care for their young, while birds do.

Organismal Biology

Aᴌʟ ᴏʀɢᴀɴɪsᴍs ᴍᴜsᴛ ʙᴇ ᴀʙʟᴇ ᴛᴏ ᴍᴀɪɴᴛᴀɪɴ the proper balances necessary for life in a somewhat hostile world. Every organism must be able to coordinate its life processes; gain food and oxygen; circulate that food and oxygen; eliminate waste; and reproduce. As organisms have evolved from single-celled to multi-cellular, they have developed increasingly sophisticated organ systems to accomplish these crucial tasks. Each organ system, such as the nervous system or circulatory system, is made up of a number of **organs** that work in concert to carry out one or a number of vital body processes. Each organ, in turn, is made up a number of **tissues**. A tissue is a conglomeration of specialized cells that all perform a common function necessary to an organ's larger efforts. During the billions of years that life has existed on Earth, different organisms have developed various systems of meeting the needs of their bodies. Oak trees and alligators, for instance, have very different ways of gaining food and circulating that food within their bodies.

The SAT II Biology test focuses its many questions about organismal biology on the structure and function of humans and plants. This chapter on organismal biology is therefore split into two parts. The first deals with the structure and function of animals, the second with plants.

Structure and Function of Animals

In order to survive, animals must be able to coordinate the functions of their many specialized cells, take in and digest food, pull oxygen from the air, circulate nutrients and oxygen to their cells, eliminate wastes, move, maintain body temperature, and reproduce. Animals have also developed various behaviors that help them to survive.

Control Systems

Humans and other highly evolved animals have developed two main systems for coordinating and synchronizing the functions of their millions of individual cells. The nervous system works rapidly by transmitting electrochemical impulses. The endocrine system is a slower system of control; it works by releasing chemical signals into the circulation. In addition to coordinating essential bodily functions, these two control systems allow the animal to react to both its external and internal environments.

The Nervous System

The nervous system functions by the almost instantaneous transmission of electrochemical signals. The means of transmission are highly specialized cells known as **neurons**, which are the functional unit of the nervous system.

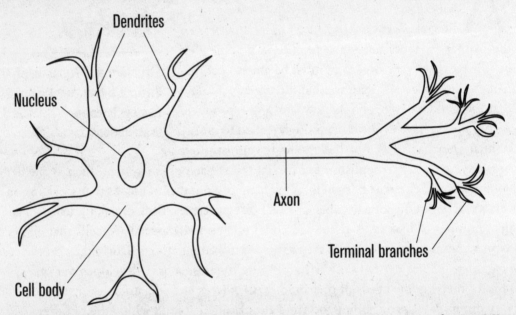

The neuron is an elongated cell that usually consists of three main parts: the **dendrites**, the **cell body**, and the **axon**. The typical neuron contains many dendrites, which have the appearance of thin branches extending from the cell body. The cell body of the neuron contains the nucleus and organelles of the cell. The axon, which can sometimes be thousands of times longer than the rest of the neuron, is a single, long projection extending from the cell body. The axon usually ends in several small branches known as the axon terminals. Neurons are often connected in chains and networks, yet they never actually come in contact with one another. The axon terminals of one neuron is separated from the dendrites of an adjacent neuron by a small gap known as a **synapse**.

The electrical impulse moving through a neuron begins in the dendrites. From there, it passes through the cell body and then travels along the axon. The impulse always follows the same path from dendrite to cell body to axon. When the electrical impulse reaches the synapse at the end of the axon, it causes the release of specialized chemicals known as **neurotransmitters**. These neurotransmitters carry the signal across the synapse to the dendrites of the next neuron, starting the process again in the next cell.

The Resting Potential

To understand the nature of the electrical impulse that travels along the neuron, it is necessary to look at the changes that occur in a neuron between when it is at rest and when it is carrying an impulse. When there is no impulse traveling through a neuron, the cell is at its resting potential and the inside of the cell contains a negative charge in relation to the outside.

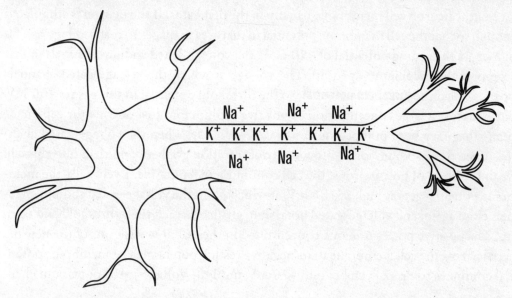

Maintaining a negative charge inside the cell is an active process that requires energy. The cell membrane of the neuron contains a protein called Na^+/K^+ ATPase that uses the energy provided by one molecule of ATP to pump three positively charged sodium atoms (Na^+) out of the cell, while simultaneously taking into the cell two positively charged potassium ions (K^+). The sodium-potassium pump builds up a high concentration of sodium ions outside the cell, and an excess of potassium ions inside the cell. These ions naturally want to diffuse across the membrane to regularize the distribution. However, one of the special properties of phospholipid cell membranes is that they bar passage to ions unless there is a special protein channel that allows a particular ion in or out. No such channel exists for the sodium that is built up outside the cell, though there are potassium leak channels that allow some of the potassium ions to flow out of the cell. The difference in ion concentrations creates a net potential difference across the cell membrane of approximately −70 mV (millivolts), which is the value of the resting potential.

The Action Potential

While most cells have some sort of resting potential from the movement of ions across their membranes, neurons are among only a few types of cells that can also form an action potential. The action potential is the electrochemical impulse that can travel along the neuron. In addition to the Na^+/K^+ ATPase and potassium leak channel proteins, the neuron membrane contains **voltage-gated proteins**. These proteins respond to changes in the membrane potential by opening to allow certain ions to cross that would not normally be able to do so. The neuron contains both voltage-gated sodium channels and voltage-gated potassium channels, which open under different circumstances.

The action potential begins when chemical signals from another neuron manage to depolarize, or make less negative, the potential of the cell membrane in one localized area of the neuron cell membrane, usually in the dendrites. If the neuron is stimulated enough so that the cell membrane potential in that area manages to reach as high as –50 mV (from the resting potential of –70 mV), the voltage-gated sodium channels in that region of the membrane open up. The voltage at which the voltage-gated channels open is called the **threshold potential**, so the threshold potential in this case is –50 mV. Since there is a large concentration of positive sodium ions just outside the cell membrane that have been pumped out by Na^+/K^+ ATPase, when the voltage-gated channels open these sodium ions follow the concentration gradient and rush into the cell. With the flood of positive ions, the cell continues to depolarize. Eventually the membrane potential gets as high as +35 mV, at which point the voltage-gated sodium channels close again, and voltage-gated potassium channels reach their threshold and open up. The positive potassium ions concentrated in the cell now rush out of the neuron, repolarizing the cell membrane to its negative resting potential. The membrane potential continues to drop, even beyond –70 mV, until the voltage-gated potassium chan-

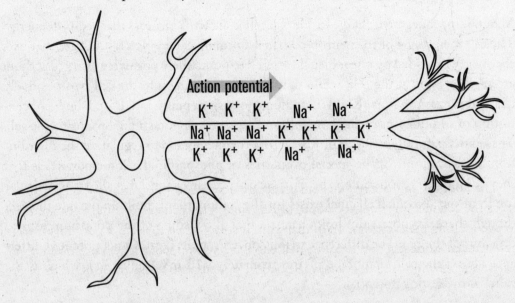

nels close once again at around −90 mV. With the voltage-gated proteins closed, the Na⁺/K⁺ ATPase and the potassium leak channels work to restore the membrane potential to its original polarized state of −70 mV. The whole process takes approximately one millisecond to occur.

The action potential does not occur in one localized area of the neuron and then stop: it travels down the length of the neuron. When one portion of the neuron's cell membrane undergoes an action potential, the entering sodium atoms not only diffuse into and out of the neuron, they also diffuse along the neuron's length. These sodium ions depolarize the surrounding areas of the neuron's cell membrane to the threshold potential, at which point the voltage-gated sodium channels in those regions open, creating an action potential. This cycle continues to occur along the entire length of the neuron in a chain reaction.

During the time it takes the neuron to repolarize back from +35 mV to −70 mV, the voltage-gated sodium channels will not reopen. This lag prevents the action potential from moving backward to regions of the cell membrane that have already experienced an action potential.

Speeding Up the Action Potential

Axons of many neurons are surrounded by a structure known as the **myelin sheath**, a structure that helps to speed up the movement of action potentials along the axon. The sheath is built of Schwann cells, which wrap themselves around the axon of the neuron, leaving small gaps in between known as the Nodes of Ranvier.

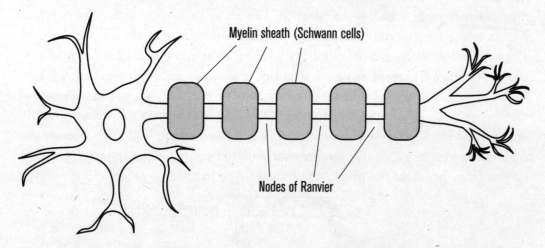

Myelin sheath (Schwann cells)

Nodes of Ranvier

The sodium and potassium ions that cause the action potential are only able to cross the cell membrane at the nodes of Ranvier, so the action potential does not have to occur along the entire length of the axon. Instead, when the action potential is triggered at one node, the sodium ions that enter the neuron will trigger an action potential at the next node. This causes the action potential to jump from node to node, greatly increasing its speed. This jumping of the action potential is called saltatory conduction. Some diseases such as multiple sclerosis can damage the myelin sheaths, greatly impeding conduction of impulses along the neurons.

Strength of the Signal

There is no such thing as a stronger or weaker action potential. If a neuron reaches the threshold to trigger an action potential, then the entire sequence of events, from depolarization to repolarization, will occur, and the same threshold potentials will be reached. But it's obvious that every signal can't trigger an identical response, or else neurons would never be able to convey any useful information. For example, if the feel of lukewarm water and the burn of a hot iron triggered the same response, our sense of touch would be rather useless.

The body communicates a stronger message not by creating a larger action potential, but by firing action potentials more rapidly. The burn of an iron may cause the heat receptors in our skin to fire action potentials at a rate of up to one hundred action potentials per second, while lukewarm water might trigger action potentials at less than half that rate.

Transmitting an Impulse Between Neurons

Neurons cannot directly pass an action potential from one to the next because of the synapses between them. Instead, neurons communicate across the synaptic clefts by the means of chemical signals known as neurotransmitters. When an action potential reaches the synapse, it causes the release of vesicles of these neurotransmitters, which diffuse across the gap and bind to receptors in the dendrites of the adjacent neuron. The neurotransmitters can be excitatory, causing an action potential in the next neuron, or inhibitory, preventing one. Excitatory neurotransmitters cause the target neuron to allow positive ions to enter it, which may or may not be enough to cause the membrane to reach the threshold potential of −50 mV that is needed to open the voltage-gated sodium channels and initiate an action potential. Inhibitory neurotransmitters cause the target neuron to allow entrance to negative ions, carrying the neuron further from threshold and preventing it from firing an action potential.

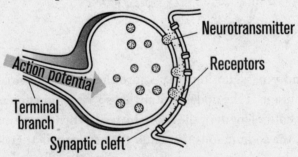

To form the nervous system, neurons are organized in a dense network. Each neuron shares a synapse with many other neurons, exposing each neuron to excitatory and inhibitory neurotransmitters simultaneously. The effects of all of the neurotransmitters working on a neuron at a given time are added up to determine whether or not an action potential will be fired. After a neurotransmitter has its effect on the target neuron, it usually either diffuses away from the synapse, is deactivated by enzymes in the synapse, or is absorbed by surrounding cells.

Nervous System Organization

As animals became more complex, their nervous systems evolved from the simple, unorganized networks of nerves that are found in cnidarians, such as jellyfish, and became more complicated and coordinated by a central control. Annelids and mollusks have simple, organized clusters of neurons known as **ganglia**. Many ganglia fuse in the head region of these organisms to form a primitive brain. Arthropods exhibit a more complex nervous system that includes many sensory organs such as antennae and compound eyes. Vertebrates mark the culmination of nervous system evolution. The vertebrate system is highly centralized, with a large brain that can process complex information and numerous specialized sensory organs.

The Vertebrate Nervous System

The vertebrate nervous system contains billions of individual neurons, but can be divided into two main parts: the central nervous system (CNS) and the peripheral nervous system (PNS). The central nervous system, as its name implies, acts as central command. It receives sensory input from all regions of the body, integrates this information, and creates a response. The central nervous system controls the most basic functions essential for survival, such as breathing and digestion, and it is responsible

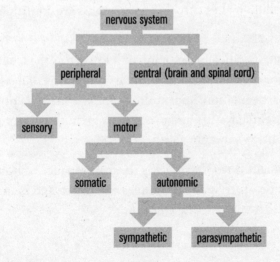

for complex behavior and, in humans, consciousness. The peripheral nervous system refers to the pathways through which the central nervous system communicates with the rest of the organism.

In highly evolved systems, such as the human nervous system, there are actually three types of neural building blocks:

Sensory Neurons: After an organisms' sense organs receive a stimulus from the environment, sensory neurons send that information back to the central nervous system. Also called afferent neurons.

Motor Neurons: In response to some stimulus or as a voluntary action, motor neurons carry information away from the central nervous system to an organ or muscle. Also called efferent neurons.

Interneurons: Provide the connection between sensory neurons and motor neurons.

The Central Nervous System

The central nervous system consists of the **brain** and the **spinal cord**. The spinal cord is a long cylinder of nervous tissue that extends along the vertebral column from the head to the lower back.

Composed of many distinct structures working together to coordinate the body, the brain is a highly complex (and poorly understood) organ. Luckily, you don't have to "understand" the brain for the SAT II Biology. You just need to know its basic structures and their functions. The brain is made up almost entirely of interneurons.

- The **cerebrum** is the largest portion of the brain and the seat of consciousness. The cerebrum controls all voluntary movement, sensory perception, speech, memory, and creative thought.

- The **cerebellum** does not initiate voluntary movement, but it helps fine-tune it. The cerebellum makes sure that movements are coordinated and balanced.

- The **brainstem**, specifically a portion of it known as the **medulla oblongata**, is responsible for the control of involuntary functions such as breathing, cardiovascular regulation, and swallowing. The medulla oblongata is absolutely essential for life and processes a great deal of information. The medulla also helps maintain alertness.

- The **hypothalamus** is responsible for the maintenance of homeostasis. It regulates temperature, controls hunger and thirst, and manages water balance. It also helps generate emotion.

The spinal cord contains all three types of neurons. Axons of motor neurons extend from the spinal column into the peripheral nervous system, while the fibers of sensory neurons merge into the column from the PNS. Interneurons link the motor and sensory neurons, and they make up the majority of the neurons in the spinal column. In addition to the neurons, cells called glial cells are present to provide physical and metabolic support for neurons. The spinal cord serves as a link between the body and the brain, and it can also regulate simple reflexes.

The brain and spinal cord are bathed in a fluid called the cerebrospinal fluid, which helps to cushion these delicate organs against damage. The cerebrospinal fluid is maintained by the glial cells.

The Peripheral Nervous System

The peripheral nervous system consists of a **sensory system** that carries information from the senses into the central nervous system from the body, and a **motor system** that branches out from the CNS to targeted organs or muscles. The motor division can be divided into the **somatic system** and the **autonomic system**.

The somatic nervous system is responsible for voluntary, or conscious, movement. The neurons only target the skeletal muscles responsible for body movement. All of the neurons in the somatic system release **acetylcholine**, an excitatory neurotransmitter that causes skeletal muscles to contract. None of the neurons in the somatic nervous system has an inhibitory effect.

The autonomic system controls tissues other than skeletal muscles, including smooth and cardiac muscle, glands, and organs. The system controls processes that an animal does not have voluntary control over, such as the heartbeat, the movements of the digestive tract, and the contraction of the bladder. Autonomic neurons can either excite or inhibit their target muscles or organs. The autonomic nervous system can itself be subdivided into the sympathetic division and parasympathetic division. These two systems act antagonistically and often have opposite effects.

- The **sympathetic division** prepares the body for emergency situations. It increases the heart rate, dilates the pupils, increases the breathing rate, and diverts blood from the digestive system so that it can be used to oxygenate skeletal muscles that may be needed for action. The sympathetic division also stimulates the medulla of the adrenal glands to release epinephrine and norepinephrine into the bloodstream, hormones that help to reinforce the direct effects of the neurons. Together, the actions of the sympathetic nervous system are often called the "fight or flight" response. The neurotransmitter most often released by sympathetic neurons is norepinephrine.

- The **parasympathetic division** is most active when the body is at rest. It slows the heart rate, increases digestion, and slows breathing. The effects of the parasympathetic are sometimes called the "rest and digest" response. The neurotransmitter most often associated with the parasympathetic division of the autonomic nervous system is acetylcholine.

The Senses

The sensory organs provide information about the environment through the peripheral nervous system to the central nervous system. Complex organs like the eyes and ears, as well as more simple sensory receptors, such as those found in the skin and joints, provide raw information about the environment by firing action potentials under special circumstances. The modified neurons of the eye fire when exposed to light, while those of the ear respond to vibration. This sensory information is processed and perceived by the brain.

Vision: The **eyes** can determine the intensity of the light as well as its color, or frequency. The retina of the eye contains specialized photoreceptors called rods and cones, which can sense the different properties of the light that hits them. Rods are very sensitive and respond to low levels of illumination, a property that is important for night vision. Cones respond to brighter light and are responsible for color vision. Pigments in the photoreceptor cells change their molecular shapes when stimulated by light, leading to the firing of an action potential from neurons in the eye. The impulse passes along the optic nerve to the occipital lobe of the brain, where the visual information is processed. Light is focused onto the retina by the lens of the eye, which can change shape in order to maintain a focused image. The pupil is the hole in the eye that regulates how much light can pass through to the lens; the diameter of the pupil is adjusted by the muscular iris. The cornea is the clear, outer layer of the eye and helps to bend light through the pupil toward the lens.

Hearing: In the **ears**, sound energy causes the eardrum, or tympanic membrane, to vibrate at the same frequency as the sound. The vibration is conducted through three small bones, the auditory ossicles, which amplify the vibration and direct it to the cochlea. Hair cells in the cochlea convert the vibrations of the cochlea into action potentials. The frequency and amplitude of the vibration affect which hair cells are stimulated and how often they fire. The action potentials are transmitted down the auditory nerve to the brain.

Balance: Everyone knows the ear is involved in hearing, but few know that the ear also helps maintain balance. Three **semicircular canals** in each ear contain specialized hair cells that detect the movement of a fluid that fills the canals. When the position of the head changes, the fluid inside the canals moves. The changing pressure on the hair cells affects the rate at which they fire action potentials. This information is transmitted to the brain along the vestibular nerve.

Taste and smell: Taste and smell detect the presence of chemical substances, either dissolved in the saliva in the case of taste, or dissolved in the mucus of the nose in the case of smell. Chemoreceptors that respond to taste are concentrated in structures known as **taste buds** present on the surface of the tongue. The taste buds respond to the four main taste sensations—sour, salty, bitter, and sweet—creating action potentials that travel to the brain along the facial and glossopharyngeal nerves. Smell originates when molecules of a substance pass along the **olfactory epithelium**, a region near the top of the nasal cavity. The molecules dissolve in the mucus that coats the olfactory epithelium and bind to surface receptors. It is believed that there are approximately one thousand different receptor types in the nose, each responding to a different chemical signal. When these receptors are activated, they transmit their signals to the brain through the olfactory nerve.

Somatic senses: In addition to the special senses discussed above, there are many sensory nerve endings throughout the body: in the skin, on the body wall, in the muscles, tendons, and joints, in the bones, and in certain organs. These senses are often called the somatic senses, and they include senses of touch, pressure, the senses of posture and movement, temperature, and pain. The specifics of these senses are not tested on the SAT II Biology, but it is important to know that the senses arise when receptor cells are stimulated to produce action potentials, which are interpreted in the brain.

The Endocrine System

The endocrine system works in concert with the nervous system to control and coordinate the functions of the other organ systems. The endocrine system, however, functions on a slower time scale than the nervous system does. The organs that make up the endocrine system are called the endocrine glands, and they communicate with the body by releasing chemical messengers known as **hormones** into the bloodstream.

The hormones released by the endocrine glands usually target specific organs in an entirely different part of the body. The cells of the target organ for a specific hormone will have receptors to which only that hormone can bind. Organs without those particular receptors will remain unaffected. A hormone can affect targeted cells for a matter of minutes, such as the regulation of blood sugar, or over several days, months, or even years, as happens in puberty.

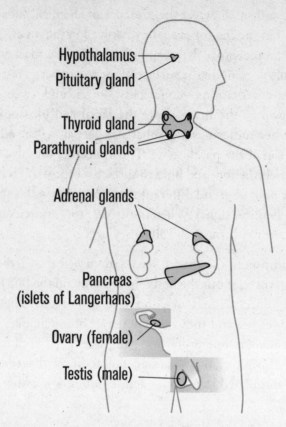

Hypothalamus
Pituitary gland

Thyroid gland
Parathyroid glands

Adrenal glands

Pancreas
(islets of Langerhans)

Ovary (female)

Testis (male)

Two major classes of hormones exist: peptide hormones and steroid hormones. Peptide hormones are composed of amino acids and can range in size from a short chain of only three or four amino acids to small polypeptides. Examples of peptide hormones include insulin and antidiuretic hormone (ADH). Because amino acids cannot freely cross cell membranes, peptide hormones must be secreted through special vesicles and also must convey their information by binding to receptors that exist on the outside of a targeted cell. By binding with the receptor, the hormone generates a chain reaction of signals into the cell that eventually causes changes in specific enzymes within the cell itself. Peptide hormones generally work rather quickly, on the order of minutes and hours rather than days and months.

Steroid hormones are ring-shaped lipids made from cholesterol. Because they are hydrophobic, steroid hormones can easily pass into the bloodstream from the endocrine cells that produce them; they can also pass directly into their target cells. The receptors for steroid hormones are located on the interior of the target cells. When hormone and receptor bind, they enter the nucleus of the cell and can activate or deactivate genes coding for specific proteins. Since steroid hormones exert their influence by changing the rates of protein synthesis, steroid hormones act more slowly than peptide hormones do. Examples of steroid hormones are testosterone, estrogen, and cortisol.

Endocrine Glands

The endocrine system contains a great variety of glands, all of which produce different hormones and regulate different processes or areas of the body. The SAT II Biology does occasionally ask questions about the major endocrine glands.

The Pituitary Gland

The pituitary gland is a tiny gland located at the base of the brain in the center of the head. It is made up of two separate lobes, the anterior pituitary and the posterior pituitary, each of which is responsible for the secretion of a different set of hormones.

The pituitary is a very important part of the endocrine system because the hormones it produces control the secretions of many of the other endocrine organs. The pituitary itself is controlled by the hypothalamus. For each of the six hormones produced by the anterior pituitary gland, the hypothalamus produces a specific hormone-like substance known as a releasing factor that stimulates the anterior pituitary to release that particular hormone. The two hormones released by the posterior pituitary are produced directly in the hypothalamus and merely stored in the pituitary gland until they are secreted into the blood. The six hormones released by the anterior pituitary are:

- **Growth hormone (GH)** stimulates growth in many body tissues. The hormone is particularly important for growing children. In adults, it affects the rate at which older cells are replaced by new ones.

- **Follicle-stimulating hormone (FSH)** stimulates the maturation of ova in the ovaries and sperm in the testes, and can cause the gonads to release sex hormones.

- **Luteinizing hormone (LH)** triggers ovulation and the development of a structure known as the corpus luteum in females. In males it stimulates the release of testosterone by the testes.

- **Prolactin**, released after pregnancy, stimulates milk production in the female mammary glands.

- **Thyroid stimulating hormone (TSH)** stimulates the thyroid, another endocrine gland, to release its hormone, thyroxine.

- **Adrenocorticotrophic hormone (ACTH)** stimulates the adrenal cortex to release its hormones, the corticoids.

The two hormones made in the hypothalamus and released by the storage facility in the posterior pituitary are:

- **Antidiuretic hormone (ADH)** — regulates the kidneys to reduce water loss in the urine.

- **Oxytocin** — stimulates uterine contraction during childbirth.

The Thyroid Gland

Located in the back of the neck, the thyroid gland produces the hormone thyroxine, which increases the metabolism of most of the cells in the body. Iodine is needed to produce thyroxine, so iodine deficiencies can greatly affect the functioning of the thyroid gland. If the thyroid gland produces too little thyroxine, a condition known as hypothyroidism develops. A person who suffers from hypothyroidism has a lower metabolic rate, which can cause obesity and sluggishness. The opposite condition, known as hyperthyroidism, occurs when the thyroid produces too much thyroxine. It can lead to excessive perspiration, high body temperature, loss of weight, and a faster heart rate.

Parathyroid Glands

Four small, but important, glands known as the parathyroid glands are embedded on the posterior surface of the thyroid gland. The parathyroid glands produce a hormone appropriately named parathyroid hormone, or parathormone, which regulates the level of calcium in the bloodstream. When parathyroid hormone is released, it stimulates the bones to secrete extra calcium into the bloodstream, raising the levels of calcium ions in the blood plasma and decreasing them in the bone tissue. Calcium is important for many reasons, including the functioning of muscles and neurons and the blood clotting process.

Pancreas

The pancreas is a large organ located behind the stomach. It serves two major functions. First, it is a digestive organ, releasing digestive enzymes into the small intestine by means of the pancreatic duct. But it also functions as an endocrine organ, releasing the hormones **insulin** and **glucagon** directly into the bloodstream from specialized cells known as the **islets of Langerhans**.

Insulin stimulates cells to absorb glucose from the bloodstream when glucose levels are high, such as after a meal. The hormone also stimulates the liver to remove glucose from the blood and store it as glycogen, decreasing blood sugar levels. Glucagon has the opposite effect. Released when blood glucose levels are low, glucagon stimulates the liver to break down glycogen into glucose and to release it into the bloodstream, raising blood sugar levels.

Adrenal Glands

The adrenal glands are located on the kidneys. They consist of two distinct parts: the **adrenal cortex**, the external portion of the gland, and the **adrenal medulla**, the interior portion.

The sympathetic nervous system stimulates the adrenal medulla to release its hormones, norepinephrine and epinephrine, into the bloodstream. Like the sympathetic nervous system, these two hormones ready the body for stress: they increase heart rate and breathing rate, they divert blood from the digestive system to the skeletal muscles, and they dilate the pupils. (The similarities between the effects of the sympathetic nervous system and adrenal medulla hormones are easy to understand, considering norepinephrine is the neurotransmitter that is released by the sympathetic neurons.) The only difference between the effects of the adrenal medulla and the sympathetic nervous system is that hormones released by the adrenal medulla remain in the bloodstream for a long time, usually several minutes and sometimes more, while the effects of the sympathetic nervous system are short-lived.

The adrenal cortex releases three types of steroid hormones. The glucocorticoids affect glucose levels in the blood. Mineralocorticoids affect the rate at which the kidneys absorb certain minerals from the blood. Sex steroids have some affect on sexual characteristics and processes, but are generally overshadowed by the hormones produced by the gonads.

The Gonads

The gonads—the testes in the male and the ovaries in the female—are the sex organs that produce gametes. In addition, the gonads produce steroid sex hormones. In males the primary sex hormone is **testosterone**, which is necessary for sperm production. In addition to facilitating the production of sperm, testosterone is responsible for developing and maintaining the secondary sex characteristics of males, starting at puberty. These characteristics include a deeper voice, facial and body hair, and broad shoulders. In females, the ovaries produce **estrogen** and **progesterone**. Estrogen helps to develop and maintain the female secondary sex characteristics, such as the development of mammary glands, a narrower waist and wider hips, axillary and pubic hair, and a higher-pitched voice. Estrogen also stimulates growth of the uterine lining for pregnancy, while progesterone prepares the uterus for embryo implantation and helps to maintain pregnancy.

The Circulatory System

In the simplest multicellular animals such as the cnidarians, almost all cells are in contact with the external environment, so there is little need to transport materials internally. Any cell can get its nutrients from the surrounding water and can expel its waste directly back from where it came. As animal body plans evolved to further complexity, however, a need developed for a circulatory system that could transport materials such as nutrients, oxygen, and waste products throughout the body. Annelids have a simple closed circuit of blood vessels with five small hearts, which are really just pulsating vessels themselves. Insects and other arthropods have an open circulatory system that bathes their internal organs. The open circulatory system consists of one dorsal vessel that pulsates, keeping the blood moving throughout the body of the insect.

Vertebrate Circulatory Systems

Vertebrates have evolved an intricate closed circulatory systems that consist of a heart and three principal types of blood vessels: **arteries**, **capillaries**, and **veins**.

Arteries carry blood away from the heart and have thick, elastic, muscular walls that can dilate or contract to control blood pressure within the vessels. Because blood in the arteries has been relatively recently pumped out of the heart, arterial blood pressure tends to be high. The blood in arteries is usually rich in oxygen, since it is being pumped out to the body to provide oxygen and other nutrients to the cells. The only exceptions are the pulmonary arteries, which carry blood to the lungs to pick up its supply of oxygen. Since blood in the pulmonary artery hasn't yet reached the lungs, it is oxygen poor.

Arteries are too large to service every little cell in the body. As arteries get further from the heart, they begin to branch into smaller and smaller vessels, which eventually branch into thousands of capillaries. The walls of the smallest capillaries are only one cell thick, allowing nutrients, waste products, oxygen, and carbon dioxide to diffuse between the blood and the surrounding tissues. After providing nutrients and oxygen and picking up waste, capillaries begin to merge into larger and larger vessels, eventually converging into veins.

Veins carry blood toward the heart. The blood in veins is not pushed by pumping of the heart, so the blood pressure and forward momentum of the blood in veins is lower than in arteries. Blood in veins is largely pushed along by the contractions of the skeletal muscles as the organism moves around. To ensure that the blood in veins flows toward the heart and away from it, veins contain unidirectional valves. Venous blood has already provided nutrients to cells, so it is usually deoxygenated, giving it a characteristic blue color. The lone exception, once again, is the pulmonary vein. Since this blood is flowing back to the heart from the lungs, it is fully oxygenated and bright red.

Patterns of Circulation in Vertebrates

As vertebrates have evolved, they have developed increasingly efficient circulatory systems. The circulatory system in fish is one closed loop: blood is pumped from the heart to the gill capillaries, where oxygen is picked up from the surrounding water. The blood then continues on to the body tissues, and the vessels eventually become capillaries again to allow for nutrient and gas exchange in the tissues. Then the deoxygenated blood is returned to the heart and pumped to the gills once more. This system is inefficient because the blood loses a lot of momentum in the gill capillaries. After leaving the gill capillaries it travels slowly and with a lower pressure, affecting the delivery of oxygen to the body tissues.

Amphibians, reptiles, birds, and mammals have overcome this problem by evolving two circuits within the circulatory system: the **pulmonary circuit** and the **systemic circuit**. After the blood is pumped from the heart to the lungs to be oxygenated, it is returned to the heart before it is pumped out to the rest of the body.

The Heart

Amphibian and reptile hearts are inefficient because they make no distinction between oxygenated and deoxygneated blood. Their hearts have only two chambers: one chamber for receiving blood from the lungs and the body, and another for pumping that blood back out. These two-chambered hearts allow oxygen-rich blood returning from the lungs to mix with oxygen-poor blood returning from the systemic circuit. The blood pumped to the body never contains as much oxygen as it could.

The avian (bird) and mammalian heart is *four*-chambered. It consists of two halves, one for oxygenated blood and the other for deoxygenated blood. Each half has one **atrium** and one **ventricle**, separated by one-way atrioventricular valves. The atrium is the chamber where blood returns to the heart, while the ventricle is the chamber where blood is pumped out of the heart. Oxygen-poor blood returning from the body enters the right atrium and then moves into the right ventricle, which pumps the blood through the pulmonary artery to the lungs where it picks up oxygen and releases carbon dioxide. This newly oxygenated blood returns to the left atrium of the heart through the pulmonary veins. Blood in the left atrium moves into the left ventricle, from where it is pumped out through the **aorta**, the largest artery, into other arteries, arterioles, and capillaries. The blood provides oxygen to the cells, picks up carbon dioxide, and gathers back into veins. Eventually the deoxygenated blood flows through the superior vena cava and inferior vena cava back into the right atrium, starting the process over again.

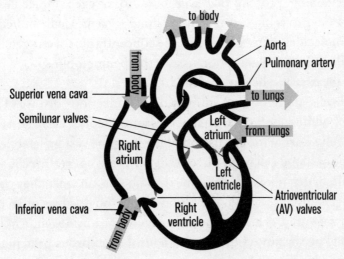

The vertebrate heart is composed of special muscle tissue called cardiac muscle. These muscles are stimulated to contract in a regular and controlled rhythm by an electric pulse generated in a region of the heart called the sinoatrial node, or pacemaker. The pacemaker cells fire impulses spontaneously, without any stimulation from the nervous system. This impulse spreads among the heart cells, stimulating the atria to contract, forcing blood into the ventricles. At the junction of the atria and the ventricles, the impulse reaches another node, called the atrioventricular node. The atrioventricular node sends an impulse that causes the ventricular walls to contract, forcing blood out of the heart and into the aorta and pulmonary arteries. Although the heartbeat can be maintained without external stimulation by the nervous system, the autonomic nervous system can regulate the heart rate by speeding it up or slowing it down.

The Blood

The entire purpose of the circulatory system is to move oxygen and nutrient-rich blood to where it needs to go. Blood is a liquid tissue that is composed of a fluid called **plasma** and three types of specialized cells: **red blood cells**, **white blood cells**, and **platelets**.

The plasma of the blood is composed mainly of water, allowing it to contain many dissolved substances, such as the glucose that provides cells with energy; carbon dioxide in the form of carbonic acid; hormones that carry important chemical signals to their target organs; salts such as calcium, potassium, and sodium; lipids; and nitrogenous waste. The plasma also contains proteins that assist in blood clotting, in the immune response, and in preventing the loss of too much blood fluid from the capillaries.

Red blood cells are biconcave discs with no nucleus and no major organelles (if you took a ball of putty and squashed it between two fingers it would look like a red blood cell). Red blood cells are the most abundant cell type in the blood. Their primary function is to transport oxygen through the blood. Red blood cells are filled with **hemoglobin**, an iron-containing protein that can bind to oxygen molecules. When the concentration of oxygen is high, as it is in the lungs, one molecule of hemoglobin can bind up to four molecules of oxygen. When the concentration of oxygen is very low, as it is in the capillaries of oxygen-poor tissue, the hemoglobin gives up its oxygen, releasing it into the tissues where it is needed.

White blood cells are important in fighting off infectious disease. There are two general classes of white blood cells: phagocytes and lymphocytes. These cells will be explained more fully during the discussion of the immune system later in this chapter.

The third type of blood cell is the platelet. Platelets are not really cells at all; they are packets of cytoplasm that release the enzyme thromboplastin when they come into contact with a foreign substance within the blood or the rough edges of an open wound. Thromboplastin sets off a chain reaction that converts fibrinogen, a soluble protein found in the blood plasma, into fibrin, a tough insoluble fibrous protein that traps red blood cells and thereby forms blood clots that stop blood loss from an open wound.

Blood Types

Red blood cells manufacture proteins called **antigens** that coat the cell surface. These proteins help the immune system to determine if a cell is a foreign invader or part of the body's normal tissues. In the case of human red blood cells, there are two major types of antigens that can be formed: antigen A and antigen B. According to genotype, an individual might have one or both of these antigens expressed, or he may have neither. If a person's red blood cells contain only antigen A, he is said to have type A blood. If only antigen B is present, the blood is type B. Type AB blood contains both antigens, and type O blood contains neither antigen A nor B.

In order to combat foreign cells, the blood plasma contains antibodies for all antigens that are *not* expressed on its own red blood cells. These antibodies would cause any foreign blood cells to clump together, forming a dangerous clot. A person with type A blood has anti-B antibodies in the plasma; a person with type B blood has anti-A antibodies in the plasma; a person with type AB blood has no antibodies in the plasma; and a person with type O blood has both anti-A and anti-B antibodies. A person with type AB blood can therefore receive a blood transfusion of any type because their blood contains no antibodies that would clump up the foreign cells. For this reason, AB blood is often called the universal recipient. In contrast, a person with type O blood can receive *only* type O blood in a transfusion because he has both anti-A and anti-B antibodies in the plasma, which would immediately clump any blood that contained antigens A or B. But since type O blood has no antigens, it could be given to a person of any type blood in a transfusion without clumping. Type O blood is called the universal donor.

Blood type is a codominant trait; we explained the inheritance patterns of blood type in the codominace section of the chapter on genetics.

The Lymphatic System

Because the capillaries are so small, the pressure inside them is often high enough to force some of the plasma out of the blood and the capillary and into the surrounding tissue. If the fluid remained in the tissue it would cause swelling. The lymphatic system is responsible for returning this fluid to the circulatory system. The fluid, known as **lymph**, collects in small lymph capillaries, which contain valves similar to veins. These lymph capillaries converge into larger lymph vessels, and they eventually drain into the subclavian vein.

The lymph is a popular route for invading microorganisms that are trying to enter the bloodstream, so it must be well defended. **Lymph nodes** contain white blood cells that can destroy bacteria or viruses that are present in the lymph. Additional organs such as the spleen and tonsils are considered part of the lymphatic system because they aid in filtering the blood to remove foreign invaders.

The Immune System

The immune system is responsible for keeping foreign invaders out of the body and destroying those entities that do manage to invade the tissues. Immune system defenses can be either passive or active. Passive defenses are physical barriers that prevent microorganisms from entering the body. Skin is the most obvious example. The sticky mucus lining the respiratory tract and stomach acid, which kills many microorganisms that might otherwise enter through the digestive system, are other examples of passive defenses.

The active defenses of the immune system are primarily made up of white blood cells. There are two classes of white blood cells: **phagocytes** and **lymphocytes**. Phagocytes resemble amoebas and can crawl through the body's tissues ingesting any foreign invaders they come upon. Lymphocytes are more specific in the invaders they target. There are three general types of lymphocytes. B cells identify pathogens by producing **antibodies** that recognize the protein coats of specific viruses or bacteria. Helper T cells coordinate the immune response by activating other immune system cells. Killer T cells kill infected cells.

The Respiratory System

All aerobic organisms need a way to exchange gases with their surrounding environment.

Oxygen must be brought to the cells in order for aerobic respiration to take place, and the carbon dioxide created as a by-product of respiration must be removed. The acquisition of oxygen and simultaneous elimination of carbon dioxide is called gas exchange. As animals have evolved they have developed increasingly efficient methods of gas exchange.

In the simplest multicellular animals, the cnidarians, gas exchange occurs by simple diffusion. Since almost all of a jellyfish or hydra's cells are in contact with its water environment, each cell has direct access to outside water as both a source of oxygen and dumping ground for carbon dioxide. Annelids also exchange gases by diffusion. In an earthworm, for example, the circulatory system comes very close to the surface skin, allowing oxygen and carbon dioxide to diffuse across the worm's skin. To make gas diffusion possible, the worm's skin must remain moist at all times. Insects and other arthropods have a system of tracheae for gas exchange. Tracheae are hollow, branched tubes that penetrate the arthropod's deep tissues. Air flows into the tracheae and oxygen and carbon dioxide diffuse into and out of the body tissues through the trachea walls. The insect does not actively draw air into the tracheae; respiration is a passive process in arthropods.

Vertebrate Respiratory Systems

Vertebrates such as fish, birds, and mammals have evolved specialized structures for gas exchange. Fish gills are made of a delicate tissue with many fine filaments that maximize surface area. The fish pumps water across the gills, and oxygen and carbon dioxide are exchanged across the filament walls. Fish gills are made especially efficient because blood flows through the gills against the current of the water. In this way, the water is always more oxygen-rich than the blood in the gills, and the concentration gradient always moves from the water to the blood.

Terrestrial vertebrates have evolved internal structures for gas exchange known as lungs. Lungs are basically inverted gills. Lungs are internal because an exposed gas exchange surface would quickly dry up when exposed to air, a problem that fish need not deal with. The amphibian lung is often shaped like one large sac. In higher vertebrates, such as mammals, the lungs divide into millions of tiny sacs known as **alveoli** which greatly increases surface area and oxygen absorptive power. After air is sucked into the lungs, gas exchange takes place across the surfaces of the alveoli, which are dense with capillaries. After the blood in the capillaries has given off its carbon dioxide and taken in oxygen, air is once again released from the lungs. Birds have evolved an even more efficient breathing system that uses air sacs to maintain a constant, countercurrent, unidirectional flow of air across the lung surfaces. Bird lungs do not contain dead-end sacs like the alveoli of mammalian lungs, but rather contain millions of tiny tubes known as parabronchi, through which air is constantly flowing in one direction.

Respiration in Humans

The human respiratory system has two parts: the upper portion channels air to the lower portion, the lungs, where the respiration takes place.

Air enters the respiratory system either through the nose or mouth. The nose contains many tiny hairs and sticky mucus that traps airborne particles and prevents them from entering the lungs. Air is also moistened and warmed in the nasal and oral passages. From the nose and mouth, air flows down the **pharynx**, through the **larynx**, and into the **trachea**. The larynx is a structure made of cartilage that contains the vocal cords. When air passes out of the larynx, the vocal cords can be tensed and made to vibrate, producing sound, which when shaped by the mouth, produces speech. The trachea is a cartilaginous tube that branches into two **bronchi**, which in turn branch into smaller and smaller **bronchioles** within the lung.

Eventually the air reaches the lungs and the clusters of alveoli. The blood is low in oxygen and the inhaled air is rich with it, while the blood contains a higher concentration of carbon dioxide than air does. These two gases passively diffuse across the thin surface of the alveoli, following the concentration gradients. After gas exchange takes place, the oxygen-poor air is expelled from the lungs. Most of the surfaces of the respiratory system, including the surfaces of the bronchioles, bronchi, trachea, and pharynx, are coated with epithelial cells that are capable of producing mucus. This mucus traps particles of dust, bacteria, and viruses that may be entering the respiratory system; cilia on these cells help to sweep this mucus up away from the lungs and eventually out of the body.

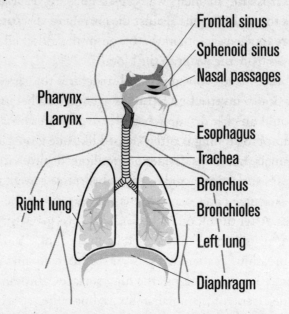

The lungs suck in air by using negative pressure. The **diaphragm** is a large, flat muscle at the base of the thoracic (chest) cavity. When it contracts during inhalation, it moves downward, expanding the volume of the thorax and lungs. Air rushes into the lungs to balance the drop in pressure caused by this expansion. To exhale, the diaphragm relaxes to its original position, increasing air pressure and forcing the air back out of the chest cavity. Breathing is only possible if the thoracic cavity remains airtight. When an accident causes any sort of puncture in the chest cavity, one or both of the lungs can collapse.

Blood pH Regulation

In addition to its obvious function of gas exchange, the respiratory system also helps maintain the pH of the blood at a constant level of about 7.4. Because carbon dioxide is transported through the blood plasma as carbonic acid, the rate of carbon dioxide exhalation can affect the pH level of the blood. Breathing faster will increase blood pH by getting rid of more carbon dioxide and carbonic acid. Breathing slower will have the opposite effect. A small receptor in the carotid artery measures blood pH and transmits this information to the medulla oblongata of the brain. The medulla then adjusts the breathing rate in order to correct for any fluctuations in blood pH. When we feel out of breath, it is not because our body is sensing that we need more oxygen; it is actually telling us that we need to get rid of more carbon dioxide.

The Digestive System

Unlike plants, animals cannot synthesize the majority of their own organic building blocks, such as fatty acids, sugars, and most amino acids. Instead, animals must ingest other organisms and digest them into the essential molecules that they need. Animals get their energy from sugars, fats, and proteins, and they use them to construct more complex molecules such as enzymes. The digestive system has evolved to process the food that animals ingest by breaking it down, or digesting it, into simple building blocks that can be used by cells.

Digestion consists of two main processes: mechanical digestion and chemical digestion. Mechanical digestion refers to the physical breaking down of food into smaller particles without changing the food's chemical nature. Chewing food is an example of mechanical digestion, as is the churning of food that takes place in the stomach. Chemical digestion, which occurs through the action of special digestive enzymes, breaks the chemical bonds in food and hydrolyzes larger molecules into simpler components.

Simple Digestive Systems

In the simplest of animals and in animal-like protists, much of the digestion process takes place within each individual cell. An amoeba engulfs its food by phagocytosis, and a lysosome fuses with the food vacuole and chemically digests its contents. Paramecia have a ciliated oral groove that facilitates the creation of the food vacuole. Cnidarians digest some of their food extracellularly by releasing enzymes into their water-filled gastrovascular cavity, but a large portion of their food is digested intracellularly as well. Flatworms, such as planarians, take food in through their mouth and into the gastrovasular cavity. The food is digested intracellularly by the cells that line the cavity and is absorbed into the tissues. Waste products are expelled back out of the mouth, which also serves as an anus in this case.

Most higher animals, such as annelids, arthropods, and vertebrates, possess a complete digestive tract, with a mouth that is separate from the anus. Food is moved in one direction through a tubular system that contains many specialized parts that perform different functions. In the earthworm, for example, food passes through the mouth, down a tube called the esophagus, and into a chamber known as the crop, which acts as a storage chamber. Next it enters the gizzard, which has thick, muscular walls that mechanically grind the food. The pulverized food passes into the intestine, where enzymes chemically break it down into simpler molecules. These molecules are absorbed into the circulatory system. In the last portion of the intestine, some water is absorbed from the food, and the indigestible portions of the food are expelled through the anus.

Organismal Biology

The Human Digestive System

The human digestive system is somewhat similar to the earthworm's in basic design, though it is more complicated and efficient. The human digestive system is composed of the **alimentary canal**, which is the actual tube through which the food travels, and the glands that aid in digestion by releasing enzymes and other secretions into the alimentary canal.

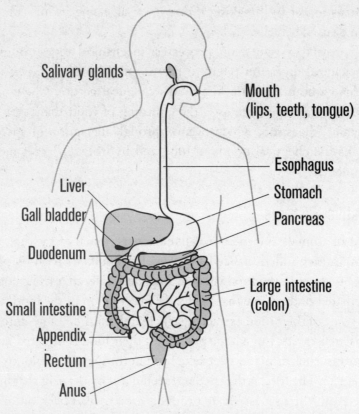

The Mouth

The alimentary canal begins with the mouth, where teeth and the tongue pulverize food through mechanical digestion into what is called a bolus. The tongue also tastes the food, which helps to determine if it is fit to be ingested. Six **salivary glands** release saliva into the mouth cavity through ducts that open under the tongue and on the roof of the mouth. Saliva is composed mainly of water, but it includes mucus and an enzyme called salivary amylase. The water and mucus in the saliva help to dissolve and lubricate the food in preparation for swallowing. Salivary amylase starts the process of chemical digestion of starches by breaking down complex polysaccharides into the disaccharide maltose. When the food is sufficiently chewed, it is swallowed. The food moves through the pharynx, or throat, to the esophagus.

The Esophagus

The esophagus is a long tube that connects the mouth and the stomach. Food in the esophagus is propelled downward by waves of muscular contraction known as **peristalsis**. Between the stomach and the esophagus is a tight ring of muscle known as the cardiac sphincter. This sphincter, which is normally closed, acts as a valve to prevent stomach contents from moving upward into the esophagus. During peristalsis the sphincter opens to allow the food to pass into the stomach.

The Stomach

The stomach has thick, muscular walls that contract to churn and mix the food, continuing the process of mechanical digestion. In addition, the walls of the stomach secrete hydrochloric acid and the enzyme pepsin. The hydrochloric acid gives the stomach a pH of less than 2, and this extremely acidic environment serves to kill many microorganisms that might be ingested along with the food. Pepsin is produced by the stomach in an inactive form known as pepsinogen. Pepsinogen is only activated into pepsin in a very low pH environment, so when it comes into contact with the hydrochloric acid, it becomes pepsin. Pepsin begins the digestion of protein by cleaving long chains of amino acids into shorter chains. In addition to its roles in mechanical and chemical digestion, the stomach temporarily stores of food.

The walls of the stomach are protected from the hydrochloric acid by a thick layer of mucus. If this mucosal lining wears away, an ulcer can develop.

The Small Intestine

The small intestine is the major site of food breakdown, chemical digestion, and cellular absorption of food. Chemical digestion is carried out by secretions from the liver and pancreas.

When the stomach empties, the partially digested food, now called chyme, passes through the pyloric sphincter into the **duodenum**, the upper portion of the small intestine. At this point the chyme encounters bile produced by the liver. Bile is a complex solution of salts, pigments, and cholesterol that is produced in the liver and stored and concentrated in a small sac called the **gallbladder** before entering the duodenum. Bile does not actually change the chemical nature of the chyme; instead it emulsifies—breaks down—fats. Because fats and oils are not soluble in water, the fat content in chyme tends to separate and collect into large globules. Bile breaks these large fat globules into tiny droplets. The surface area of many droplets of fat is much greater than the surface area of a few large globules, and so by increasing the surface area of these fat droplets, bile exposes more fat to the enzymes that will eventually digest it.

The pancreas is a large gland that sits behind the stomach. As mentioned in the section on the endocrine system, the pancreas plays an important role in regulating blood sugar levels by producing the hormones insulin and glucagon. But it plays just as vital a role in the digestive system. The pancreas produces a basic secretion that helps to neutralize the stomach acid. It also produces many digestive enzymes. Lipase digests fats into glycerol and fatty acids, while trypsin and chymotrypsin continue the breakdown of amino acid chains into shorter ones. Both trypsin and chymotrypsin are produced in inactive forms in the pancreas and are not activated until they reach the small intestine; if this were not the case, the pancreas would digest itself! The pancreas also secretes pancreatic amylase, which, like salivary amylase, breaks down polysaccharides into disaccharides, but on a much larger scale.

The walls of the small intestine secrete the remaining few enzymes necessary for digestion. Maltase, lactase, and sucrase break down the disaccharides maltose, lactose, and sucrose into monosaccharides. Aminopeptidases cleave off individual amino acids from the short chains that are left after the action of trypsin and chymotrypsin from the pancreas. At this point, digestion is completed. As the digested food travels through the long, convoluted small intestine it is absorbed through its walls into the bloodstream. The walls of the small intestine contain millions of tiny, fingerlike projections known as **villi** that increase the surface area of the intestinal wall, maximizing absorption of nutrients. The villi contain capillaries into which the digested amino acids and monosaccharides pass. Fats are processed in the cells of the intestinal lining and enter the lymphatic system before reaching the bloodstream. The blood leaving the intestines flows directly to the liver, where it enters the capillaries of the hepatic portal system for processing.

The Large Intestine and Rectum

The undigested food that is not absorbed in the small intestine is waste. It eventually passes into the large intestine, or colon, where its water content is reabsorbed into the body. A mutually symbiotic bacteria named *E. coli* lives in large intestine, feeding on waste and producing vitamin K, which is absorbed by the intestine into the body. The final segment of the large intestine is the rectum, a sac that stores feces temporarily before they are eliminated through the anus, another sphincter muscle.

Minerals and Vitamins

In addition to the nutrients that form the building blocks of proteins, fats, and carbohydrates, the body also absorbs important minerals and vitamins during digestion. Minerals are inorganic molecules that are required by the body. Important minerals are iron, a necessary component of hemoglobin; iodine, which is essential for making thyroid hormone; and calcium, which is required by the bones and for many cellular processes. Sodium, chlorine, and potassium are important components of body fluids, and phosphorus is an important ingredient of nucleic acids.

Vitamins are more complex molecules that usually serve as coenzymes, assisting in physiological processes. Vitamin A is necessary to make retinal, an important chemical for vision. Vitamin B complex contains many molecules essential for cellular respiration and DNA replication. Vitamin C is important for making collagen, a tough material that is found in the body's connective tissue. Vitamin D allows the body to absorb calcium, essential for the teeth and bones. Vitamin E helps prevent the rupture of red blood cells, and it also helps maintain healthy liver and nerve function. Vitamin K is important in the blood clotting process. Vitamins A, D, E, and K are the fat-soluble vitamins, while the vitamins of the B complex and vitamin C are water-soluble vitamins.

The Excretory System

While carrying out the physiological processes that are necessary for life, animal cells produce waste that must be eliminated. Carbon dioxide and water, two of the main waste products, are removed from the body by the respiratory system. The third type of waste produced by metabolic processes are the nitrogenous wastes urea and uric acid, which are created when amino and nucleic acids are broken down. Animals have developed a variety of systems to excrete nitrogenous waste. In many animals these excretory systems also play important roles in regulating water and salt balance as well.

Excretion in Invertebrates

As in respiration, cnidarians rely on simple diffusion to solve the problem of nitrogenous waste. Since most cells of a cnidarian are in contact with the external environment, nitrogenous wastes can diffuse across the cell membranes and into the surrounding water. Annelids have a more complex system for excretion. Two small tubes called **nephridia** exist in each of the annelid's body segments. These tubes are surrounded by capillaries. Nitrogenous waste in the form of urea is passed from the blood into the nephridia. The waste collected in the nephridia eventually exits the worm through pores in the skin. Arthropods have their own specialized means of excreting waste: a system of structures known as the **Malpighian tubules** that are bathed in the fluid of the arthropod's open circulatory system. Nitrogenous waste in the form of uric acid collects in the tubules. From there the waste empties into the digestive tract, which reabsorbs all of the water that was lost in the excretory process. Without water, urea converts to solid crystals of uric acid, which are excreted along with the solid waste produced by digestion.

Excretion in Humans

Vertebrates have evolved a different answer to the problem of water balance and nitrogenous waste excretion: the **kidneys**. The two kidneys filter blood, removing urea in the form of urine, while also regulating the levels of water and salt present in the blood plasma. From each kidney, urine travels through a large duct called the **ureter** and empties into the **urinary bladder**. The bladder is a muscular organ that expands to store urine. When the bladder contracts, urine is pushed through another duct called the **urethra** and out of the body.

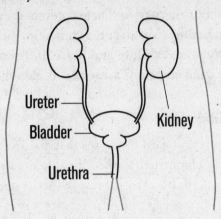

The Nephron

The basic functional unit of the kidney is the **nephron**, a tiny tubule whose special structure makes it ideal for its blood filtering task. Each nephron consists of a cluster of capillaries called the glomerulus, which is surrounded by a hollow bulb known as Bowman's capsule. The Bowman's capsule leads into a long, convoluted tubule that has four sections: the proximal tubule, the loop of Henle, the distal tubule, and the collecting duct. The collecting ducts empty into the central cavity of the kidney, the renal pelvis, which connects to the ureter that carries urine to the bladder. A kidney is made up of millions of nephrons.

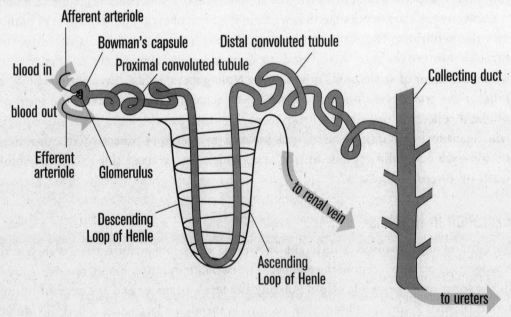

How a Nephron Filters Blood

Blood enters the kidney through renal arteries that quickly split into smaller vessels and then branch further into the very narrow clusters of capillaries that make up the glomerulus of the nephron. Because the glomerulus' capillaries are so narrow, blood pressure is high. The high pressure squeezes the liquid portion of blood through a sieve structure and into the Bowman's capsule, leaving the blood cells, platelets, and large protein molecules behind. This process is called filtration, and the liquid blood that is pushed through the sieve structure is called filtrate. The filtrate contains large amounts of water, glucose, salts, and amino acids in addition to the urea that is to be excreted.

From Bowman's capsule the filtrate enters the proximal tubule of the nephron. In the proximal tubule, important molecules for life, such as sodium, water, amino acids, and glucose, are pumped out of the proximal tubule to be reabsorbed by the blood, as they are too valuable to be excreted. The return of these molecules to the blood is called reabsorption. After reabsorption, the filtrate is called urine.

By the time urine enters the next portion of the nephron, the loop of Henle, it has already lost approximately 75 percent of its initial water content and volume. The loop of Henle descends from the outer region of the kidney, the cortex, into the medulla. The walls of the descending loop are permeable to water but not to salt. In addition, the medulla of the kidney contains a high salt concentration, creating a concentration gradient: water is drawn out of the descending loop and into the medulla, leaving the salts behind. By the time the urine reaches the ascending part of the loop of Henle, only 6 percent of the original water content remains. The ascending loop of Henle is impermeable to water, but it is permeable to salt. Because the urine lost so much water content in the descending loop, the salt content at this point is very high. Salt now diffuses from the ascending loop into the medulla of the kidney (helping to maintain the high salt content of medulla). When it is finished traveling through the ascending loop of Henle, only about 4 percent of the original salt content of the filtrate remains. With much of the water gone as well, the urine consists mainly of urea and other waste products at this point.

The urine then enters the distal tubule, which operates very similarly to the proximal tubule—salt is pumped out of the urine, and water follows osmotically. By the end of the distal tubule, only 3 percent of the original water content remains in the urine, and the salt content is negligible. In the distal tubules, a third process, in addition to filtration and reabsorption, takes place: secretion. While the salts and water are leaving the tubules, some substances, such as hydrogen and potassium ions, are actively transported from the blood into the urine of the tubule so that they can be excreted from the body.

From the distal tubule, the urine enters the collecting duct. Like the loop of Henle, the collecting duct extends deep into the medulla portion of the kidney. Because the medulla has a high salt content, as much as 3/4 of the remaining water *can* be reabsorbed as the urine travels through the collecting duct. The actual amount of water that is reabsorbed is dependent on the permeability of the walls of the duct, which is regulated by the antidiuretic hormone (ADH) secreted by the posterior pituitary gland. ADH acts on the walls of the collecting ducts to make them more permeable to water, but if ADH levels are low, less water will be reabsorbed. If a person is dehydrated and needs to conserve water, their levels of ADH will rise. In contrast, a person with sufficient levels of water in the blood will have low ADH levels, resulting in less reabsorbed water and more dilute urine. In addition to being permeable to water, the lower portions of the collecting duct are permeable to urea, allowing some of it to enter the medulla of the kidney. This release of urea allows the medulla to maintain its high ion concentration, an important factor in the functioning of the nephron.

Another hormone that has an effect on the nephron in addition to ADH is the aldosterone, which is produced in the adrenal cortex. Aldosterone increases the sodium and water reabsorption in the distal tubule, creating another method of conserving water that also increases blood volume and pressure.

The Kidneys and Blood Pressure

In addition to controlling the amount of water that is reabsorbed from the filtrate, which has an effect on blood volume and blood pressure, the kidneys release an enzyme, renin, into the blood. Renin sets off a series of reactions in the blood that results in the production of another enzyme, angiotensin II. Angiotensin II constricts blood vessels, causing a rise in blood pressure. It also causes the adrenal cortex to release more aldosterone, raising blood volume and blood pressure.

Support and Locomotion

One of the biggest differences between animals and plants is also one of the simplest: animals move, plants don't. While the simplest animals are propelled by cilia on their cell surfaces, most animals are too large for such tiny structures to have a significant effect on their locomotion. Many cnidarians have primitive contractile fibers that allow them to propel themselves through water. A number of invertebrates, such as earthworms, possess what is known as a **hydrostatic skeleton**, in which muscles are arranged longitudinally down the length of the body, and in circular rings around the body. When either of these types of muscle contract, an incompressible fluid maintains the body at a constant volume, but allows the worm to change shape. Contraction of the circular muscles lengthens the body, while longitudinal muscle contraction shortens the body. Earthworms are segmented and can control the muscles within each segment independently. By contracting the muscles in waves along its body, the earthworm can propel itself through the soil. Tiny hairs called **setae** on the worm's surface provide traction against the soil.

Arthropod muscles connect to a rigid **exoskeleton** that encloses the body and is made of chitin. When arthropod muscles contract, they pull on inward extensions of the exoskeleton, causing it to move. Range of motion is provided by joints connecting different sections of the exoskeleton. While the exoskeleton works well for animals as small as insects, it would be too heavy and impractical for larger animals.

The Vertebrate Skeletal System

In direct contrast to arthropods that live inside an exoskeleton, vertebrates have evolved a hard internal skeleton, or **endoskeleton**. The skeleton is made of two tissues: **bone** and **cartilage**.

Bones are rigid structures composed of living cells rooted in a matrix of calcium, phosphate salts, and collagen fibers. Blood vessels and nerves pass through a central canal in the bone; blood makes its way to embedded cells through tiny pores. Bones form the majority of the endoskeleton in higher vertebrates, including humans, and provide structural support to all the other tissues in the body. In addition, bones:

- Protect the soft, delicate organs and structures within the body. The skull and ribcage are examples of hard bone protecting the vital organs in the head and chest.

- Store minerals such as calcium. When the calcium supply in the blood is high, it is stored in bones. When the supply is low, bones give off calcium.

- Marrow, found in cavities at the centers of bones, produces blood cells.

Bones meet each other at joints that are held together by **ligaments** and are often bathed in a lubricating and cushioning fluid called synovial fluid. Joints allow bones to meet and bind together without actually grinding together. In this way, joints allow for smooth skeletal movement.

Cartilage is firm, but somewhat flexible. It will bend under strain and spring back to its original shape when the force is removed. The skeletons of sharks and rays are composed entirely of cartilage, as are the skeletons of developing embryos. In higher vertebrates, cartilage is retained in portions of the skeleton that need to remain flexible, such as in the rib cage that needs to expand during inhalation, the tip of the nose and ears, at the end of bones, and in joints. Cartilage contains no blood vessels or nerves, and it takes a very long time to heal when damaged.

The Muscular System

Joints allow a skeleton to move. Muscles actually *make* it move. Bones interface with muscles by way of **tendons**. Movement is achieved when muscles contract, pulling on the bones to which they are attached, bending the joints. An extensor muscle straightens the bones in a joint. An example is the triceps muscle in your upper arm, which straightens out the elbow joint. A flexor muscle bends a joint. The bicep muscle, which bends your elbow, is a flexor. (Note that both extensors and flexors perform their functions by contracting; when an extensor contracts it straightens a joint, and when a flexor contracts it bends a joint.) Muscles also help the skeleton support and protect the body. Vertebrates have three classes of muscles:

- **Skeletal muscles**, also called striated muscles, are associated with the skeletal system and are primarily involved in voluntary movement. A vertebrate generally has conscious control over its skeletal muscles. Each skeletal muscle cell contains many nuclei.

- **Smooth muscle** is found in the walls of the internal organs such as the stomach, intestines, and urinary bladder and is an involuntary muscle, and not under voluntary control.

- **Cardiac muscle** makes up the heart. Cardiac muscles are involuntary, and can contract without stimulation from the nervous system.

Muscles can be thought of as the enactors of the nervous system. Through voluntary impulse or involuntary instinct, nerves send messages to muscles. Muscles turn these messages into movement and action by contracting or relaxing.

Muscle Contraction

The interaction between two proteins, **actin** and **myosin**, is responsible for muscular contraction. In skeletal muscles, actin and myosin are arranged into units known as **sarcomeres**.

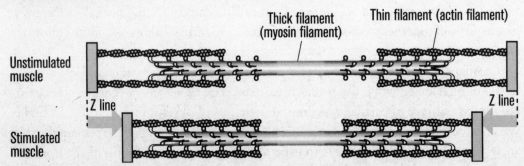

Long filaments of actin extend from each end of the sarcomere toward the middle, almost meeting, but not actually touching. In between these actin filaments are short, fat filaments of myosin that are arranged longitudinally. The myosin does not connect to the ends of the sarcomere. The ends of the sarcomere to which the actin filaments are attached are called the Z lines. When the muscle is stimulated to contract by a neuron, an influx of calcium ions (Ca^{++}) causes the myosin to pull on the actin filaments by means of tiny connections known as crossbridges. Neither the myosin nor the actin filaments change in length, but when the myosin pulls the actin together, the actin pulls the Z lines together and the whole sarcomere contracts.

Sarcomeres are arranged end to end into long fibers known as myofibrils that bundle to form the primary muscle fibers that make up the muscle. Contracting sarcomeres cause muscle fibers to contract, which, in turn, cause the whole muscle to contract.

The Skin

It's easy to think of the skin as just a thin covering for the important internal organs. But skin itself is an organ, with a multitude of functions:

- Protects against infection, abrasion, and water loss

- Contains nerve endings vital for sensation, such as touch, pain, heat, and cold

- Excretes water to maintain water and salt balance in the body

- Produces vitamin D on exposure to the UV rays in sunlight

- Regulates body temperature (thermoregulation)

Skin has three layers: the **epidermis**, the **dermis**, and the **hypodermis**. The epidermis is the topmost layer that touches the outside environment. Active cell division occurs in the lower region of the epidermis. As new cells are created, old cells are pushed toward the surface, where they form a hardened, dead layer that is constantly shed. The dermis is living tissue that contains many blood vessels, sweat glands, and sebaceous glands, which produce oils that keep the skin from drying out. The dermis also contains nerve

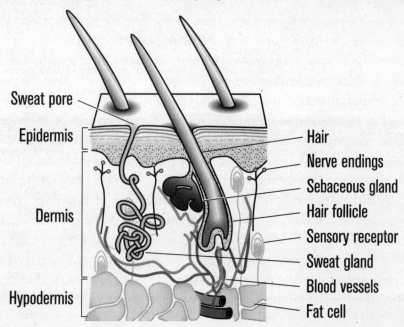

endings that are responsive to touch, pressure, heat, cold, and pain. Hair follicles originate in the inner portions of the dermis as well. The hypodermis, or subcutaneous layer of the skin, is mainly composed of loose connective tissue and fat cells.

Skin and Thermoregulation

The skin helps warm-blooded animals maintain constant body temperature in varying environmental factors. When the body becomes too warm, blood vessels in the skin dilate, allowing heat to escape through the surface of the skin. Special glands called sweat glands produce a salty secretion called perspiration that evaporates off the surface of the skin, taking heat with it. When the body becomes too cold, the opposite processes occur. Sweat glands are shut down, and blood vessels in the skin constrict, keeping the blood away from the surface of the body where heat could be lost. In addition, the muscles begin to contract rapidly and shiver, which generates significant heat.

The Reproductive System

As dictated by evolution, an organism's purpose is to reproduce and ensure the survival of the species. All of the other organ systems exist just to keep the animal alive long enough to mate and pass its genetic makeup down to its progeny.

Animals can reproduce either asexually or sexually. Asexual reproduction usually occurs among less highly evolved animals. **Budding**, which can occur in certain cnidarians like the hydra, is a process by which the offspring literally grow off the side of the parent, producing a miniature, genetically identical copy. **Regeneration** occurs when animals such as earthworms, planarians, or starfish are broken apart, and each piece then grows into a separate organism. **Parthenogenesis** occurs when an animal's egg cell begins to divide mitotically without being fertilized by a sperm. The embryo that develops from this unfertilized egg will be genetically identical to the parent. Populations of animals that reproduce parthenogenically are usually entirely female. Animals ranging from rotifers to some amphibians reproduce through parthenogenesis.

Sexual reproduction is when two haploid gametes, one from each parent, fuse to form a zygote, which develops into an offspring genetically different from the parents. This fertilization can take place externally, as is the case of many aquatic organisms that release their unfertilized gametes into the water, or internally. As animals have evolved, they have developed special structures for the production of gametes, for the fertilization process, and in the case of viviparous animals that give birth to live young, for the support and nourishment of the developing young. Collectively, these structures are known as the reproductive system. In most species, including humans, the anatomy of the male and the female reproductive systems are significantly different.

The Male Reproductive System

The male reproductive system has two major functions:

- It produces **sperm** cells, the male gametes, through the process of spermatogenesis. (Spermatogenesis is covered in the chapter on genetics.)

- It produces **semen**, a fluid that acts as vehicle and nourishment for sperm as they make their way through the female reproductive system on their way to fertilize the egg.

The **testes** are the male gonads: they produce the sperm, which is the male gamete. More specifically, sperm cells are produced in the seminiferous tubules of the testes. (In addition to producing sperm, the testes also produce the hormone testosterone.) Since sperm can only develop at a temperature slightly lower than the normal mammalian body temperature, evolution has provided the needed lower temperature by placing the testes outside the body in a sac called the scrotum.

The seminiferous tubules empty into a long tube called the vas deferens, which joins the urethra just below the bladder and thereby provides a means of exit from the body through the penis. The penis is a spongy organ that can become erect during periods of sexual excitement. During erection, arteries in the penis dilate, engorging the erectile tissue with blood. This simultaneously compresses the veins that drain blood from the penis, trapping blood in the spongy tissue, causing it to become rigid.

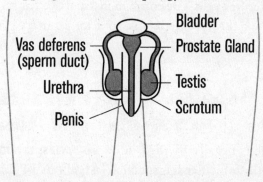

The Female Reproductive System

While the male reproductive system is designed to produce and deposit sperm in the female, the female reproductive system has the more formidable task of receiving the male gametes, producing the female gametes, and, in the event of fertilization, maintaining and supporting a pregnancy.

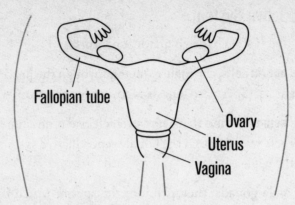

Fallopian tube

Ovary
Uterus
Vagina

The female reproductive system consists of the external genitalia, known as the vulva and vagina, the **uterus**, which supports the developing fetus, the **Fallopian tubes**, which connect the uterus with the two ovaries, and the **ovaries**, which produce the ova, or egg cells, in addition to the female sex hormones. Also included are the mammary glands, which produce milk to nourish the young.

The Menstrual Cycle

The functioning of the reproductive system in human females is dependent upon cyclical fluctuation of hormone levels that repeats regularly every 28 days. This cycle, known as the menstrual cycle, primarily affects the ovaries and the uterus. The effects of the menstrual cycle on the ovaries is called the ovarian cycle, while the effects on the uterus is called the uterine cycle. The entire menstrual cycle is regulated by a hormonal feedback loop involving the hypothalamus, anterior pituitary gland, and the ovaries.

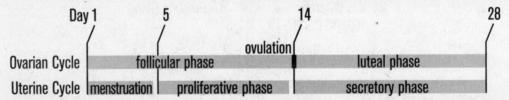

The ovarian cycle is usually divided into two stages: the **follicular stage** and the **luteal stage**. During the follicular stage, which lasts about 14 days, follicle-stimulating hormone (FSH) from the anterior pituitary gland stimulates a **follicle** in the ovary to mature. A follicle is an ovum and the cells that encapsulate it. As the ovum matures, the surrounding cells of the follicle begin to produce estrogen. After about 14 days of increasing estrogen levels, the estrogen in the blood reaches a concentration that sets in motion a series of events resulting in the release of luteinizing hormone (LH) from the anterior pituitary gland. Luteinizing hormone causes the mature follicle to release the now mature ovum into the Fallopian tube. This is called **ovulation**.

The second 14 days of the ovarian cycle are called the luteal phase. After ovulation, the remnants of the follicle form into a structure called the **corpus luteum**. Just as FSH from the anterior pituitary stimulated the follicle to mature, LH affects the corpus luteum and causes it to release progesterone and some estrogen. After about 14 days, if the ovum is not fertilized, the corpus luteum degenerates, progesterone and estrogen levels fall, and the cycle starts again with the follicular phase.

The estrogen secreted by the follicle and the progesterone and estrogen secreted by the corpus luteum affect the lining of the uterus. The cycle of hormones in the ovarian cycle push the uterus through a 28-day cycle as well. The uterine cycle contains three phases: **menstruation**, the **proliferative phase,** and the **secretory phase.**

In the first few days of the follicular phase, after the corpus luteum has disintegrated, and the follicle is in the earliest stages of maturation, estrogen and progesterone levels are relatively low. The low levels of these hormones causes the cells of the uterine lining to slough off, releasing a bloody discharge commonly referred to as menstruation, or a woman's period. The onset of menstruation marks the first day of the 28 day menstrual cycle, and usually lasts about four to five days. The nine-day long proliferative phase begins as the follicle continues to mature, estrogen levels rise, and a new uterine lining begins to build up along the uterine walls. Were fertilization to occur, the lining would support the development of an embryo. This lasts about nine days. After ovulation, the secretory phase begins as the corpus luteum develops and produces progesterone. Progesterone causes new blood vessels to grow within the uterine lining. If fertilization does not occur, the corpus luteum degenerates, hormone levels fall, and the uterine lining once again sloughs off during menstruation.

Fertilization and Development of the Embryo

As the egg is swept along the Fallopian tubes on its way to the uterus, it may encounter sperm deposited by the male. Fertilization occurs if one of these sperm cells is successful in penetrating the egg. The sperm nucleus fuses with the nucleus of the egg cell and a diploid **zygote** is formed. Within 24 hours, the zygote begins to divide by mitosis. First it divides into two cells, then four, then eight, until a solid ball of cells known as the **morula** forms. The morula eventually encounters and implants itself in the lining of the uterus.

At this point, the menstrual cycle halts. From its place in the uterine lining, the dividing embryo releases a hormone known as human chorionic gonadotropin (hCG). This hormone prevents the corpus luteum from disintegrating, prolonging the production of progesterone and estrogen. Rather than slough off, the uterine lining further thickens. The corpus luteum continues to produce estrogen and progesterone until the placenta takes over this function about three months into the pregnancy.

After it implants in the uterine lining, the solid ball of cells that is the morula begins to hollow out into a spherical ball of cells known as the **blastula**. The blastula has a round cell wall called the trophoblast, which encloses a hollow space known as the blastocoel and a small cluster of cells known as the inner cell mass.

Organismal Biology

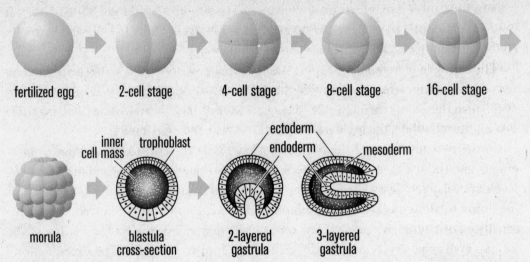

fertilized egg   2-cell stage   4-cell stage   8-cell stage   16-cell stage

morula   blastula cross-section   2-layered gastrula   3-layered gastrula

Before the formation of the blastula, all cells were identical, or undifferentiated. The cells of the inner cell mass and the trophoblast are the first sign of cell differentiation. Soon, the cells of the inner cell mass begin to divide more rapidly than the rest of the cells in the blastocyst. As development continues, the cells of the inner cell mass will go on to form the **embryo**, and the cells of the trophoblast will form the membranes that surround the developing human.

As the cells of the inner cell mass rapidly divide, a small pocket begins to form on one end of the blastocyst. This new structure is called the **gastrula**. At first the gastrula consists of two cell layers: an outer layer known as the ectoderm, and an inner layer known as the endoderm. Soon, a third layer, called the mesoderm, begins to form between the ectoderm and endoderm. These three cell layers, or germ layers, go on to form the various organs and structure of the human as they differentiate. Over the course of about eight weeks, the germ layer cells build all of the organs, and the embryo is now classified as a **fetus**. In humans, the fetus continues to grow and mature in the womb for an additional seven months, until birth.

Reproductive Support Structures

Numerous structures within the womb support the embryo as it develops. The largest and most important is the **placenta**. The blood vessels of the placenta come in close proximity with the blood vessels of the mother so that nutrients and oxygen can diffuse from the mother's bloodstream into the bloodstream of the developing embryo or fetus. There is no direct blood contact through the placenta; the mother and fetus have completely separate blood circulation. The placenta is connected to the circulatory system of the embryo or fetus through the umbilical cord.

Four membranes surround, nourish, and protect the embryo. The first membrane is the yolk sac, which provides stored nutrients to the developing embryo. The yolk sac is very small in placental mammals, which get their nutrients through the placenta, but in animals that develop in eggs, such as birds and reptiles, the yolk will be the sole source of nutrients throughout the entire course of development. The second membrane is the amnion, which is filled with a clear fluid known as the amniotic fluid. This fluid provides a cushion for the embryo so that bumps and jolts within the womb or in the external egg do not cause damage. The third membrane is the allantois. In placental mammals, the allantois develops into the umbilical cord, but in vertebrates that develop externally, the allantois is the site of waste disposal for the developing embryo. The fourth membrane is the chorion, which in humans forms the placenta. In vertebrates that develop in eggs, the chorion lines the inside of the shell and allows for gas exchange with the environment.

Animal Behavior

Animals' abilities to move create the possibility for copious interactions between organisms, giving rise to quite complex patterns of behavior. Animal behavior can come in the form of instincts and learned behavior. Instincts are inheritable, genetically coded behavior patterns that an animal possesses at birth. Learned behaviors are established and maintained as an animal responds to new situations. Learned behaviors are not passed down from parent to offspring genetically, but they can be taught.

Instinctual Behavior

Instinctual behavior can take the form of **simple reflexes** or **fixed-action patterns**. Simple reflexes are automatic responses to specific stimuli. Reflex behaviors do not originate from the brain in vertebrates. Instead, they are processed in the spinal cord. For example, if you touch a hot iron, the pain and heat receptors in your fingers send signals down a sensory neuron to your spinal cord, where a motor neuron is immediately stimulated to cause you to pull back your arm. The signal is actually sent to the brain after it has been acted upon by the spinal cord—you do not actually perceive pain until the brain processes the information.

Fixed-action patterns are complex behaviors that, like reflexes, are triggered by a specific stimulus. The stimuli that cause fixed-action behavior are often more complex than the stimulus behind simple reflex behavior. Once triggered, fixed-action patterns often proceed to completion, even if the stimulus is removed. For example, female geese demonstrate a fixed-action pattern called egg rolling. If a female goose spots an egg outside of her nest, the mother goose will use her beak to roll the egg back into the nest. If the egg is taken away in the middle of this process, she will continue to move her neck and beak as if she were rolling an egg, even though the egg is no longer there. Fixed-action patterns do not need to be learned; they are present in an individual from birth.

Many animals, most notably birds, exhibit a special type of learned behavior called **imprinting**. Imprinting occurs when an animal quickly learns, during a short critical period, to recognize an individual, object, or location. The most common example of imprinting is the case of birds that can walk soon after hatching. Newly hatched infant birds must follow their mother to survive. Soon after they hatch, these birds go through a critical period during which they treat the first moving object they see as their mother. If the first organism a young bird sees is a pig, it will imprint the pig as its mother. Imprinting is nearly impossible to reverse.

Learned Behavior

Unlike instincts, which are present at birth, an individual organism learns some behavior over the course of its life. The simplest form of learning is known as **habituation**. Habituation occurs when a non-harmful stimulus that would normally cause an animal to respond is repeated over and over again until the animal learns to ignore it. The classic example of habituation is seen in the common garden snail. When its body is poked, a snail will withdraw into its shell. However, if it is poked repeatedly without any real harm done, the snail ignores the stimulus and ceases to retreat into its shell.

Conditioning, or **associative learning**, occurs when an animal learns to associate a specific stimulus with a set behavior. There are two types of conditioning: classical conditioning and operant conditioning. Classical conditioning is merely the association of a new stimulus with a stimulus that is recognized by instinct. The most famous example of classical conditioning is Pavlov's dog. In an experiment, Russian scientist Ivan Pavlov would ring a bell a few moments before feeding a dog. Every time he fed the dog, he would first ring the bell. The sight and smell of food causes a dog to salivate instinctually. But after ringing the bell before feeding the dog a number of times, Pavlov discovered that the dog would salivate whether or not food was present. The dogs associated the sound of the bell with the stimulus of food.

Operant conditioning is sometimes called trial-and-error learning. It involves the establishment of a new behavior or the avoidance of an old behavior because of the association of a reward or punishment. For example, a rat will learn to press a lever in order to release its food. It learns a new behavior, the pressing of the lever, because it associates this behavior with a reward. Similarly, the rat can be trained to avoid a certain colored spot in its cage if standing in that spot becomes associated with a mild electrical shock. Normally the rat would have no reason to avoid such a spot, but because of the association of a punishment with this behavior, it stays away.

Both classical and operant conditioning can be undone if the association between stimulus and behavior or behavior and punishment/reward does not last. For example, if the rat presses the lever and no food comes out for several tries, it will cease to press the lever. This unlearning is called extinction.

Circadian Rhythms

Many animal behaviors, such as sleep and wakefulness, foraging times, and metabolic rate, operate according to daily cycles known as circadian rhythms. These rhythms can be traced to the periods of light and dark in the day, but the rhythms remain even if for a short time an animal cannot see the changing of the light. In other words, animals have a sort of internal clock that regulates their behavior.

Structure and Function of Plants

Plants are as intricate and complicated as animals. But you wouldn't know that from looking at the SAT II Biology. Though the test covers almost all aspects of animal organismal biology, it covers plants in much less detail. This is not to say that you can ignore plants completely while studying for the test, just that you need to study the right things.

To begin with, you need to know what plants are, how plants differ from animals on both the cellular and organismal level, and the different categories of plants that exist. You should also know about the structure and function of the three most important parts of vascular plants: leaves, stems, and roots. In addition, it's a good idea to have a basic knowledge of how plants grow. Plants also have various and unique means of reproducing themselves that the SAT II may test. And finally, you should have some sense of plant "behaviors," which are called tropisms.

The General Plant Cell

We covered plants cells back in the chapter on Cellular and Molecular Biology, but it seemed a good idea to give a summary here.

- **Plants have all the organelles animal cells have.** Nucleus, ribosomes, mitochondria, endoplasmic reticulum, Golgi apparatus, etc.—all there.

- **Plants have chloroplasts.** Chloroplasts are special organelles that contain chlorophyll and allow plants to carry out photosynthesis.

- **Plant cells can sometimes have big vacuoles for storage.**

- **Plants are surrounded by a rigid cell wall made of cellulose,** in addition to the cell membrane that surrounds animal cells. These walls provide support.

Types of Plants

Just as there are many different kinds of animals, there also a variety of kinds of plants. The earliest plants had no special vascular tissues devoted to transport, meaning they could not grow to great heights because they couldn't transport necessary liquids and minerals over long distances. These plants are called **nonvascular** or **nontracheophyte**. **Tracheophytes**, also called vascular plants, do have special vascular tissues for transport.

Vascular Tissues

Vascular tissues are composed of specialized cells that create "tubes" through which materials can flow throughout the plant body. These vessels are continuous throughout the plant, allowing for the efficient and controlled distribution of water and nutrients. In addition to this transport function, vascular tissues also support the plant. The two types of vascular tissue are xylem and phloem.

Xylem

Xylem consists of a "pipeline" of dead cells arranged end to end for water and mineral transport. When the cells that form xylem die at maturity, the nucleus and cytoplasm disintegrate, leaving a hollow tunnel through which fluids can move. The xylem carries water and dissolved minerals upward from the roots through the stem and leaves of the plant. In larger seed plants, xylem cells are specialized into tracheids and vessel elements. Vessels are wider and better at conducting water than the tracheids.

In addition to distributing nutrients, xylem provides structural support. In fact, the material commonly known as "wood" is actually xylem. After a time, the xylem at the center of older trees (woody dicots) ceases to function in transport and takes on a purely supportive role.

Phloem

Unlike xylem, the cells that make up phloem are living at maturity and can carry materials both up *and* down the plant body. Phloem is comprised of sieve elements, which are arranged end to end to form passageways, and companion cells, which are closely associated with the sieve elements, even though their exact function is unknown. Mature companion cells have both a nucleus and cytoplasm, while the mature sieve elements contain only cytoplasm; for this reason it is thought that the nuclei of companion cells may control the activities of neighboring sieve elements. Phloem is responsible for distributing the products of photosynthesis, such as amino acids and carbohydrates, from the leaves to the rest of the plant.

Types of Tracheophytes

There are also distinctions among the tracheophytes. Ferns were the first tracheophytes to evolve. Ferns are notable because they reproduce through the use of spores, and do not use seeds. Otherwise, in SAT II Biology world, you don't really have to worry about them. The two tracheophytes that are more important are gymnosperms and angiosperms.

Gymnosperms

Gymnosperms were the first tracheophytes to use seeds for reproduction. The seeds develop in protective structures called cones. A gymnosperm will contain some cones that are female and some that are male. Female cones produce spores that, after fertilization, become eggs are enclosed in seeds that fall to the ground. Male cones produce pollen, which is taken by the wind and fertilizes female eggs by that means. Coniferous trees such as pines and firs are good examples of gymnosperms.

Angiosperms

Angiosperms, the flowering plants, are the most highly evolved plants, and the most dominant in present times. Angiosperms are also the type of plant that the SAT II mainly focuses on. In fact, you don't really need to know anything about nontracheophytes, ferns, and gymnosperms beyond what we've already told you. The further discussions of plant biology in this chapter will focus on angiosperms (though what is true for angiosperms is also often true for the other types of plants).

As for angiosperms, there are actually two kinds: **monocots** and **dicots**. Monocots include grasses, grains, and other narrow-leaved angiosperms. Monocots are named for the presence of a single cotyledon (seed leaf) during embryonic development. In general, the veins of monocot leaves are parallel, the flower parts occur in multiples of three, and a fibrous root system is present. Bundles of vascular tissue are scattered throughout the stem instead of appearing in a single ring. Dicots, such as maples, oaks, elms, sunflowers, and roses, originate from embryos with two cotyledons. They are further distinguished from monocots by the branched network of veins in their leaves, the occurrence of their flower parts in groups of four or five, and the presence of a taproot, which is a single main root with tributaries off of it. The vascular bundles of dicots are arranged in a tubular pattern in the stem.

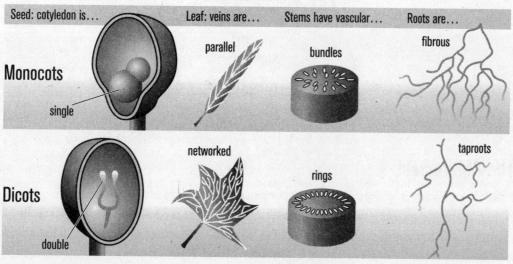

Seed: cotyledon is... | Leaf: veins are... | Stems have vascular... | Roots are...

Monocots — single — parallel — bundles — fibrous

Dicots — double — networked — rings — taproots

Leaves

Leaves are the sites of photosynthesis in plants. The leaves' broad, flattened surfaces gather energy from sunlight, while apertures on their undersides bring in carbon dioxide and release oxygen. On its two exteriors, the leaf has layers of epidermal cells that secrete a waxy, nearly impermeable **cuticle** to protect against water loss and fungal or bacterial attack. The only way gases can diffuse in or out of the leaf is though **stomata**, small openings on the underside of the leaf. The opening and closing of the stomata occurs through the swelling or relaxing of **guard cells**. If the plant wants to limit the diffusion of gases and the transpiration of water, the guard cells swell together and close the stomata.

The tissues between the epidermal cells are called **mesophyll**. The mesophyll can be further broken down into two layers, the **palisade layer** and the **spongy layer**. Both layers are packed with chloroplasts, the factories of photosynthesis. In the palisade layer, chloroplasts are lined in columns just below the epidermal cells, to facilitate the capture of light. In the spongy layer, cells are less ordered and more diffuse, leaving large intracellular spaces that facilitate the exchange of carbon dioxide and oxygen.

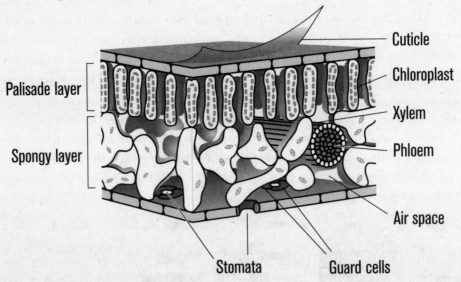

Overall, it is to the plant's advantage to maximize the gas exchange and sunlight trapping surface area, while keeping leaf thickness to a minimum so that once gases enter the leaf through the stomata, they can diffuse easily throughout the leaf cells.

The Chloroplast

Like mitochondria, chloroplasts are comprised of a double membrane layer, with an intermembrane space between. The inner membrane is folded into multiple stacks of flattened, disk-shaped compartments. Each such compartment is called a **thylakoid**, and a stack of thylakoids is called a **granum**. The thylakoid membrane separates the chloroplast interior into two very different compartments: the thylakoid space inside the thykaloids where the photosynthetic **chlorophyll** resides, and the **stroma**, a fluid that lies outside the stacked disks and takes up the rest of the organelle.

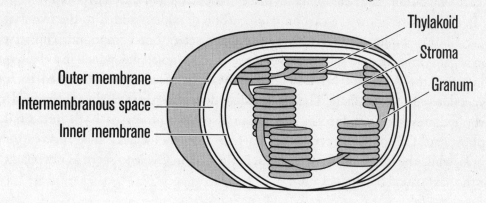

Photosynthesis

In photosynthesis, plants (and other photosynthetic autotrophs) use the energy from sunlight to create the carbohydrates necessary for cell respiration. More specifically, plants take water and carbon dioxide and transform them into glucose and oxygen:

$$6CO_2 + 6H_2O + \text{light energy} \rightarrow C_6H_{12}O_6 + 6O_2$$

This general equation of photosynthesis represents the combined effects of two different stages. The first stage is called the light reaction, since it is dependent on light. The dark reaction, the second stage, does not need light.

The Light Reaction

The light reaction, also called the light-dependent reaction, takes place within the thylakoid spaces of the grana in the chloroplast. When sunlight strikes the chlorophyll contained within the thylakoid spaces, electrons become excited and infused with energy, and they are transferred down an electron transport chain similar to the one found in aerobic respiration. The energy in the electrons is used to set up a proton gradient across the membrane of the thylakoid spaces. Protons flowing back across the thylakoid membrane according to the concentration gradient are harnessed to produce ATP and NADPH. As a by-product of this process, molecules of water are split into molecular hydrogen and oxygen. The plant needs the hydrogen to produce ATP. The oxygen you're breathing right now is some of that waste product.

The purpose of the light reaction is to make the usable energy necessary to run the dark reaction.

Organismal Biology

The Dark Reaction

The dark reaction is also referred to as the light-independent reaction, the **Calvin Cycle**, or carbon fixation. The reaction takes place in the stroma of the chloroplast.

In the dark reaction, the carbon from carbon dioxide is added to the five-carbon sugar, ribulose biphosphate (RuBP) to produce a six-carbon compound. This six-carbon sugar is immediately split into two three-carbon molecules, which in a chain reaction using the ATP and NADPH from the light reaction are modified to form glyceraldehyde 3-phosphate. The glyceraldehyde 3-phosphate can be synthesized into carbohydrates such as glucose, and it can also be synthesized back into ribulose biphosphate. One of the glyceraldehyde 3-phosphate molecules is made into carbohydrates, while the other molecules remain in the Calvin Cycle to serve as raw materials for the next round of production.

Roots

The roots of a plant draw water and minerals from the soil and pass them upward through xylem and phloem to the stem and leaves. Roots are also responsible for storing the plant's organic nutrients, which are passed downward from the leaves through the phloem. Radiating from the roots is a system of root hairs, which vastly increase the absorptive surface area of the roots. Roots also anchor the plant in the soil.

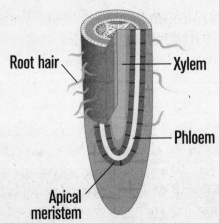

Growth in Vascular Plants

Vascular plants undergo two kinds of growth, primary growth and secondary growth. Primary growth occurs in the apical meristems, located at the tip of both root and shoot, and is mainly a growth of vertical length. The **meristems** are regions of rapid mitotic division, almost a cell-making factory. When a cell divides, one of its offspring moves down into the plant body where it elongates, and the other remains in the meristem to divide again.

Secondary growth is a growth of thickness. Secondary growth is a product of two different, though related, tissues, which both fall under the umbrella-term lateral meristems. **Vascular cambium** exists between xylem and phloem; on its inside the cambium produces what is known as secondary xylem; on its outside it forms secondary phloem. The primary xylem and phloem are pushed further inward and outward. The vascular cambium is more productive during the growing seasons. During the rest of the year it creates little growth. This phenomenon creates distinct rings of growth, each ring representing a single growing season. By studying these rings, it is possible to calculate the age of a plant, and it's even possible to determine the specific conditions of a particular growing season. The second lateral meristem is called cork cambium and is responsible for the formation of cork (bark), which replaces the epidermis to form the protective covering of shoot and root.

Controlling Growth: Plant Hormones

Plant growth is controlled by plant hormones, which influence cell differentiation, elongation, and division. Some plant hormones also affect the timing of reproduction and germination.

- **Auxins.** The primary function of the auxin hormones is to elongate plant cells in the stem. Auxins are also responsible for root development, secondary growth in the vascular cambium, inhibition of lateral branching, and fruit development.

- **Kinins** promote cell division and tissue growth in leaf, stem, and root. Kinins are also involved in the development of chloroplasts, fruits, and flowers. In addition, they have been shown to delay senescence (aging), especially in leaves, which is one reason that florists use cytokinins on freshly cut flowers.

- **Gibberellins** stimulate growth, especially elongation of the stem, and can also end the dormancy period of seeds and buds by encouraging germination. Additionally, gibberellins play a role in root growth and differentiation.

- **Ethylene** controls the ripening of fruits. It also contributes to the senescence (aging) of plants by promoting leaf loss and other changes. Ethylene can bring buds and seeds out of dormancy, initiate flower development, and promote radial (horizontal) growth in roots and stems.

- **Inhibitors** restrain growth and maintain the period of dormancy in seeds and buds.

Plant Behavior: Tropisms

When people think about plants growing, they generally think of them growing straight up, or growing wider. But plants also display other types of growth in response to the stimuli within their environment. These responses to stimuli are called tropisms, and are controlled by plant hormones. There are three main tropisms:

- **Phototropism** is the tendency of a plant to move toward light. Phototropism results from the rapid elongation of cells on the dark side of the plant, which causes the plant to bend in the opposite direction.

- **Gravitropism** refers to a plant's tendency to grow toward or against gravity. A plant that displays positive gravitropism will grow downward, toward the earth. A plant that displays negative gravitropism will grow upward, away from the earth. Most plants are negatively gravitropic. Gravitropism is also controlled by auxin. In a horizontal root or stem, auxin is concentrated in the lower half, pulled by gravity. In a positively gravitropic plant, this auxin concentration will *inhibit* cell growth on that lower side, causing the stem to bend downward. In a negatively gravitropic plant, this auxin concentration will *inspire* cell growth on that lower side, causing the stem to upward downward.

- **Thigmotropism**, a reaction to touch, causes parts of the plant to thicken or coil as they touch or are touched by environmental entities. Tree trunks, for instance, grow thicker when exposed to strong winds and vines tend to grow straight until they encounter a substrate to wrap around.

Photoperiodism

Plants have a wide variety of flowering strategies involving what time of year they will flower and, consequently, reproduce. In many plants, flowering is dependent on the duration of day and night; this is called photoperiodism.

All flowering plants have been placed in one of three categories with respect to photoperiodism: short-day plants, long-day plants, and day-neutral plants. Despite their names, however, scientists have discovered that it is the uninterrupted length of *night* rather than length of day that is the most important factor in determining when and whether plants will bloom. Short-day plants begin to bloom when the hours of darkness in a 24-hour period rise above a critical level, as when days shorten in the autumn. These plants include poinsettias, chrysanthemums, goldenrod, and asters. Long-day plants begin to flower when the duration of night decreases past a critical point, as when days lengthen in the spring and summer. Spinach, lettuce, and most grains are long-day plants. Finally, many plants are day-neutral, which means that the onset of flowering is not controlled by photoperiod at all. These plants, which are independent both of night length and day length, include tomatoes, sunflowers, dandelions, rice, and corn.

Plant Reproduction

Plants can reproduce both asexually and sexually. Each type of reproduction has its benefits and disadvantages.

Asexual Reproduction

Through asexual reproduction, many plants can produce genetically identical offshoots (clones) of themselves, which then develop into independent plants. This process is also called **vegetative propagation**. The many modes of vegetative propagation include the production of specialized structures such as tubers, runners, and bulbs. Grafting is an artificial form of vegetative propagation. The advantages to this kind of asexual reproduction, which can occur either naturally or artificially, stem from the fact that it can occur more rapidly than seed propagation and can allow a genetically superior plant to produce unlimited copies of itself without variation.

Tubers: As seen in potatoes, tubers are fleshy underground storage structures composed of enlarged parts of the stem. A tuber functions in asexual propagation as a result of the tiny scale leaves equipped with buds that grow on its surface. Each of these buds can form a new plant, genetically identical to the parent.

Runners: Such as those found on strawberry plants, runners are slender, horizontal stems that spread outward from the main plant. Entirely new plants can develop from nodes located at intervals on the runners; each node can give rise to new roots and shoots.

Bulbs: Bulbs such as onions and tulips are roughly spherical underground buds with fleshy leaves extending from their short stems. Each bulb contains several other buds that can give rise to new plants.

Grafting: In grafting, two young plants are joined together, first by artificial means and then by tissue regeneration. Typically, a twig or bud is cut from one plant and joined to a rooted plant of a related species or variety. The twig or bud is called the scion, and the plant onto which is it grafted (and that provides the roots) is called the stock. The scion eventually develops into an entire shoot system. Grafting often allows horticulturalists to combine the best features of two different plants into one plant. Sometimes the stock and scion retain independent characteristics, and sometimes the stock alters the characteristics of the scion in some desirable way.

Organismal Biology

Sexual Reproduction in Plants

All plants undergo a life cycle that takes them through both haploid and diploid generations. The multicellular diploid plant structure is called the **sporophyte**, which produces spores through meiotic division. The multicellular haploid plant structure is called the gametophyte, which is formed from the spore and gives rise to the haploid gametes. The fluctuation between these diploid and haploid stages that occurs in plants is called the **alternation of generations**. The way in which the alternation of generations occurs in plants depends on the type of plant. In nonvascular plants, the dominant generation is haploid, so that the gametophyte comprises what we think of as the main plant. The opposite is true for tracheophytes, in which the diploid generation is dominant and the sporophyte comprises the main plant. The SAT II Biology only deals with the specifics of the tracheophyte alternation of generations, though nonvascular plants have a similar life cycle.

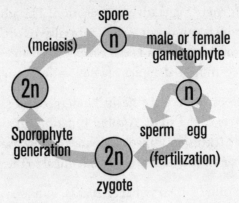

The dominant phase in the tracheophyte life cycle is the diploid (sporophyte) stage. The gametophytes are very small and cannot exist independent of the parent plant. The reproductive structures of the sporophyte (cones in gymnosperms and flowers in angiosperms), produce male and female haploid spores: microspores (male) and megaspores (female). These spores give rise to similarly sexually differentiated gametophytes, which in turn produce gametes. Fertilization occurs when a male and female gamete join to form a zygote. The resulting embryo, encased in a seed coating, will eventually become a new sporophyte.

Reproduction in Flowering Plants

Angiosperms are special because they have developed special reproductive systems, which are none other than the flowers you should always take time to stop and smell. To understand angiosperm reproduction, then, the first thing you have to do is know the structure of the flower.

The Flower

Flowers, the reproductive structures of angiosperms, are adaptations designed to attract insects and other pollen-bearing animals to the plant to aid in pollen dispersal. For this reason, flowers are most often colorful and showy; not surprisingly, plants that rely on wind (instead of insects) for pollen dispersal have flowers that are more likely to be small and drab.

The flower is composed of four organs: the **sepal**, **petal**, **stamen**, and **pistil**. Sepals and petals are not directly involved in reproduction, while the stamen and pistil are the male and female reproductive organs. The stamen holds **pollen**, which is the male gamete, and the stigma is the site where a pollen grain must land in order to fertilize the female **ovules** that are located in the **ovary** at the base of the pistil. This ovary, an exclusive feature of angiosperms, encloses the ovules and develops into a fruit after fertilization.

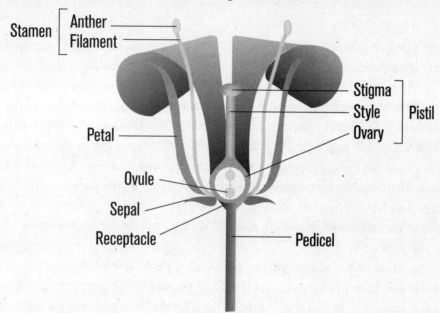

Angiosperm Fertilization

The female reproductive organ of angiosperms is the pistil, located in the middle of the flower. As in gymnosperms, the male gametophyte is the pollen grain. In order for fertilization to occur in most flowering plants, insects or other animals must transport the pollen to the pistil. A major distinguishing feature of angiosperms is the process of **double fertilization**, in which an angiosperm ovule contains an egg cell and a diploid fusion nucleus, which is created through the joining of two polar nuclei within the ovule.

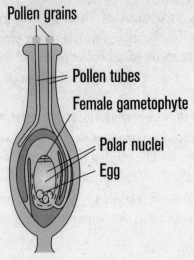

Pollen grains

Pollen tubes

Female gametophyte

Polar nuclei

Egg

When a pollen grain comes into contact with the stigma, or top of the pistil, it sends a pollen tube down into the ovary at the pistil's base. As the pollen tube penetrates the ovule, it releases two sperm cells. One fuses with the egg to create a diploid zygote, while the other joins with the fusion nucleus to form a triploid nucleus. This triploid nucleus turns into an endosperm, which nourishes the developing embryo (filling the role of gametophyte tissue in the gymnosperm seed). As in gymnosperms, the ovule becomes a seed, encasing the embryo and endosperm in a seed coat. But unlike gymnosperms, in angiosperms, the ovary containing the ovules develops into a fruit after fertilization. The fruit gives the embryos the double benefit of added protection against desiccation and increased dispersal, since it is eaten by far-ranging animals that then excrete the seeds.

Angiosperms either self-pollinate, in which a particular plant fertilizes itself, or cross-pollinate, in which one plant is fertilized by another of the same species. Cross-pollination generally produces far more vigorous plants, and is encouraged through differential development of the male and female gametophytes on a flower, or through the positioning of these gametophytes so that self-pollination is difficult.

Review Questions

1. A disease that causes a defect in the Myelin sheath would be dangerous because

    A. action potentials would be conducted too slowly along the neurons
    B. muscles would not contract when stimulated
    C. the thyroid gland would not be able to produce thyroxine
    D. bone tissue would not be properly maintained
    E. the body would not be able to fight disease

2.   All of the following are considered to be endocrine glands EXCEPT

    A.   the pituitary gland
    B.   the thyroid gland
    C.   the salivary glands
    D.   the ovaries
    E.   the adrenal glands

3.   Which of the following statements are true?

    I.   Arteries have muscular walls that can regulate the flow of blood passing through them.
    II.   Arteries contain valves that prevent the flow of blood in the wrong direction.
    III.   Veins have muscular walls that can regulate the flow of blood passing through them.

    A.   I only
    B.   III only
    C.   I and II only
    D.   I and III only
    E.   I, II, and III

4.   What is the primary advantage of the four-chambered heart?

    A.   It increases blood pressure.
    B.   It pumps blood to the lungs more often, so blood is better oxygenated.
    C.   It separates oxygenated and deoxygenated blood.
    D.   It lowers blood pressure and the threat of heart attacks.
    E.   It supplies the brain with more blood for cognition.

5.   The respiratory system is important in obtaining oxygen for the tissues and

    A.   regulating pH of the blood by controlling how much oxygen is dissolved in the plasma
    B.   regulating pH of the blood by controlling how much carbon dioxide is dissolved in the plasma
    C.   regulating blood pressure by releasing hormones from the lungs that control heart rate
    D.   playing a role in regulating the level of cholesterol in the blood
    E.   obtaining some nutrients, such as vitamin K, from the atmosphere when supplies are limited

6.   After the ovarian follicle releases the mature ovum into the Fallopian tube, the follicle

    A.   dissolves within the ovary, ceasing to produce estrogen
    B.   remains in the ovary, producing estrogen until the end of the ovarian cycle
    C.   forms the corpeus luteum and begins to produce progesterone
    D.   begins to support another developing oocyte
    E.   is shed from the ovary and released in the menstrual fluid

7.   A man goes swimming in a pond. As he walks back to his car, he notices that several newly hatched ducklings are following his moves. This is an example of

A.   tropism
B.   conditioning
C.   sympathetic nervous system
D.   associative learning
E.   imprinting

8.   The elimination of carbon dioxide from the body is completed by the

I.   circulatory system
II.   respiratory system
III. excretory system

A.   I only
B.   II only
C.   III only
D.   I and II only
E.   I, II, and III

9.   Which of the following contains the highest concentration of chloroplasts?

A.   stomata
B.   epidermal layer
C.   palisade mesophyll
D.   phloem
E.   cuticle

10. During photosynthesis, carbohydrates are made

A.   during the light reaction
B.   from oxygen, water, and a three-carbon molecule
C.   in the grana
D.   in the stroma
E.   in order to begin the light reaction

Explanations

1.   (A)
The myelin sheath surrounds the axon of neurons and speeds up the propagation of action potentials by allowing them to skip along the axon.

2.   (C)
Of the glands in the answer choices, only the salivary glands do not release any hormones into the bloodstream. They release saliva into the mouth by way of ducts.

3.   (A)
Only arteries have muscular walls that can regulate blood flow. Because arterial blood pressure tends to be high compared to blood pressure in the veins, arteries do not contain valves to prevent backflow of blood. Veins do contain valves, however, because blood flows relatively sluggishly through them.

4.   (C)
The four-chambered heart is an evolutionary advance over the two-chambered heart. By splitting up oxygenated and deoxygenated blood, the four-chambered heart ensures that more highly oxygenated blood reaches the cells that need it. The four-chambered heart does not raise or lower blood pressure. Neither does it increase blood flow to the lungs or the brain.

5.   (B)
Because carbon dioxide is dissolved in the blood as carbonic acid, when levels of carbon dioxide in the blood are high, the pH tends to drop (the blood becomes more acidic). When carbon dioxide levels are low, the blood can become slightly more basic. Respiratory rate is adjusted to control for these factors. A safe pH level is extremely important for the operation of proteins, hormones, and enzymes.

6.   (C)
After the follicle releases the ovum during ovulation, it changes form to become the corpus luteum. The corpus luteum remains in the ovary producing progesterone and begins to disintegrate if fertilization does not take place.

7.   (E)
When a newly hatched bird first sees another moving object, it instinctually believes that the object is its mother and will follow it. This phenomenon is called imprinting. Tropisms occur in plants. Conditioning is a learned rather than instinctual behavior, as is associative learning. The sympathetic nervous system operates on the body in emergency situations.

8.   (D)
Carbon dioxide, a waste-product of cell respiration, diffuses from cells into the circulatory blood stream, and is expelled from the body through the lungs of the respiratory system.

9.   (C)
Most of photosynthesis takes place in the palisade layer of the leaf, so the cells of the palisade layer have the highest concentration of chloroplasts.

10. (D)
Chloroplasts make carbohydrates during the Calvin cycle, which occurs in the intermembrane space of the chloroplast called the stroma. The light reaction creates the ATP and NADPH that powers the Calvin cycle. Oxygen is a by-product of photosynthesis, not a raw material. Grana are the locations of the light reaction.

Ecology

THE EARTH IS A GREAT WEB OF INTERACTION between various biotic organisms and nonliving, abiotic factors that make up their environment. The study of this web, and of the interactions that shape both living organisms and the environment in which they live, is called ecology.

Ecology is a critical component of biology; in some sense, it is the place where everything we have learned up until now fits together and functions in the real world. Up until this chapter we have studied biology in an increasing hierarchy:

1. Biochemistry
2. The Cell
3. Tissue
4. Organ
5. Organism

Ecology takes individuals and puts them into larger contexts:

6. Population
7. Community
8. Ecosystem
9. Biome
10. Biosphere

Ecology is important on the SAT II Biology for another reason: it makes up about 13 percent of the questions on the core of the test. In addition, if you choose to take the Biology E—rather than the Biology M—version of the SAT II Biology, then another

25 percent of the test will have some relation to ecology. In other words, this chapter and the material it covers are crucial.

Populations

Ecologists are interested in the interactions between organisms. Since it takes more than one organism to have an interaction, the basic unit of ecology is the population. A population is a group of individuals that interbreed and share the same gene pool. While every individual in a species has the capacity to interbreed with any other individual, a population is a group of organisms that exist in the same specific geographic locale and actually *are* interbreeding. All the killer whales in the ocean make up a species, but only the killer whales that actually live and migrate together—only the killer whales that actually interbreed—make up a specific population.

Populations are much more than the sum of their parts: a population displays patterns and concerns that are not applicable to an individual organism. Whereas an individual is concerned with living for as long as possible and having as many offspring as it can, a population is concerned with maintaining its number given the resources at hand.

Population Growth

A vital characteristic of a population is the rate at which it grows. The rate of population growth depends upon a variety of factors, including birth rate, death rate, initial population size, and resources. With unlimited resources, a population can expand very rapidly. Two rabbits that live in Rabbit Utopia and have five male and five female offspring every four months will produce a population of 12 rabbits after four months and 72 rabbits after eight months. Sounds like nothing, right? After one year, the population will be 432 rabbits. After two years, there will be 93,312 rabbits. And after three years, the population will be more than 20 million rabbits. This rabbit population is following the trend of **exponential population growth**, in which there is nothing to limit the growth of a population, and that population correspondingly grows by exponential factors. A graph of exponential growth looks like this:

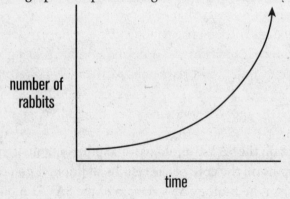

Perhaps Rabbit Utopia can grow enough lettuce to support 20 million rabbits, but normal nature cannot. In nature, when a population is small, the resources surrounding it are relatively large and the population will grow at near exponential levels. But as populations grow larger they need more food and take up more space, and resources become tight. Within the population, competition for food and space grows fierce, predators move in to sample some of the bounty, and disease increases. These factors slow the growth of the population well before it reaches into stratospheric levels. Eventually, the rate of population growth approaches zero, and the population comes to rest at a maximum number of individuals that can be maintained within a given environment. This value is the **carrying capacity** of the population, the point at which birth and death rates are equal.

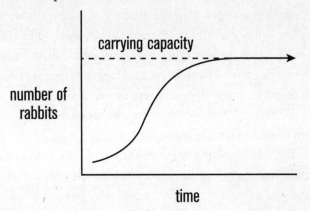

The carrying capacity of an environment will shift as an environment changes. When there is a drought and less vegetation, the carrying capacity of rabbits in a population will decrease since the environment will not be able to produce enough food. When there is a lot of rain and lush vegetation, the carrying capacity will increase.

Population Growth and Types of Reproduction

Population growth is affected by species' methods of reproduction. The two most important types of reproduction are asexual and sexual reproduction. Each type of reproduction has benefits and costs.

Asexual reproduction—such as that found in plants that reproduce by shoots or organisms that reproduce through parthenogenesis—requires less energy than its sexual counterpart. Because it requires less time and effort, asexual production allows a population to grow very quickly. For example, parthenogenesis occurs when an unfertilized egg develops offspring. Parthenogenesis creates female organisms that are identical to their mothers; the eggs of these female organisms undergo parthenogenesis and produce more females. By eliminating the necessity of males from the reproductive equation, parthenogenesis doubles the rate at which a population can grow. However, by eliminating males and sexual reproduction, populations that employ asexual reproduction limit their gene pool and the resulting diversity among members. In times when an environment is changing or competitive, the lack of variation damages these populations' ability to survive.

Sexual reproduction exhausts more energy and therefore progresses slowly. A population that reproduces through sexual reproduction will not grow as rapidly as an asexually reproducing population, but the sexual population will maintain the diversity of its gene pool. A sexually reproducing population is therefore more fit to survive in a changing or competitive environment.

Sexually reproducing organisms have two reproductive sub-strategies. Organisms such as insects have many small offspring that receive very little or no parental care, reach sexual maturity at a young age, and reproduce only one or few times. In an environment with abundant resources, this life-history strategy allows species to quickly reproduce and exploit opportunities for population growth. The disadvantage of this strategy is that it produces high mortality and great instability when resources dwindle. The alternative strategy is to bear fewer and larger offspring that receive intensive parental attention, mature gradually, and reproduce several times. Humans employ this strategy and are better suited to thrive in a competitive environment, exhibiting lower mortality rates and longer life spans. The disadvantage here is that the concerted investment of time and energy into a few individuals makes it difficult for a population to surmount large decreases in population size due to disasters or disease.

Communities

Just as individuals live within a population, populations exist within communities. A community refers to all the populations that interact with each other in a given environment and geographical area. The specific role and way of life of each population is called a niche. When populations have overlapping niches, a variety of types of interaction may occur, including competition, symbiosis, predation, and other food relationships. Communities are shaped over time by ecological succession.

The Niche

Each population in a community plays a unique role in the community. This role is referred to as a niche, and ranges from where the members of a population live, what they eat, when they sleep, how they reproduce, and every other characteristic that defines a population's lifestyle within a community. You can think of the niche as a sort of node in the network of interactions that make up a community. Wherever the niches of two populations overlap, interaction follows.

Competition

When two populations share some aspect of a niche, such as a nesting site or a food source, competition results. There are two basic outcomes of competition between populations.

One population will be a more effective competitor. The population that is more effective will eventually "win" the competition and drive the second, less effective population from the niche. With the niche freed, the winning population will grow to the carrying capacity of the niche.

The two populations will evolve into less competitive niches. If two populations compete on even terms, it may be beneficial for both populations to modify their niches so that the populations' niches overlap less, or not at all. In these cases, natural selection will favor individuals in both populations that have non-overlapping niches, and over time the two populations will evolve into different niches.

Symbiosis

Symbiosis refers to an intimate association between organisms, called symbionts. The symbiotic relationship may or may not be beneficial to the organisms involved. There are three kinds of symbiosis: **parasitism**, **commensalism**, and **mutualism**. Each type of symbiosis describes a different relationship of benefits between the two symbionts. A tapeworm is a parasite that lacks a digestive tract, and therefore infects a host and steals predigested food; parasites benefit while their hosts suffer. In commensalism, one species benefits and the other remains unaffected. Barnacles and whales live in a commensal relationship. Finally, in mutualism, both species benefit from the presence of and interactions with each other. Lichens, which consist of a fungus and alga that provide for each other, respectively, moisture and food through photosynthesis, are a good example of a mutualist relationship.

Predation

Predation refers to one organism eating another. Predation does *not* only refer to carnivores. Just as an eagle eating a rodent is a form of predation, so is a rodent munching on some grass. In fact, predation doesn't always result in the death of the prey. An antelope that gets eaten by a lion will die, but a tree that loses a few leaves to a hungry giraffe will go right on living.

Carrying capacity shifts in a periodic manner based on the cycles of predation. When the population of rabbits increases, the population of coyotes that eat the rabbits will also increase, since there's more food for the coyotes. However, at some point, there will be so many coyotes eating so many rabbits that the rabbit population will fall in number. The coyotes' great success in eating rabbits has eliminated their food source, and as the rabbit population declines, so will the coyote population. But wait! As the coyote population dwindles, the lack of predators allows the rabbit population to grow again, and so on.

Evolution Caused by Predation

The change in a population due to a shift in environment is one of the engines of evolution. Imagine the rabbits and their predators, the coyotes. As the coyotes increase in number, the rabbit population ceases to grow, and many rabbits are caught and eaten. As the coyotes increase in number, the carrying capacity of the rabbit population shrinks. But it is important to notice that not *all* rabbits are caught by the coyotes. The faster rabbits escape capture by the coyotes far more often than the slower rabbits. Fast rabbits survive and breed and have offspring, while slower rabbits get eaten. The next generation of rabbits will therefore be faster, since they are descended from faster parents—this is directional selection in action. The population of increasingly fast rabbits means that the coyotes have to be faster in order to catch the rabbits. More fast coyotes catch rabbits and live to reproduce, creating a next generation of faster coyotes. When two populations affect their mutual evolution in this manner it is called **coevolution**.

It is arguable that predation is actually helpful to the prey population. Since predators want to capture prey with the least possible effort, the weakest members of the prey population are usually targeted. In this way, the predators often remove from the gene pool of a population those prey animals that have the weakest and least fit alleles.

Food Relationships

Every organism needs food in order to live and has to get that food from somewhere. Every organism can be classified by where they fit into the food chain. Most broadly, all organisms fit into one of three camps: producers, consumers, and decomposers.

Producers

Producers are able to produce carbohydrates from the energy of the sun through photosynthesis, or, in some instances, from inorganic molecules through **chemosynthesis**. Because they can produce their own food, producers are also called **autotrophs**. Producers form the foundation of every food chain because only they can transform inorganic energy into energy that all other organisms can use. On land, plants, mosses, and photosynthetic bacteria are producers. In marine environments, green plants and algae are the main producers. In deep water environments near geothermal vents, chemosynthetic organisms are the main producers.

Consumers

Consumers cannot produce the energy and organic molecules necessary for life; instead, consumers must ingest other organisms in order to get these materials. Consumers are also called **heterotrophs** because they must consume other organisms in order to get the energy necessary for life. There are three types of consumers; the categories of consumers are based on which organisms a particular consumer preys upon. **Primary consumers**, such as sheep, grasshoppers, and rabbits, feed on producers. Since all producers are plants or plantlike, all primary consumers are herbivores, which is the name for a plant-eating animal. **Secondary consumers** eat primary consumers, making them carnivores—animals that eat other animals. Foxes and insect-eating birds are examples of secondary consumers. **Tertiary consumers** eat secondary consumers and are therefore carnivores. Polar bears that eat sea lions are tertiary consumers. Consumers that eat both producers and other consumers are called omnivores.

Decomposers

Also called **saprophytes**, decomposers feed on waste or dead material. Since they must ingest organic molecules in order to survive, decomposers are heterotrophs. In the process of getting the energy they need, decomposers break down complex organic molecules into their inorganic parts—carbon dioxide, nitrogen, phosphorous, etc.

Food Chains and Food Webs

All predatory interactions between producers and consumers in a community can be organized in food chains or more complex and realistic food webs. A food chain imagines a strictly linear interaction between the levels of producers and consumers we described above. An abstract food chain appears below on the left, with examples of animals that fit each category appearing on the right:

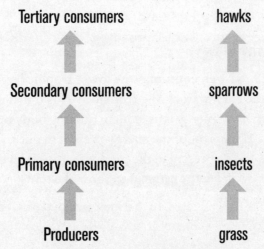

Each step in the food chain is referred to as a **trophic level**.

Food chains are simple and help us to understand the predation interactions between organisms, but because they are so simple, they aren't really accurate. For instance, while sparrows do eat insects, they also eat grass. In addition, the food chain makes it seem as if there are only four populations in a community, when most communities contain far more. Most organisms in a community hunt more than one kind of prey, and are hunted by more than one predator. These numerous predation interactions are best shown by a food web.

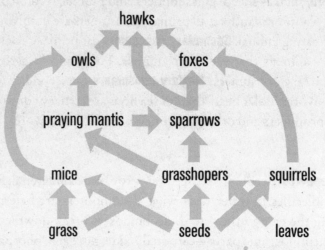

In fact, the more diverse and complicated the food relationships are in a community, the more stable that community will be. Imagine a community that was correctly described by the food chain grass → insects → sparrows → hawks. If some blight struck the grass population, the insect population would be decimated, which would destroy the sparrow population, etc. A more complex food web is able to absorb and withstand such disasters. If something were to happen to the grass in the food web, the primary consumers would all have some other food source to tide them over until the grass recovered.

Food Webs and Energy Flow

Each trophic level in a food web consumes the lower trophic level in order to obtain energy. But not all of the energy from one trophic level is transferred to the next. At each trophic level, most of the energy is used up in running body processes such as respiration. Typically, just 10 percent of the energy present in one trophic level is passed along to the next. If the energy present in the producer trophic level of of a food web is 10^7 kcal, you could draw an **energy pyramid** to show the transfer of energy from one trophic level to the next:

Tertiary consumers (10^4 kcal)

Secondary consumers (10^5 kcal)

Primary consumers (10^6 kcal)

Producers (10^7 kcal)

The energy lost between each trophic level affects the number of organisms that can occupy each trophic level. If the secondary consumer trophic level contains 10 percent of the energy present in the primary consumer level, it follows that there can only be about 10 percent as many secondary consumers as there are primary consumers. The energy pyramid is therefore also a **biomass pyramid** that shows the number of individuals in each trophic level.

Biological Magnification

Because biomass drops so dramatically from one trophic level to the next, any chemical present in a lower trophic level becomes heavily concentrated in higher trophic levels. Beginning in the 1940s, a pesticide called DDT was sprayed on crops to stop invading insects. The concentration of DDT in any local area was enough to kill insects, but not enough to hurt any of the larger organisms. But as each predator ate its prey, the DDT became concentrated in successive trophic levels. The small levels of DDT found in the insects became much more concentrated as it was swallowed and digested by predators. Eagles, sitting at the top of the food web, took in massive amounts of DDT in the course of eating their prey. The DDT caused the eagles to lay soft eggs that could not protect the developing embryos inside.

Ecological Succession

Just as the people living in your neighborhood can come and go, ecological communities change over time. One way a community can change is if external conditions shift. If the weather in a certain geographical area suddenly gets colder, certain populations will be better off and will thrive, while others will shrink and disappear.

However, change in communities is not always caused by external factors: populations can change the environments in which they live simply by living in them. The success of a particular population in a particular area will change the environment to the advantage of other populations. In fact, the originally successful population often changes the environment to its own detriment. In this way, the populations within a community change over time, often in quite predictable ways. The change in a community caused by the affects of the populations within it is called ecological succession.

The first population to move into a geographical area is referred to as a **pioneer organism**. If this pioneer population is successful in its new location, it will change the environment in such a way that new populations can move in. As populations are replaced, changing plant forms bring with them different types of animals. Typically, as a community moves through the stages of succession, it is characterized by an increase in total biomass, a greater capacity to retain nutrients within the system, increasing species diversity, and increasing size and life spans of organisms. Eventually, the community will reach a point where the mixture of populations creates no new changes in the environment. At this point, the specific populations in the stable community are said to make up a **climax community**. While individuals within a climax community will come and go, the essential makeup of the populations within the climax community will stay constant.

Which species are dominant in a particular climax community is determined by unique factors of that geographical area, such as temperature, rainfall, and soil acidity. Since a climax community does not change the environment, it also does not affect its own dominance; a climax community will remain dominant unless destroyed by a significant change in climate, or some catastrophic event such as a fire or volcanic eruption.

Succession in Action

Ready for some action? Imagine a catastrophic event: a forest fire rages through the Green Mountains of Vermont. The fires burn everything and leave behind a barren, rocky expanse.

The population of trees that once lived in this area can't grow back because the fire has changed the ground composition. Without tree roots to act as anchors, rain washes away the soil and the ground becomes rocky and barren. This rocky ground, however, proves ideal to lichens, the pioneer population. The lichens colonize the rocks and thrive. As part of their life process, lichens produce acids that break down rock into soil. Lichens need solid places to survive: they are victims of their own success. Mosses and other herbs are well suited to living in the shallow soil environment created by the lichen, and they replace the lichen as the dominant population.

The mosses and herbs continue to build up the soil. As the soil deepens, the conditions favor plants with longer roots, such as grasses. Eventually the land becomes suitable for shrubs, and then for trees. The early dominant trees in the community will be species like poplar, which thrive in bright, sunlit conditions. As more trees come to live in the area, though, there is less sunlight for growing trees, and the poplar do less well than trees such as maples that can grow in shade. Eventually, the maples come to dominate the community, since they do not change the soil and the shade they give off proves most helpful to the growth of their own kind. The community has reached its climax community, with maple as the dominant species. During all this time, don't forget, the changing vegetation has brought with it various changes in animal populations.

The SAT II Biology is most likely to test your knowledge of ecological succession in an originally rocky area, as we just covered, or in a pond. Succession in a pond follows a general pattern. Originally, the pond will contain protozoa, some small fish, and algae. As individual organisms die and water runs into the pond, sediment begins building up at the bottom and the pond grows shallower. The shallower pond becomes marshlike and fills with reeds and cattails. The standing water eventually disappears, and the land is merely moist: grasses and shrubs come to dominate. As the land grows even less moist, it becomes woodland. And as trees come to dominate, the climax community will arise from a species that can grow in the shade of its neighbors.

Ecological Succession vs. Evolution

For the SAT II Biology, do not get confused between ecological succession and evolution. In ecological succession, the populations that make up a community change, but the characteristics of the individuals within the population will not change over time. Ecological succession is something that happens to communities, while evolution happens to populations. Although succession has different rates, it is much faster overall than evolution.

Ecosystems

The dominant species in a climax community interact with and depend on nonliving (abiotic) factors in that environment. The most important abiotic factors in an environment, and for the SAT II Biology, are the chemical cycles, the availability of sunlight and oxygen, the character of the soil, and the regulation of these various phenomena. Together, the biotic and abiotic elements make up an ecosystem.

Chemical Cycles

Inorganic elements such as carbon, nitrogen, and water pass through the environment in various forms. These elements are vital to life: they are consumed, excreted, respired, and otherwise utilized by living things. The passages of these elements between organisms and the abiotic environment are called the chemical cycles.

The Carbon Cycle

The carbon cycle begins when plants use CO_2 from the air to produce glucose, which both animals and plants use in respiration and other life processes. Animals consume some of these plants as a source of food. Animals use what they can of the carbon matter and excrete the rest as waste that decays into CO_2. Plant and animal respiration releases gaseous CO_2. The carbon that plants and animals do use remains in their bodies until death. After death, decay sends the organic compounds back into the Earth and CO_2 back into the atmosphere.

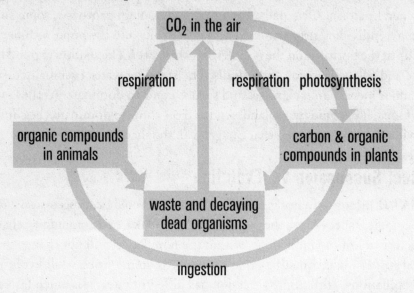

The Nitrogen Cycle

Nitrogen is a vital component of amino acids and nucleic acids, which are the fundamental units of proteins and DNA. The nitrogen cycle begins with inert atmospheric nitrogen (N_2), which is generally unusable by living organisms. Nitrogen-fixing bacteria in the soil or on the roots of legumes transform the inert nitrogen into nitrates (NO_3^-) and ammonium (NH_4^-). Plants take up these compounds, synthesize the 20 amino acids found in nature, and transform them into plant proteins; animals, typically only able to synthesize 8 of the 20 amino acids, eat the plants and produce protein using the plant's materials. Plants and animals give off nitrogen waste and death products in the form of ammonia (NH_3). One of two things can happen to the ammonia: 1) nitrifying bacteria transform the ammonia into nitrites (NO_2) and then to nitrates (NO_3^-), which re-enter the cycle when they are taken up by plants; 2) Denitrifying bacteria break down the ammonia to produce inert nitrogen (N_2).

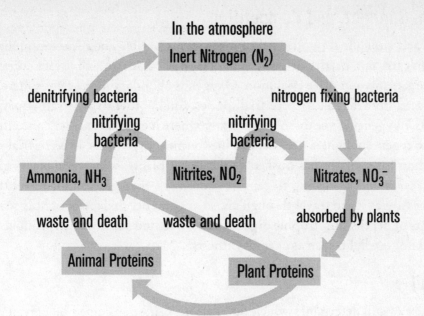

In the atmosphere
Inert Nitrogen (N_2)

denitrifying bacteria   nitrogen fixing bacteria

nitrifying bacteria   nitrifying bacteria

Ammonia, NH_3 Nitrites, NO_2 Nitrates, NO_3^-

waste and death   waste and death   absorbed by plants

Animal Proteins   Plant Proteins

animals eat plants

The cycling of water and phosphorus are also important, as these substances are limited and vital to the life processes of most organisms.

The Water Cycle

The majority of the Earth's water resides in the oceans and lakes, which act as water storage depots. This water escapes into the atmosphere through evaporation and condenses into clouds. Precipitation in the form of rain, snow, hail, etc. returns water to the ocean and lakes, and also brings water to dry land. Water on land may either return to the oceans and lakes as runoff, or penetrate into the soil and seep as groundwater.

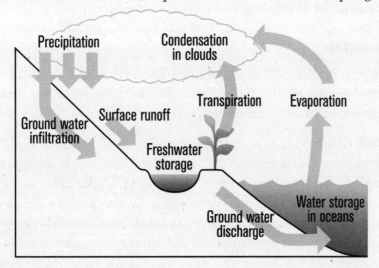

Precipitation   Condensation in clouds

Transpiration   Evaporation

Ground water infiltration   Surface runoff

Freshwater storage

Ground water discharge   Water storage in oceans

Ecology

Oxygen, Sunlight, and Competition

Oxygen and sunlight are both vital to most forms of life. The relative abundance or lack of oxygen in a particular geographic or physical locale will create competition among organisms and drive evolution. Oxygen is abundant in the atmosphere, and is therefore readily available to terrestrial species. But in order to penetrate aquatic environments, oxygen must be dissolved in water where it exists in smaller concentration.

Like oxygen, sunlight is necessary to life for most organisms. In terrestrial species, competition for sunlight has pushed evolution of plants, with some plants growing broader leaves and branching to capture more rays. Sunlight cannot travel through water as easily as it can travel through air, so at great ocean depths, light is scarce. At these sorts of depths, autotrophic organisms have to find some way to produce energy that does not use light, such as chemosynthesis.

The Soil

The nature of soil determines which populations can be sustained in a given ecosystem. High acidity inhibits most plant growth, but may be ideal for some plants that are better adapted to acidic soil. The texture of the soil and amount of clay it contains affects its ability to retain water, while the presence of minerals and decaying organic matter influence the types of plant life that can be supported.

Biomes

Different climatic conditions are produced by the geography and uneven heating of the Earth. Plant and animal forms that are characteristic of a particular geographic area with a common climate constitute biomes. Each biome is characterized by specific climax communities. All the biomes together form the biosphere.

Terrestrial Biomes

The various biotic and abiotic factors at play on Earth result in six major terrestrial biomes. Terrestrial biomes are categorized according to the types of plants they support. The fundamental characteristics of each type are described in the list below.

Tropical rain forest. Rain forests have the highest rainfall of all biomes (100–180 inches per year), which results in the greatest animal and plant diversity. Trees form canopies that block sunlight from reaching the ground. Most animal species live in the canopy, while the forest floor is inhabited predominantly by insects and saprophytes and consists of soil low in nutrients. Decomposed products on the forest floor are washed away or quickly reabsorbed by plants. Tropical rainforests can be found in Central America, the Amazon basin in South America, Central Africa, and Southeast Asia.

Savanna. This biome is characterized by grassland with sparse trees, with extended dry periods or droughts. Tropical savanna generally border rain forests and receive a yearly total of 40–60 inches of rainfall. They support large herbivores, such as antelope, zebra, elephants, and giraffe. Most tropical savanna exist in Africa. Temperate savanna, such as the Pampas in Argentina and the prairies east of the Rocky Mountains in the United States, receive only about 10–30 inches of rain a year. Grasses and shrubs dominate the landscape and support insects, birds, smaller burrowing animals, and larger, hoofed animals such as bison.

Desert. Deserts are the driest biome, receiving less than 10 inches of rain per year. They exhibit radical temperature changes between day and night. Animals of the desert such as lizards, snakes, birds, and insects are typically small and have adapted to the dry, hot climate by being nocturnally active. Plants, such as cactus, have evolved waxy cuticles, fewer stomata, spiky leaves, and seeds capable of remaining dormant until sufficient resources are available. Deserts exist in Asia, Africa, and North America.

Temperate deciduous forest. Rainfall in temperate deciduous forests is evenly distributed throughout the year. The biome has distinct summer and winter seasons. It has long growing seasons during the summer. In winter, the deciduous plants drop their leaves and enter a period of dormancy. Beech and maple dominate in colder variations of this biome, while oak and hickory are more prevalent where temperatures are warmer. Animals in deciduous forests are both herbivorous and carnivorous, such as deer, fox, owl, and squirrel. The forest floor is fertile and contains fungi and worms. Temperate deciduous forests exist mainly on the east coast of North America and in central Europe.

Taiga. The taiga is a forest biome, but is colder and receives less rainfall than deciduous forests. Coniferous (cone-bearing) trees, especially spruce, dominate the taiga. The trees also have needle-shaped leaves that help conserve water. Taiga forests sustain birds, small mammals such as squirrels, large herbivorous mammals such as moose and elk, and large carnivorous mammals such as wolves and grizzly bears. Taiga exist mainly in Russian and northern Canada.

Tundra. This biome is located in the far north and is covered by ice sheets for the majority of the year. The soil, down to a few feet, remains permanently frozen, though in the summer, the topsoil can melt and support a short growing season. Very few plants grow in the northernmost parts of the Tundra, but lichens, mosses, and grasses occupy some more southern areas. Animals must be well suited for extreme cold or must migrate. The tundra supports large herbivores such as reindeer and caribou, large predators such as bear, and some birds.

Aquatic Biomes

Aquatic biomes account for 70 percent of the Earth's surface and contain the majority of plant and animal life. Aquatic biomes also account for a vast portion of the photosynthesis, and therefore oxygen production, that occurs on Earth. There are two types of aquatic biomes, based on the type of water found in each: marine and freshwater.

Marine

Marine biomes refer to the oceans that all connect to form a single, great body of water. Since water has an immense capacity to absorb heat with little temperature increase, conditions remain uniform over these large aquatic bodies. Marine biomes are divided into three zones: **intertidal/littoral**, **neritic**, and **pelagic**.

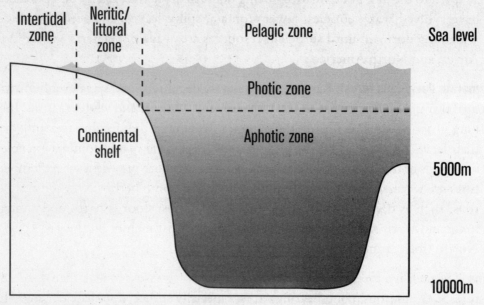

The intertidal zone, also called the littoral zone, is the region where land and water meet. It experiences periodic dryness with changing tides and is inhabited by algae, sponges, various mollusks, starfish, and crabs.

The neritic zone extends to 600 feet beneath the water's surface and sits on the continental shelf, hundreds of miles from shores. Algae, crustaceans, and numerous fish inhabit this region.

The pelagic zone consists of a **photic zone** (reaching 600 feet below sea level) and below that, an **aphotic zone**. Light penetrates the photic zone, which is why it contains photosynthetic plankton. The photic zone also is home to heterotrophs such as fish, sharks, and whales that prey on these producers as well as on each other. No light penetrates the aphotic zone, which is a kind of watery circus of the bizarre, where extreme cold water, darkness, and high pressure have spurred strange evolutionary paths. The region is home to some chemosynthetic autotrophs. Other denizens of the deep are scavengers that feed upon dead organic matter falling from the higher realms, and predators who feed on each other.

Freshwater

Freshwater biomes include rivers, lakes, and marshes. Life here is affected by temperature, salt concentration, light penetration, depth, and availability of dissolved CO_2 and O_2. Freshwater biomes are much smaller than marine biomes, so conditions are less stable. Organisms that live in these regions must be able to handle the greater extremes. The very nature of freshwater also demands special characteristics of the organisms that live within it. In freshwater environments, the salt concentration within the cell of an organism is higher than the salt concentration in the water. A concentration exists between the interior of cells and the exterior environment: water from the environment is constantly diffusing into the organism. Organisms in freshwater need homeostatic systems to maintain proper water balance.

Review Questions

1. How is an ecosystem organized, from least to most comprehensive?

    A. Individual, community, population, biome
    B. Individual, population, community, biome
    C. Individual, population, niche, community
    D. Individual, niche, community, population
    E. Individual, population, biome, niche

2. Why is energy lost as it moves from producers to primary consumers?

    A. Saprophytic activity
    B. Biomass decreases
    C. Secondary consumers eat primary consumers
    D. Respiration and metabolic activity
    E. None of the above

3. Which of the following organisms participate in the nitrogen cycle?

    A. Denitrifying bacteria
    B. Chemosynthetic bacteria
    C. Saprophytes
    D. All of the above
    E. None of the above

4. When resources are abundant and the environment is stable, which reproductive strategy is most effective?

    A.   Sexual reproduction, with intense parental care and slow development
    B.   Sexual reproduction, with slight parental care and quick development
    C.   Parthenogenesis
    D.   All of the above
    E.   None of the above

5. Why might growth slow from an exponential rate in a population of sheep?

    A.   Disease
    B.   Lack of space
    C.   Wolves
    D.   All of the above
    E.   None of the above

6. What is a relationship in which two organisms both benefit from their association?

    A.   Symbiosis
    B.   Mutualism
    C.   Commensalism
    D.   Parasitism
    E.   Competition

7. Which is true of ecological succession?

    A.   Pioneer species move into new communities first.
    B.   Climax communities have lower total biomass than preceding communities.
    C.   Species diversity is greatest in the early stages of succession.
    D.   Climax communities shift constantly.
    E.   All of the above

8. Tundra is characterized by

    A.   trees such as beech, maple, and oak
    B.   high biodiversity
    C.   barrenness
    D.   a short growing season following rainfall
    E.   none of the above

9. Which of the following releases carbon dioxide into the atmosphere?

    A.   Animal consumption of producers
    B.   Photosynthesis
    C.   Chemosynthesis
    D.   Bacterial decay
    E.   None of the above

10. In a plains community, the population with greatest biomass would be

    A.   hawks
    B.   foxes
    C.   prairie dogs
    D.   grasses
    E.   beetles

Explanations

1.   (B)
Individual organisms occupy particular niches (geographical locations as well as roles). Populations consist of individuals of an interbreeding species. Many coexisting populations constitute a community, and many communities coexist within a biome.

2.   (D)
Only 10 percent of energy moves between trophic levels, because it is lost to sustain respiration and metabolic processes. Saprophytic activity does not explain the loss of energy as you move up a food pyramid. Biomass decreases because energy is lost, not the other way around. While it is true that secondary consumers eat primary consumers, this scenario does not effect the change in energy capacity between trophic levels.

3.   (E)
All organisms are involved in the nitrogen cycle. Decaying (saprophytic), nitrifying (chemosynthetic), denitrifying, and nitrogen-fixing bacteria all play roles in the nitrogen cycle. Decaying bacteria produce ammonia (NH_3), which is transformed into nitrites (NO_2) and nitrates (NO_3^-) by nitrifying bacteria. Denitrifying bacteria convert ammonia into free N_2 in the atmosphere.

4.   (C)
Asexual reproduction such as parthenogenesis takes greatest advantage of unlimited space and resources in a stable environment. This mode of reproduction facilitates rapid population growth. Although species diversity created through sexual reproduction is sacrificed, it is not necessary in a noncompetitive atmosphere. Organisms (no matter how similar) in an environment without limitations do not compete with one another.

5.   (D)
Depleted resources, competition for food and space, predation, and disease all slow population growth. These factors shape carrying capacity for populations in any given community.

6.   (B)

The first answer is a bit of a trick: symbiosis refers to a number of different relationships between organisms, including a mutually beneficial relationship, but it does not refer specifically to that sort of relationship. Mutualism does refer to a relationship beneficial to both organisms. Commensalism helps one organism and does not harm the other, while parasitism benefits one organism and harms the other. Competition refers to a battle for resources and survival between populations.

7.   (A)

As an ecosystem moves through the stages of succession, it is characterized by an increase in total biomass, a decrease in net productivity relative to biomass, a greater capacity to retain nutrients within the system, increasing species diversity, increasing size of organisms, increasing life spans, and complex life cycles. Climax communities will not shift unless there is a cataclysmic event.

8.   (C)

Beech, maple, and oak populate the temperate deciduous forest. High biodiversity is not a characteristic of the barren tundra. The desert exhibits short growing seasons immediately after precipitation.

9.   (D)

Carbon dioxide in the atmosphere is directly produced by bacterial decay of waste and dead organic material. (Respiration also produces CO_2, but it is not listed among the answer choices.) Photosynthesis and the animal consumption of producers contribute to the carbon cycle, but are not directly responsible for the production of CO_2. Chemosynthesis is not involved in the carbon cycle.

10.   (E)

Biomass decreases from producers up through each level of consumers. Grasses, the only producer in the group, must have the largest biomass.

Glossary

A

abiotic   Nonliving materials in the environment—such as elements, sunlight, and soil—that influence and are influenced by living (biotic) entities on the planet.

acetylcholine   A neurotransmitter released by neurons to excite an action potential or trigger a muscle to contract.

acid   Hydrogen ion (H^+) donors. Acids are very important in the chemical reactions of life because they are highly reactive. Acids have pH values below 7. They are the opposite of bases.

actin   Protein filaments that, along with myosin, allow muscles to contract.

active site   The part of an enzyme that binds the substrate or substrates. The induced fit model states that the active site molds to fit the substrate.

active transport   The movement of molecules across a cell membrane from a region of lower concentration to a region of higher concentration. Because active transport involves moving the molecule against the natural flow of the concentration gradient, the process requires energy.

adaptive radiation   The evolutionary process by which ancestral forms of an organism are diversified through adaptation to new environments.

adenosine triphosphate (ATP)   The energy storage molecule for the cell. ATP is comprised of an adenosine molecule bonded to three phosphates groups. Each phosphate bond contains energy; by breaking these bonds, the cell can get the energy it needs for chemical reactions. Cells build ATP during cell respiration, using the raw material of glucose.

adrenal glands   Two glands, the adrenal cortex and adrenal medulla, located on the kidney.

aerobic respiration   A form of cell respiration requiring oxygen (as opposed to anaerboic respiration, which does not need oxygen). Aerobic respiration is much more efficient than anaerobic respiration; it produces 36 ATP for every molecule of glucose. Aerobic respiration proceeds in three stages: glycolysis, the Krebs cycle, and the electron transport chain.

allele   A specific form or possible version of a gene having multiple versions. Alleles may be dominant or recessive.

allelic frequency   The frequency with which a particular allele for a certain characteristic appears among all possible alleles for that characteristic in a population.

alternation of generations   The fluctuation between the diploid (sporophyte) and haploid (gametophyte) life stages that occur in plants.

amino acid   The monomer of a protein. A central carbon attached to an amino group ($-NH_2$), a carboxyl group ($-COOH$), and a hydrogen atom ($-H$). The fourth group is variable and defines the amino acid's chemical identity.

anaerobic respiration   A form of cell respiration that does not use oxygen (as opposed to aerobic cell respiration, which does use oxygen). Anaerobic respiration is less efficient than the aerobic variety, and produces just 2 ATP per molecule of glucose. Anaerobic respiration has two stages: glycolysis and fermentation.

analogous trait   A trait that is morphologically and functionally similar to that of a different species, but which arose from a distinct, ancestral condition.

anaphase   The stage of mitosis in which sister chromosomes are separated and pulled to opposite ends of the cell by microtubules; the fourth stage of the first meiotic division (meiosis I), during which maternal and paternal homologous pairs are separated on microtubules; the fourth stage of the second meiotic division (meiosis II), during which either maternal or paternal sister chromatids are separated on microtubules.

angiosperm   A vascular flowering plant in which seeds are enclosed inside of protective ovaries, such as fruit or flowers. Angiosperms can be monocots or dicots.

anther   Pollen-producing structure at the top of the stamen, the male reproductive organ of flowers.

anticodon   The sequence of three nucleotides on tRNA that pairs with a codon of mRNA at the A-site of a ribosome during translation.

antigen   A protein coat on the surface of red blood cells; a red blood cell may have a protein coat of type A, B, or AB. If the cell has no antigens, it is called type O. The presence of a foreign antigen in a body will cause blood to clot.

aorta   The largest artery in the body; carries oxygenated blood from the left ventricle of the heart.

aphotic zone   Literally, zone without light. The aphotic zone is part of the marine pelagic zone and begins 600 feet below the surface of the ocean. Only chemosynthetic organisms, scavengers, and predators are able to survive in this habitat.

artery   Vessel that carries blood away from the heart and has thick, elastic, muscular walls that can dilate or contract to control blood pressure within the vessels. Blood in arteries is oxygenated, with the exception of the blood in the pulmonary artery.

autonomic nervous system   The involuntary half of the peripheral nervous system. The autonomic nervous system is in two antagonistic parts: the sympathetic and parasympathetic nervous systems. Their interactions control smooth and cardiac muscle, glands, and organs; and processes such as heartbeat, the movements of the digestive tract, and the contraction of the bladder.

autosome   Any chromosome that is not a sex chromosome. Humans have 44 autosomes, in 22 homologous pairs. The two sex chromosomes comprise the twenty-third pair of chromosomes.

autotroph   An organism that can produce the organic molecules and energy necessary for life through the processes of photosynthesis or chemosynthesis. Autotrophs do not rely on other organisms for food. In a food web, autotrophs are producers.

auxin   One in a class of plant hormones that stimulates (among other things) cell elongation, secondary tissue growth, and fruit development.

B

base   An ion or compound that removes H^+ ions from solution. Often bases are substances that release hydroxide ions (OH^-). Bases have pH values above 7. They are the opposite of acids.

bile   An emulsifier of fats secreted by the liver and stored in the gallbladder for release in the small intestine.

Glossary

binary fission   Asexual reproduction found in prokaryotes in which a cell divides into two equal daughter cells by a non-mitotic process.

biomass   The amount of living matter in a given ecosystem. Because only 10 percent of energy is transferred between trophic levels, the biomass of lower trophic levels is greater than the biomass of subsequent trophic levels: biomass of producers > biomass of primary consumers > biomass of secondary consumers > biomass of tertiary consumers.

biome   A particular geographic area with a common climate and characteristic plant and animal life. There are six major terrestrial biomes and two aquatic biomes. The six terrestrial biomes are tropical rain forest, savanna, desert, temperate deciduous forest, taiga, and tundra. The two aquatic biomes are marine and freshwater. Each biome is characterized by specific climax communities.

blood   The liquid that carries nutrients and oxygen to the cells and carries carbon dioxide and nitrogenous wastes away. The liquid fluid of blood is called plasma. Red blood cells contain hemoglobin, an iron-containing protein that binds oxygen. White blood cells fight disease. Platelets clot to prevent extreme blood loss through injury.

bone   Rigid structures composed of living cells rooted in a matrix of calcium, phosphate salts, and collagen fibers. Bones are the primary component of most vertebrate skeletons.

brain   The center of the central nervous system. The brain coordinates the processes of the body. It is composed of various distinct regions, all of which have different functions, including the cerebrum, cerebellum, medulla oblongata, and hypothalamus.

bryophyte   A lower terrestrial plant (often a moss or liverwort) that lacks a vascular system and is dependent on environmental moisture for reproductive and nutritive functions.

budding   Asexual reproductive process in which a small portion of the cell membrane and cytoplasm receive a nucleus and pinch off from the parent cell.

buffer   Solutions that resist change in pH even when acids and bases are added.

bulb   Roughly spherical underground bud containing additional buds that can develop asexually into new plants.

C

Calvin cycle   Light-independent phase of photosynthesis, where carbon dioxide is fixed to a three-carbon compound used to form glucose. ATP and NADH are consumed in this cycle. Also called the Calvin-Benson cycle, or the dark reactions.

capillary   Tiny blood vessels able to branch through the body and deliver oxygen and nutrients to every cell.

carbon   The central element of life. Carbon has the ability to form bonds with up to four other elements or molecules at the same time.

carrying capacity   The maximum number of individuals in a population that can be sustained in a given environment. As populations become increasingly concentrated, competition for food and space, predation, and disease all determine carrying capacity.

cartilage   A firm but flexible substance, found in regions of the vertebrate skeletons that need to bend.

cell   The smallest unit of life, consisting of a solution of organic molecules enclosed by a plasma membrane.

cell cycle   A process in which cells reproduce. First the cell replicates its DNA, and then divides into two daughter cells. The two main phases of the cell cycle are interphase and mitosis.

cell membrane   The phospholipid bilayer that surrounds all cells, regulating the passage of molecules in and out of the cell.

cellular respiration   The process in which the cell burns glucose to create ATP with the aid of oxygen. Cells have two different methods of turning food into usable fuel: aerobic respiration and anaerobic respiration.

cell theory   The doctrine that every living organism is composed of cells and that all cells come only from other preexisting cells.

cell wall   A rigid structure that surrounds the outer membrane of some cells and helps maintain their shape. In plants, the cell wall contains cellulose; in fungi it contains chitin; in prokaryotes it typically contains peptidoglycan.

cellulose   A complex carbohydrate that constitutes the cell walls of plants and protist molds.

central nervous system (CNS)   The brain and the spinal cord. The CNS acts as the central command center of the body. Made up mostly of interneurons.

centriole   A structure in the cell that plays an important role in cell replication. During prophase, the centrioles migrate to the poles of the cell and form the mitotic spindle that allows the chromosomes to be organized and split when the cell divides.

cerebellum   Part of the brain. Makes sure that movements are coordinated and balanced.

cerebrum   Part of the brain. Controls all voluntary movement, sensory perception, speech, memory, and creative thought.

chemical cycles   The cycles in which inorganic elements move through the biotic and abiotic aspects of an ecosystem. The two most important chemical cycles are the carbon and nitrogen cycles.

chemosynthesis   Synthesizing organic compounds by energy derived from chemical reactions rather than from the energy of the sun. Chemosynthetic organisms are autotrophs.

chitin   A rough polysaccharide that constitutes the cell wall of fungi and exoskeleton of arthropods.

chlorophyll   A pigment located within a chloroplast that absorbs light in plant cells, helping to convert light energy into biological energy through the process of photosynthesis.

chloroplast   A double membrane-bound organelle that contains chlorophyll and is found in plant cells. Chloroplasts are responsible for mediating photosynthesis.

chromatin   The stringy web of genetic material and histone proteins found in the nucleus of eukaryotic cells. During cell division, each strand of DNA coils to form a chromosome.

chromosome   A physical structure composed of a single long strand of DNA (and associated proteins), containing along its length many genes. The human genome consists of 46 chromosomes contained within the nucleus of each cell.

cilia   Short, hairlike projections found on eukaryotic cells that can help the cell move or can sweep food particles toward the mouth.

circadian rhythms   Behavior cycles that depend on time of day.

circulatory system   System of organs and blood that brings nutrients and oxygen to cells and carries away wastes. In higher vertebrates, the system has a pulmonary and systemic circuit. The pulmonary circuit carries blood to the lungs to be oxygenated, while the systemic circuit carries oxygenated blood to the body. Vertebrates have a closed circulatory system, while arthropods have an open system.

citric acid cycle   See Krebs cycle.

climax community   A combination of plant and animal forms that dominate mature ecological communities. Climax communities are unique and shaped by various factors including temperature, rainfall, and soil acidity.

codominance   A phenomenon in which two alleles of the same gene are fully expressed in the phenotype when both are present in a heterozygote. Blood type is an example of codominance.

codon   A three-nucleotide sequence in a DNA or mRNA molecule. Each codon specifies a single amino acid.

coenzyme   A compound that regulates activity by binding to an enzyme to tell it when to catalyze a reaction.

cold-blooded   Animals that are unable to retain heat produced by metabolic activities. Also known as ectothermic. The metabolism of cold-blooded animals is greatly influenced by climate and temperature.

community   The many populations that interact in a given geographical locale constitute ecological communities. Communities exhibit particular interactions such as competition, symbiosis, predation, and food relationships. They also undergo ecological succession.

competition   The struggle for survival between organisms or populations that use similar resources and occupy similar niches. Interspecific competition refers to competition between populations that may drive a population out of a community or push it to evolve a different niche to reduce competition. Intraspecific competition refers to competition between individuals of the same species.

consumer   Consumers are heterotrophic organisms within the food web of a community. Primary consumers consume producers. Secondary consumers consume primary consumers, and tertiary consumers consume secondary consumers.

Glossary

contractile vacuole   An organelle often found in protozoa that pumps excess water out of the cell to keep the cell from bursting in a hypotonic environment (like freshwater).

corpus luteum   After releasing its ovum (ovulation), the follicle becomes the corpus luteum, which produces progesterone for the continued buildup of the uterine wall.

crossing-over   The exchange of genetic information between homologous chromosomes during meiosis I. Crossing-over can disrupt the normal linkage between genes on the same chromosome.

cytokinesis   The final part of mitosis, in which a cell with duplicated contents splits into two independent cells.

cytoplasm   The entire content of the cell outside the nucleus, including the membrane-bound organelles and the cytosol.

cytoskeleton   A system of protein filaments found throughout the cytoplasm of eukaryotic cells, which provides structural support for the cell. The cytoskeleton also helps with the movement of organelles within the cell. It is composed of microfilaments and microtubules.

cytosol   The main component of the cytoplasm. It is a grayish, gel-like liquid containing the nucleus, organelles, and cytoskeleton.

D

Darwin, Charles   English naturalist (1809–1882) who proposed the modern theory of evolution through natural selection. Traveled aboard the *HMS Beagle* to the Galapagos Islands where his revolutionary observations took shape.

decomposer   Organisms that consume waste products and dead organic material and constitute part of the food web, which also includes producers and consumers. Also called saprophytes. Decomposers liberate inorganic elements such as nitrogen and carbon and allow those elements to move back into their respective chemical cycles. Examples of decomposers are bacteria and fungi.

dehydration synthesis   A common biochemical reaction in which a new compound is formed by the joining of two compounds to release water. Occurs in the synthesis of polysaccharides and polypeptides. The reverse of hydrolysis.

deoxyribonucleic acid (DNA)   A type of nucleic acid polymer built from sugar-phosphate backbones and nitrogenous bases. DNA's sugar, deoxyribose, has one fewer oxygen atom than ribose found in RNA. The nitrogenous bases adenine, cytosine, guanine, and thymine are used in DNA.

dicot   A flowering plant (angiosperm) that possesses two cotyledons during embryonic development. Usually has tap roots, flower parts in multiples of fours and fives, and branching veins in leaves.

diffusion   The transport or natural drift of molecules traveling from an area of higher concentration to an area of lower concentration. Diffusion does not require outside energy from the cell.

digestive system   The system of organs that converts food to usable nutrients through mechanical and chemical breakdown. Important components of the system are the alimentary canal, glands, esophagus, stomach, small intestine, large intestine, and rectum.

diploid number   The total number of chromosomes present in a somatic cell. The diploid number is twice the haploid number. In humans, the diploid number is 46.

disaccharide   A sugar compound consisting of two carbohydrate monomers.

dominant   Refers to an allele that controls the phenotype even when a different allele is also present, as in a heterozygote. Can also refer to the trait or phenotype produced by a dominant allele. Also known as Mendel's law of dominance based on his observations that when two purebred individuals with different forms of the same trait are mated, only one of the two forms appears in the first generation of offspring. He called the apparent form dominant, and the suppressed form recessive.

E

---

ear   Sensory organ capable of detecting sound.

ecological succession   The progression of plant life and attendant animal life in a given geographic location, from pioneer plant to climax community.

ecology   The study of the interactions and relationships of populations with each other and their abiotic environments.

ecosystem   A community of organisms and its abiotic environment.

ectotherm   See cold-blooded.

egg   The female gamete in sexual reproduction; also called an ovum.

electron microscope   An instrument that uses an electron beam to form clear and highly magnified images of microscopic structures. Electron microscopes cannot take pictures of living organisms.

electron transport chain   The final stage of aerobic respiration. The electron transport chain establishes an electrochemical gradient across the inner mitochondrial membrane that powers the synthesis of ATP in oxidative phosphorylation.

embryo   Before birth, the maturing cells that will grow into a fully formed organism.

endocrine system   Control system of the body that functions by releasing hormones into the bloodstream.

endocytosis   Process by which liquids or small, solid particles are taken into a cell in the form of small vesicles that are produced through the invagination of the cell membrane.

endoplasmic reticulum   A network of membrane-bound tubes and sacs in the cytoplasm. The endoplasmic reticulum is a major site of protein and lipid synthesis.

endoskeleton   An interior skeleton found in vertebrates made of bone and cartilage.

endotherm   See warm-blooded.

energy pyramid   Energy in a community can be depicted as a pyramid of food or biomass. The availability of food, biomass, and energy from the trophic level of producers up through each subsequent level on the food web is approximately 10 percent of that available in the previous trophic level.

enzymes   Biological catalysts made from proteins. Enzymes have attachment locations for substrates called active sites.

estrogen   Hormone that stimulates the growth of the uterine lining during pregnancy, and which develops and maintains the female secondary sex characteristics, such as the development of mammary glands, a narrower waist and wider hips, axillary and pubic hair, and a higher pitched voice.

eukaryote   An organism whose cells have membrane-bound intracellular organelles, including a nucleus containing multiple chromosomes. Eukaryotes, unlike prokaryotes, can undergo sexual reproduction via meiosis. Compared to prokaryotes, eukaryotes are more complex and arose later in evolutionary history. Protists, fungi, plants, and animals are all eukaryotic organisms.

excretory system   The organ system that filters blood and removes nitrogenous wastes from the body in the form of urea or uric acid. In humans, the two kidneys are the vital organs of blood filtration. In annelids, nephridia fill the filtering role; malpighian tubules do the same in arthropods. In humans, other important structures of the system are the ureters, the urinary bladder, and the urethra.

exocytosis   Process by which molecules are secreted from the cell. Exocytosis occurs when a vesicle fuses with the cell membrane and releases its contents to the outside.

exoskeleton   A rigid, chitinous protective structure that surrounds the bodies of arthropods and provides support.

eye   Sensory organ capable of detecting light.

F

F_1 generation   The first generation of offspring from a cross between two varieties or individuals. In Mendel's experiments, all the F_1 offspring were heterozygous hybrids with a dominant phenotype.

F_2 generation   The second generation of offspring in a breeding experiment; the offspring from a mating between two F_1 hybrids. In Mendel's monohybrid experiments, the ratio of dominant to recessive phenotypes in the F_2 generation was 3:1.

facilitated diffusion   Diffusion of molecules that cannot pass through the cell membrane independently, but rather through permeable protein channels embedded in the membrane. Facilitated diffusion does not require outside energy.

$FADH_2$ A molecule that stores energy for harvest by the electron transport chain.

fallopian tube   Duct that connects the ovaries with the uterus; the passage through which the ovulated egg travels from the ovaries to the uterus.

fermentation   The second stage of anaerobic respiration, which produces the NAD^+ necessary for glycolysis. There are two types of fermentation: alcoholic fermentation and lactic acid fermentation. Yeast engage in alcoholic fermentation, while muscle cells lacking oxygen produce lactic acid.

fetus   The name given to an embryo after it has developed organs.

flagellum   A whiplike structure projecting from the surface of some cells and single-celled organisms; coordinated waving of the flagellum allows the organism to swim. Prokaryotic flagella are made of a single helical chain of flagellin proteins; eukaryotic flagella are made of multiple chains of microtubule proteins.

fluid-mosaic model   Theory describing the cell membrane as a dynamic structure with proteins floating, yet partially embedded, in a sea of phospholipids.

food chain   A linear relationship of predators and prey.

food web   Many connected food chains that exhibit the relationships of all predators to all prey constitute a food web.

fossil record   The grouping of fossilized remains according to relative and absolute age.

G

gallbladder   An organ that stores the bile produced by the liver and releases it to the small intestine during digestion.

gamete   A haploid sex cell (either an egg or sperm cell); male and female gametes join during fertilization to create a diploid zygote. Gametes are created out of germ cells and are passed down to offspring.

gametophyte   A haploid plant or plant structure that produces haploid gametes through mitosis.

ganglion   A simple cluster of nerve cells that acts as a coordinating center. In more sophisticated organisms, ganglia evolved into a brain and spinal cord.

gene   The fundamental unit of heredity, composed of a stretch of DNA. In general, a single gene encodes the information needed to produce one kind of protein. Each gene resides in a specific spot on a chromosome.

gene flow   The movement of genes, within a population or between populations, through mating.

genetic code   The series of codons that make up an organism's DNA.

genotype   The entire set of specific alleles present in an organism or cell: the genetic information that (together with the environment) defines the phenotype. Often refers only to the alleles controlling a particular trait of interest.

germ cell   Cells that lead to the production of gametes. Produced by meiosis.

glucose   A monosaccharide with the chemical formula $C_6H_{12}O_6$. Used as the raw material for cellular respiration.

glycolysis   The first step of aerobic and anaerobic respiration. Glycolysis produces ATP while converting glucose to pyruvate, which is the raw material for the rest of aerobic respiration.

Golgi apparatus   A series of membrane-bound sacs in the eukaryotic cytoplasm. The Golgi apparatus takes proteins produced by the endoplasmic reticulum and packages and secretes them to various destinations inside and outside of the cell.

gonads   Sex organs that produce gametes. The gonads also release sex hormones, such as testosterone, estrogen, and progesterone. In humans, the male gonads are the testes; in females, the ovaries.

grafting   An artificial form of vegetative propagation in which parts of two young plants are joined together, first by artificial means and then by tissue regeneration.

Gram staining   A process by which components of bacterial cell walls are bound to Gram's stain. Depending on the amount of peptidoglycan in their cell walls, bacteria stain differently and are classified as Gram-negative or Gram-positive.

guard cells   Epidermal plant cells found in pairs surrounding the stomata of leaves. By increasing or decreasing their size, guard cells regulate gas exchange by opening and closing individual stoma.

gymnosperm   A vascular nonflowering plant (commonly known as a conifer) in which seeds are "naked"—collected in a cone and not protected by an ovary. The dispersion of their spermatozoids often relies on wind.

H

haploid number   The number of homologous pairs in a cell. Equal to half the diploid number. Gametes, cells that are passed on to offspring, contain the haploid number of chromosomes. In humans, the haploid number is 23.

Glossary

heart   The muscular organ that pumps blood through the circulatory system. Mammals and birds have a four-chambered heart, with a left atrium and ventricle, and a right atrium and ventricle. The right half of the heart receives deoxygenated blood from the body and pumps it to the lungs, while the left half receives oxygenated blood from the lungs and pumps it to the body.

heredity   The genetic transmission of traits from parents to offspring, so that offspring resemble their parents. Traits transmitted this way are called hereditary traits.

heterotrophs   Organisms that can only get the organic molecules and energy necessary for life through the consumption of other organic matter. In the food web, all consumers and decomposers are heterotrophs. Heterotrophs can be herbivores, carnivores, or omnivores.

heterozygous   A situation in which an individual (heterozygote) possesses two dissimilar alleles for the same gene. The opposite is homozygous.

homologous chromosomes   Chromosomes containing the same series of genes; they may or may not carry the same alleles. Humans receive one set of 23 paternal chromosomes from their male parent, and another set of 23 maternal chromosomes from their female parent. Each set matches up to the other for a total of 23 different pairs of homologous chromosomes. During meiosis, homologous pairs line up and are separated. In males, the X and Y chromosomes act as a homologous pair, although they are only partially homologous.

homologous trait   A trait found in different species that are morphologically and functionally similar and that come from the same ancestral condition. A whale's fin and a human's arm are homologous structures.

homozygous   A situation in which an individual (homozygote) with the exact same allele on both homologous chromosomes. Mating of two individuals with the same homozygous genotype will produce only offspring with that same identical genotype. The two identical alleles may be dominant or recessive (e.g., RR or rr). The opposite of homozygous is heterozygous.

hormones   A chemical messenger that can be made of either peptides or lipids. Secreted by glands in one part of the body, hormones affect glands or organs in another part.

hybrid   A genetic mixture; the offspring of two genetically different parents. Hybrids are usually heterozygous for a variety of genes.

hydrogen bond   A weak bond between hydrogen and a set of other elements including oxygen. Hydrogen bonds are a subset of dipole-dipole interactions.

hydrolysis   A common biochemical reaction in which the bond between two molecules is split by the addition of a water molecule. Hydrolysis is the process that breaks down polymers and dimers. The reverse is dehydration synthesis.

hydrophilic   Having an affinity for water; usually polar molecules. For the SAT II Biology, this is principally important in relation to the phospholipid bilayer.

hydrophobic   Having a reluctance to mix with water; usually nonpolar molecules. The fatty acids that form the interior pocket between the two layers of the cell membrane are hydrophobic.

hydrostatic skeleton   A fluid skeleton in many soft-bodied invertebrates, including annelids, that allows an organism to change shape but not volume.

hypothalamus   Part of the brain responsible for temperature regulation, controlling hunger and thirst, and managing water balance. It also helps generate emotion.

hypertonic   A situation in which the concentration of solutes in a solution is higher than what it contains. For example, a sodium solution of 10 percent would be hypertonic to an animal cell (with a sodium concentration of about 0.9 percent), causing water to leave the cell by osmosis.

hypotonic   A situation in which the concentration of solutes in a solution is lower that what it contains. An example is a paramecium in pond water: the organism has more solutes than its environment, so water flows into the cell by osmosis. Paramecia have evolved contractile vacuoles to keep from exploding.

I

imprinting   Instinctual behavior in which social bonds are formed during early development. Typically used with the example of a newly hatched bird or other animal identifying and treating the first moving object it sees as its mother.

incomplete dominance   Occurs when two different alleles of the same gene are both partially expressed in a heterozygote. The resulting phenotype is intermediate between the homozygous phenotypes of the two alleles. Color in a four o'clock flower is an example of incomplete dominance.

independent assortment   Mendel's conclusion that during gamete formation, the segregation of one pair of genes has no influence over the segregation of another pair of hereditary units. Two different traits will thus be inherited independently of one another. This law holds true, except for linked genes. It is often called Mendel's Second Law.

inheritance of acquired traits   A crucial, and incorrect, aspect of Lamarck's theory of evolution. Lamarck believed that the traits a parent acquired during its lifetime would be passed on to its offspring.

instincts   Behavior that is hardwired into the brain of an organism; behavior that does not have to be learned.

insulin   Hormone secreted by the pancreas that reduces blood sugar levels. A lack of insulin can result in diabetes.

interphase   The phase of the eukaryotic cell cycle in which the cell prepares for division, primarily be replicating its DNA. After interphase, the cell enters mitosis.

intertidal zone   The most shallow zone in a marine habitat. Periodically dry or wet with the changing tides. Algae, sponges, mollusks, starfish, and crabs inhabit this zone. Also called the littoral zone.

ion   An atom or molecule that has lost or gained an electron and consequently has a positive or negative charge.

isotonic   A situation in which the concentration of solutes in a solution is equivalent to what it contains. There is no concentration gradient in isotonic solutions, and no net flow of solutes or water.

K

karyotype   A photograph of the chromosomes from an individual cell, usually lined up in homologous pairs, according to size. Missing, extra, or abnormal chromosomes can then be easily identified, aiding the diagnosis of genetic disorders.

kidney   The organ of blood filtration in humans. The functional unit of the kidney is the nephron.

kingdom   The broadest category of biological taxonomy.

Krebs cycle   A metabolic pathway in aerobic organisms in which acetyl-CoA combines with oxaloacetic acid to form citric acid. For this reason, the Krebs cycle is also known as the citric acid cycle. The cycle produces energy in the forms of ATP, NADH, and $FADH_2$.

L

Lamarckism   An evolutionary theory (proved false by Darwin) stating that species change over time by the use and disuse of structures, and the inheritance of acquired traits.

learned behavior   Behavior that an organism picks up over the course of its life. Three types of learned behavior are habituation, conditioning, and associative learning.

Leeuwenhoek, Antonie van   Dutch clothing salesman (1632–1723) who made the first observations of bacteria and protozoa using single-lens microscopes of his own design.

ligament   Connective tissue between bones.

linked genes   Genes that are located close together on the same chromosome. Linked genes will not undergo independent assortment during gamete formation, constituting an exception to the law of independent assortment. Crossing-over will disrupt the linkage of two genes on the same chromosome if they are far enough apart.

lymphatic system   A means of returning blood fluid, lymph, that has escaped from capillaries back into the blood stream. Defended against foreign bodies by lymphocytes.

lymphocyte   White blood cells that are specialized to kill specific invading bacteria. Three types of lymphocytes work in coordination: B cells, helper T cells, and killer T cells.

M

malpighian tubules   The organ of blood filtration in arthropods.

medulla oblongata   Part of the brain responsible for the control of involuntary functions such as breathing, cardiovascular regulation, and swallowing.

meiosis   A type of cellular reproduction that results in the formation of four haploid cells from one diploid cell. Contains two cellular divisions, meiosis I and meiosis II, that follow only one round of DNA replication. Meiosis produces germ cells.

Mendel, Gregor   Gregor Mendel (1822–1884) was an Austrian monk and scientist. Through a series of experiments with pea plants, he discovered the basic laws of heredity, including dominance, segregation, and independent assortment.

menstrual cycle   A 28-day hormone sequence that defines the production, ovulation, and menstruation of eggs in the female reproductive system. If fertilization of the egg occurs, the menstrual cycle stops.

mesophyll   The internal tissue of a leaf between the epidermal cells; specialized for photosynthesis. Contains the palisade and spongy layer.

messenger RNA (mRNA)   An RNA molecule that specifies the amino acid sequence of a protein. In transcription, messenger RNA molecules copy the genetic information stored in DNA. The mRNA then bring the recipes for proteins from the nucleus to ribosomes in the cytoplasm.

metaphase   The second stage of mitosis in which microtubules align the chromosomes in the center of the cell along the metaphase plate; the stage of meiosis I and II during which the chromosomes align at the center of the cell.

minerals   Inorganic molecules required by the body to carry out life processes. Important minerals are iron, a necessary component of hemoglobin; iodine, which is essential for making thyroid hormone; and calcium, which is required by the bones and for many cellular processes.

mitochondria   Double membrane-bound organelles that produce most of the energy in eukaryotic cells through the process of aerobic (cellular) respiration, which generates ATP.

mitosis   The phase of the eukaryotic cell cycle in which the cell divides. The four steps of mitosis are prophase, metaphase, anaphase, and telophase.

mitotic spindle   A complex of microtubules that forms between opposite poles of a cell during mitosis. The mitotic spindle is formed by the centrioles and serves to separate and move chromosomes to opposite ends of the cell for division.

molecular clock   A molecule or gene sequence that has a constant rate change through accumulation of neutral substitutions, and is therefore a good measuring stick for the relatedness of different species.

monocot   A flowering plant (angiosperm) that possesses one cotyledon during embryonic development. Usually has fibrous roots, flower parts in threes, and parallel veins in leaves.

monomer   Each of the repeating units that make up a polymer.

monosaccharide   A carbohydrate monomer. Glucose and fructose are common examples.

muscle   Structures that create movement in an organism by contracting under a stimulus from a neuron. There are three types of muscle: skeletal, which is responsible for voluntary movement; smooth, which is responsible for involuntary movement; and cardiac, which makes up the heart.

mutation   An error in the sequence of nucleotides in DNA or RNA that in turn affects the production of proteins. There are two main types of mutations: substitution mutations and frameshift mutations. A substitution mutation occurs when one nucleotide is replaced by another; these mutations can range from ineffectual to drastic, depending on how the new nucleotide changes the protein coded for. Frameshift mutations occur when a nucleotide is either inserted or deleted into the code; these mutations are always drastic, since an insertion or deletion will affect *every* codon in a particular genetic sequence by throwing the entire three-by-three codon frame out of whack.

myelin sheath   A structure that speeds the movement of action potentials along the axon of a neuron. The sheath is built of Schwann cells, which wrap themselves around the axon of the neuron, leaving small gaps in between known as the Nodes of Ranvier.

myosin   Protein filaments that, along with actin, allow muscles to contract.

N

NADH   An energy-carrying coenzyme produced by glycolysis and the Krebs cycle. NADH carries energy to the electron transport chain where it is stored in ATP.

natural selection   The theory, first proposed by Darwin, which holds that organisms produce as many offspring as possible, which compete for limited resources. Organisms' characteristics vary, and certain characteristics will allow organisms to survive and reproduce more effectively. These adaptive characteristics will be more prevalent in subsequent generations. Natural selection is the engine of evolution, by choosing the most fit genes to pass from one generation to the next.

Glossary

nephridium   A blood filtration and excretory organ characteristic of segmented worms.

nephron   Tiny, tubule structures responsible for the filtering of blood in the kidneys of vertebrates.

neritic zone   The medium depth zone of the marine biome. Extends to 600 feet beneath the water's surface and sits on the continental shelf, hundreds of miles from any shore. Algae, crustaceans, and fish inhabit this region.

nervous system   Control system of the body that functions by sending impulses through neurons to receive information and spur muscles to action.

neuron   The functional unit of the nervous system. A neuron is a specialized cell able to carry an action potential and made up of dendrites, a cell body, and an axon. There are three types of neurons: sensory, motor, and interneurons.

niche   The unique role a population plays in a community. A niche ranges from where the members of a population lives, what they eat, when they sleep, how they reproduce, and across every other characteristic that defines the way a population lives in a community.

nitrogenous base   One of the nitrogen-containing bases in DNA and RNA nucleotides. There are five nitrogenous bases in living organisms. DNA is composed of adenine, thymine, guanine, and cytosine. RNA is composed of adenine, uracil, guanine, and cytosine.

nondisjunction   Occurs when a pair of homologous chromosomes fails to separate during gamete formation. The offspring produced from these gametes have either one too many or one too few of a particular chromosome. Nondisjunction is the cause of genetic disorders like Down's syndrome.

notochord   A longitudinal rod of cells that forms in the least developed chordates and in embryonic stages of more developed chordates.

nucleolus   A dense, spherical body inside the nucleus of a cell. The nucleolus makes the RNA that is a structural component of the ribosomes.

nucleotide   The monomer of a nucleic acid. Nucleotides consist of (1) a phosphate group, a group of atoms containing phosphorous; (2) a sugar; and (3) a nitrogenous base, a compound containing nitrogen that removes H^+ ions from solution. Nucleotides are grouped into two general classes, depending on the sugar group that they carry: deoxyribonucleic acids (DNA) contain the sugar deoxyribose and ribonucleic acids (RNA) contain the sugar ribose. Nucleotides are further divided by the type of nitrogenous base that they carry. DNA is composed of adenine, thymine, guanine, and cytosine. RNA is composed of adenine, uracil, guanine, and cytosine.

nucleus   The large, central organelle of eukaryotes. The nucleus contains the genetic material of the cell and controls cellular activities.

O

olfactory epithelium   Region near the top of the nasal cavity with chemoreceptors and neurons that inform the sense of smell.

oogenesis   The process in which haploid eggs cells (ova) form through meiotic division.

organelle   Specialized membrane-bound structure in a cell that performs a specific function. Examples of organelles include the endoplasmic reticulum and the mitochondria.

organ   A discrete unit of tissues that work together to perform specific functions within the body.

osmosis   Process by which water naturally travels from an area of high water concentration to low water concentration.

ovary   In animals, the female gonad that produces ova and sex hormones. In plants, the ovaries are the structure at the base of the pistil that contains the eggs.

ovule   Structure that contains the female gametophyte and gametes; after fertilization, develops into a seed.

oxidative phosphorylation   Part of the electron transport chain. A process occurring in the mitochondria that results in the formation of ATP from the flow of electrons across the inner membrane to bind with oxygen.

P

pancreas   A digestive organ that releases enzymes into the small intestine. Also an endocrine gland that regulates glucose levels in the blood by the release of insulin or glucagon from specialized cells called islets of Langerhans.

parathyroid   Four small glands embedded on the posterior surface of the thyroid gland. The parathyroid glands produce a hormone that regulates the level of calcium in the bloodstream.

parthenogenesis   Asexual reproduction in which an unfertilized gamete (usually female) produces female offspring. Parthenogenesis vastly increases the speed at which a population can grow, though it results in a loss of genetic diversity among members of the population.

pelagic zone   The open-ocean zone at the greatest depth in a marine habitat. This zone is divided into a photic (down to 600 feet below the water's surface) and aphotic zone.

peptide bond   The bond between the amino acids in a protein. Formed by dehydration synthesis.

peripheral nervous system (PNS)   The pathways by which the central nervous system receives sensory information from the body and sends commands to muscles. The peripheral nervous system is divided into two halves. The sensory system brings information in from the body, while the motor system sends commands out to muscles.

peristalsis   The rolling motion of smooth muscle that moves food along the alimentary canal. Includes the passage from the esophagus to the stomach, the churning action of the stomach, and the passage through the small intestine.

pH   A scale for measuring the presence or absence of hydrogen ions in solution. Values between 0 and 7 indicate an excess of hydrogen ions. Such solutions are called acids. Values between 7 and 14 indicate the presence of compounds that counteract the effects of hydrogen ions. Such solutions are called bases. At pH 7, solutions are neutral.

phagocytes   A type of white blood cell that kills invading cells by ingesting them.

phagocytosis   A form of endocytosis in which a cell ingests a solid particle.

phenotype   The entire set of observable characteristics of an organism or cell; the physical traits of an organism. The genotype, together with environmental factors, defines the phenotype.

phloem   Vascular tissue composed of cells that are living at maturity; transports the products of photosynthesis throughout the plant body.

phospholipid   Type of lipid found in cell membranes. Phospholipids are made up of a single hydrophilic phosphate head and two nonpolar hydrophobic lipid tails.

phospholipid bilayer   A double layer of phospholipid molecules that provides the structure of the cell membrane. Formed naturally from the alignment of the two layers of lipids such that their hydrophobic tails point inward toward each other, and their hydrophilic phosphate heads point outward into the watery environments inside and outside of the cell.

photic zone   Literally, zone with light. The photic zone is part of the marine pelagic zone and extends to 600 feet below the surface of the ocean. Photosynthetic plankton as well as fish, sharks, and whales inhabit this zone.

photoperiodism   An organism's response to the length of day and night within a 24-hour period (photoperiod); in many plants, this phenomenon determines when flowering occurs.

photosynthesis   The process by which plants and other autotrophic organisms convert light energy into organic materials, such as glucose.

phylogeny   The evolutionary relationships of a genetically similar group of organisms.

pinocytosis   Form of endocytosis during which liquids are taken into the cell through the invagination of the cell membrane.

pioneer population   The first population to move into a geographic location and begin the process of ecological succession.

pistil   The female reproductive organ of the flower, composed of a stigma, style, and ovary; sometimes called the carpel.

pituitary   The "master" gland of the endocrine system. The pituitary releases hormones that control the other major glands of the endocrine system. Made up of the anterior and posterior pituitary. Controlled by the hypothalamus.

placenta   A structure that develops in the uterus during pregnancy; filter through which the embryo gains nutrition through the mother.

plasmids   Circular DNA molecules found in prokaryotes.

pollen   The male gametophyte of gymnosperms and angiosperms.

polymer   A large molecule consisting of the same or similar units attached in a series, forming a chain.

population   A group of interbreeding organisms in a particular locale exhibiting a unique set of characteristics such as patterns of growth and reproductive strategies.

Glossary

Glossary

predation   Term that refers to one organism eating another. Predation covers both carnivorous and herbivorous consumption.

producers   Autotrophic organisms such as plants, plankton, and chemosynthetic bacteria that are able to synthesize organic compounds using energy from the sun or chemical reactions. Producers do not have to consume other organisms to attain energy and are the foundation of every food web.

progesterone   Hormone that prepares the uterus for embryo implantation, and helps to maintain pregnancy.

prokaryote   A single-celled organism that completely lacks membrane-bound intracellular organelles such as a nucleus or mitochondria; prokaryotes possess only a single circular strand of DNA. Prokaryotes are simpler than eukaryotes and arose earlier in evolutionary history. All bacteria are prokaryotes. Taxonomists group all prokaryotes into the kingdom Monera.

prophase   The first stage of mitosis, meiosis I, and meiosis II, during which the chromosomes become visible and the centrioles move to opposite ends of the cell and begin to form the spindle.

pseudopods   Temporary cytoplasmic protrusions of ameboid cells that function in movement and food uptake by phagocytosis.

Punnett square   A pictorial method of showing the gene combinations (genotypes) of offspring that might result from an experimental genetic cross of two parents.

pyruvate   The 3-carbon end product of glycolysis. Pyruvate is the raw material of the Krebs cycle.

R

recessive   Refers to an allele that cannot control the phenotype unless it is the only kind of allele present, as in a homozygote or hemizygote. Refers to the trait or phenotype produced when only a recessive allele is present. The opposite of recessive is dominant.

reproductive isolation   The inability of individuals within a species to create offspring with members of any other species. The mark of a species is its reproductive isolation from all other species.

respiratory system   The organ system responsible for the intake of oxygen and diffusion of that gas into the blood, and the elimination of carbon dioxide from the body. Important structures of the system are the pharynx, larynx, trachea, bronchi, bronchioles, and lungs. Alveoli in the lungs are the location of gas exchange with the blood. The movement of the muscular diaphragm allows the lungs to inhale and exhale.

ribonucleic acid (RNA)   One type of nucleic acid polymer. RNA nucleotides' sugars contain one more oxygen atom than DNA nucleotides' sugars. RNA nucleotides can have the nitrogenous bases adenine, cytosine, guanine, and uracil.

ribosome   Organelle responsible for protein synthesis. Ribosomes are located in cytoplasm or endoplasmic reticulum.

root   The part of a plant beneath the soil; responsible for collecting water and minerals from the soil, storing nutrients, and securing the plant to the ground. Can be fibrous, or a tap root.

root hair   An outgrowth of a plant root that provides an increased surface area for the absorption of water and dissolved minerals from the soil.

runner   Slender horizontal stem that can give rise via specialized nodes to form new plants.

S

saprophytes   See decomposers.

segregation   Mendel's conclusion that individuals have two copies of each gene, and that these copies separate randomly during gamete formation, one copy per gamete. This law is true except for genes on sex chromosomes in males, who have only one copy of each such gene. It is often called Mendel's First Law.

semicircular canals   Fluid-filled structure within the ear that can detect balance.

sepal   Green, leaflike structure that encloses and protects the unopened flower bud.

sex cells   See gamete.

sex chromosome   Refers to a chromosome involved in defining the sex of an individual. Humans have 2 sex chromosomes and 44 autosomes. In females, both sex chromosomes are X chromosomes. Males have one X chromosome and one Y chromosome.

Glossary

sex-linked   Refers to a gene located on a sex chromosome, or to a trait defined by such a gene. Such traits will appear with different frequencies in males and females, and males and females will differ in their ability to transmit the trait to their offspring. In order for a recessive sex-linked trait such as hemophilia and color-blindness to manifest in the phenotype of a woman it must be inherited from both mother and father; such diseases will be present in the phenotype of a man if he inherits it just from his mother.

somatic cell   Any plant or animal cell that is not a germ cell, meaning it is not passed down to offspring. The class of cell formed during mitosis.

somatic nervous system   One half of the motor system of the peripheral nervous system. Responsible for voluntary, or conscious, movement. Neurons in this system target skeletal muscles and release the neurotransmitter acetylcholine.

speciation   The development of a species through evolution. A species forms when its members become reproductively isolated from all other organisms. Speciation can occur through geographic separation that eliminates gene flow, or through adaptive radiation.

species   A group of organisms defined by their ability to interbreed with only each other.

sperm   The male gamete in sexual reproduction.

spermatogenesis   The process in which haploid sperm cells form through meiotic division.

spinal cord   A long cylinder of nervous tissue that extends along the vertebral column from the head to the lower back. It controls some autonomic responses and connects the brain to the peripheral nervous system.

spores   Usually unicellular and microscopic, spores are produced by protist molds, fungi, and plants and are able to develop into new individuals. Spores are able to survive without food or water for long periods. Most fungi spend part of their lifecycle as hyphae and part as spores.

sporophyte   A diploid plant or plant structure that produces haploid spores through meiosis.

stabilizing selection   When selection pressures favor the average form of a trait.

stamen   The male reproductive organ of the flower, comprised of an anther and filament.

stigma   The top part of the pistil, where pollen grains are received.

stoma   A very small epidermal pore, surrounded by two guard cells, through which gases diffuse and water transpires in and out of a leaf. Plural: stomata.

stop codon   A codon on mRNA that signals the termination of DNA translation. There are three stop codons: UAA, UAG, or UGA.

style   The shaft of the pistil that leads from the stigma down into the ovary.

substrate   The starting material that will undergo chemical change in a chemical reaction facilitated by an enzyme.

symbiosis   A type of interaction within a community that falls into one of three categories: a parasitic relationship benefits one organism and hurts the other; a commensal relationship benefits one and does not affect the other, a mutualistic relationship benefits both organisms.

synapse   The gap between two neurons, spanning the space between the axon of one and the dendrites of the other. In order to pass an impulse across a synapse, neurons must release neurotransmitters.

T

taste bud   Structures on the tongue that allow for the sense of taste.

taxonomy   The study of biological classification.

telophase   The final stage of mitosis before cytokinesis. In telophase, the nuclear envelope re-forms around separated sister chromatids, and kinetochore microtubules disappear. Cell elongation also occurs during this phase. The final stage of the first meiotic division (meiosis I), during which chromosomes arrive at the poles of the cell and begin to recondense; the final stage of the second meiotic division (meiosis II), during which chromosomes arrive at the poles of the cell, the nuclear envelope begins to reform, and the chromosomes begin to recondense.

tendon   Connective tissue between bones and muscles.

testes   The male gonads; sperm and testosterone are produced here.

testosterone   A hormone necessary for sperm production in men. Also responsible for developing and maintaining the secondary sex characteristics of males, starting at puberty.

thyroid   Gland that produces the hormone thyroxine, which increases the metabolism of most of the cells in the body. Located in the neck.

tissue   A group of closely connected and similar cells that cooperate to generate a specific structure or specialized function within an organism.

tracheophyte   A terrestrial plant with a vascular system.

trait   Any observable feature or characteristic of an organism.

transfer RNA (tRNA)   An RNA molecule used in protein synthesis as a link helping to convert messenger RNA into amino acids.

transpiration   The process by which a plant loses water to its environment through evaporation.

trophic level   Steps on a food/biomass pyramid that are defined by organisms within a community which are the same distance from the primary producers in a food web.

tropism   Long-term growth of a plant toward or away from a stimulus.

tuber   Fleshy underground storage structure composed of an enlarged portion of the stem that has on its surface buds capable of producing new plants.

U

uterus   Structure in the female reproductive system in which the embryo develops.

V

vascular cambium   Tissue that produces new vascular cells; lies between the xylem and phloem in dicot stems.

vascular tissue   A conductive component (either xylem or phloem) of the vascular system that transports food and nutrients throughout the plant body.

vegetative propagation   A form of asexual reproduction in which plants produce genetically identical offshoots (clones) of themselves, which then develop into independent plants.

vein   A blood vessel that carries blood back to the heart. The blood in veins is not oxygenated, with the exception of the pulmonary vein.

vertebrate   An animal that has a skeletal rod of bone or cartilage running up its back, surrounding the nerve cord. Segments of this rod are called vertebrae. All vertebrate animals belong to subphylum Vertebrata, part of phylum Chordata.

vestigial structures   Bodily structures that developed in the past, but no longer serve any function for an organism.

villi   Fingerlike projections in the small intestine that increase surface area and maximize the absorption of nutrients.

vitamins   Complex molecules that usually serve as coenzymes, assisting in physiological processes.

W

warm-blooded   Animals that have developed fat and fur, hair, or feathers in order to retain heat produced by metabolic activities. Also known as endothermic. Warm-blooded animals are able to thrive in various climates, because they are minimally affected by environmental fluctuations in temperature.

X

xylem   Vascular tissue composed of cells that are dead at maturity; transports water and dissolved minerals upwards from the roots to the shoot.

Z

zygote   In sexual reproduction, the diploid product of the fusion of the father's haploid sperm cell and the mother's haploid ovum (egg) cell. The single-celled zygote divides billions of times to form a whole individual.

Glossary

PRACTICE
TESTS

Practice Tests Are Your Best Friends

IN THIS CRAZY WORLD, THERE'S AT LEAST ONE thing that you can always take for granted: the SAT II Biology test will stay the same. From year to year and test to test, of the 60 core questions you have to answer on the SAT II Biology, about 10 will deal with genetics, 8 will cover ecology, 10 will deal with cellular biology, and so on. Obviously, different versions of the SAT II Biol-

ogy aren't *exactly* the same: individual questions won't repeat from test to test. But the subjects you'll be tested on, and the way in which you'll be tested, *will* remain constant. This constancy can be of great benefit to you as you study for the test.

To show how you can use the similarity between different versions of the SAT II Biology test to your advantage, we provide a case study.

Taking Advantage of the Test's Regularity

One day, an eleventh grader named Molly Bloom sits down at the desk in her room and takes a practice test for the SAT II Biology. She's a bright young woman, and she gets only one question wrong. Molly checks her answers and then jumps from her chair and does a little happy dance that would be embarrassing if anyone else were around to see her.

After her euphoria passes, Molly begins to wonder which question she got wrong and returns to her chair. She discovers that the question dealt with mitosis. Looking over the question, Molly at first thinks the test made a mistake and that she was actually right, but then she realizes that she answered the question wrong because she had thought that anaphase preceded metaphase, when really it is the other way around. In thinking about the question, Molly realizes she didn't have the strongest grasp of the processes of mitosis in general. She takes a few minutes to study up on cell reproduction, and sorts out when the different phases take place and what happens in each. All this takes her about ten minutes, after which she vows never again to make a mistake on a question involving mitosis.

Analyzing Molly Bloom

Molly's actions seem minor. All she did was study a question she got wrong until she understood why she got it wrong and what she should have done to get it right. But think about the implications. Molly answered the question incorrectly because she didn't understand the topic it was testing, and the practice test pointed out her mistaken understanding in the most noticeable way possible: she got the question wrong.

After doing her admittedly goofy little dance, Molly wasn't content simply to see what the correct answer was and get on with her day; she wanted to see *how* and *why* she got the question wrong, and what she should have done, or needed to know, in order to get it right. So, with a look of determination, telling herself, "I will figure out why I got this question wrong, yes I will, yes," she spent a little while studying the question, discovered her mistaken understanding of mitosis, and then eliminated her misunderstanding of mitosis by studying the subject. If Molly were to take that same test again, she definitely would not get that question wrong.

"But she never will take that test again, so she's never going to see that particular question again," some poor sap who hasn't read this book might sputter. "She wasted her time. What a dork!"

Why That Poor Sap Really Is a Poor Sap

In some sense, that poor sap is correct: Molly never will take that exact practice test again. But the poor sap is wrong to call Molly derogatory names, because, as we know, the SAT II Biology is remarkably similar from year to year—both in the topics it covers and in the way it poses questions about those topics. Therefore, when Molly taught herself about mitosis, she actually learned how to answer the similar questions dealing with cell reproduction that will undoubtedly appear on every future practice test, and on the SAT II Biology that counts.

In studying the results of her practice test, in figuring out exactly why she got her one question wrong and what she should have known and done to get it right, Molly targeted a weakness and overcame it.

Molly and You

Molly has it easy. She took a practice test and only got one question wrong. Less than one percent of all people who take the SAT II Biology will be so lucky. Of course, the only reason Molly got that many right was so that we could use her as an easy example.

So, what if you take a practice test and get 15 questions wrong, and your errors span many of the major topics in biology? Well, you should do exactly what Molly did: take your test and study it. Identify every question you got wrong, figure out why you got it wrong, and then teach yourself what you should have done to get the question right. If you can't figure out your error, find someone who can.

Think about it. What does an incorrect answer mean? That wrong answer identifies a weakness in your test taking skills, whether that weakness is unfamiliarity with a particular topic or a tendency to be careless. If you got 15 questions wrong on a practice test, then each of those questions identifies a weakness in your ability to take the SAT II Biology or your knowledge about the topics the SAT II Biology tests. As you study each question and figure out why you got that question wrong, you are actually learning how to answer the very questions that will appear some Saturday in the future on the real SAT II Biology. You are discovering exactly where your weaknesses in biology lie and addressing them. You are learning not just to understand the principles you're being tested on, but also *the way* that ETS will test you. Practice tests do for you what simply studying biology cannot: beyond helping you understand biology, they prepare you specifically for the test you're going to take.

True, if you got 15 questions wrong, the first time you study your test will take a bit of time. Think of that time as an investment. If you study your practice test properly, you will be eliminating future mistakes. Since practice tests allow you to target your weaknesses, on each successive practice test you take, you will get fewer questions wrong, meaning less time spent studying those errors. Also, and more importantly, you'll be pinpointing what you need to study to get the score you want on the SAT II Biology, identifying and overcoming your weaknesses, and learning to answer an increasing variety of questions on the specific topics covered by the test. Taking practice tests and studying them will allow you to teach yourself how to recognize and handle whatever the SAT II Biology has to throw at you.

Practice Tests Are Your Best Friends

Taking a Practice Test

Through the example of Miss Molly Bloom, we've shown you why studying practice tests is an extremely powerful study tool. Now we'll explain how to use that tool.

Controlling Your Environment

Although a practice test is practice, and no one but you ever needs to see your scores, you should do everything in your power to make the practice test feel like the real SAT II Biology. The closer your practice resembles the real thing, the more helpful it will be. When taking a practice test, follow these rules:

Time yourself: Don't give yourself any extra time. Be stricter with yourself than the meanest administrator would be. Don't give yourself time off for bathroom breaks. If you have to go to the bathroom, let the clock keep running; that's what would happen during the real SAT II.

Take the test in a single sitting: Training yourself to endure an hour of test taking is part of your preparation.

Eliminate distractions: Don't take the practice test in a room with lots of people walking through it. Go to a library, your bedroom, a well-lit closet—anywhere quiet.

Following these rules ensure that you won't cheat yourself as you study. If you aren't strict with yourself about the little details, it can be quite easy to put in hours of study time in which you're mostly staring into space or singing along with the radio. If you're going to take the time to study, you might as well make that time as productive and fruitful as possible.

Practice Test Strategy

You should take each practice test as if it were the real deal: go for the highest score you can get. This doesn't mean you should be more daring than you would be on the actual test, guessing blindly even when you can't eliminate an answer. It doesn't mean that you should speed through the test carelessly. The more closely your attitude and strategies during the practice test reflect those you'll employ during the actual test, the more accurately the practice test will reflect your strengths and weaknesses: you'll learn what areas you should study and how to pace yourself during the test.

Scoring Your Practice Test

After you take your practice test, you'll no doubt want to score it and see how you did. But don't just tally up your raw score. As a part of your scoring, you should keep a precise list of every question you got wrong and every question you skipped. This list will be your guide when you study your test.

Studying Your . . . No, Wait, Go Take a Break

You know how to have fun. Go do that for a while. Come back when you're refreshed.

Studying Your Practice Test

After grading your test, you should have a list of the questions you answered incorrectly or skipped. Studying your test involves going down this list and examining each question you answered incorrectly. As you study a question, make sure not just to learn the right answer but also to understand why you got the question wrong, and what you could have done to get the question right.

Why Did You Get the Question Wrong?

There are three main reasons why you might have gotten an individual question wrong:

1. You thought you knew the answer, but, actually, you didn't.

2. You couldn't answer the question directly, but you knew the general principles involved. Using this knowledge, you managed to eliminate some answer choices and then guessed among the remaining answers; sadly, you guessed incorrectly.

3. You knew the answer, but somehow made a careless mistake.

You should know which of these reasons applies to every question you got wrong.

What You Could Have Done to Get the Question Right

The reasons you got a question wrong affect how you should think about it while studying your test.

If You Got a Question Wrong for Reason 1—Lack of Knowledge

A question answered incorrectly for Reason 1 identifies a weakness in your knowledge of the biology tested on the SAT II Biology. Discovering this wrong answer gives you an opportunity to target and eliminate that weakness, and perhaps related weaknesses as well.

For example, if you got a question wrong that dealt with the structure of RNA, first figure out why you were confused about RNA's structure, and then study up on the correct structure. But don't stop there. If you had some trouble with RNA structure, it's possible you're not so hot with RNA function. Take a quick look through RNA function to see if what you remember about it is complete and correct. If it is: great! If it isn't, take some time to study up on that as well. Remember, you will *not* see a question exactly like the question you got wrong, so there's no use in making sure you won't get that exact question wrong a second time. Instead, cut to the heart of the problem and understand the principles that would lead you to a correct answer on this question and any other related question.

If You Got a Question Wrong for Reason 2—Guessing Wrong

If you guessed wrong, review your guessing strategy. Did you guess intelligently? Could you have eliminated more answers? If yes, why didn't you? By thinking in this critical way about the decisions you made while taking the practice test, you can train yourself to make quicker, more decisive, and better decisions.

If you took a guess and chose the incorrect answer, don't let that sour you on guessing. Even as you go over the question and figure out if there was any way for you to have answered the question without having to guess, remind yourself that as long as you eliminated at least one answer and guessed—even if you got the question wrong—you followed the right strategy.

If You Got a Question Wrong for Reason 3—Carelessness

If you discover you got a question wrong because you were careless, it might be tempting to say to yourself, "Oh I made a careless error," and assure yourself you won't do that again. That is not enough. You made that careless mistake for a reason, and you should try to figure out why. While getting a question wrong because you didn't know the answer constitutes a weakness in your knowledge about biology, making a careless mistake represents a weakness in your *method* of taking the test.

To overcome this weakness, you need to approach it in the same critical way you would approach a lack of knowledge. Study your mistake. Reenact your thought process on the problem and see where and how your carelessness came about. Were you rushing? Did you jump at the first answer that seemed right instead of reading all the answers? Do you have trouble telling the difference between the letters C and D? Know your error, and look it in the eye. If you learn precisely what your mistake was, you are much less likely to make that mistake again.

If You Left a Question Blank

It is also a good idea to study the questions you left blank on the test, since those questions constitute a reservoir of lost points. A blank answer is a result either of:

Total inability to answer a question. Look to see if there was some way you might have been able to eliminate an answer choice or two and put yourself in a better position to guess. You should also make a particular point to study up on that topic in biology, since you clearly have a good deal of trouble with it.

Lack of time. Look over the question and see whether you think you could have answered it. If you definitely could, then you know that you are throwing away points and probably working too slowly. If you couldn't, then carry out the steps above: study the relevant material and review your guessing strategy.

The Secret Weapon: Talking to Yourself

Yes, it's embarrassing. Yes, you'll look silly. But, first of all, no one will be around while you study. And second, talking to yourself is perhaps the best way to pound something into your brain. As you go through the steps of studying a question, you should talk them out. When you verbalize something to yourself, it makes it much harder to delude yourself into thinking that you're working if you're really not. Talking out the words makes you really think about them, and taking an active grip on your studying will make all the difference between a pretty good score and a great score.

SAT II Biology

Practice Test I

BIOLOGY E/M TEST

FOR BOTH BIOLOGY-E AND BIOLOGY-M, ANSWER QUESTIONS 1–60

Directions: Each set of lettered choices below refers to the numbered questions or statements immediately following it. Select the one lettered choice that best answers each question or best fits each statement, and then fill in the corresponding oval on the answer sheet. A choice may be used once, more than once, or not at all in each set.

Questions 1–3 refer to the following molecules:

    (A)   proteins
    (B)   monosaccharides
    (C)   lipids
    (D)   DNA
    (E)   RNA

1. Contain carbon, hydrogen, and oxygen in a 1:2:1 ratio

2. Are often not soluble in water

3. Enzymes, which catalyze biological reactions, are protein molecules, consisting of one or more chains of amino acids.

Questions 4–6 refer to the following groups:

    (A)   producer
    (B)   primary consumer
    (C)   secondary consumer
    (D)   tertiary consumer
    (E)   decomposer

4. The group in the food pyramid with the fewest number of members

5. Creates glucose from carbon dioxide in the atmosphere

6. Omnivores most often fall into this group

Questions 7–9 refer to the following processes:

    (A)   Krebs Cycle
    (B)   oxidative phosphorylation
    (C)   aerobic respiration
    (D)   glycolysis
    (E)   anaerobic respiration

7. Stage at which one molecule of 6-carbon glucose is broken in half to produce two molecules of pyruvate. Two ATP are generated in this stage.

8. Process occurring in the mitochondria of eukaryotes and resulting in the total oxidation of acetyl-CoA to carbon dioxide. Two ATP are generated in this stage.

9. Occurs in the fermentation of alcohol

Questions 10–12 refer to the following behavior types:

    (A)   imprinting
    (B)   habituation
    (C)   conditioning
    (D)   insight learning
    (E)   fixed-action patterns

10. When confronted with a non-harmful stimulus many, many times, an animal will learn to ignore it.

11. When an animal associates two unrelated events that occur simultaneously, this is known as

12. This behavior involves an animal's recognition of its mother.

GO ON TO THE NEXT PAGE

Directions: Each of the questions or incomplete statements below is followed by five suggested answers or completions. Some questions pertain to a set that refers to a laboratory or experimental situation. For each question, select the one choice that is the best answer to the question and then fill in the corresponding oval on the answer sheet.

13. Of the following, which group's members have the LEAST in common with each other?

    (A) Species
    (B) Order
    (C) Family
    (D) Phylum
    (E) Kingdom

14. A culture of animal cells and a culture of plant cells are pulverized and tested for the presence of several different molecules. Which of the following molecules should be significantly more prevalent in the plant cell sample?

    (A) Glucose
    (B) Deoxyribonucleic acid
    (C) Adenosine triphosphate
    (D) Cholesterol
    (E) Cellulose

15. Which of the following is the best example of exponential population growth?

    (A) A population of pigeons in a small town grows until there are few nesting areas left.
    (B) The salmon population in the Yukon River grows rapidly, greatly increasing the food supply for bears in the area.
    (C) Dandelions grow in a field until they cover the entire expanse.
    (D) Bacteria in a laboratory grow in many petri dishes, and are transferred to new, empty dishes as the old dishes begin to get filled.
    (E) The population of buffalo in the Great Plains is severely diminished by hunting and development.

16. A person becomes anemic when they are not getting enough oxygen to their body. Which of the following could cause someone to be anemic?

    (A) A deficiency in white blood cells
    (B) A deficiency in red blood cells
    (C) A low platelet count
    (D) Too little plasma in the bloodstream
    (E) An abnormally high T-cell count

17. Natural selection refers to all of the following EXCEPT

    (A) Individual organisms differ from one another.
    (B) Competition exists between individuals.
    (C) The best-adapted organisms are most likely to survive.
    (D) The best-adapted organisms are most likely to reproduce.
    (E) The traits an organism acquires in its lifetime are passed down to its offspring.

18. Which of the following is the best example of an ecological community?

    (A) All of the pigeons inhabiting a city
    (B) A school of trout in the Mississippi river
    (C) Tropical rainforests worldwide, and all of the organisms that inhabit them
    (D) All of the plants, insects, rodents, and predators inhabiting a small island
    (E) An ant colony

19. Which of the following is the best description of a protein molecule?

    (A) Small building blocks called amino acids linked together in one or more chains
    (B) Small building blocks called amino acids linked together in a ring
    (C) Small building blocks called nucleotides linked together in a helical structure
    (D) Small building blocks called monosaccharides linked together in a chain
    (E) A glycerol molecule linked to three hydrocarbon chains

20. The DNA sequence TTATTAGACCT is transcribed to the RNA sequence

    (A) TCCAGATTATT
    (B) GGCGGCUCAAG
    (C) TTUTTUGUCCT
    (D) UUTUUTCUGGU
    (E) AAUAAUCUGGA

GO ON TO THE NEXT PAGE

21. When a fertilized egg implants in the uterine lining, the lining is not shed in menstruation, but instead stays to support the pregnancy. What initially signals this change?

    (A) The release of hormones by the newly developing embryo
    (B) The release of estrogen by the ovaries
    (C) The release of enzymes by the uterine wall
    (D) The release of enzymes by the placenta
    (E) The release of hormones from the pituitary gland

22. Gaps in the fossil record, the only direct evidence for historical evolution, may be attributed to all of the following EXCEPT

    (A) fossilization is an improbable event
    (B) fossilization requires sedimentary rock
    (C) erosion
    (D) many fossils have yet to be found
    (E) specimens were enclosed in rocks formed from hardened sediments

23. You are told that an unidentified cell contains a single, circular DNA molecule but no defined nucleus. Which of the following is it also possible for the cell to possess?

    I.   Chloroplasts
    II. Cell wall
    III. Ribosomes

    (A) I only
    (B) III only
    (C) I and II only
    (D) II and III only
    (E) I, II, and III

24. Nitrogen in the atmosphere gets converted into a usable form by

    (A) photosynthesis
    (B) respiration
    (C) digestion
    (D) nitrogen-fixing bacteria
    (E) decomposition

25. Monerans are

    (A) eukaryotes
    (B) fungi
    (C) prokaryotes
    (D) multicellular
    (E) plants

26. Which of the following was NOT a component of the Earth's early atmosphere?

    (A) Oxygen
    (B) Water
    (C) Methane
    (D) Hydrogen
    (E) Ammonia

27. A blood vessel has thick muscular walls. This blood vessel is

    I.   an artery
    II. carrying oxygenated blood
    III. carrying blood away from the heart

    (A) I only
    (B) III only
    (C) I and II only
    (D) I and III only
    (E) I, II, and III

GO ON TO THE NEXT PAGE

28. Which of the following statements is true about the flow of energy through the food pyramid?

   (A) The most energy is at the top of the pyramid, with the tertiary consumers, because the energy increases at each level.
   (B) The most energy is at the bottom of the food pyramid because some is lost as it is passed from producer to each level of consumer.
   (C) The energy is distributed equally at each level of the pyramid; very little is lost or added moving from producers to tertiary consumers.
   (D) Energy doesn't flow through the food pyramid; each level receives energy from the sun.
   (E) It depends on the ecological community; in some, there is more energy at the top of the food pyramid, and in others, there is more energy at the bottom.

29. The toxic chemical produced by anaerobic respiration is

   (A) pyruvate
   (B) lactic acid
   (C) acetyl-CoA
   (D) NADH
   (E) coenzyme

30. One of the functions of human white blood cells is to ingest and destroy harmful agents, such as bacteria, that find their way into the bloodstream. In order to perform this function, you could expect a white blood cell to have a higher than average number of

   (A) ribosomes
   (B) peroxisomes
   (C) chloroplasts
   (D) lysosomes
   (E) chromosomes

GO ON TO THE NEXT PAGE

<u>Questions 31–35</u> refer to the diagram below.

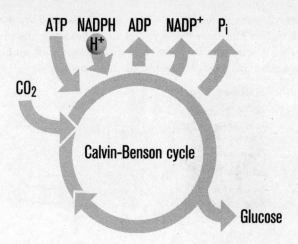

31. The depicted process is also known as

    (A) aerobic respiration
    (B) photophosphorylation
    (C) light-dependent photosynthesis
    (D) light-independent photosynthesis
    (E) anaerobic respiration

32. This process occurs in the

    (A) stroma of chloroplasts
    (B) cytoplasm of palisade cells
    (C) inner membrane of mitochondria
    (D) nucleus
    (E) endoplasmic reticulum

33. ATP stands for

    (A) accelerated transport protein
    (B) adenosine triphosphate
    (C) activated transphosphate
    (D) adenine tripeptide
    (E) adenosine diphosphate

34. The synthesized glucose will most likely be stored as

    (A) sucrose
    (B) starch
    (C) cellulose
    (D) glycogen
    (E) glucose

35. How is the Calvin cycle similar to the Krebs cycle?

    (A) The starting compound is regenerated at the end of the cycle.
    (B) Multiple molecules of ATP are produced.
    (C) Both occur in mitochondrial inner membranes.
    (D) Both produce oxygen gas.
    (E) Each is present in all prokaryotes.

GO ON TO THE NEXT PAGE

Questions 36–39 refer to the diagram below.

In an experiment, pre-soaked bean seeds were placed in three sterile petri dishes. They were covered with tissue paper and cotton, which was subsequently wet with tap water. The dishes were closed and taped shut. Dish 1 was affixed to the wall of a dark box with the transparent bottom facing out. Dish 2 was attached to the side of the windowsill, and Dish 3 was laid flat on the sill, each with bean seeds visible. After several days, the experimenter checked the new seedlings.

36. In Dish 1, several pale shoots have started to reach downwards. This is most likely an example of

    (A) thigmotropism
    (B) negative phototropism
    (C) positive gravitropism
    (D) negative gravitropism
    (E) wilting

37. The seeds in Dish 1 were kept in a dark box to

    (A) study the effect of light on their emergence
    (B) decrease experimental variables
    (C) simulate conditions when planted
    (D) study the effects of phototropism
    (E) keep the temperature down

38. The physical growth associated with tropisms is caused by

    (A) auxin
    (B) lactic acid
    (C) associative behavior
    (D) nitrogen
    (E) excess carbon dioxide

39. What process is NOT occurring in the Dish 1 seedlings

    (A) Photosynthesis
    (B) Respiration
    (C) Mitosis
    (D) Glycolysis
    (E) Absorption

GO ON TO THE NEXT PAGE

Questions 40–44 refer to the following illustration of a cell in solution, where a "+" indicates the presence of a sodium ion.

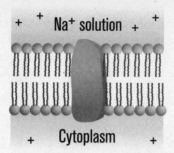

40. The figure depicts an animal cell in a 10% sodium solution. What likely occurs?

   (A) Water exits the cell by osmosis.
   (B) Sodium ions enter by diffusion.
   (C) The cell swells and bursts.
   (D) Sodium is pumped out of the cell.
   (E) No change

41. Relative to the cell, the sodium solution is

   (A) hypotonic
   (B) hydrophobic
   (C) isotonic
   (D) hypertonic
   (E) equivalent

42. The process by which the carrier protein might bring sodium into the cell is called

   (A) simple diffusion
   (B) facilitated diffusion
   (C) active transport
   (D) osmosis
   (E) phosphorylation

43. The cell membrane is composed of two layers of

   (A) phospholipids
   (B) enzymes
   (C) amino acids
   (D) proteins
   (E) steroids

44. Which of the following molecules could NOT easily and independently pass through the membrane?

   (A) Nitrogen
   (B) Water
   (C) Glucose
   (D) Carbon dioxide
   (E) Oxygen

GO ON TO THE NEXT PAGE

A copperhead snake (*Agkistrodon contortrix*) and a canary (*Serinus canaries*) are both being studied in a zoological laboratory.

45. During the night, the air temperature in the lab falls. What happens to the two organisms' metabolic rates?

    (A) both remain stable
    (B) both increase
    (C) snake's decreases, canary's remains stable
    (D) both decrease
    (E) canary's decreases, snake's increases

46. The copperhead has tiny leg bones along its skeleton. These structures are

    (A) mutations
    (B) homologous
    (C) analogous
    (D) vestigial
    (E) convergent

47. All of the following are true about endotherms EXCEPT

    (A) They inhabit a wide range of environments.
    (B) They typically become more active with warmer temperatures.
    (C) They maintain body temperatures higher than their surroundings.
    (D) They are all heterotrophs.
    (E) They evolved relatively later than ectotherms.

48. Which of the following characteristics distinguishes the canary from the copperhead?

    (A) Four-chambered heart
    (B) Thick-shelled eggs for survival on land
    (C) Vertebral column
    (D) Bony skeleton
    (E) Closed circulatory system

GO ON TO THE NEXT PAGE

Red cabbage (*Brassica oleracea capitata rubra*) can serve as a natural indicator—its pigments change color in response to varying pH levels. A student chops and boils half a red cabbage head for ten minutes, and then strains it to obtain a purple liquid. The liquid is then cooled to room temperature and separated into beakers. The student adds various substances to each beaker and observes the changes.

Additive	pH	Solution Color
Lemon Juice	2.0	Pink
Vinegar	2.2	Pink-red
Baking Soda	8.3	Blue-green

49. What can the student determine about red cabbage as a natural indicator?

    (A) It turns pink in the presence of acids.
    (B) It turns red in the presence of bases.
    (C) It turns blue-green in the presence of acids.
    (D) It is purple at a pH lower than 7.
    (E) It is a poor indicator of acidic or basic solutions.

50. What would the student observe if sodium hydroxide (NaOH) was slowly added to the vinegar solution?

    (A) The solution would turn from pink-red to purple to blue-green.
    (B) The solution would turn from pink-red to pink to yellow.
    (C) Nothing -- the reaction has already occurred.
    (D) A white precipitate would form at the bottom.
    (E) The solution would turn clear.

51. Plants get much of their color from pigments, such as chlorophyll. What is the function of red cabbage pigments in nature?

    (A) Indicate the pH of the soil
    (B) Contribute to photosynthesis
    (C) Keep down heat absorption
    (D) None: vestigial structure
    (E) Attract animals

52. When added directly to leaves of red cabbage, such as in salad, vinegar affects no color change. What best explains why?

    (A) Vinegar is too weak a substance to change the indicator
    (B) Nothing can penetrate the epidermis of plant cells
    (C) Red cabbage neutralizes the vinegar
    (D) Hydrogen ions cannot independently cross cell membranes
    (E) The indicator only works at higher temperatures

GO ON TO THE NEXT PAGE

The common fruit fly (*Drosophila melanogaster*) is usually found with red eyes and normal wings. A series of experimental crosses were run to examine their recessive traits: white eyes and vestigial (shrunken) wings. In the F_0 generation, a female with red eyes and normal wings was crossed with a male having white eyes and vestigial wings. The results are given below.

Phenotype	F_1 Males	F_1 Females
Red eyes, normal wings	21	20
White eyes, normal wings	0	0
Red eyes, vestigial wings	0	0
White eyes, vestigial wings	0	0

Phenotype	F_2 Males	F_2 Females
Red eyes, normal wings	62	123
White eyes, normal wings	59	0
Red eyes, vestigial wings	18	39
White eyes, vestigial wings	21	0

53. Based on the data, which of these characteristics is sex-linked in fruit flies?

    (A) Wing shape
    (B) Eye color
    (C) Vestigial wings
    (D) Red eyes
    (E) All of the above

54. What is the likelihood of observing female offspring with white eyes and vestigial wings in the F_3 generation?

    (A) Impossible: females cannot have white eyes
    (B) Much less likely than any other phenotype
    (C) As likely as seeing males with white eyes and vestigial wings
    (D) As likely as seeing females with red eyes and vestigial wings
    (E) Unable to determine without actually breeding flies

55. What is the ratio of phenotypes in F_2 males?

    (A) 4:1
    (B) 3:1
    (C) 3:3:1:1
    (D) 3:0:1:0
    (E) 1:1:1:1

56. If the allele for white eyes was dominant, approximately how many F_2 males would have white eyes (out of a possible 160 males)?

    (A) 20
    (B) 40
    (C) 60
    (D) 80
    (E) 120

GO ON TO THE NEXT PAGE

An experimenter was testing the effects of temperature on egg production and hatching rates in fruit flies. She kept separate communities of 50 fruit flies at different temperatures, counting the eggs produced and hatchlings for each day of the experiment.

		Day 2	Day 3	Day 4	Day 5
5°C	Eggs (total)	0	8	19	31
	Hatchlings	0	0	0	0
20°C	Eggs (total)	3	15	45	51
	Hatchlings	0	0	13	39
30°C	Eggs (total)	4	20	62	76
	Hatchlings	0	1	44	69
45°C	Eggs (total)	0	2	4	4
	Hatchlings	0	0	1	1

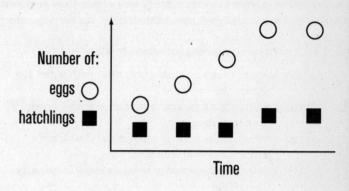

57. According to this data, the experimenter can conclude fertility rates of fruit flies are highest at temperatures near

   (A) 5°
   (B) 15°
   (C) 30°
   (D) 40°
   (E) 50°

58. The majority of egg production occurs between days

   (A) 1–2
   (B) 2–3
   (C) 3–4
   (D) 4–5
   (E) after day 5

59. This graph best represents the experiment at

   (A) 10°
   (B) 20°
   (C) 30°
   (D) 40°
   (E) 50°

60. Constructing a hypothesis about fertility rates for fruit flies at different temperatures could be strengthened by

   (A) conducting tests at temperatures higher than 45°
   (B) measuring the growth of the individual organisms
   (C) increasing temperatures by 5° each day
   (D) testing different species of insects
   (E) charting the survival of the original 50 flies on each day

GO ON TO THE NEXT PAGE

BIOLOGY-E SECTION

If you are taking the Biology-E test, continue with questions 61–80.
If you are taking the Biology-M test, go to question 81 now.

Directions: Each of the questions or incomplete statements below is followed by five suggested answers or completions. Some questions pertain to a set that refers to a laboratory or experimental situation. For each question, select the one choice that is the best answer to the question and then fill in the corresponding oval on the answer sheet.

61. A particularly strong sensation is felt when

    (A) a neuron fires an action potential with a greater charge than normal
    (B) a neuron fires an action potential with a lower charge than normal
    (C) a neuron fires an action potential that lasts a longer time than usual
    (D) a neuron fires action potentials more frequently than usual
    (E) interneurons rather than sensory neurons carry the action potential

62. All of the following are part of the cytoskeleton EXCEPT

    (A) microtubules
    (B) microfilaments
    (C) flagella
    (D) cilia
    (E) ribosomes

63. As a means to avoid predators, an insect and a squirrel both develop flaps between their legs that allows them to glide in the air. This is an example of

    (A) divergent evolution
    (B) speciation
    (C) convergent evolution
    (D) coevolution
    (E) biological magnification

64. The common house cat is inadvertently introduced to a small island that previously contained no cats. The cats begin to feed on local rodents, and their population grows very rapidly in the first few years, after which it begins to level off. At this point, the cat population of cats has reached the

    (A) maximum yield
    (B) carrying capacity
    (C) tertiary level
    (D) climax community
    (E) extinction point

65. In addition to gas exchange, the respiratory system helps regulate

    (A) the immune response
    (B) body temperature
    (C) pH balance in the blood
    (D) enzyme production
    (E) osmotic pressure

66. A particular food chain consists of mice, which feed on grass, snakes that feed on the mice, and hawks, which feed on both mice and snakes. Rank the animals from most to least numerous in this particular environment.

    (A) mice, snakes, hawks
    (B) hawks, snakes, mice
    (C) hawks, mice, snakes
    (D) mice, hawks, snakes
    (E) snakes, mice, hawks

GO ON TO THE NEXT PAGE

Questions 67–70 refer to the following diagram, depicting a cross-section view of the ocean divided into standard zones

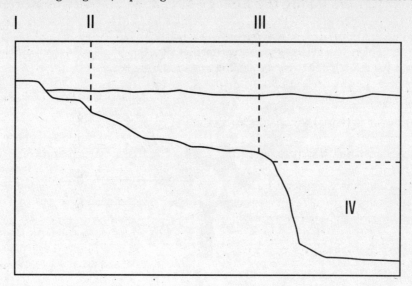

67. The area from II to III is known as the

   (A) pelagic zone
   (B) neritic zone
   (C) abyssal plain
   (D) intertidal zone
   (E) aphotic zone

68. What organismal characteristics are most likely found in zone IV?

   (A) Autotrophic
   (B) Exclusively unicellular
   (C) Heterotrophic
   (D) Highly advanced eyesight
   (E) Silicate shells

69. Of the following, which organism is LEAST likely to be found in the intertidal zone?

   (A) Heterotrophic clams
   (B) Photosynthetic kelp
   (C) Heterotropic starfish
   (D) Chemosynthetic bacteria
   (E) Photosynthetic algae

70. The ocean participates in which of the following cycles?

   I.   Water cycle
   II. Carbon cycle
   III. Nitrogen cycle

   (A) I only
   (B) I and II only
   (C) I and III only
   (D) II and III only
   (E) I, II, and III

GO ON TO THE NEXT PAGE

Questions 71–75 refer to the following diagram.

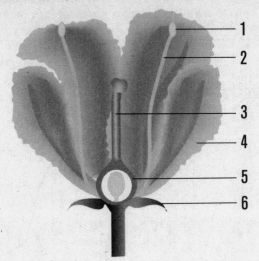

71. Structure 6 is called a

   (A) petal
   (B) sepal
   (C) ovule
   (D) leaf
   (E) stamen

72. The pollen tube runs through structure

   (A) 1
   (B) 2
   (C) 3
   (D) 4
   (E) 5

73. The function of structure 1 is to

   (A) spread pollen
   (B) receive gametes
   (C) photosynthesize
   (D) release pheromones
   (E) emit spores

74. If pollinated, fruit will grow from structure

   (A) 1
   (B) 3
   (C) 4
   (D) 5
   (E) 6

75. This could be an illustration of a

   (A) bracheophyte
   (B) conifer
   (C) fungus
   (D) dicot
   (E) fern

GO ON TO THE NEXT PAGE

A field biologist was studying the behavior of several similar species of warblers that had all recently been introduced to a national park. All the birds fed on the same leaf-eating insects on the same spruce trees at the same time of day. Over a period of several years, she observed the species' ranges of typical appearance in spruce trees, in terms of height.

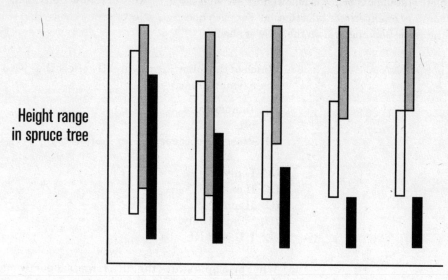

Height range in spruce tree

Time

□ Bay-breasted warbler
▨ Cape May warbler
■ Blackburnian warbler

76. The segregation of warblers in the tree demonstrates

(A) convergent evolution
(B) adaptation
(C) predation
(D) mutation
(E) climax community

77. An organism's niche is determined by which of the following factors?

(A) Habitat location
(B) Food
(C) Temperature
(D) Behavior
(E) All of the above

78. What is the primary consumer in this community?

(A) Cape May warbler
(B) Spruce
(C) Bay-breasted warbler
(D) Insect
(E) Blackburnian warbler

79. What can the experimenter conclude from her observations?

(A) Inter-species competition sorts warblers into different niches.
(B) Competing warblers kill off any intruders in their zone.
(C) The population of Blackburnian warblers falls dramatically in the presence of other species.
(D) Warblers will change their diets under new selection pressure.
(E) Spruce trees cannot support multiple species of warblers.

80. If a fungus killed off a large percentage of the spruces' insect populations in the park, which of the following is a predictable result?

(A) The warblers consume all the available insects and die off.
(B) The Bay-breasted warbler replaces the other species.
(C) Each population of warbler species falls in number until a new carrying capacity is reached.
(D) Warblers migrate to new insect-rich forests.
(E) Different species mate to give rise to better adapted warblers.

GO ON TO THE NEXT PAGE →

BIOLOGY-M SECTION

**If you are taking the Biology-M test, continue with questions 81–100.
Be sure to start this section of the test by filling in oval 61 on your answer sheet.**

<u>Directions:</u> Each of the questions or incomplete statements below is followed by five suggested answers or completions. Some questions pertain to a set that refers to a laboratory or experimental situation. For each question, select the one choice that is the best answer to the question and then fill in the corresponding oval on the answer sheet.

81. A nitrogenous base found in RNA but not in DNA is

    (A) adenine
    (B) guanine
    (C) cytosine
    (D) thymine
    (E) uracil

T=tall, t=short

82. Which of the following can be inferred from the Punnett Square above?

    I.   The genotypic ratio is 50% hybrid tall, 25% pure tall, and 25% pure short.
    II. The genotypic ratio is 75% tall, 25% short.
    III. The phenotypic ratio is 50% hybrid tall, 25% pure tall, and 25% pure short.
    IV. The phenotypic ratio is 75% tall, 25% short.
    V.   These results are typically found in sex-linked inheritance.

    (A) I, IV
    (B) I, III, V
    (C) I, III
    (D) II, III
    (E) II, IV, V

83. Divergent evolution might result in

    (A) biological magnification
    (B) reproductive isolation
    (C) analogous traits
    (D) mutations
    (E) succession

84. Which of the following can greatly effect the speed of an enzymatic reaction?

    I.   Temperature
    II. pH
    III. Presence of coenzymes or inhibitors

    (A) I only
    (B) II only
    (C) III only
    (D) I and III only
    (E) I, II, and III

85. What principle states that in a large, randomly mating population in which evolutionary forces such as selection, migration, and mutation do not occur, the allele and genotype frequencies will remain constant from generation to generation?

    (A) Natural selection
    (B) Homeostasis
    (C) Balanced mutation
    (D) Stabilizing selection
    (E) Hardy-Weinberg equilibrium

86. Of the following, which statement is true of glycolysis?

    (A) Breaks glucose down to pyruvate
    (B) Also called fermentation
    (C) Produces no ATP
    (D) Not part of the aerobic respiratory pathway
    (E) Occurs inside mitochondria

GO ON TO THE NEXT PAGE

Cystic fibrosis (CF) is caused by gene mutation on an autosomal chromosome, where a single nucleotide is omitted during the copying of a normal DNA sequence.

87. This type of mutation is known as

    (A) frameshift
    (B) point mutation
    (C) insertion
    (D) silent mutation
    (E) crossing-over

88. The CF gene is recessive. Assuming his genes are not the product of mutations, a CF patient must have inherited CF genes from

    (A) mother only
    (B) father only
    (C) both parents
    (D) mother if the child is male
    (E) one parent who is a CF patient

89. Mutations can occur during

    I.   transcription
    II. translation
    III. meiosis

    (A) I only
    (B) II only
    (C) III only
    (D) I and II only
    (E) I, II, and III

90. Why are frameshift mutations particularly dangerous?

    (A) They shorten the length of chromosomes.
    (B) No other mutation changes phenotypes.
    (C) They prevent transcription from occurring.
    (D) They affect all codons following the mutation.
    (E) Future offspring will be sterile.

GO ON TO THE NEXT PAGE

Questions 91–95 refer to the following figures of molecules.

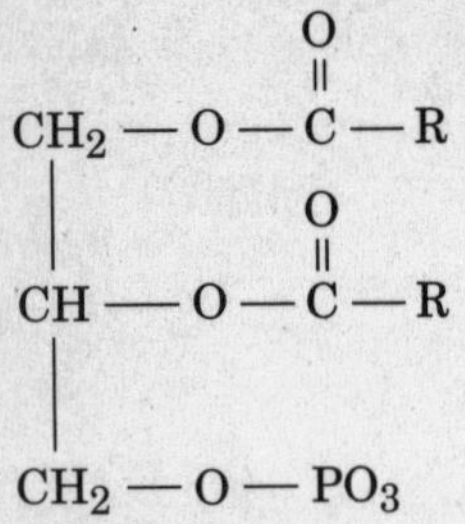

Figure 1 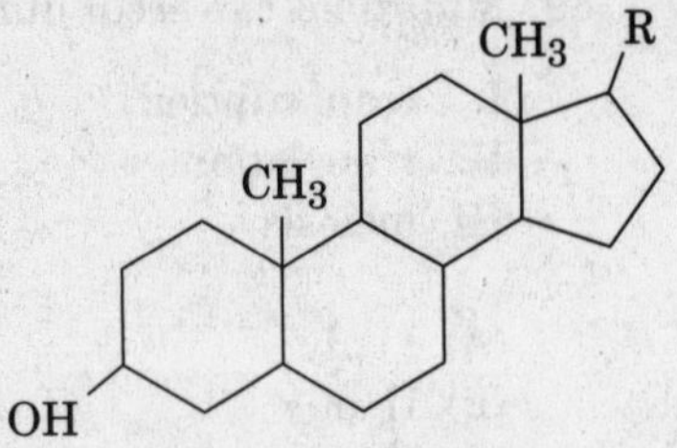 Figure 2 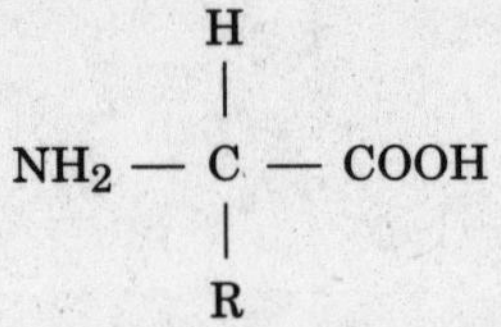 Figure 3 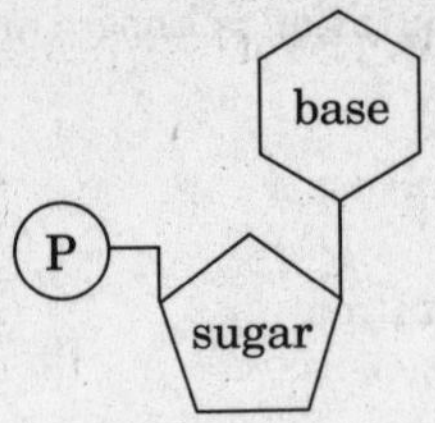 Figure 4 Figure 5

$C_6H_{12}O_6$

91. What reaction occurs when two molecules of Figure 3 combine?

(A) Glycolysis
(B) Dehydration synthesis
(C) Hydrolysis
(D) Phosphorylation
(E) Oxidation

92. What type of bond is formed in the above reaction?

(A) Hydrogen
(B) Peptide
(C) Double
(D) Triple
(E) Polymer

93. When two molecules of Figure 5 combine, what is the resulting chemical formula?

(A) $C_nH_{2n}O_n$
(B) $C_nH_nO_n$
(C) $C_nH_{n-1}O_{n-1}$
(D) $C_nH_{2n-1}O_{n-1}$
(E) $C_nH_{2n-2}O_{n-1}$

94. Which of these molecules readily forms polymers?

I.   Figure 1
II. Figure 2
III. Figure 4

(A) I only
(B) II only
(C) III only
(D) II and III only
(E) I, II, and III

95. The phosphate group in Figure 1 becomes the molecule's

(A) hydrophilic head
(B) hydrophobic head
(C) active site
(D) functional group
(E) hydrophobic tail

96. Figure 2 is a

(A) nucleotide
(B) carbohydrate
(C) polypeptide
(D) steroid
(E) triglyceride

GO ON TO THE NEXT PAGE

In constructing evolutionary relationships, scientists examine sequences of nucleotides or amino acids from molecules common to all organisms, such as hemoglobin. By identifying the relative differences in the sequences between species, scientists can chart degrees of evolutionary relatedness: the smaller the dissimilarity, the closer the relation. The following table records differences in the amino acid sequences of beta hemoglobin from seven different species of primates.

	human	chimpanzee	gorilla	gibbon	rhesus monkey	squirrel monkey	lemur
human							
chimpanzee	0						
gorilla	1	1					
gibbon	3	3	4				
rhesus monkey	8	8	8	8			
squirrel monkey	11	11	12	10	13		
lemur	31	30	30	31	29	30	

Figure 1

A phylogenic tree can be built from this data to show when and how organisms diverged.

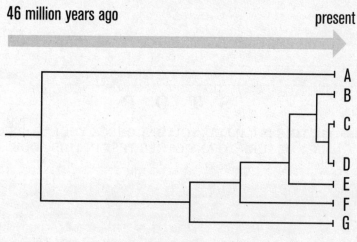

Figure 2

97. What organism should be listed in the branch labeled E?

(A) Lemur
(B) Squirrel monkey
(C) Gorilla
(D) Gibbon
(E) Rhesus monkey

GO ON TO THE NEXT PAGE

98. Based on this evidence, which of these organisms share the most recent common ancestor?

    I.   Humans and gorillas
    II. Gorillas and chimpanzees
    III. Humans and gibbons

    (A) I
    (B) II
    (C) III
    (D) I and II
    (E) I, II, and III

99. Which of the following statements is true?

    (A) Humans evolved from modern-day lemurs.
    (B) Humans and lemurs share a common ancestor.
    (C) Humans are not related to lemurs.
    (D) Lemurs look just like their ancestors did millions of years ago.
    (E) Humans and lemurs demonstrate convergent evolution.

100. Relative to the other primates, a horse actually demonstrates fewer differences in amino acids (~28) for beta hemoglobin than does a lemur. What best explains this?

    (A) Humans are more closely related to horses than lemurs.
    (B) The horse is a mutant.
    (C) The same amino acids can be coded for by very different sequences of nucleotides.
    (D) Molecular methods for identifying evolutionary relationships don't work.
    (E) The evolutionary tree for horses has few branches.

S T O P

IF YOU FINISH BEFORE TIME IS CALLED, YOU MAY CHECK YOUR WORK ON THIS TEST ONLY.
DO NOT TURN TO ANY OTHER TEST IN THIS BOOK.

SAT II Biology
Practice Test I
Explanations

Answers to SAT II Biology Practice Test I

Question Number	Correct Answer	Right	Wrong	Question Number	Correct Answer	Right	Wrong
1.	B	___	___	51.	B	___	___
2.	C	___	___	52.	D	___	___
3.	A	___	___	53.	B	___	___
4.	D	___	___	54.	B	___	___
5.	A	___	___	55.	C	___	___
6.	C	___	___	56.	D	___	___
7.	D	___	___	57.	C	___	___
8.	A	___	___	58.	C	___	___
9.	E	___	___	59.	A	___	___
10.	B	___	___	60.	E	___	___
11.	C	___	___	61.	D	___	___
12.	A	___	___	62.	E	___	___
13.	E	___	___	63.	C	___	___
14.	E	___	___	64.	B	___	___
15.	D	___	___	65.	C	___	___
16.	B	___	___	66.	A	___	___
17.	E	___	___	67.	B	___	___
18.	D	___	___	68.	C	___	___
19.	A	___	___	69.	D	___	___
20.	E	___	___	70.	E	___	___
21.	A	___	___	71.	B	___	___
22.	E	___	___	72.	C	___	___
23.	D	___	___	73.	A	___	___
24.	D	___	___	74.	D	___	___
25.	C	___	___	75.	D	___	___
26.	A	___	___	76.	B	___	___
27.	D	___	___	77.	E	___	___
28.	B	___	___	78.	D	___	___
29.	B	___	___	79.	A	___	___
30.	D	___	___	80.	C	___	___
31.	D	___	___	81.	E	___	___
32.	A	___	___	82.	A	___	___
33.	B	___	___	83.	B	___	___
34.	B	___	___	84.	E	___	___
35.	A	___	___	85.	E	___	___
36.	C	___	___	86.	A	___	___
37.	B	___	___	87.	A	___	___
38.	A	___	___	88.	C	___	___
39.	A	___	___	89.	E	___	___
40.	A	___	___	90.	D	___	___
41.	D	___	___	91.	B	___	___
42.	B	___	___	92.	B	___	___
43.	A	___	___	93.	E	___	___
44.	C	___	___	94.	C	___	___
45.	C	___	___	95.	A	___	___
46.	D	___	___	96.	D	___	___
47.	B	___	___	97.	D	___	___
48.	A	___	___	98.	D	___	___
49.	A	___	___	99.	B	___	___
50.	A	___	___	100.	C	___	___

Test I Explanations

Calculating Your Score
on SAT II Biology Practice Test I

Your raw score for the SAT II History test is calculated from the number of questions you answer correctly and incorrectly. Once you have determined your composite score, use the conversion table on page 23 of this book to calculate your scaled score.

To Calculate Your Raw Score

Count the number of questions you answered correctly: _____

A

Count the number of questions you answered incorrectly, and multiply that number by $\frac{1}{4}$:

_____ X $\frac{1}{4}$ = _____

B C

Subtract the value in field C from value in field A: _____

D

Round the number in field D to the nearest whole number. This is your raw score: _____

E

Biology E/M Classification Questions

1.   (B)   Organic and Biochemistry

Monosaccharides, such as glucose, are carbohydrates that contains carbon, hydrogen, and oxygen in a 1:2:1 ratio.

2.   (C)   Organic and Biochemistry

Lipid compounds usually contain nonpolar hydrocarbon chains, which are not soluble in water.

3.   (A)   Organic and Biochemistry

Enzymes, which catalyze biological reactions, are protein molecules, consisting of one or more chains of amino acids.

4.   (D)   Ecology

Because energy is lost between each level of the food pyramid, there is progressively less biomass as the levels become more complex. Tertiary consumers, at the top of the pyramid, therefore have the fewest organisms.

5.   (A)   Ecology

Producers create glucose molecules from carbon dioxide and sunlight through the process of photosynthesis.

6.   (C)   Ecology

Omnivores are animals that eat both plants and other animals. They are not primary consumers because of the fact that they eat other animals, but they are usually not tertiary consumers because they eat plants as well. They are most often secondary consumers.

7.   (D)   Cell Processes

In glycolysis, glucose is enzymatically broken down to pyruvic acid. Glycolysis leads the way for either anaerobic or aerobic respiration (Krebs cycle), depending on the presence of oxygen. Glycolysis is one of the oldest energy-producing reactions that evolved in living organisms.

8.   (A)   Cell Processes

In the Krebs cycle (or Citric acid cycle), acetyl coenzyme A reacts with oxaloacetate to form citric acid. The oxaloacetate is regenerated while acetyl-CoA is oxidized to CO_2.

9.   (E)   Cell Processes

In fermentation, yeast are added to a sugar solution (like fruit juice) and denied oxygen. Anaerobic respiration occurs, with the byproduct of ethanol.

10.   (B)   Organismal Biology

Habituation is when an animal's reaction to a repeated stimulus is lessened or disappears, so long as the stimulus does not cause any damage. This is a temporary behavior: if the stimulus is halted for a period of time and restarted, the animal will no longer ignore it.

11. **(C)** Organismal Biology

Conditioning is when an animal learns to associate two stimuli, one of which is usually neutral. The classic example is Pavlov's experiment. Whenever Pavlov fed his dogs, he rang a bell. Soon the dogs would begin to salivate at the sound of the bell, even if there was no food in sight.

12. **(A)** Organismal Biology

Imprinting is an instinctive reaction to a stimulus that triggers a social bond, such as when a baby bird imprints "mother" on the first moving thing it sees. This moving object is usually its mother when in the wild, but scientists have gotten birds to imprint on a variety of objects, including balloons and humans.

Biology E/M Solitary Multiple Choice

13. **(E)** Evolution and Diversity

Similarities between organisms are most pronounced at the species level. Differences between organisms are most obvious at the kingdom level. A Persian cat and a tabby cat (species level) are far more similar than a sponge and an elephant (kingdom level). The sequential order of taxonomic divisions is Kingdom-Phylum-Class-Order-Family-Genus-Species. Members of a family will have more in common than members of an order. Members of a phylum will have more in common than members of a kingdom but less in common than members in a class, order, family, or species.

14. **(E)** The Cell

Levels of cellulose would be significantly higher in the plant cell sample because the cell walls of plants are made out of cellulose, while animal cells do not have cell walls or cellulose.

15. **(D)** Ecology

Only (D) fits the definition of exponential growth, which refers to unlimited growth. All of the other answers are examples of limited growth, except for answer (E), which is not growth at all and should be eliminated right off the bat. Note that exponential growth is not really possible in nature, as there will always be some factor limiting this growth.

16. **(B)** Organismal Biology

Red blood cells contain hemoglobin, which binds to oxygen in the lungs and delivers it to the body's tissues. If there are too few red blood cells, or if their hemoglobin content is too low, then this could cause a person to become anemic. A common variant is sickle cell anemia, a condition in which red blood cells are distorted and sickly, unable to carry as much oxygen to the body.

17. **(E)** Evolution and Diversity

Natural selection refers to the mechanism of evolution proposed by Charles Darwin. It asserts that organisms produce more offspring than can survive, and these organisms compete for limited natural resources. Because of variations in genotype within species, some organisms have phenotypes that offer a better chance for reproduction and survival. Therefore, these adaptive characteristics will appear in future generations by natural selection. The theory of acquired characteristics (E), was part of an evolutionary theory, proposed by Lamarck, that collapsed under scientific scrutiny.

18. **(D)** Ecology

An ecological community consists of a group of populations that coexist and interact within a specific environment. Combined with nonliving factors such as soil, weather, geography, etc., the community is known as an ecosystem.

19. **(A)** Organic and Biochemistry

Proteins are amino acids linked together in a chain called a polypeptide. Answer (B) is wrong because amino acids do not generally form rings. Answer (C) describes a nucleic acid, answer (D) describes a carbohydrate, and answer (E) describes a lipid molecule.

20. **(E)** Genetics

When DNA is transcribed to RNA, RNA bases pair with DNA bases to form an RNA molecule that is the inverse copy of the original DNA strand. DNA's thymine pairs with RNA's adenine, guanine pairs with cytosine, cytosine pairs with guanine, and adenine pairs with uracil (because RNA does not contain thymine). In other words, in the RNA sequence, DNA's T becomes A, G becomes C, C becomes G, and A becomes U. Therefore, choice (E) is the correct RNA sequence. Given that thymine (T) is not present in RNA, you should have been able to eliminate choices (A), (C), and (D) quite easily.

21. **(A)** Organismal Biology

The correct answer is (A). When an embryo implants into the uterine lining, it releases human chorionic gonadotropin (hCG), which prolongs the life of the corpus luteum in the ovary. The corpus luteum then continues to release progesterone, and the uterine lining remains to support the developing embryo.

22. **(E)** Evolution and Diversity

Far from describing how a gap in the fossil record might arise, (E) actually describes the first phase of fossil formation. All of the other choices give plausible reasons why gaps in the fossil record might appear.

23. **(D)** The Cell

The fact that the DNA molecule is circular and the cell does not have a nucleus means that the cell is prokaryotic. Prokaryotes do not contain membrane-bound organelles, such as chloroplasts, so we can eliminate choices (A), (C), and (E). Prokaryotic cells can, however, possess a simple cell wall made of peptidoglycan, and every living cell contains ribosomes. Thus, the correct answer is (D), II and III only.

24. **(D)** Ecology

In the nitrogen cycle, special nitrogen-fixing bacteria take the N_2 from the atmosphere and convert it into a form that plants can use, such as ammonia (NH_3) or nitrate (NO_3).

25. **(C)** Evolution and Diversity

Monerans are prokaryotes—single-celled organisms that lack a membrane-bound nucleus and membrane-bound organelles. Fungi and plants are single-celled or multicellular eukaryotes and have a membrane-bound nucleus and organelles.

26. **(A)** Evolution and Diversity

The Earth's early atmosphere was composed of water, methane, hydrogen, and ammonia. Anaerobic organisms that didn't require oxygen predominated. Early autotrophs released oxygen as a waste product, and over time, free oxygen gas became a major component in the atmosphere.

27.   **(D)**   Organismal Biology

If a blood vessel has muscular walls, it is clear that it is an artery and not a vein. It is also clear that it will be carrying blood away from the heart, as all arteries do. Remember that while arteries typically carry oxygenated blood, this is not *always* true. The pulmonary arteries, carrying blood from the heart to the lungs, are arteries that carry deoxygenated blood.

28.   **(B)**   Ecology

The producers, at the bottom of the food pyramid, receive their energy from the sun, and possess the largest energy of all the trophic levels. As it is passed from level to level, energy is lost to heat and biological processes (e.g. respiration), and in the end only about 10% of it gets passed on to each succeeding level.

29.   **(B)**   Cell Processes

If, while doing strenuous exercises, your muscles use up available oxygen, the cells will produce lactic acid, which causes a burning sensation, muscle fatigue, and muscle soreness. (A) and (D) are components of glycolysis. (A), (C), (D) and (E) are found in the Krebs Cycle.

30.   **(D)**   The Cell

Lysosomes are small, membrane-bound packages of enzymes that have the ability to break down aging cell structures, or in the case of white blood cells, foreign bodies that are ingested into the cell by endocytosis. A good strategy would be to eliminate answer (C) right away, because chloroplasts are not found in animal cells, and answer (E) because chromosomes are simply formations of genetic material that condense during cell division, which has nothing to do with the function of the white blood cell. Ribosomes serve as the sites of protein synthesis, a function unrelated to the digestion of harmful bacteria. Peroxisomes, like lysosomes, are membrane bound structures containing enzymes, but the enzymes in peroxisomes help to break down fats and protect the cell from toxic hydrogen peroxide.

Biology E/M Group Multiple Choice

31.   **(D)**   Cell Processes

You should know that the Calvin-Benson cycle is the last stage of photosynthesis. Since light affects the earliest part of photosynthesis, the Calvin cycle is also known as light-independent photosynthesis, or the "dark reactions." ATP and NADPH produced by the "light reactions" of photosynthesis provide the energy for the fixation of carbon from CO_2 into glucose; however, the Calvin cycle itself needs no light to operate.

32.   **(A)**   Cell Processes

All of photosynthesis occurs inside the chloroplasts of plant cells. Since no other answer choice is inside chloroplasts, you should quickly identify (A) as correct. The inner space of the chloroplast, called the stroma, is the site of the Calvin cycle.

33.   **(B)**   Organic and Biochemistry

Adenosine triphosphate is the energy currency of all cells. Its three phosphate groups (tri-phosphate) form high-energy bonds, one of which is broken to provide energy for photosynthesis. When a molecule of ATP loses a phosphate group, it becomes ADP, or adenosine diphosphate.

34. (B) Cell Processes

Photosynthesis produces 3-carbon molecules which combine to form glucose ($C_6H_{12}O_6$). However, plants store glucose as starch, a polysaccharide comprised of long chains of glucose molecules. Sucrose (A) is a disaccharide of glucose and fructose molecules, and not the preferred storage molecule. Although some glucose is synthesized into cellulose (C) for cell walls, plants do not retrieve glucose from cellulose, so it is not storage. Glycogen (D) is the glucose storage favored by animals.

35. (A) Cell Processes

In comparing the similarities of the Calvin and Krebs cycles, you can immediately eliminate the wrong answers for either one. The Calvin cycle consumes ATP rather than producing it, as apparent in the diagram, which rules out (B). Photosynthesis occurs in chloroplasts, which negates (C). The Krebs cycle of aerobic respiration consumes oxygen rather than producing it (D). Finally, many prokaryotes are heterotrophs, unable to photosynthesize (E). You could also answer this question with the definition of the word "cycle." The Calvin cycle starts when ribulose biphosphate (RuBP) joins with carbon dioxide. After a series of chemical changes, the RuBP is regenerated to start the whole thing over. Similarly, the Krebs cycle, sometimes called the citric acid cycle, begins when oxaloacetic acid joins acetyl-CoA to form citric acid. By the end of the cycle, oxaloacetic acid is regenerated.

36. (C) Organismal Biology   *Laboratory*

Tropisms are plants' responses to specific stimuli, including light, gravity, and touch. They are "positive" when the plant responds in the direction of the stimulus, and "negative" when the plant draws away from the stimulus. In the case of the shoots, they turn downward in the direction of gravity, which is positive gravitropism. Since there is no light allowed in the box, the shoots cannot react either positively or negatively to it; phototropism is not an option. Thigmotropism (A) is a plant's response to touch.

37. (B) Organismal Biology   *Laboratory*

Keeping the seeds in a dark box eliminates the possibility of phototropism. In effect, it decreases the variables acting upon the seeds. (A) is incorrect, as the experimenter does not observe what occurs after their emergence from the box; temperature (E) is also not part of the experiment. Although the box may simulate subterranean darkness, this is part of the control for testing tropisms, which occur in many different environments.

38. (A) Organismal Biology   *Laboratory*

You should know that auxin is a common plant hormone effecting cell elongation. Auxin has been shown to function in plants' growth in response to stimuli. Lactic acid (B) is a byproduct of anaerobic respiration. Associative behavior (C) implies that plants can learn and have brains. Nitrogen (D) is an important chemical for plants, but does not directly cause cell growth. Excess carbon dioxide (E) is incorrect, as plants exhibit tropisms in equal distributions of carbon dioxide, such as in nature.

39. (A) Organismal Biology   *Laboratory*

Since the Dish 1 seedlings are kept in the dark, photosynthesis cannot occur. All of the other answer choices can be eliminated. The plants do undergo glycolysis (D) as a part of respiration (B). The plants must undergo mitosis (C) to grow. They also absorb the water from the damp cotton (E).

40. **(A)** The Cell

Concentration differences across a membrane will cause diffusion to balance the concentrations; for water, this diffusion is called osmosis. In the diagram, the concentration of sodium ions is higher outside the cell. However, since they are ions, they cannot diffuse across the cell membrane's hydrophobic interior by themselves. Instead, water flows out of the cell by osmosis to try and balance the concentrations across the membrane.

41. **(D)** The Cell

The tonicity of a solution is defined by how much solute it has relative to what's in it. The diagram shows a higher concentration of sodium ions outside the cell. Therefore, the solution is hypertonic: it has a higher concentration of solute than the cell it surrounds. As a guideline, cells commonly shrink in hypertonic solutions. Solutions are isotonic (C) when they have the same concentrations of solutes as whatever is in them. A hypotonic solution (A) is the opposite of hypertonic, having less solute than what it contains, as when cells are put in distilled water.

42. **(B)** The Cell

When solutes cannot pass membranes on their own, they must be transported. Sodium ions want to move down their concentration gradient into the cell by diffusion. However, since ions cannot cross the membrane by themselves, simple diffusion is out (A). They require a protein to facilitate their diffusion. Think of it as passive transport. Active transport (C) pumps ions against their concentration gradient; in this case, as if sodium ions were moving out of the cell. Osmosis (D) refers to water alone. Phosphorylation (E) has nothing to do with this scenario.

43. **(A)** The Cell

Cell membranes are made up of many molecules of phospholipids, which arrange themselves into two opposing layers, often called bilayers. The phospholipids' hydrophilic heads (the phospho- part) align to form membranes' external surfaces, while hydrophobic tails (the lipid part) arrange themselves in the interior space of the membrane.

44. **(C)** The Cell

To pass through cell membranes independently, a molecule must be very small and have no charge. Water easily passes through cell membranes by osmosis. Other small, uncharged molecules may pass by diffusion, including the gases nitrogen (N_2), carbon dioxide (CO_2), and oxygen (O_2). Glucose ($C_6H_{12}O_6$) is too large to cross the membrane by itself.

45. **(C)** Evolution and Diversity

To answer this question, you must know that snakes, like all reptiles, are ectothermic, or cold-blooded. Their body temperatures and processes are affected by the surrounding temperature; hence, a snake's metabolism will slow down in colder air. Birds and mammals are endothermic, or warm-blooded, and able to maintain a constant temperature in fluctuating temperatures. The canary's metabolic rate will remain stable.

46. **(D)** Evolution and Diversity

The withered leg bones serve no use to the copperhead and are remnants of a distant ancestor. They are vestigial structures. (A) is incorrect, because although evolution works through random mutation, the appearance of legs is extremely unlikely to result from a single mutation. Homologous structures (B) are versions of a particular feature from an ancestor that, through divergent evolution, have taken on varying forms in different animals, such as the forelegs of a horse and the flippers of a whale. Analogous structures (C), such as the wings of birds and butterflies, are a product of convergent evolution, and share no direct ancestral source.

47. **(B)** Evolution and Diversity

Because they can regulate body temperature to maintain a constant level, the activity or metabolic rates of endotherms are not directly affected by changes in surrounding temperatures, so (B) is the answer.

48. **(A)** Evolution and Diversity

This question asks about evolutionary diversity, and what animals have evolved greater complexity. As vertebrates, both birds and snakes share answers (C), (D), and (E). Reptiles also have tough-skinned eggs for laying on land (B), though amphibians do not. However, both reptiles and amphibians have three-chambered hearts, while all birds and mammals evolved four-chambered hearts. Memorize this progressive sequence of evolution in major groups of animals: fish, amphibians, reptiles, birds, and mammals.

49. **(A)** Organismal Biology *Laboratory*

This question asks you to identify the general properties of an indicator from specific data. The solution turns pink in the presence of acids, such as lemon juice and vinegar. Acids have a pH lower than 7. The indicator solution is purple at neutral pH (7), and blue-green in the presence of bases, which have pHs higher than 7.

50. **(A)** Organic and Biochemistry *Laboratory*

Indicators can change gradually during a pH change, which makes them effective at distinguishing between solutions. Sodium hydroxide (NaOH) is a strong base, and the vinegar solution is acidic. If NaOH was slowly added to the solution, the indicator would change from pink-red (acidic) to purple (neutral) and finally to blue-green (basic). (B) and (E) are wrong, as there is no data suggesting that the solution would turn yellow or clear. (C) is false, as indicators can change gradually, and (E) is wrong, as the addition of a base to an indicator does not form white precipitate.

51. **(B)** Organismal Biology *Laboratory*

If you don't know about plant pigments, the mention of chlorophyll should give this away. Pigments absorb light and transform the energy for use in photosynthesis. Chlorophyll is not the only pigment that contributes to this process. There are two types of chlorophyll, a and b, as well as other pigments in plants. (A) is incorrect, as cabbages could not perceive their own color change. (C) is false, as color absorbs rather than reflects light energy for heat. There is no reason to believe that redness is a vestigial characteristic (D). It is also not in the best interests of a cabbage to be eaten (E).

52. **(D)** Organismal Biology
Laboratory

Acids and bases can be defined by the types of ions they release. Acids, such as HCl, release a hydrogen ion (H^+) into solution, and bases, such as NaOH, release a hydroxide ion (OH^-). These ions cannot cross cell membranes on their own to interact with the indicator inside the red cabbage. Remember: the red cabbage had to be pulverized and boiled, which broke membranes and released the indicator pigment into solution. Answers (A), (C), and (E) are directly contradicted by the data given for the experiment. (B) is wrong, because the epidermis of plants is frequently crossed during gas exchange and transpiration.

53. **(B)** Organismal Biology
Laboratory

Sex-linked traits appear in different ratios between male and females. Because males have only one X chromosome, they are much more likely to express X-linked traits. The table data shows that there are no females with white eyes, whereas there are males with white eyes, so eye color is an X-linked trait. Answer (D) is incorrect, as eye color has two alleles for red and white. Male and female offspring with normal vs. vestigial wings have a common phenotype ratio of 3:1, common to autosomal traits, so (A) and (C) are also false.

54. **(B)** Genetics
Laboratory

Punnett squares are good for numbers and ratios, but you can answer this question about the probability of offspring by elimination and logic. Throw out (E) right away: the core of Mendelian genetics is that the results of genetic crosses are predictable. Since white eyes are a recessive trait, they will not occur more frequently than dominant red eyes, so (D) can be quickly eliminated. Similarly, as always with X-linked traits, its frequency in males is much higher than in females, eliminating (C). (A) is incorrect, as it is possible for a female to express an X-linked recessive trait, if she receives the allele from both male and female parents. Although no F_2 females have white eyes, some are carriers of the recessive white eyes allele. These F_2 females need only mate with a white-eyed male with at least one recessive allele for vestigial wings to have a chance at producing a white-eyed, vestigial winged female.

55. **(C)** Organismal Biology
Laboratory

Phenotype ratios are comparisons of different traits appearing in individuals. By looking at the data, you can see that there are four different phenotypes (eye colors and wing shapes) for F_2 males. Therefore, you can immediately eliminate (A) and (B), which have only two phenotypes, and also (D), which has zeros. Some phenotype counts are three times as large as others, so (E) is also false. Calculating the ratio is simple arithmetic: divide each amount by the largest possible factor that still gives whole numbers; in this case, 20. Often, the numbers will not be exact, but you should be able to round to the nearest value that gives sensible results.

56. **(D)** Genetics
Laboratory

Although X-linked traits are typically recessive, males with the allele will express the trait whether it's dominant or recessive, because males only have one X chromosome to begin with. You would observe the same number of white-eyed males in either case. Count up the total number of white-eyed F_2 males to get 80. Wing shape has no bearing on eye color, and doesn't affect your count.

57. **(C)** Organismal Biology
Laboratory

Fertility rates would be highest when egg production and hatchlings are both at their maximums. Data in the table shows that the highest numbers of eggs and hatchlings produced are found at 30° C.

58. **(C)** Organismal Biology   *Laboratory*

To find the time of greatest egg production, look at successive columns in the table for the largest day-to-day increases in eggs. Although there are more total eggs on day 5, the greatest net increase occurs between days 3 and 4. No information is given about egg production after day 5, so (E) is not valid.

59. **(A)** Organismal Biology   *Laboratory*

This graph shows egg production increasing with time, but with a very low rate of hatching. The closest measurement to this trend in the table is at 5° C, and (A) is the closest match. Temperatures above 10° would have higher hatchling rates. Temperatures near 45° produce few hatchlings, but there are also virtually no eggs produced.

60. **(E)** Organismal Biology   *Laboratory*

Experiments are strengthened by identifying and controlling variables. This question asks you to consider what variable is important to fertility rates in fruit flies when temperature is tested. (A) would likely add no significant data, as very few eggs or hatchlings would be produced at high temperatures. (B) could possibly relate to fertility, but does so indirectly. (C) changes the variable being tested—temperature, and (D) would shed no light on fruit flies. (E) is correct: if the fruit flies themselves do not survive, they cannot produce eggs. Losses in the parental generation greatly affects the ability to compare data across the table.

Biology E Solitary Multiple Choice

61. **(D)** Organismal Biology

A strong sensation has nothing to do with a "stronger" action potential, or a longer lasting potential. In fact, the voltage and duration of action potentials usually remain constant in a neuron. Sensation also has nothing to do with the type of neuron carrying the potential. Rather, the frequency of action potentials affects the intensity of the sensation as perceived by the brain.

62. **(E)** The Cell

The cytoskeleton is a network of protein fibers within the cellular cytoplasm that gives shape and movement to the cell. Microtubules are strong hollow rods that act as internal scaffolding, and microfilaments are protein fibers made of actin found on the perimeter of the cell. Flagella and cilia are built from microtubules and thrash around as the cell's propulsion source. Among the answer choices, only (E), ribosomes, are not a part of the cytoskeleton.

63. **(C)** Evolution and Diversity

Convergent evolution describes the evolution of similar traits, either physical or behavioral, in two unrelated species responding to similar selection pressure. Divergent evolution and speciation result in two related populations becoming more dissimilar; hence, choices (A) and (B) can be eliminated. Coevolution refers to the evolution of adaptations in one species in response to new adaptations in other species; for instance, the hummingbird's long, narrow bill for obtaining nectar has co-evolved with long, tubular flowers that depend upon the bird for fertilization. Bioaccumulation (or biological accumulation or biological magnification) refers to the accumulation up the trophic layers of toxic substances occurring in the environment.

64. (B) Ecology

The carrying capacity of an environment is the maximum population of a particular organism that that environment can sustain, limited by food supplies, space, and other factors. When the population of the cats on the island levels off, it has reached the point of carrying capacity on the island.

65. (C) Organismal Biology

The respiratory system helps regulate pH balance by speeding up or decreasing respiration rate based on the levels of carbonic acid in the blood. By regulating the levels of carbon dioxide (the source of carbonic acid) through gas exchange in the lungs, the system regulates the overall blood pH.

66. (A) Ecology

In the food pyramid, the organisms at the bottom of the pyramid will be more numerous, and as you go higher up the pyramid, the numbers will decrease. Tertiary consumers, such as the hawk in this example, will be fairly uncommon.

Biology E Group Multiple Choice

67. (B) Ecology

The marine (saltwater) biome can be divided into several parts, or zones. Closest to the shore, with alternating states of being submerged and dry, is the intertidal zone (D), also known as the littoral zone. The next zone out, and the correct answer for this question, is the neritic zone, which extends to the continental shelf, or a depth of about 300 meters. Beyond that is open ocean, or the pelagic zone (A). The abyssal plain (D) refers to land at the deep bottom of the ocean. The aphotic zone (D) is deep ocean laying beyond the penetration of sunlight.

68. (C) Ecology

Based on the diagram, zone IV is below the continental shelf and at a depth beyond the reach of sunlight. This is the aphotic zone: "a-" for absence, and "-photo" for light. Of the answer choices, the correct organismal characteristic for this zone is heterotrophism. Because there is no light, autotrophs (A) cannot photosynthesize. Additionally, there is no light for advanced eyesight (D) to be useful. There are many multicellular organisms found here (e.g. giant squid), which eliminates (B), and these organisms do not necessarily have silicate shells (E).

69. (D) Ecology

Chemosynthetic bacteria are autotrophs that make their own food in the presence of certain chemicals. In the oceans, they are typically found near deep geothermal vents. All of the other answer choices are organisms frequently found in the intertidal (or littoral) zone.

70. (E) Ecology

As they cover 2/3 of the Earth's surface, you wouldn't be reaching to guess that oceans participate in the water, carbon, and nitrogen cycles. Obviously, they participate in various aspects of the water cycle, including evaporation and runoff. Carbon dioxide dissolved in the ocean and the organic materials from organisms are examples of the ocean's involvement in the carbon cycle. Nitrogen-fixing bacteria and organic excretion found in the ocean represent aspects of the nitrogen cycle.

71. **(B)** Organismal Biology

When a plant forms flower buds, it encases the developing structures in a case of specialized leaves, called sepals. Once the flower opens, these greenish leaf-like structures have served their protective purpose, and remain under the petals.

72. **(C)** Organismal Biology

Pollen grains land on the flower's stigma, which is the uppermost part of the pistil—the female sexual organ of flowering plants. The pistil's long supporting column is called the style (C), through which pollen grains descend in a pollen tube to reach the ovule and fertilize the plant.

73. **(A)** Organismal Biology

A flowering plant's male sexual component is called the stamen. Unlike the pistil, there are typically more than one stamen found in flowers. A stamen is comprised of a supporting column, called a filament, and a pollen-producing head, called an anther, which is identified as structure #1 in the diagram. The anther's function is the production and distribution of pollen.

74. **(D)** Organismal Biology

Pollen grains, having landed on the pistil's stigma, descend through a pollen tube to reach the plant's female gametes called ovules. The mature ovules become the plant's seeds, and the surrounding ovary tissue develops into its fruit.

75. **(D)** Organismal Biology

Flowers only appear in angiosperms. Among the answer choices, only (D), dicot, is a member of the angiosperm division.

76. **(B)** Ecology   *Laboratory*

Species sharing the same niche will compete for resources and survival until one is displaced, eliminated, or their niches have diverged sufficiently for coexistence. When the different warbler species are simultaneously introduced to the same habitat, they compete for food. Over time, each species begins to feed at different locations within the spruce trees, as a result of behavioral adaptation. An adaptation is any biological or behavioral change that allows an organism to increase its chances of survival. The only other conceivable answer choice, mutation (D), refers to changes in genetic code, which is not necessarily required for behavioral adaptations to appear.

77. **(E)** Ecology   *Laboratory*

An organism's niche describes its unique position within a community, including physical factors such as food, climate temperature, and habitat location; and behavioral factors, such as the feeding locations of different species of warblers in spruce trees.

78. **(D)** Ecology   *Laboratory*

Primary consumers feed on autotrophic primary producers. In this community, the primary producer is the spruce, and the primary consumer is the leaf-eating insect.

79. **(A)** Ecology   *Laboratory*

The warblers all initially share the same niche. This competitive situation creates new selection pressures, and the warblers adapt different feeding locations to survive. Based on the given observations, competition between species sorts them into different niches. (B) is false, as there are no observations of violence among the warblers. (C) seems logical, but the experimenter observed feeding locations and not population size; it is also conceivable that the Blackburnian warbler population didn't shrink. The warblers continue to eat the same insect, ruling out (D), and their segregation into different zones in spruce trees falsifies (E).

80. **(C)** Ecology   *Laboratory*

Prey and predator relationships often follow cycles of boom and bust. An increase in available prey will likely increase the predator population. With more predators, more prey is eaten, and eventually this consumption causes a drop in the prey population. The predator population subsequently falls without an abundant food source. Though dynamic, these cycles find an equilibrium through time. If the warblers' food source dramatically drops, so will the carrying capacities of warbler populations, which will fall to levels that the food source can sustain. (A) is unlikely. There is no evidence to support (B), or that any warbler species has a distinct advantage over the others. (D) is a possibility, but not a *predictable* result. (E) defies the common definition of species, which are typically unable to successfully interbreed.

Biology M Solitary Multiple Choice

81. **(E)** Cell Processes

Uracil is found exclusively in RNA. Thymine occurs only in DNA. The other bases all occur in both.

82. **(A)** Genetics

A Punnett Square depicts possible combinations of genetic crosses and the resulting offspring. The dominant allele is capitalized; hence, in this example, T (tall) is dominant over t (short). The male contribution is listed on top of the square and the female contribution is listed on the left-hand side of it. The Punnett Square above indicates that the genotypic ratio (that is, the composition of the genes) is 25 percent tall (TT), 25 percent short (tt), and 50 percent hybrid tall (Tt). The phenotypic ratio, which refers to the physical characteristics of the offspring, indicates that 75 percent are tall (TT and Tt) and 25 percent are short (tt). These Punnett Square results are typical of a simple single-trait Mendelian cross and do not reflect the outcome of a cross involving sex-linked traits.

83. **(B)** Evolution and Diversity

Divergent evolution is the process in which organisms with a common ancestor evolve in different directions. Ultimately, divergent evolution will transform the organisms into distinct species because they will be so different that they can no longer reproduce. Divergent evolution therefore leads to reproductive isolation. Biological magnification (A) is an ecological phenomenon in which chemical substances become more concentrated as they travel up the food pyramid. Analogous traits (C) are produced by convergent evolution. Mutations (D) might help cause divergent evolution, but they are not caused by it. And succession (E) refers to the changing ecological characteristics of a certain geographical location.

84. **(E)**   Organic and Biochemistry

All of these factors can change the speed of an enzymatic reaction or even cause it to completely stop. Enzymes usually operate under very narrow temperature and pH conditions, and many work in conjunction with smaller proteins known as coenzymes, or only in the absence of other molecules known as inhibitors that can stop the reaction.

85. **(E)**   Evolution and Diversity

The Hardy-Weinberg equilibrium describes allele and genotype frequencies in the absence of evolutionary forces. It states that in the absence of selective or geographic pressures, the overall allele frequencies in a population remain constant, and evolution stops. Natural selection (A) is the mechanism of evolution proposed by Darwin. Homeostasis (B) refers to maintaining a stable internal equilibrium (such as a constant core body temperature) or physiological environment. Balanced mutation (C) describes the rate at which copies of an allele are lost to mutation equals the rate at which new copies of the allele are created by mutation. Stabilizing selection (D) refers to a type of natural selection in which extreme individuals (mutant forms) are eliminated.

86. **(A)**   Cell Processes

Glycolysis breaks glucose down into two molecules of 3-carbon pyruvate, which, depending on the presence of oxygen, then follows either an aerobic or anaerobic respiratory pathway. Therefore, (B) is false: glycolysis is a part of fermentation, but it is not all of fermentation. Glycolysis produces two ATP, eliminating (C). Glycolysis is also the first step of the respiratory chain (D). It occurs outside the mitochondria (E), in the cytoplasm.

Biology M Group Multiple Choice

87. **(A)**   Genetics

Genetic mutations can find frequent opportunities to occur during the copying and translating of millions of nucleotides in the lifetime of DNA strands. If a single nucleotide is omitted or added during the copying of DNA, a frameshift error results. There are two types of frameshift errors: insertion (C), when a new nucleotide is sandwiched into the existing sequence; and deletion, when a nucleotide is skipped or omitted. Cystic fibrosis is a deletion frameshift error. A point mutation (B) is the substitution of an original nucleotide for a different one; it does not shift the frame for codons. A silent mutation (D) is any genetic mutation that does not express a phenotypical change. Crossing-over (E) occurs when chromosomes overlap and exchange genetic material in mitosis or meiosis.

88. **(C)**   Genetics

Autosomal recessive traits appear only if the offspring receives a recessive allele from both parents. (As initially stated in this question group, CF appears on an autosomal chromosome.)

89. **(E)**   Genetics

Mutations can occur during the copying of DNA, its transcription to mRNA, and translation during protein synthesis. Mutations can also occur during meiosis, when all of a cell's chromosomes (wrapped strands of DNA) are copied. Meiosis is also an occasion for the exchange of genetic materials on overlapping chromosomes in an event called crossing-over.

90. **(D)** Genetics

Nucleotides are grouped in threes, called codons, which are translated into amino acids during protein synthesis. With the insertion or deletion of a single nucleotide, a frameshift error changes which nucleotide triplets are read as codons for the entire length of the DNA sequence following the error.

91. **(B)** Organic and Biochemistry

You should be able to identify Figure 3 as the generic chemical model for an amino acid. In all amino acids, a central carbon is connected to an amino group (NH_2), a carboxyl group (COOH), and a functional group (R). Differences in the functional group distinguish amino acids from each other. When two amino acids combine to form a polypeptide, the opposing amino and carboxyl groups join and release a single molecule of water. Thus, this reaction is known as dehydration synthesis.

92. **(B)** Organic and Biochemistry

The linking of amino acids by dehydration synthesis forms a polypeptide, also known as a protein. The bond forged between them is called a peptide bond, which links the carbon in the carboxyl group of one amino acid, and the nitrogen in the amino group of the next.

93. **(E)** Organic and Biochemistry

Figure 5 is the chemical formula for a monosaccharide (e.g. glucose). The dehydration synthesis reaction also occurs in the formation of polysaccharides, such as when two molecules of glucose combine to form maltose. Separate, two glucose molecules have 12 carbons, 24 hydrogens, and 12 oxygens total. This ratio of 1:2:1 or $C_nH_{2n}O_n$ holds true for all monosaccharides. When they combine, they release a single molecule of water (H_2O) and form maltose with the formula $C_{12}H_{22}O_{11}$. Thus, two atoms of hydrogen and one atom of oxygen are subtracted from the general monosaccharide formula: $C_nH_{2n-2}O_{n-1}$.

94. **(C)** Organic and Biochemistry

To answer this question, identify each of the depicted molecules. Figure 1 resembles a triglyceride, with one hydrocarbon chain replaced by a phosphate group. It is indeed a phospholipid, with two hydrocarbon chains and a phosphate head. Phospholipids align to form bilayers in membranes, but their association is based on polarity—hydrophilic heads aligning with each other, and hydrophobic tails aligning with each other—and not chemical bonds; therefore, bilayers are not polymers. With several hydrocarbon rings, Figure 2 is another lipid called a steroid, which also does not readily form polymers. With sugar and phosphate groups supporting a nitrogenous base, Figure 4 depicts a generic nucleotide. Nucleotides definitely form long polymers, of which DNA and RNA are typical examples.

95. **(A)** Organic and Biochemistry

Phospholipids have a characteristic form of two long hydrocarbon "tails" and a single phosphate "head." The nonpolar hydrocarbon chains are hydrophobic ("afraid" of polar water molecules), while the polar phosphate group is hydrophilic, having an affinity for water. When phospholipids are in abundance, their components align based on polarity to form the bilayer found in cell membranes: hydrophilic phosphate heads on the outside, hydrophobic hydrocarbon tails on the inside.

96. **(D)** Organic and Biochemistry

At their core, steroids have several connected hydrocarbon rings: three are hexagons, and a fourth is pentagonal. Steroids are lipids; examples of steroids include cholesterol and the sex hormones testosterone and estrogen.

97. **(D)**   Evolution and Diversity   *Laboratory*

Evolutionary relationships can be reconstructed based upon organisms' common ancestors, or when different organisms were last the same. In the molecular analysis of beta hemoglobin, the differences in amino acid sequence represent the proximity of relation between organisms. Organisms with large differences in amino acid sequence are more distantly related (i.e. shared a more distant common ancestor) than organisms with fewer differences. With this in mind, build out the chart based upon the table data. The first major division (A) is pretty obviously the lemur, which has a large difference in amino acid sequence with all of the other organisms. The next branch to split off is the squirrel monkey (G), then the rhesus monkey (F), the gibbon (E), the gorilla (D), and the chimpanzee and human share the closest branch (C, B).

98. **(D)**   Evolution and Diversity   *Laboratory*

Both humans and chimpanzees have only a single difference with gorillas in amino acid sequence for beta hemoglobin. Humans and gibbons have three differences in this amino acid sequence. As you can see in the reconstructed chart, based on this evidence, gorillas shared the same common ancestor with chimpanzees as with humans.

99. **(B)**   Evolution and Diversity   *Laboratory*

All the primates share a common ancestor, including humans and lemurs. (A) is false, as humans evolved from an ancestor of lemurs, not the modern variety. (C) is obviously incorrect. (D) is wrong: even though lemurs split off from the rest of the primate tree millions of years ago, they did not stop evolving. Humans and lemurs demonstrate divergent evolution, not convergent (E).

100. **(C)**   Evolution and Diversity   *Laboratory*

This is a tricky question. To answer it, you must recall that the genetic code is "degenerate," which means that some nucleotide triplets, or codons, call for the same amino acid. There are only 20 amino acids found in nature, and 64 possible codons. A horse's genetic sequence can be dramatically different from primates, but by the redundancy of some codons, this nucleotide sequence can code for many of the same amino acids.

SAT II Biology

Practice Test II

BIOLOGY E/M TEST

FOR BOTH BIOLOGY-E AND BIOLOGY-M, ANSWER QUESTIONS 1–60

Directions: Each set of lettered choices below refers to the numbered questions or statements immediately following it. Select the one lettered choice that best answers each question or best fits each statement, and then fill in the corresponding oval on the answer sheet. A choice may be used once, more than once, or not at all in each set.

Questions 1–3 refer to the following tissues.

    (A)   xylem
    (B)   stamen
    (C)   monocot
    (D)   phloem
    (E)   chloroplast

1.   Site of photosynthesis

2.   Male reproductive organ of a flower

3.   Living vascular tissue

Questions 4–6 refer to the following organisms.

    (A)   Hawk
    (B)   Salamander
    (C)   Snake
    (D)   Amoeba
    (E)   Salmon

4.   Breathes through simple lungs or skin

5.   Has a powerful four-chambered heart

6.   The oldest in evolutionary terms

Questions 7–9 refer to the following chemicals.

    (A)   water
    (B)   carbon dioxide
    (C)   glucose
    (D)   nitrogen
    (E)   carbon monoxide

7.   Returned to the atmosphere by living organisms through evaporation and transpiration

8.   Converted by bacteria from an atmospheric gas to a form usable by organisms

9.   A product of photosynthesis

Questions 10–12 refer to the following cell components.

    (A)   DNA
    (B)   Mitochondria
    (C)   Cytoplasm
    (D)   RNA polymerase
    (E)   RNA

10.   Active in the translation of proteins

11.   An enzyme used in transcription

12.   Cellular location of protein synthesis

GO ON TO THE NEXT PAGE

Directions: Each of the questions or incomplete statements below is followed by five suggested answers or completions. Some questions pertain to a set that refers to a laboratory or experimental situation. For each question, select the one choice that is the best answer to the question and then fill in the corresponding oval on the answer sheet.

13. Which of the following is a possible path of blood flow?

    (A) right atrium, right ventricle, lungs
    (B) left atrium, right atrium, lungs
    (C) left ventricle, left atrium, body
    (D) left ventricle, left atrium, lungs
    (E) right ventricle, right atrium, lungs

14. Which of the following is the best example of an ecological population?

    (A) A group of field mice living on a small island
    (B) All of the field mice found on a small island, the plants they eat, and the animals that pray on them
    (C) All of the field mice in North America
    (D) A single nest of field mice, including the mother and her young
    (E) All of the rodents on a small island, including many species of mice, rats, and squirrels

15. Which of the following are characteristics of every organic molecule?

    I.   Very simple structure
    II. Contains carbon
    III. Contains nitrogen

    (A) I only
    (B) II only
    (C) I and III only
    (D) II and III only
    (E) I, II, and III

16. Viruses reproduce themselves by

    (A) binary fission
    (B) mitosis
    (C) budding
    (D) producing and dispersing spores
    (E) injecting their genetic material into a living cell

17. The mechanism responsible for evolution is called

    (A) eugenics
    (B) artificial selection
    (C) natural selection
    (D) Lamarckism
    (E) succession

18. If one species of bird hunts insects in the canopy of the rainforest during the day, and a second hunts only at night, and closer to the ground, these two species can be said to

    (A) inhabit separate communities
    (B) have found distinct ecological niches
    (C) live in different biomes
    (D) possess the same biological cycles
    (E) have reached their carrying capacities

19. The number of chromosomes found in a human germ cell is

    (A) 46
    (B) 23
    (C) 48
    (D) 20
    (E) 44

20. If a single-celled protist that is used to living in a saltwater environment is suddenly placed into freshwater, which of the following is likely to happen?

    (A) The cell membrane, which is soluble in freshwater, will disintegrate, destroying the cell.
    (B) Due to osmosis, water will flow out of the cell into the surrounding environment, causing the cell to shrivel and die.
    (C) Due to osmosis, water will flow into the cell and cause it to swell and possibly burst.
    (D) Nothing will happen; the cell will pump water in from its surrounding environment to maintain its fluid content.
    (E) Nothing will happen; the cell membrane does not allow water to flow into or out of the cell.

GO ON TO THE NEXT PAGE

21. The function of the myelin sheath is to

    (A) strengthen the action potential of a neuron
    (B) speed up the conduction of an action potential along a neuron
    (C) regulate the frequency of action potentials fired along a neuron
    (D) prevent the neuron from firing if the action potential is too weak
    (E) make sure the action potential is traveling in the correct direction along the neuron

22. Physical structures in an organism that no longer serve a function in its current environment, but which were once developed and functional, are called

    (A) adaptations
    (B) homologous structures
    (C) forelimbs
    (D) vestigial structures
    (E) analogous structures

23. Which structures form part of a flower's male component?

    I. Anther
    II. Filament
    III. Stamen

    (A) I only
    (B) II only
    (C) III only
    (D) I and II only
    (E) I, II, and III

24. DNA and RNA are both nucleic acids that are essential to life. However, they differ in several ways. Which of the following is NOT true about the differences between DNA and RNA?

    (A) DNA is double stranded, while RNA is single stranded.
    (B) DNA is found in the nucleus of the cell, while RNA is mainly found in the cytoplasm.
    (C) DNA contains the nitrogenous base thymine, while RNA uses uracil in its place.
    (D) DNA and RNA have different sugars in their sugar-phosphate backbones.
    (E) DNA is found in eukaryotes, while RNA is found only in prokaryotes and viruses.

25. The majority of food digestion and absorption takes place in the

    (A) stomach
    (B) liver
    (C) pancreas
    (D) small intestine
    (E) large intestine

26. An individual's genotype has the all of the following characteristics EXCEPT

    (A) determines the phenotype
    (B) is an organism's genetic composition
    (C) depends on the phenotype
    (D) can be homozygous
    (E) can be heterozygous

GO ON TO THE NEXT PAGE

27. Members of the same phylum are also members of the same

    (A) kingdom
    (B) species
    (C) class
    (D) order
    (E) family

28. Which of the following proportions of nitrogenous bases describes a valid DNA molecule?

    (A) adenine 35%, cytosine 15%, guanine 15%, thymine 35%
    (B) adenine 35%, cytosine 15%, guanine 15%, uracil 35%
    (C) adenine 35%, cytosine 15%, guanine 35%, thymine 15%
    (D) adenine 20%, cytosine 20%, guanine 40%, thymine 20%
    (E) adenine 35%, cytosine 35%, guanine 15%, thymine 15%

29. All of the following describe the electron transport chain EXCEPT

    (A) the reactions occur on the inner membrane of mitochondria
    (B) the reactions occur on the outer membrane of mitochondria
    (C) the reactions are an aerobic process
    (D) hydrogen ions and electrons recombine and are then used to reduce oxygen to form water
    (E) NADH is oxidized

30. All of the following cause changes in the gene pool of a population from generation to generation EXCEPT

    (A) cloning
    (B) migration
    (C) mutation
    (D) disruptive selection
    (E) stabilizing selection

GO ON TO THE NEXT PAGE

Questions 31–35 refer to the following illustration of structures in the human body.

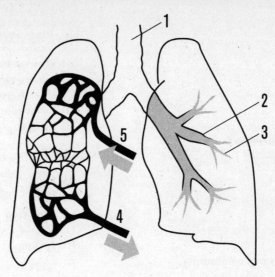

31. The structure labeled 4 is classified as a/n

   (A) artery
   (B) vein
   (C) arteriole
   (D) bronchiole
   (E) capillary

32. Gas exchange occurs in structure/s

   (A) 1 only
   (B) 2 only
   (C) 3 only
   (D) 2 and 3 only
   (E) 1, 2, and 3

33. Oxygenated blood from 5 is headed directly for the heart. Which structure does it enter first?

   (A) Right atrium
   (B) Vena cava
   (C) Right ventricle
   (D) Left atrium
   (E) Aorta

34. The body regulates respiration rate based upon blood pH and the concentration of

   (A) CO_2 in the blood
   (B) O_2 in the blood
   (C) CO_2 in alveolar sacs
   (D) O_2 in the brain
   (E) lactic acid in the muscles

GO ON TO THE NEXT PAGE

Over time, a small pond in a field becomes muddy, filled with vegetation, and is eventually filled in completely with land and trees.

35. This process is called

    (A) succession
    (B) dispersion
    (C) adaptation
    (D) degradation
    (E) mutation

36. In comparison to evolution, this process is

    (A) slower
    (B) faster
    (C) similar in rate
    (D) temporary
    (E) chaotic

37. The resulting forest is called a climax community. Why?

    (A) There is no room left for any new organisms
    (B) It continually undergoes dynamic changes
    (C) The trees create a high canopy of leaves
    (D) Its ecological characteristics remain essentially stable
    (E) It exhibits the most biological diversity of any biome

38. Compared to the pond, the forest will exhibit all of the following EXCEPT

    (A) greater biomass
    (B) more species
    (C) more heterotrophic species
    (D) fewer pioneer organisms
    (E) no change in resident species

39. Which of the following is a pioneer organism?

    (A) Fern
    (B) Kelp
    (C) Pine tree
    (D) Maple
    (E) Lichen

GO ON TO THE NEXT PAGE

Blood typing is frequently used to determine biological fatherhood. Two men—candidates X and Y, both possible fathers—are tested for blood type in relation to a child, who has blood type B.

40. If the mother has blood type AB, what blood types could the father potentially have?

    (A) A
    (B) B
    (C) AB
    (D) O
    (E) all of the above

41. What blood type would a candidate have to exhibit to determine with certainty that he is NOT the father?

    (A) Homozygous A
    (B) Heterozygous B
    (C) AB
    (D) O
    (E) Heterozygous A

42. If the child required a transfusion, what scenario best describes the concerns of getting a donor?

    (A) He can only receive blood from a direct relative.
    (B) His antibodies would attack any other blood type besides B.
    (C) If he receives the wrong type, anti-A antibodies in his plasma could cause clotting.
    (D) Adding a different antigen, such as A, would change his blood type.
    (E) He would require blood from a person of his approximate age.

43. For a couple who both have blood type AB, what percent chance will their offspring exhibit type A?

    (A) 0%
    (B) 25%
    (C) 33%
    (D) 50%
    (E) 75%

44. The alleles for A and B blood types are

    (A) mutations
    (B) haploid
    (C) recessive
    (D) commensalistic
    (E) codominant

An experimenter runs a simple combination reaction and charts the results as line A. She then reruns the reaction with the original solution plus substance B, and again after adding substance C to the new solution.

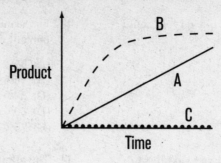

45. For the initial reaction (A), which best describes the relationship of product to time?

    (A) Directly proportional
    (B) Inverse square
    (C) Exponential growth
    (D) Inversely proportional
    (E) Limited growth

46. Substance B most likely contains

    (A) more reactants
    (B) an enzyme
    (C) hormones
    (D) a strong acid
    (E) extra product

47. The addition of substance C failed to produce any product. Which of the following is the LEAST LIKELY explanation for what might have occurred?

    (A) A pH change decreased the efficiency of the catalyst.
    (B) Substance C reacted separately with the substrate.
    (C) It catalyzed a different reaction.
    (D) Simple reactions cannot run with more than two reactants.
    (E) It contained multiple unknowns that interfered with the reaction.

48. The addition of a catalyst can effect the reaction in the following ways EXCEPT

    (A) decreases the activation energy
    (B) temporarily binds substrates to its active sites
    (C) speeds up the reaction rate
    (D) increases reaction temperature
    (E) produces an unlimited amount of product

GO ON TO THE NEXT PAGE

Questions <u>49–52</u> refer to the diagram below, which represents a cross-section of a leaf.

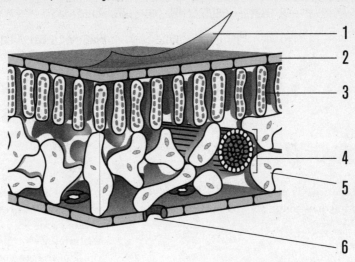

49. Where does the majority of photosynthesis occur?

   (A) 1
   (B) 2
   (C) 3
   (D) 4
   (E) 5

50. The opening in the lower epidermis layer is termed the

   (A) xylem
   (B) cuticle
   (C) phloem
   (D) stoma
   (E) leak channel

51. The release of water vapor through structure 6 is called

   (A) transpiration
   (B) transduction
   (C) exhalation
   (D) photosynthesis
   (E) capillary effect

52. This leaf could represent any of the following EXCEPT

   (A) dicot
   (B) monocot
   (C) fern
   (D) moss
   (E) angiosperm

GO ON TO THE NEXT PAGE

In pea plants, two separate alleles code for the shape and color of peas. Round shape is dominant over wrinkled, and green color is dominant over yellow. In a controlled experiment, a plant with round green peas is crossed with a plant with wrinkled yellow peas.

F_0 Plant with round   x   Plant with wrinkled
green peas   yellow peas

F_1 13 plants with round green peas

F_2 ?

53. If a cross of F_1 plants produces 31 plants in the F_2 generation, approximately how many should have wrinkled green peas?

(A) 0
(B) 3
(C) 6
(D) 10
(E) 15

54. What is the expected ratio of phenotypes for the F_2 generation?

(A) 1:3:3:1
(B) 1:9:9:1
(C) 1:3:1
(D) 9:3:3:1
(E) 1:1:1:1

55. An experimenter wanted to determine whether a plant with wrinkled green peas from the F_2 generation was homozygous for color. In a test cross with a plant with wrinkled yellow peas, what ratio of offspring would confirm that the test subject was homozygous green?

(A) 1 wrinkled green to 1 wrinkled yellow
(B) all wrinkled green
(C) all wrinkled yellow
(D) 1 wrinkled green to 1 round green
(E) 1 wrinkled yellow to 1 round green

56. If a randomly selected plant from F_2 is crossed with the original F_0 plant with round green peas, what is the probability that their offspring will have round green peas?

(A) 6%
(B) 19%
(C) 56%
(D) 94%
(E) 100%

GO ON TO THE NEXT PAGE

BIOLOGY-E SECTION

If you are taking the Biology-E test, continue with questions 61–80.
If you are taking the Biology-M test, go to question 81 now.

<u>Directions:</u> Each of the questions or incomplete statements below is followed by five suggested answers or completions. Some questions pertain to a set that refers to a laboratory or experimental situation. For each question, select the one choice that is the best answer to the question and then fill in the corresponding oval on the answer sheet.

An experimenter attempted to determine how nerves operate on muscles. Two frog hearts were placed in isotonic solutions in adjoining containers; the fluid was allowed to flow between the containers. The first heart was still connected to the vagus nerve, which serves in the body as the heart's pacemaker by slowing the heart rate. Using an electrode, the experimenter stimulated the vagus nerve and observed that the rate of heart #1 slowed down. A few seconds later, heart #2 also slowed down.

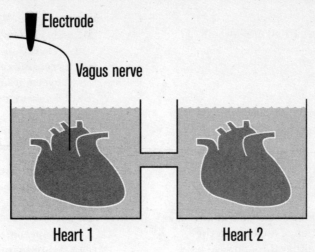

57. The scientist, an Austrian named Otto Loewi, hypothesized that heart #2 received stimulation from something in the fluid, and named it "Vagusstoff." It has since become known to be

    (A) an action potential of 70 mV
    (B) the neurotransmitter acetylcholine
    (C) sodium cations
    (D) potassium cations
    (E) the depolarizing threshold

58. The vagus nerve is part of the nervous system called the

    (A) autonomic nervous system
    (B) medulla oblongata
    (C) central nervous system
    (D) somatic nervous system
    (E) hypothalamus

59. Arrange in order the following events in the neuron when it is stimulated with an electrode:

    I.   sodium channels open
    II. the depolarizing current reaches a threshold voltage
    III. potassium channels open

    (A) I, II, III
    (B) II, I, III
    (C) II, III, I
    (D) III, II, I
    (E) III, I, II

60. The vagus nerve does not actually "touch" the heart. The microscopic gap is called a(n)

    (A) axon
    (B) resting potential
    (C) Node of Ranvier
    (D) dendrite
    (E) synapse

GO ON TO THE NEXT PAGE ➤

61. Which of the following is probably better developed in an intelligent animal species than in a more primitive species?

    (A) Cerebrum
    (B) Cerebellum
    (C) Medulla
    (D) Hypothalamus
    (E) Brainstem

62. Of the following, all are vertebrates EXCEPT

    (A) frog
    (B) trout
    (C) shark
    (D) lizard
    (E) crab

63. Of the following, what best explains how animals obtain the nitrogen and amino acids they require to survive?

    (A) By eating plants that have obtained nitrogen from bacteria, or other animals which have eaten these plants
    (B) By ingesting nitrogen-fixing bacteria from the soil
    (C) Through simple respiration of nitrogen in the atmosphere, absorbed either through skin or lungs
    (D) By providing nitrogen-fixing bacteria a habitat within their own bodies
    (E) By drinking water that contains dissolved nitrogen

64. What results if overlap between the niches of two organisms decreases?

    (A) Competition between the organisms is unaffected
    (B) Competition between the organisms decreases
    (C) Competition between the organisms increases
    (D) Coevolution occurs in both organisms
    (E) Biomagnification

65. Of the following, evolutionary fitness is best characterized by

    (A) changes in the gene pool of a population
    (B) an organism's ability to contribute to the next generation's gene pool
    (C) increasing complexities in the features of a species
    (D) the formation of a new species
    (E) the development of more human-like traits

66. The hormone epinephrine, or adrenaline, produced in the adrenal medulla

    (A) regulates the level of glucose in the blood
    (B) regulates the level of calcium in the blood
    (C) regulates the body's pH balance
    (D) operates in stressful situations with the sympathetic nervous system
    (E) stimulates other glands to produce their respective hormones

GO ON TO THE NEXT PAGE

Questions 67–71 refer to the following bar chart of available energy (kilocalories) based on a food web of organisms within a given community. (The chart is not drawn to scale.)

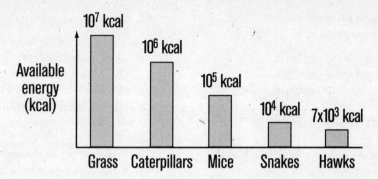

67. Who is the primary consumer in this community?

    (A) Grass
    (B) Caterpillars
    (C) Mice
    (D) Snakes
    (E) Hawks

68. What happens to the energy that is NOT transferred to consumers?

    (A) Used in respiration
    (B) Lost in the nitrogen cycle
    (C) Used for temperature control in endotherms
    (D) Taken up by decomposers
    (E) Lost to entropy

69. Which of the following would a decomposer be?

    (A) Primary producer
    (B) Autotroph
    (C) Primary consumer
    (D) Heterotroph
    (E) Tertiary consumer

70. What is the lowest trophic level that can include a carnivore?

    (A) Primary producer
    (B) Primary consumer
    (C) Secondary consumer
    (D) Tertiary consumer
    (E) Decomposer

71. Energy transfer between trophic levels typically runs at 10% efficiency. What is the most likely explanation for the 30% energy loss between snakes and hawks?

    (A) Hawks eat both snakes and mice.
    (B) Hawks are efficient at catching snakes.
    (C) Snakes provide more nutrition than mice.
    (D) Hawks span all of the trophic levels.
    (E) Some snakes eat hawks.

GO ON TO THE NEXT PAGE

After fertilization of the egg in humans, the ball of rapidly dividing cells arrives and lodges itself in the nutrient-rich lining of the female uterus.

72. From fertilization, the correct sequence of development of the embryo-to-be is:

    (A) zygote—blastula—gastrula—morula
    (B) zygote—blastula—gastrula—morula
    (C) zygote—morula—blastula—gastrula
    (D) gastrula—blastula—zygote—morula
    (E) morula—zygote—gastrula—blastula

73. The build-up of the uterine lining is facilitated by the corpus luteum and its production of

    (A) progesterone
    (B) estrogen
    (C) luteinizing hormone (LH)
    (D) oxytonin
    (E) prolactin

74. If the egg is not fertilized, which of the following occurs?

    (A) Ovulation
    (B) Menstruation
    (C) Spike in estrogen levels
    (D) Buildup of uterine wall
    (E) Spike in progesterone levels

75. Which of these structures will the human embryo NOT form at some point before birth?

    (A) Notochord
    (B) Gills
    (C) Tail
    (D) Eyelids
    (E) Scales

GO ON TO THE NEXT PAGE

**If you are taking the Biology-M test, continue with questions 81–100.
Be sure to start this section of the test by filling in oval 61 on your answer sheet.**

<u>Directions:</u> Each of the questions or incomplete statements below is followed by five suggested answers or completions. Some questions pertain to a set that refers to a laboratory or experimental situation. For each question, select the one choice that is the best answer to the question and then fill in the corresponding oval on the answer sheet.

Questions 76–80 refer to the following diagrams referring to the growth of a rabbit population over time.

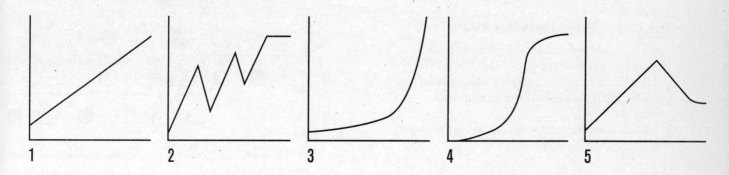

76. Which of the charts shows exponential growth to carrying capacity?

   (A) 1
   (B) 2
   (C) 3
   (D) 4
   (E) 5

77. The introduction of natural predators could affect the population according to which curve?

   I.   1
   II. 4
   III. 5

   (A) I only
   (B) II only
   (C) III only
   (D) I and II only
   (E) II and III only

78. The shape of the curve in chart 4 is "sigmoidal." All of the following factors can be responsible for this population curve EXCEPT

   (A) food scarcity
   (B) disease
   (C) waste accumulation
   (D) niche competition
   (E) individual mutations

79. Rabbits use what reproductive strategy?

   (A) Vast numbers of offspring with no parental care
   (B) Large, fast-developing litters with some parental care
   (C) One or two offspring with delayed sexual maturity
   (D) Offspring only under non-predatory conditions
   (E) Parthenogenesis

80. A population of squirrels is introduced to the rabbits' environment. The two groups could share all of the following EXCEPT

   (A) niche
   (B) biome
   (C) community
   (D) water
   (E) trophic level

GO ON TO THE NEXT PAGE

81. Which of the following molecules is NOT considered a basic building block of larger, more complex organic molecules?

    (A) Ribose, a monosaccharide
    (B) Guanine, a nitrogenous base
    (C) Lysine, an amino acid
    (D) Sucrose, a disaccharide
    (E) Amylase, an enzyme

82. Which of the following statements are true?

    I.   All chemical reactions of life occur in or in association with cells.
    II. All cells carry genetic information in the form of DNA, which is passed from parent cell to daughter cell.
    III. All cells contain a nucleus that coordinates the basic functions of the cell.

    (A) I only
    (B) III only
    (C) I and II only
    (D) II and III only
    (E) I, II, and III

83. The correct chronology of the evolution of the five kingdoms is

    (A) Monera, Fungi, Plantae, Protista, Animalia
    (B) Protista, Monera, Fungi, Plantae, Animalia
    (C) Protista, Monera, Plantae, Animalia, Fungi
    (D) Fungi, Monera, Protista, Animalia, Plantae
    (E) Monera, Protista, Plantae, Fungi, Animalia

84. Transcription involves which two types of nucleic acids?

    (A) DNA and tRNA
    (B) DNA and mRNA
    (C) mRNA and tRNA
    (D) mRNA and rRNA
    (E) rRNA and tRNA

85. Which of the following organisms is classified in Phylum Chordata?

    (A) Lobster
    (B) Minnow
    (C) Earthworm
    (D) Clam
    (E) Hydra

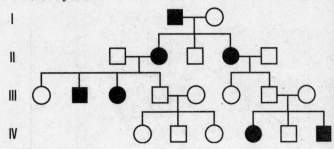

86. In the above pedigree, males are indicated by squares, and females by circles. The shaded individuals have a disorder caused by a recessive allele. Which of the following can therefore be true?

    (A) All the unaffected individuals on the chart are heterozygous
    (B) The allele appears on the X chromosome
    (C) All the males in generation II are heterozygous
    (D) The disorder will not appear in any subsequent generations
    (E) In generation IV, individuals 1, 2, and 3 must be homozygous

GO ON TO THE NEXT PAGE

A student conducted an experiment to determine how different wavelengths of light affect photosynthesis in the common green pondweed, *Elodea*. A sample of the aquatic plant was submerged in distilled water under a measuring pipette filled with water.

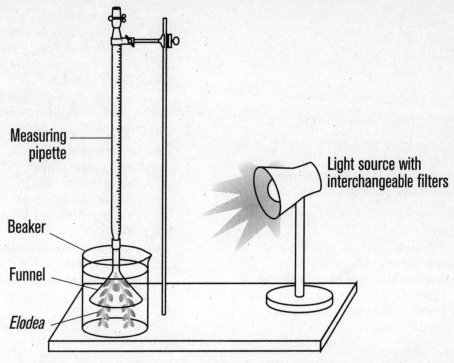

Several colored filters were used to change the wavelength of the light produced by the light source. The experimenter counted bubbles the *Elodea* sprig produced during a 5-minute period of exposure to each filter, including without a filter and without light, and recorded the results in a graph.

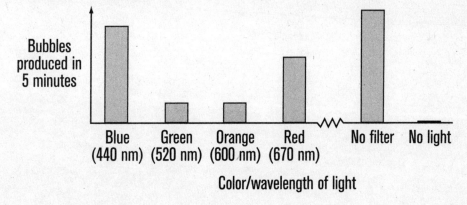

87. The gas being produced as bubbles in this experiment is

    (A) oxygen
    (B) carbon dioxide
    (C) water vapor
    (D) hydrogen
    (E) chlorine

GO ON TO THE NEXT PAGE

88. Which of the following act(s) as a control for this experiment?

    I.   No filter
    II. No light
    III. Using the same plant

    (A) I only
    (B) II only
    (C) III only
    (D) I and II only
    (E) I, II, and III

89. Green light produced few bubbles. Which of the following statements explains why?

    (A) Light with wavelengths near 520 nm is reflected off the water.
    (B) Chlorophyll reflects all the light near 520 nm, making plants appear green.
    (C) Green light is totally absorbed, exciting electrons and driving photosynthesis.
    (D) Green light doesn't penetrate *Elodea* leaves.
    (E) *Elodea* has no chlorophyll.

90. How much gas would the *Elodea* produce when exposed to a yellow filter (~580 nm)?

    (A) More than blue
    (B) More than green, less than blue
    (C) About the same as green or orange
    (D) More than orange, less than red
    (E) More than red

91. What could the student conclude from this experiment?

    (A) The rate of photosynthesis is variable with wavelength of light.
    (B) The shorter the wavelength of light, the faster the rate of photosynthesis.
    (C) Photosynthesis has different rates in different plants.
    (D) The rate of photosynthesis increases with temperature.
    (E) Plants cannot survive in filtered light.

GO ON TO THE NEXT PAGE

Bacteriophage viruses replicate by latching on to bacteria and programming them to make more viruses. In an experiment, two groups of bacteriophage viruses were labeled with radioactive isotopes: Group I had sulfur-labeled protein coats, and Group II had phosphorous-labeled genetic cores. The groups were introduced to separate colonies of bacteria. After ten minutes, each culture was vigorously stirred to detach the viruses from the bacteria, then spun in a centrifuge to separate the components: bacteria at the bottom, and the remaining solution (called the "supernatant") at the top. The components were then tested for radioactivity.

Group I: viruses with sulfur-protein coats	Radioactivity?	Group II: viruses with phosphorous-DNA coats	Radioactivity?
Bacteria	No	Bacteria	Yes
Supernatant	Yes	Supernatant	No

92. Why does the supernatant liquid show radioactivity in Group I?

    (A) It contains the viruses' radioactive protein coats.
    (B) It contains radioactive genetic material.
    (C) Bacteria synthesized radioactive sulfur.
    (D) The bacteria exploded with new viruses.
    (E) Bacteria expelled the isotopes by active transport.

93. The bacteriophage virus is classified in

    (A) Kingdom Monera
    (B) Kingdom Protista
    (C) Kingdom Fungi
    (D) Kingdom Animalia
    (E) none of the above

94. This experiment, called the Hershey-Chase experiment and conducted in 1952, was a milestone in genetics. What was its breakthrough?

    (A) It demonstrated that the viruses' DNA is the key to their replication.
    (B) It detailed the makeup of bacteriophages.
    (C) It showed how bacteria replicate.
    (D) It used radioactive isotopes to track molecules.
    (E) Bacteria were able to synthesize new radioactive viruses.

95. If this virus reproduces using the lytic cycle, all of the following will occur in the host bacteria EXCEPT

    (A) rupture of cell membrane
    (B) viral DNA replication
    (C) new protein synthesis
    (D) manufacture of virus coats
    (E) exponential growth of bacteria

GO ON TO THE NEXT PAGE

A standard process in genetic testing is to replicate individual segments of DNA over and over into quantities large enough for tests. One such test is electrophoresis, where the replicated DNA segments are lined up at the base of a regular, stable magnetic field.

Figure 1 (before)

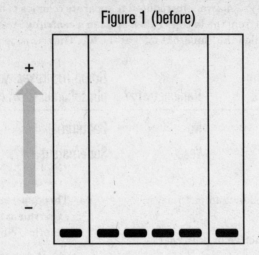

Due to its polarity, the clumps of DNA migrate across the electrophoresis plate; the distance of migration relates to the size of the DNA segments. In the following test, two specific genes from two adults and four children were tested using electrophoresis. Each column represents the replicated DNA segments from one individual.

Figure 2 (after)

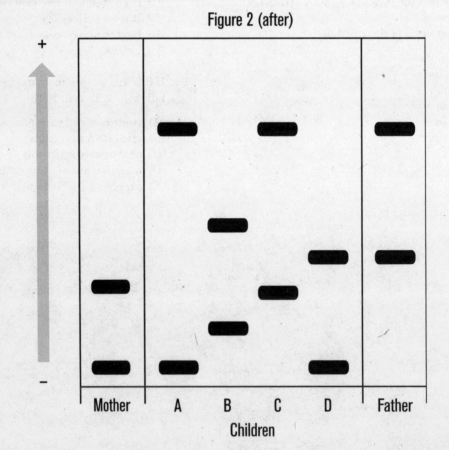

GO ON TO THE NEXT PAGE

96. Which column represents the child who is not a genetic offspring of these parents?

    (A) A
    (B) B
    (C) C
    (D) D
    (E) They could all belong

97. What explains why some segments would move farther towards the positive end of the electrophoresis plate?

    (A) The magnetic field increases towards one end.
    (B) Those DNA segments are more polar.
    (C) The segments closer to the positive end are smaller.
    (D) The farther segments are RNA.
    (E) There are more copies of the gene.

98. After the test is run, what is an experimenter likely to find in an analysis of one of the bands?

    (A) High levels of uracil
    (B) Many copies of DNA code for a single gene
    (C) DNA from both the father and mother
    (D) A complete chromosome
    (E) A high pH level

99. In the body, the replication of DNA segments is carried out by a(n)

    (A) enzyme
    (B) ribosome
    (C) chance association of nucleotides
    (D) hormone
    (E) sugar phosphate backbone

100. The copying of DNA segments in the beginning of the experiment most resembles

    (A) conjugation
    (B) translation
    (C) transduction
    (D) gene mapping
    (E) transcription

S T O P

IF YOU FINISH BEFORE TIME IS CALLED, YOU MAY CHECK YOUR WORK ON THIS TEST ONLY.
DO NOT TURN TO ANY OTHER TEST IN THIS BOOK.

SAT II Biology
Practice Test II
Explanations

Answers to SAT II U.S. History Practice Test I

Question Number	Correct Answer	Right	Wrong	Question Number	Correct Answer	Right	Wrong
1.	E	——	——	51.	A	——	——
2.	B	——	——	52.	D	——	——
3.	D	——	——	53.	C	——	——
4.	B	——	——	54.	D	——	——
5.	A	——	——	55.	B	——	——
6.	D	——	——	56.	E	——	——
7.	A	——	——	57.	B	——	——
8.	D	——	——	58.	A	——	——
9.	C	——	——	59.	B	——	——
10.	E	——	——	60.	E	——	——
11.	D	——	——	61.	A	——	——
12.	C	——	——	62.	E	——	——
13.	A	——	——	63.	A	——	——
14.	A	——	——	64.	B	——	——
15.	B	——	——	65.	B	——	——
16.	E	——	——	66.	D	——	——
17.	C	——	——	67.	B	——	——
18.	B	——	——	68.	A	——	——
19.	B	——	——	69.	D	——	——
20.	C	——	——	70.	C	——	——
21.	B	——	——	71.	A	——	——
22.	D	——	——	72.	C	——	——
23.	E	——	——	73.	A	——	——
24.	E	——	——	74.	B	——	——
25.	D	——	——	75.	E	——	——
26.	C	——	——	76.	D	——	——
27.	A	——	——	77.	E	——	——
28.	A	——	——	78.	E	——	——
29.	B	——	——	79.	B	——	——
30.	A	——	——	80.	A	——	——
31.	A	——	——	81.	E	——	——
32.	C	——	——	82.	C	——	——
33.	D	——	——	83.	E	——	——
34.	A	——	——	84.	B	——	——
35.	A	——	——	85.	B	——	——
36.	B	——	——	86.	C	——	——
37.	D	——	——	87.	A	——	——
38.	E	——	——	88.	E	——	——
39.	E	——	——	89.	B	——	——
40.	E	——	——	90.	C	——	——
41.	A	——	——	91.	A	——	——
42.	A	——	——	92.	A	——	——
43.	B	——	——	93.	E	——	——
44.	E	——	——	94.	A	——	——
45.	A	——	——	95.	E	——	——
46.	B	——	——	96.	B	——	——
47.	D	——	——	97.	C	——	——
48.	E	——	——	98.	B	——	——
49.	C	——	——	99.	A	——	——
50.	D	——	——	100.	E	——	——

Calculating Your Score on SAT II Biology Practice Test II

Your raw score for the SAT II History test is calculated from the number of questions you answer correctly and incorrectly. Once you have determined your composite score, use the conversion table on page 23 of this book to calculate your scaled score.

To Calculate Your Raw Score

Count the number of questions you answered correctly: _____
A

Count the number of questions you answered incorrectly, and multiply that number by $\frac{1}{4}$:

$$\underline{\hspace{2cm}}_{B} \quad X \quad \frac{1}{4} \quad = \quad \underline{\hspace{2cm}}_{C}$$

Subtract the value in field C from value in field A: _____
D

Round the number in field D to the nearest whole number. This is your raw score: _____
E

Biology E/M Classification Questions

1. (E) Organismal Biology
Photosynthesis takes place in the chloroplast.

2. (B) Organismal Biology
The stamen is the male reproductive organ in a flower. The pistil is the female reproductive organ.

3. (D) Organismal Biology
Both xylem and phloem are types of vascular tissue, but xylem cells die at maturity and only carry out their function as dead cells. Phloem cells live as they carry out their function of transporting water and nutrients throughout the plant.

4. (B) Evolution and Diversity
The salamander, an amphibian, breathes through simple lungs or skin. The hawk, a bird, and snakes, a reptile, both have better developed lungs and do not really breathe through their skin. Salmon, a fish, breathe through gills, and Amoeba can't be said to breathe in the proper sense (amoebas also don't have skin, they have a cell membrane).

5. (A) Evolution and Diversity
Birds have powerful four chambered hearts, in part to help them maintain energy for the rigors of flight. Hawk is the right answer.

6. (D) Evolution and Diversity
The amoeba, a single-celled protist, evolved before any of the more complex organisms in the list.

7. (A) Ecology
An important part of the water cycle is the release of water into the atmosphere by evaporation and transpiration. You might have been tempted to answer carbon dioxide, since that is given off by animals and plants also. But carbon dioxide is given off by respiration, not evaporation or transpiration.

8. (D) Ecology
Special bacteria living in the soil or in the roots of plants convert atmospheric nitrogen to more usable forms for organisms. These "nitrogen-fixing" bacteria break the triple bond in nitrogen gas to allow it to be used by organisms to make protein.

9. (C) Ecology
In the carbon cycle, plants use carbon dioxide from the atmosphere and, powered by the energy of the sun, convert it to glucose. Carbohydrate energy is passed through the food chain when herbivores eat the plants and carnivores and omnivores eat the herbivores.

10. (E) Cell Processes
In translation, mRNA travels from the nucleus of the cell to the cytoplasm, where it works with ribosomes to create proteins. DNA is involved in the transcription half of protein synthesis, but not the translation half.

11. **(D)** Cell Processes

An enzyme ends with the suffix "ase," so RNA polymerase is the only possible answer. RNA polymerase uses DNA as a template to synthesize compliment strands of mRNA.

12. **(C)** Cell Processes

Protein synthesis occurs in the cytoplasm. Mitochondria are locations of much of cell respiration, not protein synthesis.

Biology E/M Solitary Multiple Choice

13. **(A)** Organismal Biology

The proper blood circuit is right atrium, right ventricle, lungs, left atrium, left ventricle, body, right atrium, etc. Blood never crosses directly from one side of the heart to the other, and it always flows from atria to ventricles.

14. **(A)** Ecology

An ecological population is a group of individuals that interbreed and share the same gene pool. Since individuals can only breed with members of their own species, we can eliminate answers (B) and (E) right away. A group of field mice consisting of a mother and her young (D) is too small to be a population, because they will breed with others outside the nest. Answer (C) is too broad and would consist of several populations, since all of the field mice on the entire continent do not come in contact with all of the other groups of field mice.

15. **(B)** Organic and Biochemistry

By definition, an organic molecule will contain carbon. Organic molecules tend to be very complex, so choice I can be eliminated, and it is not a requirement that they contain nitrogen, eliminating choice III.

16. **(E)** Organismal Biology

The correct answer is (E). Viruses cannot reproduce on their own, and they must rely on living cell hosts. They inject their DNA or RNA into the host cell, and this DNA or RNA replicates inside the cell and produces new virus particles. These new viruses eventually break free and infect other cells.

17. **(C)** Evolution and Diversity

Natural selection is the mechanism of evolution proposed by Darwin. Eugenics (A) refers to the study of how genetics can improve the inherited characteristics of the human race. Artificial selection (B) occurs with human interference, such as breeding dogs. Larmackism (D) refers to the inheritance of acquired traits, an evolutionary theory which Darwin debunked. Succession (E) refers to the physical changes within an ecosystem.

18. **(B)** Ecology

An ecological niche is the way an organism lives in a particular environment, including how it hunts for food, where it lives, and so on. Organisms compete with one another if their niches are similar, and they can better coexist if their niches do not overlap, as in this example.

19. **(B)** Cell Processes

Germ cells (sperm and egg cells) are haploid, which is to say they possess half of the total number of chromosomes found in somatic cells. Somatic cells in humans have two sets of 23 unique chromosomes for a total of 46 chromosomes.

20. **(C)** The Cell

Because the concentration of solutes is higher in the cell than in the surrounding freshwater, the cell is hypertonic to its environment, and water will flow into the cell due to osmosis, trying to maintain a solute balance. Cells that normally live in freshwater contain contractile vacuoles to pump out this excess water, but a cell not accustomed to this environment most likely would not. Note the cell membrane is not soluble in water, eliminating choice (A), and that water is small enough to easily pass through the cell membrane, eliminating choice (E).

21. **(B)** Organismal Biology

The myelin sheath, which is comprised of cells known as Schwann cells, allows the action potential to "jump" down the axon, greatly increasing the speed of conduction.

22. **(D)** Evolution and Diversity

Vestigial structures have little or no utility in an organism's current environment; an example is the human appendix. Such structures did have utility in an earlier stage of evolutionary development. Though these structures may have originally been adaptations (A), they are no longer adaptive, or useful. Homologous structures correspond to other structures in origin and form, but not necessarily in function: A bird's wing and horse's leg are homologous. (C) is overly specific, and can be eliminated. Analogous structures are similar in function but not in origin: A bee's wing and a hummingbird's wing are analogous structures.

23. **(E)** Organismal Biology

The male part of the flower, or the stamen, is comprised of a supporting filament and a pollen-producing head, called the anther.

24. **(E)** Organic and Biochemistry

DNA and RNA are both found in both eukaryotes and prokaryotes. Most viruses contain DNA, but some, known as retroviruses, contain RNA. All of the other answers are true.

25. **(D)** Organismal Biology

Almost all of food digestion and absorption takes place in the small intestine. The stomach produces strong acids and pepsin to break down foods, and churns them into a mush called chyme. Bile from the liver and enzymes from the pancreas released into the small intestine break down the chyme further, and the nutrients are absorbed through microscopic projections called villi covering the intestinal wall.

26. **(C)** Genetics

An organism's phenotype is the physical expression of its genotype, which is its genetic composition (B). As such, the phenotype is dependent upon the genotype (A). An organism can have a homozygous genotype (D), that is, two copies of the same allele. On the other hand, an organism can have a heterozygous genotype (E), which means the organism has two different alleles of the gene.

27. (A) Evolution and Diversity

In terms of inclusiveness, a broader taxonomic category is more inclusive than a narrower one. A kingdom, such as "Animalia," includes phyla, classes, orders, families, genera, and species. Remember the classification scheme, from most broad to narrowest identifier, is kingdom, phylum, class, order, family, genus, species.

28. (A) Organic and Biochemistry

The correct answer must have equal proportions of adenine-thymine and cytosine-guanine, which demonstrates that these bases are paired with one another in a double helix. Answer (B) can be eliminated right away because DNA does not contain uracil, while answer (D) can be eliminated because it does not demonstrate any sort of equal pairing among the bases.

29. (B) Cell Processes

The electron transport chain takes products from the aerobic Krebs cycle and puts them through a series of oxidation-reduction reactions. Electrons harvested from glucose are carried by NADH molecules to the inner mitochondrial membrane. NADH releases its high-energy electrons and is oxidized to NAD+. The energy from these electrons drives proton pumps in the membrane which will eventually make ATP. At the end of the electron transport chain, oxygen (O_2) is reduced, or accepts the electrons, to form water (D). Given that choices (A) and (B) are opposites, the answer is likely to be one of these two choices.

30. (A) Evolution and Diversity

A gene pool is comprised of all the genes in a population found in individuals capable of reproduction. Clones are identical genetic copies of a single individual produced by asexual reproduction; hence, clones do not introduce changes to the gene pool. A mutation (B) is a random change in a gene that can alter an inheritable characteristic. If organisms migrate (B) so that different populations mix, the gene pool can also change. Natural selection, including both disruptive (A) and stabilizing (A) selection, can change the gene pool over generations by favoring the survival and reproductive success of certain genotypes over others.

Biology E/M Group Multiple Choice

31. (A) Organismal Biology

Blood flowing into the lungs for oxygenation is pumped through the pulmonary artery. Arteries carry blood away from the heart; veins (B) return blood to the heart. Arterioles (C) are smaller branches from a main artery, and capillaries (E) are the tiniest branches of the circulatory system. Bronchioles (E) are branches of respiratory tubes for air passage.

32. (C) Organismal Biology

Gas exchange occurs across the thin membranes of alveolar sacs, packed with capillaries, which are found at the ends of the respiratory pathway. The trachea (A) and bronchus/bronchiole (B) are structural tubes with strong, cartilaginous-ringed walls, and do not participate in gas exchange.

33. (D) Organismal Biology

Know the pathway of blood through the heart and lungs. Oxygen-poor blood from the body travels through the vena cava into the right atrium of the heart, and gets pumped out by the right ventricle though the pulmonary artery to the lungs. Oxygenated blood from the lungs is collected by the pulmonary vein, and then enters the left atrium of the heart. It subsequently arrives in the left ventricle, which pumps the oxygen-rich blood out through the aorta to the body.

34. (A) Organismal Biology

An important function of the respiratory system is to control the pH of the blood. Carbon dioxide becomes carboxylic acid in solution, and excess CO_2 can lower the blood's pH to dangerous levels. The brain controls breathing by monitoring the levels of carbon dioxide in the blood. With an increase in CO_2 levels, the brainstem responds by increasing the respiration rate to expire the gas through the lungs.

35. (A) Ecology

Ecological succession is the set of cumulative biotic changes within a community. Succession happens when one set of organisms replaces another according to an orderly progress and leading to a climax community. Both adaptation (C) and mutation (E) refer to individual changes. Dispersion (B) refers to the way the individuals of a population are arranged. Degradation (D) is the opposite effect of succession.

36. (B) Ecology

Although it varies in rate, succession is much faster than evolution overall. For instance, ponds can fill with trees within the span of a human lifetime, whereas evolution works across many, many generations of individuals. Succession is dynamic, but the changes are not temporary (D), and it is an orderly progress as opposed to chaotic (E).

37. (D) Ecology

The climax community is the final phase of succession, where the community reaches a state of equilibrium. The climax community is subject to change in its individuals, and even resident species may come and go, but the overall biological characteristics of the community are stable. (e.g. The forest will not become a pond again.) This implies that (A) is false. (B) is also incorrect; although some change can occur, it does not necessarily do so, and it does not change the community's overall makeup. Tree height (C) has nothing to do with this sense of "climax." (E) refers to the tropical rainforest, which climax communities do not always represent.

38. (E) Ecology

This question asks you to compare characteristics of communities at different stages of succession. These details can be deduced. Later successional stages have greater biomass (think of trees vs. pond reeds) and more species as the area becomes more habitable for more organisms. As the ecosystem gains complexity, there are more heterotrophs feeding on other organisms. Pioneer organisms (E) appear in very early successional stages. Though this forest is a climax community, the individual species living there may change, as long as the entire community retains its ecological characteristics, so (E) is the correct answer.

39. (E) Ecology

Pioneer organisms are the first to establish themselves in a new habitat. Among these answer choices, lichen is the pioneer organism. Since it can thrive on bare rock, lichens need very little or no organic support, and can infiltrate a barren habitat to begin the process of ecological succession.

40. **(E)** Genetics

Questions about blood type refer to combinations of the codominant alleles for blood types A and B, and the recessive allele for type O. It's a good idea to keep track of them while you go: I_A for the A allele, I_B for B, and i for O. With blood type AB, the mother has two alleles to contribute to her offspring: I_A or I_B. The son has blood type B, so his genotype is either I_BI_B or I_Bi. Therefore, he could only have received the I_B allele from his mother. This means that the father contributed either an I_B allele or a recessive i allele. The I_B and i alleles appear in numerous combinations of blood types, including all of the first four answer choices: A (I_Ai); AB (I_AI_B); B (I_Bi); and O (ii).

41. **(A)** Genetics

As established in the previous explanation, the son received an I_B allele from his mother. He cannot have an I_A allele and still exhibit blood type B. If the male candidate has only I_A genes to contribute (homozygous A), he cannot be the father.

42. **(A)** Genetics

Blood type is determined by the antigens appearing on the surfaces of blood cells. Blood can have A antigens (type A), B antigens (type B), both kinds (type AB), or no antigens at all (type O). Blood also has antibodies in its plasma to attack foreign antigens. For example, antibodies in blood type B would attack the A antigens of blood type A. The son could only receive blood without A antigens, including types B and O. (Type O has no antigens to attack, which is why it is called "the universal donor.") If the son is given blood of types A or AB, his antibodies would attack the A antigens and cause clumping and clotting.

43. **(B)** Genetics

This question asks you about probable phenotypes in a simple heterozygous cross. Sketch out (or visualize) a Punnett Square. Each parent has two alleles to contribute, I_A and I_B.

	I^A	I^B
I^A	I^AI^A	I^AI^B
I^B	I^AI^B	I^BI^B

There is one chance in four, or 25%, that offspring will have blood type A (I_AI_A).

44. **(E)** Genetics

The alleles for blood types A and B are codominant, meaning that if both alleles are present in the genotype, both will be expressed in the phenotype. For example, if alleles for blood types A (I_A) and B (I_B) combine in offspring, the individual will exhibit blood type AB (I_AI_B). One will not subsume the other, as in the case of the recessive allele for type O (i). Mutations (E) are alterations to genetic code. Haploid (E) refers to the number of chromosomes in gametes. Commensalism (E) is a symbiotic relationship between organisms.

45. **(A)** Organic and Biochemistry   *Laboratory*

You can identify common types of mathematical relationships by the shape of their curves. A straight line describes a proportional relationship. For line A, the amount of product increases as time increases, so the relationship is direct. In an inversely proportional relationship (E), product would decrease with time, and the line would slope downwards. Inverse square (B) and exponential growth (C) would both give pronounced curves. Limited growth (E) refers to population size rather than chemical reactions.

46. **(B)** Organic and Biochemistry   *Laboratory*

Catalysts increase reaction rates. From the diagram's increased rate in line B, you should recognize the presence of a catalyst. Enzymes typically work as catalysts in chemical reactions by binding at least one of the substrates and facilitating the reaction. (A) is false, as the reaction's rate is not determined by the amount of reactants. Hormones are enzymes, but they (C) do not function as reaction catalysts. You can eliminate (D), as there is no general rule about the effect of a lowered pH increasing reaction rate. (E) would likewise not affect reaction rate.

47. **(D)** Organic and Biochemistry   *Laboratory*

Enzyme catalysts have unique properties. They are sensitive to pH and temperature changes, and work best within a given range. Radical changes in pH and temperature can "denature" proteins (i.e., alter their structure) in the enzyme, disabling its function in the reaction. Answer choices (B), (C), and (E) suggest similar corruptions or unknowns which are all possible and unaccounted for. The least likely explanation is (D), as simple reactions can run with more than two reactants.

48. **(E)** Organic and Biochemistry   *Laboratory*

Catalysts increase the rates of reactions by making it easier for the substrates (the name for reactants in the presence of a catalyst) to combine. In effect, this decreases the activation energy required for the reaction to run. As the reaction runs faster, the temperature increases (analogous to an engine). Enzyme catalysts bind certain substrates to specialized places called active sites. Among these answer choices, the only effect a catalyst does NOT have is producing an unlimited amount of product. The final amount of product depends upon the initial amount of reactants available to form it. Since the catalyst is not used up in the reaction, nor is it a part of the product, (E) is the correct option.

49. **(C)** The Cell

The majority of photosynthesis occurs in the palisade layer of cells in plant leaves. This closely packed layer of cells tucked against the upper epidermis is exposed to plenty of light, and the palisade cells have many chloroplasts. Epidermal layers protect the plant from its environment; vessel tissue is not active in photosynthesis. The spongy mesophyll layer has air pockets, and although photosynthesis occurs in these cells, it is not to the scale of the photosynthesis taking place in the palisade layer.

50. **(D)** The Cell

An opening in the lower epidermis of a plant leaf is called a stoma (plural: stomata). These apertures are opened and closed by the turgidity (swelling) of neighboring guard cells. Xylem (A) is vascular tissue inside the plant that transports water. The cuticle (B) is a waxy covering on the surface of the leaf. Phloem (C) is also vascular tissue; it transports food. Leak channels (E) are gaps or carrier proteins in the membranes of cells.

51. **(A)** The Cell

The release of water vapor through the stomata is called transpiration. Through these pores, plants also take in carbon dioxide and give out oxygen. Transduction (B) refers to the recombination of DNA in bacteria. Since they have no lungs or diaphragm, plants do not "exhale" (C). Photosynthesis (D) is a carbon-fixation process that involves gas exchange. Capillary effect (E) refers to the action of polar liquids as they climb tiny vessels, such as water in xylem.

52. **(D)** The Cell

This question asks you to classify plants based on leaf characteristics. The diagram shows the leaf as having a bundle of vascular tissue. Moss is the only answer choice that is not a vascular plant. Moss, like lichens and liverworts, is a bryophyte. These non-flowering plants do not have true leaves or roots.

53. **(C)** Genetics   *Laboratory*

In the first cross, a homozygous dominant plant is crossed with a homozygous recessive for two alleles. The entire F_1 generation is heterozygous for both traits. The ratio of phenotypes in F_2 offspring is 9:3:3:1. If you didn't know that, draw a Punnett square for a cross of RrGg and RrGg, where R is the dominant round shape, and G is dominant green color.

	RG	Rg	rG	rg
RG	RRGG	RRGg	RrGG	RrGg
Rg	RRGg	RRgg	RrGg	Rrgg
rG	RrGG	RrGg	rrGG	rrGg
rg	RrGg	Rrgg	rrGg	rrgg

Count up the results for phenotypes. Out of 16 possible genotypes, 9 show round green peas (1 RRGG, 2 RrGG, 2 RRGg, 4 RrGg); 3 show round yellow peas (1 RRgg, 2 Rrgg); 3 show wrinked green peas (1 rrGG, 2 rrGg); and 1 has wrinkled yellow peas (1 rrgg). Therefore, out of a possible 31 plants (about 16 doubled), approximately 6 will show wrinkled green peas.

54. **(D)** Organismal Biology   *Laboratory*

Refer to the above Punnett square to see the ratio of phenotypes. This ratio is 9:3:3:1, which is standard in this type of cross of heterozygous organisms with two alleles.

55. **(B)** Genetics   *Laboratory*

You can solve this question about phenotype ratio by knowing the characteristics of dominant alleles. A plant with wrinkled green peas that is homozygous for color has the genotype rrGG. It only has a dominant green allele to give to its offspring. In this test cross, the plant with wrinkled yellow peas is also homozygous (as both wrinkled and yellow traits are recessive) with the genotype rrgg. The offspring will all have the genotype rrGg, so all will have wrinkled green peas.

56. **(E)** Genetics   *Laboratory*

Remember that this particular F_0 plant is homozygous for its dominant alleles: RRGG, round green peas. It can only give dominant alleles to its offspring; therefore, its offspring will express the dominant alleles (round green peas) in a cross with any genotype.

57. **(B)** Organismal Biology

To answer this question, you need to know how nerves operate. When neurons are stimulated, they release tiny vesicles of a chemical neurotransmitter to the adjacent neuron or muscle. In this experiment, the vagus nerve released its neurotransmitter to the first heart and into the solution, gradually reaching and slowing the second heart. The most common neurotransmitter in motor neurons is acetylcholine. Choices (A) and (E) can be eliminated, as an electrical impulse would have affected the second heart instantaneously. Sodium (C) and potassium (D) work to propagate an action potential along a nerve, but no nerves were connected to the second heart.

58. **(A)** Organismal Biology

The nervous system is divided into two main parts: the central nervous system (brain and spinal cord) and the peripheral nervous system (nerves to the rest of the body). Because it contacts the heart, the vagus nerve is peripheral. The peripheral nervous system reaches out to muscles along two pathways: what we can consciously control, called the voluntary or somatic system; and what is automatic, or under the brain's control, called the autonomic nervous system. Heart rate is unconsciously controlled, so the vagus nerve is part of the autonomic nervous system.

59. **(B)** Organismal Biology

Think of the events surrounding an action potential. At rest, neurons maintain a constant voltage difference across their membranes, called a resting potential. This is achieved by pumping sodium ions out of the cell, and potassium ions into the cell. A stimulus to the neuron, such as an electrical "depolarizing" current, increases the membrane potential to a certain threshold voltage. At this point, sodium channels in the membrane open and allow sodium ions to flood the neuron's interior. This creates a drastic change in voltage, and causes potassium channels to open in turn, bringing the voltage down again. Sodium-potassium pumps then work to restore the resting potential. In this way, the action potential propagates down the neuron.

60. **(E)** Organismal Biology

The gap between neurons or between a neuron and muscle tissue is called the synapse, or synaptic gap. Vesicles of neurotransmitters cross this juncture to transmit a nerve impulse. An axon (A) is the fiber traveling away from the nerve's main body; dendrites (D) are the spindly receptive fibers opposite axons. The resting potential (B) is a voltage measurement. Nodes of Ranvier (C) are the spaces between Schwann cells, or gaps in the myelin sheath of some neurons.

Biology E Solitary Multiple Choice

61. **(A)** Organismal Biology

The cerebrum is the part of the brain responsible for complex reasoning and higher thought, so that region would probably be better developed in intelligent animal species. The cerebellum (B) controls motor coordination and balance. The medulla (C) is part of the brainstem (E), and both are involved with unconscious mechanisms such as heart rate and digestion. The hypothalamus (D) regulates homeostasis, including body temperature, water balance, blood pressure, etc.

62. **(E)** Evolution and Diversity

Vertebrates have an internal skeleton of cartilage or bone, and a segmented vertebral column surrounding a nerve cord. Crabs are arthropods and have a hard exoskeleton rather than an endoskeleton; crabs have no backbone. All of the other choices do have vertebral columns of bone or cartilage (shark).

63. **(A)** Ecology

Animals procure usable nitrogen and amino acids by eating plants that have obtained fixed nitrogen from bacteria. The bacteria convert the nitrogen in the atmosphere into a usable form. It is eventually returned to the soil when animals and plants die or excrete the nitrogen, and other bacteria can then return it to the atmosphere.

64. **(B)** Evolution and Diversity

If the ecological niches of two organisms overlap, they will compete for the limited supplies of available resources. As the overlap between niches decreases, so does the competition between organisms. Coevolution (D) refers to the evolution of species that have affected one another's selection pressures, such as increased leg muscles for running in prey and predators. Biomagnification refers to the increase in tissue concentrations of a chemical substance as it passes along trophic consumer levels.

65. **(B)** Evolution and Diversity

An organism's ability to transmit its genotype into new generations, or contribute to the gene pool, is a measure of that particular organism's fitness. (A) is false, as changes in the gene pool are not always adaptive or beneficial. Fitness is not defined by complexity (C) or specific features, such as human-like traits (E), but by how well organisms respond to selection pressure and produce viable offspring in the next generation. The formation of a new species (D) is not a necessary component of fitness.

66. **(D)** Organismal Biology

Epinephrine, also known as adrenaline, acts in conjunction with the sympathetic nervous system to prepare the body for a stressful situation by increasing heart rate, blood pressure, and respiration rate, and by diverting blood flow away from the digestive system to the muscles, preparing the body to act. This response is commonly known as "fight or flight."

Biology E Group Multiple Choice

67. **(B)** Ecology   *Laboratory*

Primary consumers occupy the first trophic level above autotrophic primary producers. Because of this, primary consumers are also known as herbivores. In the diagram, grass is the primary producer, and caterpillars are the grass-eating (herbivorous) primary consumer.

68. **(A)** Ecology   *Laboratory*

Only about 10% of possible energy is transferred between the tropic levels in a food web. The remaining 90% is used for respiration (in other words, to keep the organism alive) and other biological process, and some is lost to heat.

69. **(D)** Ecology   *Laboratory*

Decomposers break down the remains of organisms across all of the trophic levels. Decomposers are heterotrophs, but they are distinct from consumers, as they do not consume living organisms. Knowing these characteristics, you can eliminate all the incorrect answer choices.

70. **(C)** Ecology   *Laboratory*

Carnivores are meat eaters; to find their lowest trophic level, think through the hierarchy. Primary producers are all photosynthesizing autotrophs (plants, plankton, algae, etc.). Primary consumers are herbivores, and eat the primary producers. The lowest trophic level to find meat eaters is secondary consumers, which eat primary consumers. In this scenario, caterpillar-eating mice are the lowest trophic level of carnivores.

71. **(A)** Ecology   *Laboratory*

Energy charts and hierarchical food pyramids can give false impressions of the actual relationships between organisms in a community. A more accurate depiction is the food web, illustrating multiple links between organisms. Such is the case with the hawk in this scenario: it consumes both mice and snakes at tertiary and quaternary consumer levels, respectively. Only about 10% of energy is conserved down a trophic level. If hawks consumed mice alone, they would be approximately equivalent in energy with snakes (10^4 kcal). If hawks consumed just snakes, their energy level would be nearer to 10^3 kcal. Instead, hawks' combined diet puts their energy level in-between.

72. **(C)** Organismal Biology

The correct sequence of development after fertilization is zygote—morula—blastula—gastrula. An egg and sperm first combine to create a single fertilized cell called a zygote. This cell undergoes rapid cleavage, or cell divisions, until it becomes a solid ball of cells called a morula. Cells continue to divide, and the morula starts to hollow out with a mass of cells collected to one side; the entire structure is now known as a blastocyst, or blastula. In a process called gastrulation, the inner cell mass divides into three layers, and the structure becomes known as a gastrula. The gastrula's three layers will differentiate and give rise to the tissues and structure of the body during the embryonic period.

73. **(A)** Organismal Biology

During ovulation, a follicle containing a mature ovum ruptures to release the egg into the Fallopian tube. The ruptured follicle becomes a structure known as the corpus luteum, which produces the hormone progesterone to continue the buildup of the uterine wall in case of a pregnancy. In addition to developing secondary sexual characteristics in women, estrogen (B) helps build the uterine wall in the first half of the menstrual cycle; however, it is secreted by the ovaries rather than the corpus luteum. Luteinizing hormone (C) triggers ovulation. Oxytonin (D) helps stimulate labor in childbirth, and prolactin (E) increases breast milk production.

74. **(B)** Organismal Biology

Menstruation occurs if the egg is not fertilized. The uterine wall is broken down and flushed out of the body with the egg, and the cycle starts anew. Ovulation (D) is the release of the ovum during the middle of the cycle. Estrogen levels (C) are at their highest to help build up the uterine wall (D), as are levels of progesterone (E) following ovulation.

75. **(E)** Organismal Biology

Embryonic development has unique pathways in each species. However, among all the chordates, there are remarkable similarities. At some point in their development, all vertebrate embryos will have a notochord, gills, and tail. In the case of humans, the latter two disappear before birth. Eyelids certainly form on human fetuses. Among the answer choices, scales (E) are not found in human or in any mammalian embryos.

76. **(D)** Ecology   *Laboratory*

Exponential growth is the sequential doubling (or tripling, or quadrupling, etc.) of a value, such as population size. This type of growth produces a distinctive curve with a very steep climb. Carrying capacity is the maximum population that a given community can sustain; it appears on population charts as a horizontal line. The steep curve that levels off is the correct response.

77. **(E)** Ecology   *Laboratory*

The introduction of predators would slow the growth of a population or shrink its size. Charts 4 and 5 depict declining growth and population shrinking effects, respectively. The first chart, with an unaffected straight line, can be eliminated.

78. **(E)** Ecology   *Laboratory*

Population growth can be affected by a variety of factors, including food availability, climate changes, disease, and predation. The appearance of a competitor for the niche and the accumulation of waste could also slow population growth. Among the answer choices, individual mutations (E) would not inhibit the population as a whole.

79. **(B)** Ecology   *Laboratory*

Organisms employ different reproductive strategies to increase their chances of survival. Like all mammals, rabbits reproduce sexually, but they give birth to large litters of offspring. Large mammals and birds limit the size of their broods; these offspring have delayed sexual maturity, and parents invest a great deal of care in them. Rabbit offspring reach sexual maturity quickly, until which time the rabbits invest parental care.

80. **(A)** Ecology   *Laboratory*

A niche describes an organism's ecological circumstances, including its habitat, food source, behaviors, etc. When two species occupy the same niche, competition results until only one species remains. Biomes (B) and communities (C) are shared by numerous organisms. Water (D), unless it is a limited resource, could also be shared. Both squirrels and rabbits are primary consumers; trophic level (E) does not imply competition.

Biology M Solitary Multiple Choice

81. **(E)** Organic and Biochemistry

Enzymes are large, complex proteins, while the other four choices are building blocks of larger molecules. Monosaccharides and disaccharides can combine in chains to form larger carbohydrates known as polysaccharides, and amino acids link in chains to form proteins. Nitrogenous bases are important components of nucleic acids like DNA and RNA.

82. **(C)** The Cell

The first two statements are true: all of the chemical processes essential to life take place in a cellular environment, and all cells contain DNA. However, the third statement is false, since only eukaryotic cells (plant and animal cells, for example) contain a nucleus, while prokaryotic cells, such as bacteria, do not.

83. **(E)** Evolution and Diversity

The general order in which organisms evolved was from unicellular anaerobic organisms to more complex eukaryotic, multicellular aerobic organisms. The correct evolutionary ordering of the five kingdoms is Monera, Protista, Plantae, Fungi, and Animalia.

84. **(B)** Cell Processes

Transcription involves the transfer of information from DNA to mRNA through complementary base pairing. The mRNA then travels from the nucleus into the cellular cytoplasm, where it serves as a blueprint for protein synthesis in a process called translation. tRNA and rRNA are both involved in translation.

85. **(B)** Evolution and Diversity

Chordates have a hollow notochord at some point in their development. Many chordates have a backbone (vertebrates). Fish are in this category. Lobsters are arthropods with exoskeletons and jointed appendages, earthworms are annelids (segmented worms), clams are mollusks (soft-bodied animals with hard external shells), and a hydra is a cnidarian with body walls made of two layers of cells, radial symmetry, and a sac-like digestive system.

86. **(C)** Genetics

This is a complex question about phenotype ratios and probability. Start by deciding whether or not this is a sex-linked or an autosomal recessive trait. If the allele is Y-linked, no female would express the disorder, which is not the case. In generation II, individuals 1 and 2 produce an affected female. This female (individual 3 in generation III) received an X chromosome from each parent. If the allele were X-linked recessive, her father would have had the disorder. Therefore, the allele is autosomal recessive (d), and individuals must be homozygous (dd) to exhibit the disorder. Knowing this, go back to the top and look at the original parents. The unaffected female in generation I must be heterozygous (Dd); if she only had the dominant allele (DD), she would only pass dominant alleles to her offspring, none of whom would then exhibit the disorder. This cross (Dd x dd) produces a 1:1 ratio of genotypes: 50% Dd (unaffected), and 50% dd (affected). Therefore, unaffected individual 3 in generation II must be heterozygous. The same test can be applied to the unaffected male individuals in generation II: they must be heterozygous (Dd), or else they could not have offspring exhibiting the disorder. All of the other answer choices are either eliminated by this reasoning, or otherwise untrue.

Biology M Group Multiple Choice

87. **(A)** Cell Processes   *Laboratory*

In photosynthesis, oxygen is produced as a byproduct from the splitting of water. Oxygen gas is released to the atmosphere, or in this experiment, into the measuring pipette. Carbon dioxide (B) is consumed in the reaction to synthesize glucose. Water molecules (C) are broken apart in photosynthesis rather than produced. The hydrogen (D) from water sets up a proton gradient for the production of ATP. Chlorine (E) does not participate in photosynthesis.

88. **(E)** Cell Processes   *Laboratory*

To run a successful experiment and obtain meaningful data, all relevant variables must be controlled save the one being tested. The observations can then be attributed to this single variable. In the *Elodea* experiment, wavelength of light is the changing condition. Running the experiment without a filter and without light serve as controls against which to compare the data. Using the same plant insures that the amount of surface area for photosynthesis remains constant.

89. **(B)** Cell Processes *Laboratory*

This question combines chemical and physical problems. Photosynthesis starts with light absorbed by chloroplasts exciting electrons to a higher energy. Green light does not facilitate much photosynthesis at all, as evident in the very few bubbles produced by *Elodea* under a 520 nm filter. Therefore, you can rightly guess that green light is almost entirely reflected, which is why green appears as the dominant color in plants. In order to perceive color, light of that color must reach our eyes. For example, if an object appears green, it is reflecting light with a wavelength of 520 nanometers. By way of comparison, blue light (440 nm) produces a high rate of photosynthesis. Because it is almost entirely absorbed by plants, there is no blue light reaching your eyes from plants, which is why they do not appear blue.

90. **(C)** Cell Processes *Laboratory*

If you didn't know the acronym ROYGBIV for the spectrum of visible light (red-orange-yellow-green-blue-indigo-violet), you can place the 580 nm wavelength of yellow light between orange and green on the graph. Estimate by the distribution of bubbles produced that yellow light gives a comparably low rate of photosynthesis.

91. **(A)** Cell Processes *Laboratory*

The main variable under consideration in this experiment is the changing wavelength of light. The only correct conclusion is the first. (B) is false, as the rate of photosynthesis is not directly proportional with wavelength. Only one plant was tested, so (C) is eliminated. Temperature (D) was not part of the experiment. There is no evidence to support (E); in fact, it is possible that photosynthesis rates from some filters are high enough to sustain the plant.

92. **(A)** Organismal Biology *Laboratory*

When a bacteriophage virus lands on a bacteria, it injects its genetic material while its protein coat remains outside the cell. In Group 1, the sulfur-radiolabeled protein coats were removed from the bacteria during stirring. The radioactive coats were separated in the supernatant liquid, which tested positive for radioactivity. The bacteria do not show radioactivity in Group 1, as the genetic material injected by the viruses was not radiolabeled.

93. **(E)** Organismal Biology *Laboratory*

Unlike all of the taxonomic kingdoms, a virus does not meet strict definitions of being "alive." A virus is not a cell; organisms in all other kingdoms are comprised of at least one cell. Though viruses contain genetic material encoded in nucleic acids, can mutate and reproduce, viruses cannot carry out metabolism. Viruses are more commonly known as microbes or particles. The answer is (E), none of the above.

94. **(A)** Organismal Biology *Laboratory*

When bacteriophage viruses attach themselves to host bacteria, they inject DNA to hijack the bacteria's biosynthetic processes and start manufacturing new bacteriophage viruses. The Hershey-Chase experiment showed that the viruses' genetic material, rather than the protein coats, appeared inside of bacteria. Therefore, the genetic material is the key and code for the production of new viruses.

95. **(E)** Organismal Biology *Laboratory*

Bacteria-attacking viruses follow two different pathways to reproduce themselves, both of which result in the destruction of the host bacteria. In the typical cycle, called the lytic cycle, viral DNA uses the bacteria's cellular mechanisms to replicate itself and produce more viruses. Eventually, the bacterial membrane breaks in cytolysis and releases the viral progeny to attack more bacteria. The original host bacteria is destroyed, and has no chance for its own replication (E). In the lysogenic cycle, viral DNA integrates itself with the bacterial chromosome, and lies dormant as the bacteria divides normally, producing more bacteria with dormant viral DNA. A change in the bacteria's chemistry or an extracellular signal causes the dormant genetic code to begin manufacturing new viruses, which eventually rupture and destroy the host cell, as in the lytic cycle.

96. **(B)** Genetics   *Laboratory*

Knowing only that children get their genetic information from their parents, you can answer this question by choosing the "odd man out." Two different genes are being tested. Children will acquire one gene from each parent, so there are four possible combinations. Each band on the electrophoresis plate represents a clump of identical DNA segments, or in other words, the DNA sequence of one of the genes being tested. Compare bands of DNA in each vertical column to the parents. Every child shares one gene with each parent except in column B; this child cannot be the parents' offspring.

97. **(C)** Genetics   *Laboratory*

The magnetic field in an electrophoresis experiment is consistent and even. DNA segments are all equally polar, and move through the field based on their mass. With lesser mass, the smaller segments (with fewer nucleotide base pairs) will move farther along the plate than large segments.

98. **(B)** Genetics   *Laboratory*

When the bands of DNA segments migrate along the electrophoresis plate, they are effectively segregated based on their mass/size, with shorter segments traveling further towards the positive electrode. After this separation, each band on the plate will have many copies of a single gene sequence. (A) is false, as DNA does not contain the uracil base; only RNA molecules do. Each band represents a gene from either father or mother, so (C) is also false. The DNA segments are only tiny parts of a complete chromosome, ruling out (D). There is no suggestion of a high pH in DNA, eliminating (E).

99. **(A)** Cell Processes   *Laboratory*

The replication of DNA in the body is carried out by special enzymes, the primary enzyme being DNA polymerase. Ribosomes (B) function in the assembly of amino acids into proteins. Replication does not occur by chance (C). Hormones (D) are chemical messengers that facilitate interactions between cells. The sugar phosphate backbone (E) is the structural support for DNA.

100. **(E)** Cell Processes   *Laboratory*

Since strands of DNA are being copied, this process most resembles transcription. In cells, mRNA in the nucleus transcribes strands of DNA to take to the nucleus for protein synthesis. In translation (B), molecules of tRNA matches amino acids to nucleotide sequences of mRNA. Conjugation (A) and transduction (C) refer to exchanges of genetic material in bacteria. Gene mapping (D) is a technique of genetic engineering.

SAT II Biology
Practice Test III

BIOLOGY E/M TEST

FOR BOTH BIOLOGY-E AND BIOLOGY-M, ANSWER QUESTIONS 1–60

<u>Directions:</u>   Each set of lettered choices below referes to the numbered questions or statements immediately following it. Select the one lettered choice that best answers each question or best fits each statement, and then fill in the corresponding oval on the answer sheet. <u>A choice may be used once, more than once, or not at all in each set.</u>

Questions 1–3 refer to the following structures.

(A)   chloroplast
(B)   mitochondrion
(C)   ribosome
(D)   nucleus
(E)   cytoplasm

1. Site of DNA transcription in eukaryotes.

2. Locations of aerobic respiration

3. Found in autotrophic cells

Questions 4–6 refer to the following chemicals.

(A)   enzymes
(B)   amino acids
(C)   glucose
(D)   fatty acids
(E)   nitrogenous bases

4. About twenty different forms exist naturally

5. Usually are paired up with one another by hydrogen bonds

6. An important source of energy for many living organisms

Questions 7–9 refer to the following parts of the circulatory system.

(A)   left ventricle
(B)   left atrium
(C)   capillary
(D)   pulmonary artery
(E)   aorta

7. Carries oxygen-deficient blood

8. Pumps blood to the tissues in the body

9. A blood vessel with walls that can be just one cell thick

Questions 10–12 refer to the following terms.

(A)   population
(B)   community
(C)   ecosystem
(D)   niche
(E)   biome

10. A single species in a localized area

11. Examples include desert, tundra, and tropical rainforest

12. Predators, prey, and the physical environment of a geographic location

GO ON TO THE NEXT PAGE

Directions: Each of the questions or incomplete statements below is followed by five suggested answers or completions. Some questions pertain to a set that refers to a laboratory or experimental situation. For each question, select the one choice that is the best answer to the question and then fill in the corresponding oval on the answer sheet.

13. Which of the following statements are true about amino acids?

    I.   There are hundreds of varieties common in nature.
    II. They form the basic components of protein molecules.
    III. They are the primary source of energy for the cell.

    (A) I only
    (B) II only
    (C) I and II only
    (D) II and III only
    (E) I, II, and III

14. For which of the following tasks would the use of an electron microscope NOT be appropriate?

    (A) Examining the structure of a bacterial flagellum
    (B) Observing the feeding behavior of *Paramecium*
    (C) Identifying a virus by the shape of its protein coat
    (D) Differentiating between smooth and rough endoplasmic reticulum
    (E) Determining whether or not a cell contains centrioles

15. A person with blood type A can

    I.   donate blood to someone with type O
    II. receive blood from someone with type AB
    III. receive blood from someone with type O

    (A) I only
    (B) III only
    (C) I and II only
    (D) I and III only
    (E) I, II, and III

16. If two organisms occupy the same ecological niche, which of the following is LEAST likely to happen?

    (A) They will coexist peacefully.
    (B) One of the organisms will, over a long period of time, begin to change its habits so that it occupies a different niche.
    (C) One of the organisms will go extinct.
    (D) Both organisms will slightly modify their habits over time, dividing up what used to be only one ecological niche into two.
    (E) The population of one of the organisms will decrease dramatically.

17. Of the following, which organism is an annelid?

    (A) Flatworm
    (B) Earthworm
    (C) Grasshopper
    (D) Spider
    (E) Scallop

18. Which of the following describes the physical passage of an action potential through a neuron?

    (A) dendrite, cell body, axon
    (B) cell body, dendrite, axon
    (C) axon, cell body, dendrite
    (D) axon, dendrite, cell body
    (E) dendrite, axon, cell body

19. Which of the following statements most accurately describes the structure of the cell membrane?

    (A) A single layer of phospholipid molecules with larger proteins interspersed throughout
    (B) A double layer of protein molecules with larger phospholipid molecules interspersed
    (C) A double layer of phospholipids with no associated proteins
    (D) A double layer of phospholipids with protein molecules that are rigidly attached and fixed in position
    (E) A double layer of phospholipids with protein molecules that are free to move throughout the membrane

20. Which of the following organisms are heterotrophs?

    I.   Ferns
    II. Deer
    III. Tigers

    (A) I only
    (B) III only
    (C) I and II only
    (D) II and III only
    (E) I, II, and III

GO ON TO THE NEXT PAGE

BIOLOGY E/M TEST—*Continued*

21. Which of the following is the greatest component of human blood, by volume?

    (A) Plasma
    (B) Red blood cells
    (C) Platelets
    (D) Lymphocytes
    (E) Phagocytes

22. Which of the following is the best example of a biome?

    (A) A rocky cave
    (B) A dry riverbed
    (C) An expansive deciduous forest
    (D) A tern nesting area and the terns that inhabit it
    (E) The fish that inhabit the area around a coral reef

23. Which of the following organs is NOT a part of the alimentary canal?

    (A) Stomach
    (B) Liver
    (C) Esophagus
    (D) Small intestine
    (E) Large intestine

24. The 5-carbon sugar in DNA is

    (A) deoxyribose
    (B) ribose
    (C) glucose
    (D) fructose
    (E) pentane

25. A protein's tertiary structure refers to the

    (A) amino acid sequence
    (B) attachment sites for ribosomes
    (C) three-dimensional folding of the polypeptide
    (D) sequence of nucleotides
    (E) binding sites for oxygen

26. A forest is cleared for the lumber industry and the land is left bare. Soon afterwards, lichens and mosses begin to grow on the rocks and stumps of the former forest. These organisms are called

    (A) pioneer organisms
    (B) heterotrophs
    (C) primary consumers
    (D) decomposers
    (E) climax organisms

27. Thyroid cells need to maintain a high concentration of iodide in order to produce the hormone thryoxin. Which of the following is most likely about the flow of iodide into the thyroid cells?

    (A) The iodide passively diffuses through the cell membrane into the thyroid cells, requiring no ATP.
    (B) The iodide passively diffuses through specialized channels in the cell membrane, requiring no ATP.
    (C) The iodide is transported into the cell by the Golgi apparatus of the thyroid cells, requiring ATP.
    (D) The iodide flows into the cell by osmosis, requiring no ATP.
    (E) The iodide is actively transported through the cell membrane, requiring ATP.

28. Which of the following statements is true about an enzymatic reaction?

    (A) The substrates always remain unchanged and are reusable.
    (B) The enzymes always remain unchanged and are reusable.
    (C) Enzymes often combine to form new enzymes.
    (D) They can take place in a wide temperature range.
    (E) They require a pH below 3.0.

29. The correct sequence of the progressive phases of mitosis is

    (A) telophase—metaphase—anaphase—prophase
    (B) anaphase—telophase—metaphase—prophase
    (C) prophase—anaphase—metaphase—telophase
    (D) prophase—metaphase—anaphase—telophase
    (E) metaphase—anaphase—telophase—prophase

30. Which of the following individuals is the MOST fit in evolutionary terms?

    (A) A healthy three-year-old child
    (B) A 49-year-old woman with three adult children and one grandchild
    (C) A healthy 30-year-old male with no children
    (D) A 40-year-old male with cancer and three young children
    (E) A 27-year-old woman with two young children who can no longer reproduce

GO ON TO THE NEXT PAGE

dent prepared a slide with a longitudinal section of a stained onion root tip, and drew this rendering at 400x magnification.

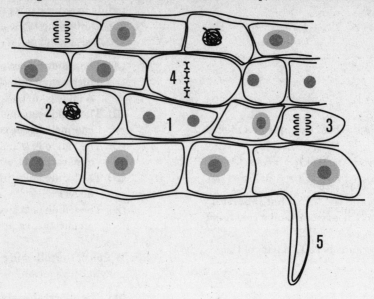

31. Approximately how many cells in this sample are in mitotic prophase?

    (A) 0
    (B) 2
    (C) 4
    (D) 5
    (E) 7

32. The cell labeled 1 has yet to undergo

    (A) cytolysis
    (B) interphase
    (C) metaphase
    (D) telophase
    (E) cytokinesis

33. Onion cells have a diploid number of 16. How many chromosomes are in cell number 3?

    (A) 4
    (B) 8
    (C) 16
    (D) 32
    (E) 64

34. The protruding structure labeled 5 is most likely a

    (A) daughter cell
    (B) petiole
    (C) meristem
    (D) root hair
    (E) mitotic division

35. Why are root tips good places to observe mitosis?

    (A) They are a region of rapid growth.
    (B) They receive disproportionate amounts of water.
    (C) Underground tissues are not rendered sterile by UV rays.
    (D) Root cells are larger than other plant cells.
    (E) Nitrogen in the soil increases cellular reproduction rates.

GO ON TO THE NEXT PAGE

BIOLOGY E/M TEST—*Continued*

A population of deer is split in half after a landslide diverts the course of a massive river. Much time passes.

36. Which of the following is NOT a possible result of this division?

    (A) Homologous structures
    (B) Speciation
    (C) Adaptive mutations
    (D) Divergent evolution
    (E) Convergent evolution

37. A male and female from the separated populations were brought together by experimenters to breed. The offspring was sterile. This is a probable result of the two parents no longer sharing the same

    (A) drinking water
    (B) species
    (C) genus
    (D) biome
    (E) community

38. If both populations are in the Hardy-Weinberg equilibrium, which of the following CANNOT be true?

    (A) Evolution proceeds slowly and evenly.
    (B) Individuals mate at random.
    (C) No migration between populations.
    (D) Natural selection does not occur.
    (E) Populations are large.

Questions 39–43 refer to the following sequence of nucleotides on a strand of mRNA: AUGGCAGGUGAAUA.

39. What is the sequence of nucleotides on the strand of DNA it translated?

    (A) UACCGUCCACUUAU
    (B) AUCCGACCUCAAUA
    (C) GTCCGTAGAATAGT
    (D) TACCGTCCACTTAT
    (E) UTCCGUCCTCUUTU

40. Which substance does this strand of mRNA NOT possess?

    (A) Phosphate
    (B) Deoxyribose
    (C) Nitrogen
    (D) Adenine
    (E) Cytosine

41. When the mRNA's code is used to synthesize a protein, the process is called

    (A) transcription
    (B) splicing
    (C) translation
    (D) transduction
    (E) crossing over

42. Molecules of tRNA have three-nucleotide sequences that line up with mRNA during protein synthesis. This sequence on a tRNA molecule is called a(n)

    (A) anticodon
    (B) A site
    (C) allele
    (D) P site
    (E) gene

43. Of the following, where in a eukaryotic cell does protein synthesis occur?

    (A) Nucleus
    (B) Golgi apparatus
    (C) Mitochondria
    (D) Nuclear membrane
    (E) Endoplasmic reticulum

GO ON TO THE NEXT PAGE

ions 44–48 refer to the diagram below, which represents a single cell of an organism.

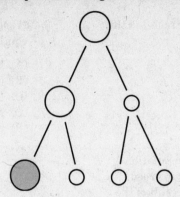

44. The structure in which this process occurs is called the

 (A) cervix
 (B) uterus
 (C) Fallopian tube
 (D) testes
 (E) ovary

45. The shaded cell in the figure will have how many chromosomes?

 (A) 0
 (B) 12
 (C) 23
 (D) 46
 (E) 92

46. In human males, how many total chromosomes are eventually produced from a single germ cell after spermatogenesis?

 (A) 12
 (B) 23
 (C) 46
 (D) 69
 (E) 92

47. Immediately upon fertilization, the fused egg and sperm become a(n)

 (A) zygote
 (B) embryo
 (C) gastrula
 (D) haploid
 (E) follicle

48. The release of the mature egg (ovulation) is triggered by which hormone?

 (A) Luteinizing hormone (LH)
 (B) Prolactin
 (C) Progesterone
 (D) Estrogen
 (E) Epinephrine

GO ON TO THE NEXT PAGE

A student observes three unicellular organisms under a light microscope, and makes these renderings.

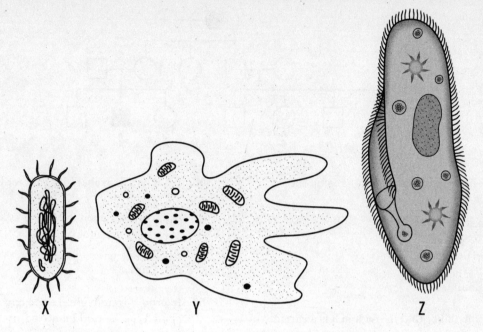

X   Y   Z

49. Which of these cells are protists?

    I.   Cell X
    II. Cell Y
    III. Cell Z

  (A) I only
  (B) II only
  (C) III only
  (D) II and III only
  (E) I, II, and III

50. The oozing arms of Cell Z are called

  (A) pseudopods
  (B) flagellates
  (C) vacuoles
  (D) cilia
  (E) lysosomes

51. What structure is common to all three cells?

  (A) Cell wall
  (B) Nucleus
  (C) Mitochondria
  (D) Cilia
  (E) Ribosomes

52. Cell X could be all of the following EXCEPT

  (A) moneran
  (B) prokaryotic
  (C) heterotrophic
  (D) autotrophic
  (E) eukaryotic

53. The cell wall in Cell X is composed of

  (A) chitin
  (B) cellulose
  (C) glucose
  (D) glycogen
  (E) peptidoglycan

GO ON TO THE NEXT PAGE

...or..s 54–57 refer to the following pedigree chart, in which squares indicate males and circles indicate females.

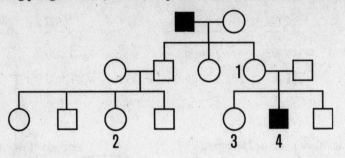

54. Based on this information, the allele causing the shaded trait is likely

(A) codominant
(B) x–linked recessive
(C) autosomal dominant
(D) y–linked
(E) x–linked dominant

55. What is the probability that individual 3 is a carrier?

(A) 0%
(B) 25%
(C) 50%
(D) 75%
(E) 100%

56. What is the probability that individual 2 is a carrier?

(A) 0%
(B) 25%
(C) 50%
(D) 75%
(E) 100%

57. In order for individual #4 to have a son expressing the phenotype, he could mate with

I. A female carrier (heterozygous)
II. An affected female (homozygous)
III. A non-carrier female

(A) I only
(B) II only
(C) III only
(D) I and II only
(E) I, II, and III

GO ON TO THE NEXT PAGE

A student makes the following observations about three plant samples.

Structure	Plant X	Plant Y	Plant Z
Flower	6 petals	none	8 petals
Leaf	veins in parallel	none	branched veins
Roots	fibrous	none	tap

58. Which plant/s could be classified as an angiosperm?

    I.   Plant X
    II. Plant Y
    III. Plant Z

    (A) I only
    (B) II only
    (C) III only
    (D) I and II only
    (E) I and III only

59. Plant Y is most likely a/n

    (A) fern
    (B) gymnosperm
    (C) bryophyte
    (D) angiosperm
    (E) fungus

60. In which plant/s could the student expect to find seeds with two halves?

    I.   Plant X
    II. Plant Y
    III. Plant Z

    (A) I only
    (B) II only
    (C) III only
    (D) I and II only
    (E) I and III only

GO ON TO THE NEXT PAGE

BIOLOGY-E SECTION

If you are taking the Biology-E test, continue with questions 61–80.
If you are taking the Biology-M test, go to question 81 now.

<u>Directions:</u> Each of the questions or incomplete statements below is followed by five suggested answers or completions. Some questions pertain to a set that refers to a laboratory or experimental situation. For each question, select the one choice that is the best answer to the question and then fill in the corresponding oval on the answer sheet.

61. The correct order of plant and animal classification is

   (A) Kingdom, Phylum, Order, Family, Genus, Class, Species
   (B) Species, Genus, Family, Class, Order, Phylum, Kingdom
   (C) Kingdom, Phylum, Class, Order, Family, Genus, Species
   (D) Class, Order, Family, Genus, Kingdom, Species, Phylum
   (E) Species, Family, Genus, Order, Class, Phylum, Kingdom

62. Which of the following is the best example of an ecosystem?

   (A) All crocodiles in northeastern Australia
   (B) The snakes, birds, cacti, rodents, sand, and weather patterns of the desert in Arizona
   (C) The temperate forests of the world
   (D) The squirrels, birds, chipmunks, and other animals of Central Park
   (E) A large herd of bison

63. Which of the following digestive secretions helps to emulsify fats?

   (A) Lipase
   (B) Amylase
   (C) Saliva
   (D) Bile
   (E) Hydrochloric acid

64. All of the following are homologous structures EXCEPT

   (A) horse forelimb
   (B) whale flipper
   (C) human arm
   (D) lobster claw
   (E) dog's front paw

65. In the nitrogen cycle, nitrogen returns to the environment when organisms

   I. die and decompose
   II. excrete waste
   III. exhale

   (A) I only
   (B) II only
   (C) III only
   (D) I and II only
   (E) I, II, and III

66. All of the following describe characteristics of bryophytes EXCEPT

   (A) they grow to great heights
   (B) they lack vascular tissue
   (C) they live in damp areas
   (D) they are eukaryotic
   (E) they lack roots

GO ON TO THE NEXT PAGE

A scientist incubates several geese eggs in a laboratory until they hatch.

67. The goslings' first experience outside the shell is an encounter with a ticking clock, which they take to be their "mother." What best describes their reaction?

    (A) fixed-action pattern
    (B) imprinting
    (C) conditioned reflex
    (D) associative learning
    (E) intuitive reasoning

68. The experimenter rings a small bell before each feeding of the goslings. After a few days, the goslings scramble towards the hatch of their pen at the sound of the bell. This is due to

    (A) imprinting
    (B) instinctual behavior
    (C) associative learning
    (D) habituation
    (E) intuitive reasoning

69. What experiment would best test the goslings' capacity for intuitive reasoning?

    (A) Placing their food at the end of a maze
    (B) Ringing a bell but no longer bringing food
    (C) Providing food after a gosling presses a small switch
    (D) Hanging the food out of reach with a moveable step nearby
    (E) Bringing more food than the goslings can eat

GO ON TO THE NEXT PAGE

Three types of mites were introduced to three groups of rats to observe their interactions. The mites and rats established a symbiotic relationship in each case. The experimenter observed the groups and their individual rats for two weeks.

End of 2 weeks	Rat individuals	Rat population
Group 1	More vigorous and healthy	Shows increase
Group 2	No observable change	No change
Group 3	Sickly and dessicated	Decrease

70. What relationship exists between the two species in Colony 1?

    (A) Parasitism
    (B) Commensalism
    (C) Mutualism
    (D) Predation
    (E) Competition

71. During the observation period, the mite population could potentially increase in

    I.   Group 1
    II. Group 2
    III. Group 3

    (A) I only
    (B) II only
    (C) III only
    (D) I and II only
    (E) I, II, and II

72. A month after the initial observations, the population of rats in Group 3 remains constant. What best explains this?

    (A) Parasites commonly do not eradicate their hosts.
    (B) The hosts establish a commensalistic relationship with the parasites.
    (C) The hosts begin to prey on the parasites.
    (D) The parasites die off from starvation.
    (E) Pathogenic bacteria kills off the parasites.

73. The introduction of a new organism into a population can create

    (A) new mutations
    (B) new selection pressure
    (C) adaptive radiation
    (D) genetic drift
    (E) biological magnification

GO ON TO THE NEXT PAGE

A species of finch was under observation on a small, isolated island in the south Pacific ocean. Scientists measured the beak width of a wide selection of individuals.

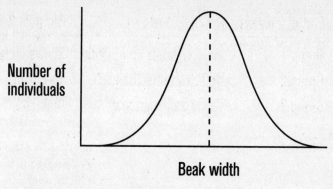

Figure 1: Initial measurement

Forty years later, a second team of scientists returned to the island to check up on the finch population. After measuring beaks and counting individuals, they found a population with a new distribution of beak widths.

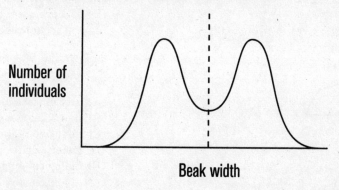

Figure 2

74. What has happened to the finch population over time?

(A) It reached Hardy-Weinberg equilibrium
(B) Directional selection
(C) Speciation
(D) Stabilizing selection
(E) Disruptive selection

GO ON TO THE NEXT PAGE

75. A strong beak is needed to crack open a big seed. What would have happened to beak width of the original population if seeds on the island grew progressively larger for 40 years and no other changes in the environment occurred? (Graphs show number of individuals vs. beak width.)

(A)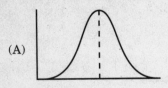

(B)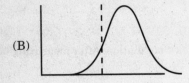

(C)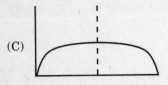

(D)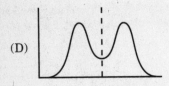

(E)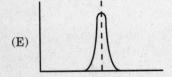

76. Which of the following individuals is the most fit in evolutionary terms?

(A) Short-beaked male finch with 4 offspring
(B) Long-beaked female finch with 6 unhatched eggs
(C) Long-beaked male finch just before sexual maturity
(D) Median-beaked female finch with three suitors
(E) Median-beaked hatchling finch

GO ON TO THE NEXT PAGE

Farmers frequently grow legume crops, such as alfalfa, as "green cover" during winter seasons. By their association with nitrogen-fixing bacteria of the genus *Rhizobium*, legumes produce a great deal of nutrients, so much so that alfalfa is sometimes plowed directly into the ground to improve the soil for the next rotation of crops.

77. Of the following, which explains the behavior of *Rhizobium* bacteria and legumes?

    (A) *Rhizobium* cause legumes to grow nitrogen-fixing fungus
    (B) *Rhizobium*, in the legumes' root nodules, fix nitrogen from the soil
    (C) Legumes synthesize *Rhizobium* and release them into the soil
    (D) *Rhizobium* break down nitrogen gas absorbed through legumes' leaves
    (E) *Rhizobium* steadily decompose the roots of legumes to fix nitrogen

78. The relationship between legumes and nitrogen-fixing bacteria demonstrates

    (A) mutualism
    (B) commensalism
    (C) parasitism
    (D) predation
    (E) convergent evolution

79. Plants may use the ammonia (NH_3) released by nitrogen-fixing bacteria to synthesize all of the following EXCEPT

    (A) cytosine
    (B) methionine
    (C) enzymes
    (D) carrier proteins
    (E) cellulose

80. The process by which some bacteria transform ammonia (NH_3) into gaseous N_2 and N_2O in the atmosphere is called

    (A) transpiration
    (B) nitrogen fixation
    (C) denitrification
    (D) ammonifying
    (E) nitrification

GO ON TO THE NEXT PAGE

BIOLOGY-M SECTION

**If you are taking the Biology-M test, continue with questions 81–100.
Be sure to start this section of the test by filling in oval 61 on your answer sheet.**

<u>Directions:</u> Each of the questions or incomplete statements below is followed by five suggested answers or completions. Some questions pertain to a set that refers to a laboratory or experimental situation. For each question, select the one choice that is the best answer to the question and then fill in the corresponding oval on the answer sheet.

81. When examined under a microscope, the cytoplasm of an amoeba can be seen moving across the cell in a process known as cytoplasmic streaming that allows the amoeba to change shape and move in its environment. Which of the following cell structures are most likely to play a direct role in this process?

   (A) Endoplasmic reticulum
   (B) Mitochondria
   (C) Chloroplast
   (D) Cytoskeleton
   (E) Golgi apparatus

82. Plants store glucose in long starch chains. What byproduct results when molecules of glucose are linked into the growing polysaccharide?

   (A) Water
   (B) Carbon dioxide
   (C) Oxygen
   (D) Peptide bonds
   (E) ATP

83. An example of a gymnosperm is a

   (A) moss
   (B) brown alga
   (C) Sequoia redwood
   (D) daisy
   (E) mold

84. A woman with type B blood and a man with type AB blood can produce offspring with blood type(s)

   (A) A only
   (B) A, B, and AB only
   (C) B only
   (D) A, B, and O only
   (E) B and O only

85. An organism lays soft eggs, breathes through primitive lungs, and has a metabolism that slows down when the temperature drops. It is most likely a(n)

   (A) protist
   (B) arthropod
   (C) amphibian
   (D) reptile
   (E) bird

86. In order to travel from the outside of a plant cell to the innermost part of one of its chloroplasts, a molecule would have to pass through a minimum of how many separate phospholipid bilayer membranes?

   (A) 1
   (B) 2
   (C) 3
   (D) 4
   (E) The molecule would not have to travel through an phospholipid membranes.

GO ON TO THE NEXT PAGE

Brewer's yeast (*Saccaromyces cerevisiae*) is commonly used in the fermentation of alcoholic beverages. Tanks with a carbohydrate food source are sealed off to force the yeast into anaerobic respiration.

87. Yeast cells possess all of the following characteristics EXCEPT

   (A) cell wall
   (B) mitochondria
   (C) asexual reproduction
   (D) prokaryotic
   (E) anaerobic respiration

88. Yeast cannot produce alcohol concentrations greater than 12%. Why?

   (A) At 12%, the toxicity of the alcohol is lethal to yeast.
   (B) They begin the Krebs Cycle.
   (C) They succumb to lactic acid buildup.
   (D) There is no longer any oxygen in concentration.
   (E) They run out of sugar food supply.

89. What is the byproduct of anaerobic respiration in muscle tissue?

   (A) Ethanol
   (B) Oxygen
   (C) Glucose
   (D) Glycolysis
   (E) Lactic acid

GO ON TO THE NEXT PAGE

A scientist conducted an experiment with three strains of bacteria: a normal or "wild type" strain, and two mutant strains that were unable to synthesize one essential amino acid, either arginine or tryptophan. The strains were inoculated on four test plates covered with glucose-containing agar; agar on some of the plates contained supplemental arginine or tryptophan, as indicated below. The scientist recorded colony growths for each test.

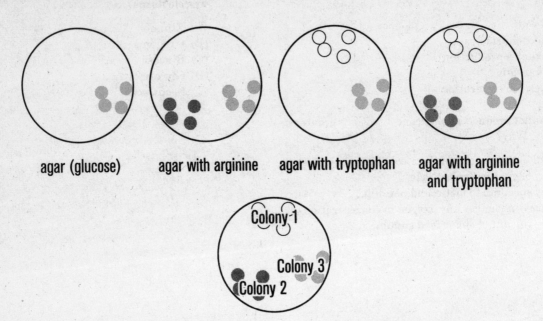

agar (glucose)   agar with arginine   agar with tryptophan   agar with arginine and tryptophan

90. The ability or inability of bacteria to synthesize a particular amino acid is indicated by a superscript + or –, respectively. For example, bacteria capable of synthesizing arginine are arg^+; bacteria unable to synthesize tryptophan are trp^-. Colony 2 is

    (A) $arg^+ trp^+$
    (B) $arg^+ trp^-$
    (C) $arg^- trp^+$
    (D) $arg^- trp^-$
    (E) wild type

91. What would the experimenter observe if an $arg^- trp^-$ strain were inoculated in the agar with tryptophan plate?

    (A) Bacteria would convert tryptophan to arginine
    (B) A large bacterial lawn would form
    (C) The strain would mutate to $arg^- trp^+$
    (D) Colonies would form on half of the plate
    (E) No growth

92. Colonies 1 and 2 were mixed in a test tube and left overnight in a heated incubator. The following day, the mixture was spread over four new plates prepared as above. After time, large bacterial lawns were observed in each plate. What explains why?

    (A) The bacteria formed a mutualistic relationship.
    (B) Genetic recombination created a strain of $arg^+ trp$ bacteria.
    (C) If given enough time, bacteria will form under any conditions.
    (D) The heat from incubation mutated each strain.
    (E) Each strain overproduced critical amino acids.

93. By what other method could an experimenter introduce arginine production capabilities into arg^- bacteria?

    (A) Increasing the temperature of bacteria incubation
    (B) Running the tests repeatedly in the absence of arginine
    (C) Extended incubation of the strain with arginine
    (D) Exposing the strain to intense ultraviolet light
    (E) Introducing a bacteriophage virus with arg^+ DNA

GO ON TO THE NEXT PAGE

In 1953, Stanley Miller conducted an experiment to examine how biotic life might have formed on Earth. In a closed glass vessel, he recreated the earliest conditions of Earth's atmosphere with gases and high-energy electricity. The resulting "primordial soup" in the bottom of the chamber included compounds that resembled amino acids.

94. Which of these chemicals were NOT originally present in Earth's earliest atmosphere according to current theory?

   (A) Hydrogen
   (B) Water
   (C) Methane
   (D) Ammonia
   (E) Oxygen

95. Why were these amino acids a significant discovery?

   (A) mRNA was formed in the chamber.
   (B) Amino acids are the building blocks for living cells.
   (C) It showed the spontaneous formation of ribosomes.
   (D) The "primordial soup" was cellular cytoplasm.
   (E) Showed that amino acids were present in Earth's early atmosphere.

96. The elemental composition of the Earth's crust and the human body differ significantly. What best explains why?

   (A) Biotic tissue once contained all such elements, but has discarded them in the course of evolution.
   (B) Humans evolved from aquatic life; the available elements in marine environments are different from those on land.
   (C) Not all elements in the Earth's crust are suitable or have properties compatible with living processes.
   (D) The elemental composition of the Earth has changed significantly since the ancestors of humans first appeared.
   (E) Life first reached the Earth as bacteria on a meteorite with significant chemical differences from Earth.

GO ON TO THE NEXT PAGE

Questions 97–100 refer to the following diagram, which depicts an interaction between a homologous pair of chromosomes.

97. This transfer of genetic material is called

   (A) transcription
   (B) transduction
   (C) crossing-over
   (D) translation
   (E) substitution

98. The depicted exchange of genetic material can occur during

   (A) prophase I of meiosis
   (B) anaphase I of meiosis
   (C) telophase of mitosis
   (D) metaphase II of meiosis
   (E) interphase of mitosis

99. After the chromosomes exchange material, which of the following could NOT result in the next generation?

   (A) Adaptive mutation
   (B) Same phenotype
   (C) Debilitating mutation
   (D) Change in diploid number
   (E) Further transfers of genetic material

100. The exchange of genetic material only occurs in sexual reproduction, and offers a significant advantage over asexual reproduction. Why?

   (A) Genetic recombination increases variation of species.
   (B) Random mutations are usually beneficial.
   (C) It alters the number of base pairs in the species' genetic code.
   (D) It increases reproduction rates.
   (E) It provides stability in the gene pool.

S T O P

IF YOU FINISH BEFORE TIME IS CALLED, YOU MAY CHECK YOUR WORK ON THIS TEST ONLY.
DO NOT TURN TO ANY OTHER TEST IN THIS BOOK.

SAT II Biology
Practice Test III
Explanations

Answers to SAT II Biology Practice Test III

Question Number	Correct Answer	Right	Wrong	Question Number	Correct Answer	Right	Wrong
1.	D	——	——	51.	E	——	——
2.	B	——	——	52.	E	——	——
3.	A	——	——	53.	E	——	——
4.	B	——	——	54.	B	——	——
5.	E	——	——	55.	C	——	——
6.	C	——	——	56.	A	——	——
7.	D	——	——	57.	D	——	——
8.	A	——	——	58.	E	——	——
9.	C	——	——	59.	C	——	——
10.	A	——	——	60.	C	——	——
11.	E	——	——	61.	C	——	——
12.	C	——	——	62.	B	——	——
13.	B	——	——	63.	D	——	——
14.	B	——	——	64.	D	——	——
15.	B	——	——	65.	D	——	——
16.	A	——	——	66.	A	——	——
17.	B	——	——	67.	B	——	——
18.	A	——	——	68.	C	——	——
19.	E	——	——	69.	D	——	——
20.	D	——	——	70.	C	——	——
21.	A	——	——	71.	E	——	——
22.	C	——	——	72.	A	——	——
23.	B	——	——	73.	B	——	——
24.	A	——	——	74.	E	——	——
25.	C	——	——	75..	B	——	——
26.	A	——	——	76.	A	——	——
27.	E	——	——	77.	B	——	——
28.	B	——	——	78.	A	——	——
29.	D	——	——	79.	E	——	——
30.	B	——	——	80.	C	——	——
31.	B	——	——	81.	D	——	——
32.	E	——	——	82.	A	——	——
33.	D	——	——	83.	C	——	——
34.	D	——	——	84.	B	——	——
35.	A	——	——	85.	C	——	——
36.	E	——	——	86.	C	——	——
37.	B	——	——	87.	D	——	——
38.	A	——	——	88.	A	——	——
39.	D	——	——	89.	E	——	——
40.	B	——	——	90.	C	——	——
41.	C	——	——	91.	E	——	——
42.	A	——	——	92.	B	——	——
43.	E	——	——	93.	E	——	——
44.	E	——	——	94.	E	——	——
45.	C	——	——	95.	B	——	——
46.	E	——	——	96.	C	——	——
47.	A	——	——	97.	C	——	——
48.	A	——	——	98.	A	——	——
49.	D	——	——	99.	E	——	——
50.	A	——	——	100.	C	——	——

Calculating Your Score
on SAT II Biology Practice Test III

Your raw score for the SAT II History test is calculated from the number of questions you answer correctly and incorrectly. Once you have determined your composite score, use the conversion table on page 23 of this book to calculate your scaled score.

To Calculate Your Raw Score

Count the number of questions you answered correctly: _____
A

Count the number of questions you answered incorrectly, and multiply that number by $\frac{1}{4}$:

_____ X $\frac{1}{4}$ = _____
B   C

Subtract the value in field C from value in field A: _____
D

Round the number in field D to the nearest whole number. This is your raw score: _____
E

Biology E/M Classification Questions

1.   (D)   Evolution and Diversity

DNA transcription must take place in the nucleus, since the DNA is always inside the nucleus. After DNA transcription, the messenger RNA binds with a ribosome in the cytoplasm to carry out translation.

2.   (B)   Evolution and Diversity

The processes of aerobic respiration are the Krebs Cycle and the electron transport chain, both of which occur in mitochondria.

3.   (A)   Evolution and Diversity

An autotroph is an organism that can make its own food. Autotrophs are most likely to be organisms that conduct photosynthesis. The chloroplast is the organelle in which photosynthesis takes place.

4.   (B)   Organic and Biochemistry

While it's theoretically possible to create any number of different amino acids in a lab, only twenty are commonly found in nature.

5.   (E)   Organic and Biochemistry

Nitrogenous bases pair up with each other in DNA molecules by forming weak complimentary hydrogen bonds, adenine with thymine and cytosine with guanine.

6.   (C)   Organic and Biochemistry

Monosaccharides, such as glucose and fructose, form basic, readily available energy sources for most living organisms.

7.   (D)   Organismal Biology

Normally, veins carry oxygen-poor blood and arteries contain oxygen rich blood, but the pulmonary arteries and veins are exceptions. The pulmonary arteries takes oxygen-poor blood and deliver it to the lungs, and the pulmonary veins carry the newly oxygenated blood back to the left atrium.

8.   (A)   Organismal Biology

The ventricles in the heart are the main pumping mechanisms for blood, and the left ventricle pumps blood to the body. The aorta is the primary vessel through which blood travels out to the body, but it does not do the actual pumping of blood.

9.   (C)   Organismal Biology

Capillaries are the smallest blood vessels, with minimal thickness for the exchange of gases, nutrients, and waste products.

10.   (A)   Ecology

A population is a group of interbreeding organisms, which means they must be the same species, and they must be physically close enough to each other to interbreed.

11. **(E)**   Ecology

A biome is a large area consisting of several similar ecosystems with specific characteristic flora and fauna, such as deserts, tundra, and tropical rainforests.

12. **(C)**   Ecology

An ecosystem is the conglomeration of biotic and abiotic factors in a certain area. You might have been tempted to pick community (B) as the answer, but that term refers only to the interrelated organisms in an area, excluding abiotic factors such as weather and geology.

Biology E/M Solitary Multiple Choice

13. **(B)**   Organic and Biochemistry

Amino acids form the basic components of protein molecules. A core group of only twenty amino acids are common in nature, eliminating choice I, and amino acids are not used for energy such as a molecule of glucose or ATP.

14. **(B)**   The Cell

Electron microscopes operate in a vacuum; therefore, they cannot be used to examine living organisms, so it would be impossible to observe the feeding behavior of *Paramecium*, since the organisms would be killed in the preparation process. A light microscope would be much better suited for this task.

15. **(B)**   Organismal Biology

A person with blood type A can only donate to someone whose blood already contains the type-A protein, namely people with type A or type AB blood. They can receive blood from people with either the type-A protein only (type A blood), or with no protein on the surface of their red blood cells (type O blood), but not the type-B protein (types B and AB).

16. **(A)**   Ecology

When two organisms occupy the same niche, they will compete due to the limited number of resources, whether they consist of food supplies or nesting areas. This competition will result in a change in one or both of the populations; they will not be able to coexist peacefully.

17. **(B)**   Evolution and Diversity

Earthworms are annelids, which are segmented worms with coeloms and a closed circulatory system. Flatworms are unsegmented worms found in Phylum Platyhelminthes. A grasshopper is an arthropod, with jointed appendages. A spider is an arachnid, which is a type of arthropod. A scallop is a mollusk, which is a soft-bodied animal within a hard, calcium-containing shell.

18. **(A)**   Organismal Biology

The action potential of a neuron is initially conducted from the dendrites, which are spindly receptor fibers reaching out to other neurons or stimuli. The action potential then travels through the cell body, and then down the single axon away from its cell body.

19. (E)   The Cell

The cell membrane is made up of a double layer of phospholipid molecules, with their hydrophilic regions on the inside and outside surfaces of the membrane, and their hydrophobic lipid tails forming the membrane's inner space. Interspersed throughout the membrane are large protein molecules, which serve many important functions, such as providing for the transport of larger molecules across the membrane. These protein molecules are loosely held among the phospholipids, and, according to the fluid mosaic model, are free to move among them. Note how knowing just one of the above mentioned facts can allow you to eliminate several answers at a time.

20. (D)   Ecology

A heterotroph is an organism that cannot make its own food, and therefore must consume other organisms to survive. Ferns produce their own food by photosynthesis, making them autotrophs, but deer must eat plants and tigers must eat other animals to survive, making them heterotrophs.

21. (A)   Organismal Biology

The blood plasma, which is mostly water, forms the greatest proportion of the blood—about 50% of its volume.

22. (C)   Ecology

A biome is the largest ecological categorization, containing many ecosystems of a generally similar nature and climate. Among the answer choices, only deciduous forests fits the bill.

23. (B)   Organismal Biology

The alimentary canal is the path food takes as it travels through the digestive system. Although the liver plays an important role in digestion, food never actually flows through the organ.

24. (A)   Cell Processes

DNA (deoxyribonucleic acid) uses a 5-carbon sugar called deoxyribose in its sugar-phosphate backbone. Ribose (B) is the 5-carbon sugar found in RNA (ribonucleic acid). Glucose (C) is the most common 6-carbon monosaccharide. Fructose (D), also a 6-carbon monosaccharide, is a fruit sugar. Pentane (E) is a hydrocarbon lacking oxygen, and is not a sugar.

25. (C)   Organic and Biochemistry

Proteins can have several levels of structure. A protein's primary structure refers to its sequence of amino acids. These polypeptide chains also undergo winding and coiling, called secondary structure. Tertiary structure refers to the overall folding of the protein, giving it a unique three-dimensional shape that contributes to its function.

26. (A)   The Cell

In the process of ecological succession, the first organisms to populate a desolate region are called pioneer organisms, and the final organisms to move in are called climax organisms. Lichen and moss are photosynthesizing plants, not heterotrophs, consumers, or decomposers.

27. **(E)**   Ecology

You do not really need to know anything about the thyroid in order to answer this question. The only thing you do need to know is that an ion will not flow from a region of low concentration (outside the thyroid cells) to a region of high concentration (inside the cells), and that energy must be expended to transport the solute against this gradient into the cell. You can then eliminate choices (A), (B), and (D), as these require no ATP. Choice (D) can also be eliminated, as the Golgi apparatus does not transport materials into the cell. This leaves the final choice, (E), active transport, a process that requires ATP.

28. **(B)**   Organic and Biochemistry

In enzymatic catalysis, the enzymes always remain unchanged in the reaction. An enzyme is not an enzyme if it is changed by the reaction. The substrates are often changed, however. It's also important to remember that enzymatic reactions take place in a narrow temperature and pH range, and the pH is usually not as low as 3.0.

29. **(D)**   Cell Processes

The correct sequence of mitosis begins with prophase, during which the chromosomes condense. Prophase is followed by metaphase. In metaphase, the replicated chromosomes line up along the center of the cell. In anaphase, sister chromatids on each chromosome separate, and are pulled to opposite poles of the cell. In telophase, the final phase, the chromosomes become diffuse, the nucleoli reappear in daughter nuclei and nuclear envelopes reform.

30. **(B)**   Evolution and Diversity

In comparing evolutionary fitness of individuals within a species, look at each individual's reproductive success in producing fertile offspring. To achieve maximum fitness, an individual must survive, reproduce, and bear offspring which can reproduce in turn. Choice (B) best meets these requirements: the woman has survived, mated, reproduced, and has mature children who are now reproducing themselves.

Biology E/M Group Multiple Choice

31. **(B)**   Cell Processes   *Laboratory*

In prophase of mitosis, newly duplicated chromosomes condense and differentiate to where they become visible under the microscope. (The chromosomes are not yet arranged across the middle of the cell, which occurs in metaphase.) Duplicated clumps of chromosomes are visible in two cells in the diagram. Additionally, the cell's nuclear envelope dissolves, and spindle fibers and centrioles migrate to opposite ends of the cell.

32. **(E)**   Cell Processes   *Laboratory*

The diagram shows Cell 1 with two distinct nuclei. Sister chromatids have separated and migrated to opposite ends of the cell, and nuclear envelopes have reformed around the two sets of chromosomes. This arrangement represents telophase, the last stage of mitosis. The cell will now physically divide its cytoplasm into two daughter cells in a process called cytokinesis.

33. **(D)** Cell Processes   *Laboratory*

The diploid number expresses the number of chromosomes typically found in somatic (non-sex) cells. During mitosis, all the cell's chromosomes are duplicated so that each new cell will have a full set of chromosomes. For a short time in mitosis, the cell has twice its normal number of chromosomes, or twice the diploid number. This occurs in anaphase and telophase, when the duplicated chromosomes are separated and migrate to opposite ends of the cell. Cell 3 is in anaphase, and has twice the diploid number: 2 x 16 = 32.

34. **(D)** Organismal Biology   *Laboratory*

Root hairs are slim projections from epidermal cells in plant roots. They help absorb water and minerals from the soil by increasing the surface area of the root. As seen in the diagram, there is no chromosomal replication for this projection to be a daughter cell (A) or mitotic division (E). A petiole (B) is a slender stem that supports the leaf. (C) is also incorrect, as the meristem is a region of rapidly growing plant tissue, not an individual cell.

35. **(A)** Organismal Biology   *Laboratory*

Mitosis produces new cells, and new cells contribute to the growth of their surrounding tissue. Plant cells divide rapidly in roots and stems, as these are regions of pronounced tissue growth. Since these regions appear above and below ground, answer choices (B), (C), and (E) can be dismissed. (D) is just plain wrong.

36. **(E)** Ecology

Evolutionary relationships hinge upon common ancestry. If populations are separated for a significant amount of time, as with the divided deer population, divergent evolution (D) can occur, where different pressures, adaptive mutations (C), and survival successes can change the characteristics of each population. These populations may eventually lose the ability to interbreed, becoming distinct species (B). Among the answer choices, only (E) cannot occur, as convergent evolution occurs between disparate species that develop similar structures independently.

37. **(B)** Ecology

A species is commonly defined by the capability of individuals to breed and produce fertile offspring. Answers (A), (D), and (E) reflect changes in environment, and so are false, as members of the same species are not constrained to the same habitat. (E) is also false, as the parents could still share the same genus and be different species, incapable of producing fertile offspring. (Recall the order of taxonomy: Kingdom-Phylum-Class-Order-Family-Genus-Species. A sample mnemonic for this sequence, KPCOFGS, is Kung Pao Chicken Over Funky Garlic Sauce.) The correct answer is (B).

38. **(A)** Ecology

A population in the Hardy-Weinberg equilibrium is one in which allele frequencies do not change from generation to generation. On the whole, evolution has stopped. Therefore, (E) is the right answer choice. The remaining answer choices are all requirements for the Hardy-Weinberg equilibrium.

39. **(D)** Genetics

The four nucleotide bases in DNA pair up according to fixed rules. Cytosine (C) always pairs with guanine (G), and vice versa; adenine (A) always pairs with thymine (T), and vice versa. Molecules of RNA lack thymine, and instead use uracil (U) to pair with adenine in the same way as thymine. The sequence given in the question comes from mRNA. To reconstruct the original DNA sequence, match each letter with its partner, remembering that RNA will show U for A, A for T, C for G, and G for C.

40. **(B)** Genetics

RNA (ribonucleic acid) uses ribose as the sugar in its sugar-phosphate backbone, while DNA (deoxyribonucleic acid) uses deoxyribose. Both RNA and DNA have phosphate (A) in their structural backbones, and nitrogen (C) in their nitrogenous bases, which include adenine (D) and cytosine (E).

41. **(C)** Genetics

When mRNA and tRNA interact to synthesize proteins, the process is called translation. The process of mRNA copying the nucleotide sequence of DNA is called transcription. You can think of it this way: transcription is copying nucleotides to nucleotides; there is no "language" change in copying. Translation matches nucleotide sequences to amino acids, so there is a language change. Splicing (B) is a technique of genetic engineering. Transduction (D) refers to recombination in bacteria. Crossing-over (E) is a mutation between chromosomes.

42. **(A)** Genetics

The three-nucleotide sequence on molecules of tRNA that aligns with mRNA is called an anticodon. Conversely, the three-nucleotide sequences on molecules of mRNA or DNA are called codons. The A site (B) and P site (D) are locations on the ribosome for amino acids in protein synthesis. A gene (E) is any number of nucleotides coding for a trait. An allele (C) is a gene with two possible manifestations.

43. **(E)** Cell Processes

Protein synthesis occurs on the endoplasmic reticulum (ER). Remember that rough endoplasmic reticulum (RER) is covered with ribosomes, which assemble amino acids into polypeptides. Transcription occurs in the nucleus (A); protein packaging occurs in the Golgi apparatus (B); and aerobic respiration in mitochondria (C). Protein synthesis does not occur in the nuclear membrane (D), though in eukaryotic cells, mRNA molecules must cross this membrane after transcription.

44. **(E)** Organismal Biology

Gametogenesis—the production of haploid sex cells called gametes—occurs in the gonads of humans. The male gonads are the testes, which are the sites for the production of sperm (spermatogenesis). The female gonads are the ovaries, where the production of eggs (oogenesis) occurs.

45. **(C)** Organismal Biology

Gametes have half of the normal number of chromosomes found in cells; they are haploid, whereas somatic cells are diploid. Humans have 46 chromosomes, or a diploid number of 46; human gametes (eggs and sperm) have a haploid number of 23. (Haploid eggs and haploid sperm will combine to form the full number of chromosomes in fertilized zygotes.)

46. **(E)** Organismal Biology

Meiosis is the production of gametes, and it occurs in two stages: meiosis I and II. In females, a diploid primary oocyte divides into four cells, all of which are haploid. However, only one of these cells obtains the majority of cytoplasm and becomes the ovum, or egg. The remaining three cells, called polar bodies, simply disintegrate. In males, the initial diploid cell is called a spermatogonium. It also undergoes two meiotic divisions and produces four haploid cells. However, unlike the single gamete produced in females, all of these cells become viable sperm. Therefore, the original spermatogonium gives rise to four times the haploid number of chromosomes: 4 x 23 = 92.

47. **(A)** Organismal Biology

A fused egg and sperm is a single fertilized cell called a zygote. The diploid zygote undergoes rapid cell divisions, and becomes a gastrula (C) on its way to becoming an embryo (B). Haploid (D) refers to the number of chromosomes found in gametes. A follicle (E) encases the egg during its time in the ovary.

48. **(A)** Organismal Biology

You should probably be familiar with the major hormones in the human endocrine system. Ovulation is the release of an ovum from the ovary into the Fallopian tube. It is caused by a surge in luteinizing hormone (LH) around day 14 of the menstrual cycle. Prolactin (B) is released after childbirth to stimulate the production of breast milk. Progesterone (C) furthers the enrichment of the uterine wall in the second half of the menstrual cycle. Estrogen (D) builds up the uterine wall in the first half of the cycle. Epinephrine (E) is an adrenal hormone involved in the sympathetic nervous system (including the "fight or flight" response).

49. **(D)** Evolution and Diversity   *Laboratory*

The organisms in Kingdom Protista, also known as protists, represent a diverse assembly of eukaryotic unicellular organisms. These include autotrophic algae and heterotrophic organisms such as amoebas. By the diagrams, you should recognize that Cell X lacks a nucleus; as a prokaryote, Cell X cannot be a protist. The other two organisms, paramecium and amoeba, are protists.

50. **(A)** Evolution and Diversity   *Laboratory*

Amoebas move by cytoplasmic streaming: they extend a projection of cytoplasm and then flow into the new space. These oozing arms are called pseudopods (meaning "false feet" in Greek). Flagellates (B) refer to protists with flagella—a whip-like tail that thrashes around for propulsion. Similarly, cilia (D) are small fibers on the outside of cells which beat in tandem for propulsion; paramecium is covered with cilia. Vacuoles (C) are storage containers within the cell; lysosomes (E) are vacuoles filled with digestive enzymes.

51. **(E)** Evolution and Diversity   *Laboratory*

The only structures among these answer choices common to both protists (Cells Y and Z) and monerans (Cell X) are ribosomes for protein synthesis. Protists typically lack cell walls (A), and not all protists have cilia (D), as evident with the amoeba. Since Cell X is a prokaryotic bacteria (Kingdom Monera), it has no membrane-bound organelles, ruling out answers (B) and (C).

52. **(E)** Evolution and Diversity   *Laboratory*

According to the diagram, Cell X has no nucleus; therefore, it is not a eukaryotic cell. It is prokaryotic (B) and a moneran (A). It is possible for prokaryotes to be heterotrophic (C) or autotrophic (D).

53. **(E)** Evolution and Diversity   *Laboratory*

Bacterial cell walls are built from peptidoglycan. Cell walls in plants are constructed with cellulose (B). Fungal cell walls are made from chitin (A). Glucose is a monosaccharide (C), and glycogen (D) is the storage compound of glucose in animals.

54. (B) Genetics   *Laboratory*

Recessive sex-linked alleles, and x-linked alleles in particular, express themselves with far greater frequency in males than in females. You can see this trend in the pedigree. Because of the disparity in appearance, the gene is sex-linked, not autosomal, eliminating answer (C). It cannot be codominant (A), or the trait would appear in the middle generation. You can tell is it not y-linked (D), as the affected male in the first generation does not produce an affected son in the second generation, having passed on the Y chromosome. It is not x-linked dominant (E), as both of the females in the first generation would express the allele, having received it on an X chromosome from their father.

55. (C) Genetics   *Laboratory*

Since females have two X chromosomes, it is less likely that they will express x-linked recessive traits. Individual 4 shows the trait, which means he received it from his mother, who must be a carrier (heterozygous $XX°$). His father, with only one X chromosome, does not show the trait (XY). Even if he did, males only pass Y chromosomes to their male offspring. To find the probability of offspring from this cross ($XX°$ and XY), sketch a Punnett square.

	X	Y
X	XX	XX°
X°	XY	X°Y

50% of females, or one out of two, carry the allele ($XX°$).

56. (A) Genetics   *Laboratory*

Males cannot pass x-linked traits to their male offspring. Therefore, the father of #2 did not inherit the allele, and individual #2 has no chance of being a carrier. (We have no information on individual #2's mother, and can therefore assume she is likewise not a carrier.)

57. (D) Genetics   *Laboratory*

Individual #4 cannot pass his affected X chromosome to his male offspring. For male offspring to exhibit the trait, they must receive a single X chromosome with the allele from their mother. This is possible in the case of both heterozygous ($XX°$) and homozygous ($X°X°$) females.

58. (E) Organismal Biology   *Laboratory*

All angiosperms are vascular, flowering plants. According to the observations, Plant Y cannot be an angiosperm, as it lacks flowers and vascular leaves. Plants X and Z have flowers and are angiosperms.

59. (C) Organismal Biology   *Laboratory*

This question asks about your knowledge of major plant categories. Plant Y has no flowers, apparent vascular tissue or root system, so it can only be a bryophyte. (An example of a bryophyte is liverwort.) (A) is wrong, as ferns have leaves and vascular tissue. Gymnosperms (B) have leaves, vascular tissue and well-developed roots. An angiosperm (D) has all these characteristics, plus the ability to flower. A fungus (E) is not a plant, appearing in a separate taxonomic kingdom (Fungi vs. Plantae).

60. **(C)** Organismal Biology   *Laboratory*

Angiosperms are typically divided into two categories: monocots and dicots. These names literally refer to the number of cotyledons, or seedling leaves, found in their seeds. Monocots have one cotyledon; dicots have two cotyledons, or seed halves. Monocots and dicots exhibit other distinguishing characteristics. Monocots have parallel veins in their leaves, flower parts in threes, and fibrous roots. Dicots have branching veins in leaves, flower parts in fours or fives, and tap roots. Looking at the data, you can identify Plant X as a monocot, and Plant Z as a dicot. Therefore, Plant Z will have two seed halves (di-cotyledon).

Biology E Solitary Multiple Choice

61. **(C)** Evolution and Diversity

The correct order is Kingdom, Phylum, Class, Order, Family, Genus, and Species. In phylogeny, a kingdom is the highest level in biological classification of similar, related phyla. Phylum is the primary subdivision of a kingdom in which organisms with the same body plan are grouped together. Classes are the major subdivision of a phylum and they contain Orders, which are divided into Families, which are divided into Genera, and then Species, the most specific taxonomic division.

62. **(B)** Ecology

An ecosystem consists of many interacting populations of organisms and the environment that they inhabit (the jargon: both biotic and abiotic factors). The crocodiles in northeastern Australia and a herd of bison are examples of populations. The temperate forests of the world are a biome. The animals of Central Park are a community.

63. **(D)** Organismal Biology

Bile, produced in the liver, helps emulsify fats by breaking down large fat globules into smaller ones. It does not chemically alter or digest the fat; this is the function of the enzyme lipase (A), released by the pancreas. Amylase (B) is the starch-breaking enzyme found in saliva (C). Hydrochloric acid (E), secreted by the stomach, does not directly digest foods: it kills microorganisms and lowers the pH of the stomach to activate protein enzymes.

64. **(D)** Evolution and Diversity

Homologous structures are body parts with a similar design derived from a common ancestor but used for different functions. Since answer choices (A), (B), (C), and (E) all refer to mammals, these structures for propulsion are likely derived from a common ancestor. Lobsters are crustaceans, rather than mammals, and do not share as close of a common ancestor.

65. **(D)** Ecology

Nitrogen is returned to the environment when animals decompose, or when they excrete waste such as urea. This nitrogen is then returned to the atmosphere by denitrifying bacteria. Not all organisms exhale, and nitrogen is not used in respiration.

66. **(A)** Evolution and Diversity

Bryophytes are non-vascular plants including hornworts, liverworts, and mosses. Without vascular tissue, they cannot transport nutrients effectively, which limits their growth (falsifying answer choice (A) and requires them to live in damp areas. All organisms in Kingdom Plantae are eukaryotic. Bryophytes also lack true roots.

Biology E Group Multiple Choice

67. **(B)** Organismal Biology *Laboratory*

Behavior observed in newborn organisms is typically instinctual, as opposed to learned behavior. Imprinting is the instinctual establishment of social bonds in an individual organism during its early development. Newly hatched goslings will imprint "mother" on the first object they see, such as a ticking clock. Fixed-action patterns (A) are instinctual behaviors that manifest themselves in response to stimuli; for example, when goslings are placed in water, they swim without having to be taught. Conditioned reflex (C) and associative learning (D) are similar learned behaviors linking stimuli and responses. Intuitive reasoning (E) is a problem-solving cognitive capability.

68. **(C)** Organismal Biology *Laboratory*

Associative learning occurs when the mind links two separate stimuli. Like Pavlov's famous experiment with dogs, each time the goslings hear the bell, they receive food. As this process is repeated, they associate the sound of the bell with food. This type of associative learning is also called classical conditioning. Even in the absence of the food itself, the goslings respond to the sound of the bell (an otherwise neutral stimulus) in a scrambling expectation of dinner. Answer choices (A), (B), and (E) are discussed above. Habituation (D) is a simple response to a repetitive stimulus, where the organism becomes desensitized, or learns to ignore it.

69. **(D)** Organismal Biology *Laboratory*

Intuitive reasoning, or insight learning, can occur when an organism encounters a new problem or unfamiliar situation and finds a solution beyond an associative response. Only answer choice (D) would require the goslings to creatively link the moveable step to the problem of hanging food. Answer choices (A), (B), and (C) are all examples of associative learning. (E) would provoke a physical reaction, but does not present a problem to solve by insight.

70. **(C)** Ecology *Laboratory*

For this question, you must recognize the effects of different forms of symbiosis. In mutualism, both organisms benefit, which indeed appears to be the case for Group 1. In commensalism (B), one organism benefits while the other is neither helped nor harmed. In parasitism (A), the host organism suffers while the parasite benefits. Predation (D), while sometimes associated with parasitism, is a relationship between consumers at adjacent trophic levels. Competition (E) occurs when organisms' niches overlap, or when resources are limited within a community.

71. **(E)** Ecology *Laboratory*

The original mite populations could increase in any one of these situations. Since we have no data on mite populations, the answer depends on the general possibility of growth. You should identify that Group 1 represents mutualism, Group 2 commensalism, and Group 3 parasitism. Mites benefit in each case, though the host rats might not. As mites breed, reproduce and spread, their population could potentially increase in each group, though it seems paradoxical in the case of parasitism.

72. **(A)** Ecology *Laboratory*

Parasites need their hosts to survive. For this reason, parasites that do not kill off their hosts are more likely to pass their characteristics to the next generation of parasites. Non-lethal parasites are "selected" to survive. (B) is false, as the relationship would not change from parasitism to commensalism. Rats are not likely to prey upon their microscopic parasites (C). (D) is incorrect, as there are still rats in the group to serve as hosts, or food sources. Finally, we are given no information to conclude that (E) is possible.

73. **(B)** Ecology *Laboratory*

Selection pressure is the sum of environmental and genetic factors affecting the survival rates of organisms. These pressures shape natural selection and therefore evolution. Environmental pressures can include other organisms within a community, particularly competitive, predatory, or symbiotic organisms. (A) is false, as mutations occur randomly, regardless of other organisms; however, the presence of new organisms may contribute to the selection of new mutations to survive. Adaptive radiation (C) refers to the evolution of a single population into varying forms; it results from new selection pressure, which must come first. Genetic drift (D) is the random change of allele frequencies in populations, rather than directed change. Biological magnification (E) refers to the accumulation of ingested material that cannot be metabolized or excreted.

74. **(E)** Evolution and Diversity *Laboratory*

Populations can change and diversify by natural selection. There are several types of selection, and each has a unique effect on the distribution of individual characteristics (such as beak width) within a population. Distribution of a trait is typically bell-shaped according to the number of individuals. Disruptive selection causes the trait's two extremes to be favored over the median or average, and results in two peaks of individuals. The diagram shows two peaks of finches with beaks slimmer and wider than the original median, so the correct answer is (E). Hardy-Weinberg equilibrium (A) requires that evolution has stopped, which is untrue in this case. Directional selection (B) causes the median to increase or decrease in one direction; the bell curve shifts to wider or slimmer beaks depending on the selection pressure. There is no evidence to support that the two finch peaks are now different species (C). Stabilizing selection (D) is the opposite of disruptive, and favors individuals with traits nearer the median value.

75. **(B)** Evolution and Diversity *Laboratory*

A change in food source creates new selection pressure. In this case, larger seeds favor finches with wider and stronger beaks. Over time, directional selection will drive evolution to increase the average beak width for the population, and the curve will shift to the right.

76. **(A)** Evolution and Diversity *Laboratory*

Evolutionary fitness is defined by the number of surviving, fertile offspring that carry an organism's genes into future generations. Among these choices, the finch with the most offspring will be the most fit, so (A) is correct. Although the finch in (B) has more eggs, we do not know if they are fertilized, or if they will hatch. The remaining answer choices (C), (D), and (E) have no offspring.

77. **(B)** Ecology

If you did not know that legumes characteristically grow root nodules filled with nitrogen-fixing bacteria, such as *Rhizobium*, you could have answered this question by elimination. Fungi can be involved in nitrogen-fixation, but their growth is not caused by bacteria, so (A) is false. Plants do not synthesize nitrogen-fixing bacteria themselves; the two organisms are in symbiosis, so (C) is false. Nitrogen-fixing bacteria in the soil use the soil itself as a source of nitrogen (N_2), so (D) is wrong. Finally, you can rule out (E), as *Rhizobium* is not a decomposer of legumes; rather, it fixes nitrogen from the soil.

78. (A) Ecology

Since both organisms benefit from their symbiotic relationship, *Rhizobium* and legumes exist in mutualism: *Rhizobium* gets a habitat with organic compounds from the plant, and legumes get loads of fixed nitrogen (ammonia). In commensalism (B), one organism benefits while the other is neither helped nor harmed. In parasitism (C), the parasite benefits while its host is harmed. Legumes do not consume *Rhizobium*, or vice versa, so (D) is false. Neither organism has evolved convergently (E), though their purposes serve each other well.

79. (E) Ecology

Among the answer choices, only cellulose does not contain nitrogen. Cellulose is a carbohydrate, a starch, and specifically a long chain of alternating glucose molecules (with only carbon, hydrogen, and oxygen components). Cytosine is a nitrogenous base. Methionine is an amino acid; all amino acids have amino groups ($-NH_2$). Both carrier proteins and enzymes are built from amino acids.

80. (C) Ecology

The transformation of ammonia into gaseous nitrogen (N_2) or nitrous oxide (N_2O) is the opposite of nitrogen fixation in the soil. This process is called denitrification. Transpiration (A) is gas exchange through plant leaves. Nitrogen fixation (B), as observed in *Rhizobium*, produces ammonia and nitrates (NO_3) for uptake in plants. Ammonification (D) is the action of decomposing bacteria on organic matter to produce ammonia. Nitrification (E) is the bacterial processing of ammonia into nitrites and nitrates.

Biology M Solitary Multiple Choice

81. (D) The Cell

The cytoskeleton is an array of protein filaments within the cell that provide structural support and can enable the cell to move by contracting. The other answer choices are organelles that have functions that do not directly relate to this process, and chloroplasts, answer (C), are not even found in the amoeba, an animal-like protist.

82. (A) Cell Processes

Molecules of glucose are monosaccharides which combine to form disaccharides, such as sucrose, and polysaccharides, such as starch. The combination of two monosaccharides or the addition of a monosaccharide to a long chain occurs by the dehydration synthesis reaction—literally, synthesis by the loss of water. The products of the reaction are the growing polysaccharide and one molecule of H_2O.

83. (C) Evolution and Diversity

Gymnosperms are non-flowering, primitive speed plants with seeds that are exposed to the air. Examples of gymnosperms include conifers, such as the giant redwood. A moss is a bryophyte, a brown alga is a protist, a daisy is an angiosperm (flowering plant), and a mold is a fungus.

84. (B) Genetics

The ABO blood type alleles are inherited separately from each parent. The mother could have two alleles of type A ($I^A I^A$), or one allele of type A and one allele of type O which is recessive ($I^A i$). The father has one allele each for types A and B ($I^A I^B$). Thus, the child could be type A ($I^A I^A$ or $I^A i$), type B ($I^B i$), and type AB ($I^A I^B$), but not type O (ii).

85. (C)   Evolution and Diversity

Amphibians are the only species that fit the description. Protists do not have lungs and do not lay eggs. Arthropods do not have lungs. Reptiles lay hard eggs. Birds are warm-blooded, so their metabolism doesn't slow when the temperature drops.

86. (C)   The Cell

In order to travel from the outside of the cell to the interior of a chloroplast, the molecule would first cross the plant cell membrane. It would then have to cross two membranes of the chloroplast: the outer membrane enclosing the organelle, and the inner membrane within the chloroplast. (Mitochondria are also built of two membranes.) All membranes consist of bilayers of phospholipids.

Biology M Group Multiple Choice

87. (D)   Evolution and Diversity

Yeasts are found in Kingdom Fungi, all of whose members are heterotrophic and eukaryotic. Fungi have cell walls made from chitin, and some fungi, like yeast, are capable of both sexual and asexual reproduction. Yeast undergoes anaerobic respiration during the fermentation process. Among the answer choices, (D) is incorrect, as yeast is not prokaryotic.

88. (A)   Cell Processes

If you didn't know that yeast cannot survive 12% concentrations of the ethanol they produce during anaerobic respiration, you could answer this question by elimination. Since this respiration is anaerobic, there is no oxygen available (D), and the Krebs cycle does not occur (B). Lactic acid (C) is a byproduct of anaerobic respiration in muscle tissue, whereas yeast produce alcohol. Finally, there is no reason to think that the food source is depleted (E) in either this case or every time the alcohol concentration reaches 12%.

89. (E)   Cell Processes

Ordinarily, muscle tissue uses aerobic respiration for energy, producing carbon dioxide as a byproduct. When oxygen is used up by intense aerobic respiration, mitochondria switch to anaerobic respiration, which produces far less ATP per molecule of glucose burned, and has a byproduct of lactic acid. The "burn" felt in muscles during intense exercise is a result of lactic acid buildup.

90. (C)   Genetics

Bacteria that lack the ability to synthesize a particular amino acid cannot grow in media without a supplemental supply of that amino acid. As the diagrams show, Colony 2 only grows in media infused with arginine. Colony 2 must be able to synthesize its own tryptophan, as it appears in the agar plate infused with arginine but no tryptophan. Therefore, Colony 2 is arg^- trp^+.

91. (E)   Genetics   *Laboratory*

A strain of arg^- trp^- would only grow in media supplemented with both arginine and tryptophan. No growth would occur in an agar plate with tryptophan alone. (A) is false, as bacteria cannot convert amino acids into those they lack. (If they could, each colony in the original experiment could form in all of the plates.) If the strain cannot grow, it cannot cover either half (D) or the whole plate (B), nor can it survive to mutate (C).

92. **(B)**   Genetics   *Laboratory*

Bacteria have a unique ability to exchange genetic material in a process called conjugation. Through tiny projections called pili, a bacterial cell can transfer strands or portions of its DNA to another bacteria. In this scenario, some of the bacteria from the mingling of Colony 1 (arg⁻ trp⁻) and Colony 2 (arg⁻ trp⁺) experienced this genetic recombination, and incorporated new genes for producing amino acids into their DNA. If it survives on all four agar plates, the new strain must be arg⁺ trp⁺.

93. **(E)**   Genetics   *Laboratory*

Another form of genetic recombination, and one that is frequently exploited in bioengineering, is transduction. In this process, a bacteriophage virus injects its genetic material into bacteria. Ordinarily, the virus' genetic material codes for the production of more viruses. However, because scientists can design the content of the virus' genetic material, they can introduce new capabilities into bacteria, such as the ability to produce arginine.

94. **(E)**   Organic and Biochemistry

Earth's earliest atmospheric conditions are hypothesized to have been mainly comprised of hydrogen, carbon dioxide, methane, and ammonia; there was no free oxygen gas. Free atmospheric oxygen likely appeared as a byproduct from Earth's early autotrophs.

95. **(B)**   Organic and Biochemistry

Proteins are a fundamental part of living organisms, and amino acids are the building blocks for proteins. There is no evidence for the spontaneous formation of mRNA (A), ribosomes (C), or cellular cytoplasm (D). (E) is false, as amino acids are not gaseous.

96. **(C)**   Organic and Biochemistry

The best answer for the chemical differences between the Earth's crust and the human body is the function of chemicals. Availability does not imply usefulness. Many elements are not compatible with biological systems; some chemicals are even toxic. Therefore, we can eliminate (A). (B) is also false, as chemical components of organic life do not radically differ significantly between land and sea organisms. Nor has the elemental composition of Earth's crust significantly changed (D). Some scientists have proposed a "nanobe" hypothesis of bacteria-like cells arriving from outer space (E), but it has yet to gain wide support.

97. **(C)**   Genetics

When homologous pairs of chromosomes align during meiosis, overlapping segments of their chromatid arms sometimes trade genetic material in an event called crossing-over. The location at which these homologous chromatids overlap is called the chiasma (plural: chiasmata). All of the other answer choices refer to events on the scale of DNA and RNA, rather than entire chromosomes.

98. **(A)**   Genetics

A cell's entire genetic code is copied in preparation for meiosis. Sister chromatids appear on the chromosomes as they condense during prophase I. Unlike mitosis, chromosomes arrange themselves and separate as homologous pairs: individual members of the pairs migrate to opposite poles of the cell in anaphase I. During the second stage of meiosis, individual chromosomes align in each new cell, and their sister chromatid arms are pulled apart in anaphase II. The diagram shows a homologous pair of copied chromosomes, which indicates the first stage of meiosis. Since the pair must be in proximity to exchange genetic material, this crossing-over occurs in prophase I.

99. **(E)** Genetics

An exchange of genetic material does not change an organism's number of chromosomes. There are genetic disorders with variations in chromosomal number (i.e. Down's Syndrome), but these mutations do not result from crossing-over. In general, mutations may be adaptive (A) or not (C), and although changes in genetic code often affect an organism's phenotype, some mutations are "silent" with no phenotypical change (B). Further transfers of genetic material are always possible (E).

100. **(C)** Organismal Biology

Sexual reproduction sorts parental chromosomes among offspring and allows for genetic recombination in crossing-over. These phenomena greatly increase the opportunities for variation within a species. Greater variation allows species to adapt better to changing selection pressures. (B) is false, as random mutations are beneficial as they relate to an individual's survival, but not all mutations are "good." Changes in the number of base pairs (C) does not imply an advantage. Genetic recombination has no direct bearing on the rate of reproduction (D). Exchanges of genetic material increase the diversity of the gene pool, eliminating (E).